Sam Nelson

II Chr. 4:5

SonLight

Other books by Sam Polson

In His Image

(Also available in Romanian & Mandarin)

By Faith

(Also available in Romanian)

SONLIGHT

Daily Light From the Pages of God's Word

Pastor Sam Polson

Publishing
Angel
Climbing

SONLIGHT
Written by Pastor Sam Polson

Published in 2019 by:
Climbing Angel Publishing
PO Box 32381
Knoxville, Tennessee 37930
http://www.ClimbingAngel.com

First Edition: November 2019
Printed in the United States of America

Jacket design: Tara Hayes
Cover photo: Getty Images
Interior Design by Climbing Angel Publishing

ISBN: 978-1-64370-030-4
Library of Congress Control Number: 2019942150

This book is dedicated to my mother,
Eunice Polson (1924-2005),
the most devoted reader of God's Word
I have ever known.

Contents

Foreword

I am honored to write this foreword for Sam Polson's daily devotional, *SonLight*. Reading through these pages has been the most encouraging tool for me in studying the Bible that I can recall. This book you hold in your hands, in my estimation, is directly on par with Oswald Chambers' devotional, *My Utmost for His Highest*.

I have had the privilege to know and study under Pastor Sam Polson's ministry for over 33 years now. His grasp of God's Word, and wisdom to teach God's Word, is revealed throughout these daily segments. It is a joy to anticipate the next nugget that prepares your heart to receive today's truth in Scripture. *SonLight's* thought-provoking antidotes are carefully written by a pastor who loves the Lord, loves the Word, and loves God's people.

SonLight has helped me develop a consistent habit of studying God's Word daily, and because of this consistency, I have grown in the grace and knowledge of the Lord Jesus Christ. Pastor Polson's ideas are so clearly presented, that I am prepared every day to share what I have learned with hurting people needing scriptural encouragement for their soul.

My wife and I have the privilege of facilitating a Growth Group at West Park Baptist Church and we have been using this awesome devotional as a daily Bible study guide for the group participants. I have witnessed significant spiritual growth in the members as they engage in daily Bible study as individuals and then as part of our group.

If you hunger for a more consistent, structured Bible study, want a personal introduction each day to prepare your heart to receive God's Word, or want to be more ready to encourage those in need around you, this devotional, *SonLight*, will bring you to a closer and more fulfilling walk with Him.

— Damon A. Falconnier

Introduction

The Bible teaches us that it is the entrance of God's Word that gives light. It is a "lamp for our feet and a light for our path" (Ps. 119:105). Only God's Word provides the light to see things as they really are. Most importantly, it is the Word of God that gives us *SonLight*, the light of the personal knowledge of God's Son.

Jesus said, "Search the scriptures for it is they which testify of me" (John 5:39). Yes, in the pages of the Bible, we get acquainted with the Lord of Glory and our dearest friend, Jesus Christ. It is with the goal of helping you walk in the light of the Son that this devotional is being provided.

The plan of this daily guide is one of a journey through the New Testament, and also through the pages of wisdom and worship found in Psalms and Proverbs. By following this daily Bible reading schedule, you will read through the entire New Testament as well as the books of Psalms and Proverbs in one year's time. Also, each day, devotional insights are included to bring personal application of God's truth to your life. These devotionals are no substitute for the reading of the Word, but they are shared in hopes of providing additional personal inspiration gleaned from the daily Scripture reading. It might prove beneficial for you to journal your own notes and responses during the daily time you spend with the Lord.

May God bless you richly as you take this journey with Him through His Word, and may the *SonLight* of His love shine brightly in your soul!

— Sam Polson

How to **R.E.A.P.** the Word of God

Read: Read the passage carefully and prayerfully.

Examine: Read the passage again, noting key words or phrases. Be careful to note the context surrounding the passage. Ask questions about the passage. Who is the audience? What situation is the speaker or author addressing? What is the main theme of this passage? Note in particular what you learn about the Lord from the passage.

Apply: Consider carefully the impressions on your heart as you read. How does this passage touch on specific areas or situations in your life? What wisdom are you gaining from this passage? What are you learning about your Lord in relation to your current spiritual experience?

Pray: Use what the Lord has revealed about Himself or about you personally in this time as an opportunity to respond directly to Him. Pray to Him in praise, or repentance, or in petition for others as the Holy Spirit guides you. Treat this time in God's Word not as a devotional exercise, but as a personal encounter with your holy God and your loving Savior.

JANUARY

"Behold, I am making
all things new."

"*A Genealogy of Grace*"

*"So all the generations from Abraham to David were fourteen
generations, and from David to the deportation to Babylon
fourteen generations, and from the deportation
to Babylon to the Christ fourteen generations."*
(Matthew 1:17)

The New Testament opens with the genealogy of Jesus. This might seem to us quite an unimpressive way to begin the greatest revelation ever given to mankind. But it was very important. This long list of names reveals Jesus to be the descendant and fulfillment of the covenant promises God gave to Abraham and to David. Jesus is the promised Son of Abraham through whom all the nations of the world will be blessed. Jesus is also the promised Son of David, the King of the Jews whose reign will never end.

But take a closer look at the genealogy. It is truly a story of God's amazing grace. Included in Jesus' family tree are some of the most notorious sinners *and* some of the most noted trophies of God's redeeming grace. In fact, even the people God chose to be the first recipients and first missionaries of the good news of Messiah's birth were shepherds—people of the lowest social standing in society. What a joy to begin this new year and this new journey through the New Testament knowing that Jesus includes in His spiritual genealogy flawed and failing people, people like us, to be the recipients and messengers of His salvation. Now that is amazing grace!

"Wise Guys"

Most of us cannot read this chapter of the Bible without the music of the Christmas carol "We Three Kings" playing through our minds. This beautiful song has given life to some fantastic scenes in Christmas plays and pageants for years. However, the song is mostly incorrect. Sorry! Matthew chapter 2 does not tell us that these men were kings, or that they were three in number, or that they followed the star for months, or even that they came to the baby Jesus in the manger. The story is rather about the "magi"—experts in astronomy and very familiar with the life and writings of the prophet Daniel, who centuries earlier had been appointed leader of the magi in Babylon. The story of the coming of these magi to find the one "who has been born King of the Jews" is amazing. And in the story, these men show us what it means to be truly wise:

- They were wise because they were looking for the King.
- They were wise because they pursued the King.
- They were wise because they worshiped the King.
- They were wise because they offered their possessions to the King.

Yes, these guys were really wise. May each of us determine to be "likewise" today by pursuing and worshiping our King.

MATTHEW 3
January 3

"*Preparing to Meet With the Master*"

In those days John the Baptist came preaching in the wilderness of Judea, "Repent, for the kingdom of heaven is at hand." For this is he who was spoken of by the prophet Isaiah when he said, "The voice of one crying in the wilderness: 'Prepare the way of the Lord; make his paths straight.'"
(Matthew 3:1-3)

"**R**epent" is a good word. It is a good word because it is a word of invitation and a word of preparation. The first words of the preaching shared by both John the Baptist and later by Jesus are "Repent for the kingdom of God is at hand." To repent means we change direction. It also means we change from our own direction. We turn away from self in order to turn toward the Savior.

When our Lord calls on us to repent, it is an invitation for a personal, life-changing experience with Him. Just as John the Baptist invited sinners to meet the glorious Messiah, so the Holy Spirit invites us to personally encounter Christ today. That means we must repent. We must turn from the mirror of self-absorption and look intently on the beauty of the one of whom the father said, "This is my beloved Son, with whom I am well pleased."

"Repent" is a beautiful word because it invites us to a beautiful view —experiencing the kingdom by following the King.

MATTHEW 4
January 4

"Fight Like Jesus"

The Prince of Peace was under attack all His life here on earth. The names of His enemies and their issues were quite varied, but our Lord knew who His enemy truly was—the prince of darkness, the devil. Of course, that fallen angel, Lucifer, was no match for the Lord of glory in strength and power.

But our Lord knew that His enemy would be *our* enemy as well. So, Jesus fought the devil with the completely powerful weapon that is readily available to every one of His followers—the Word of God. Jesus overcame the lies and temptations of the god of this world with the living truth of the God of the ages. Jesus attacked the devil with scripture. He used His own weapon.

> *"...and take the helmet of salvation, and the sword of the Spirit,*
> *which is the word of God..."*
> (Ephesians 6:17)

Satan couldn't handle the truth, so he fled from that sword attack. If we want to handle Satan, we must have a good handle on the Word of God. That means we must know it. That means we must read it. That means we must pray it. Hiding God's Word in our heart is how we get a good handle on the sword of the spirit, and that is how we handle the devil and fight like Jesus.

PROVERBS 1
January 5

" *Listen Up*!"

Proverbs is often described as the book of wisdom. In fact, Solomon, the human author of the book of Proverbs, uses the character Wisdom as the narrator of this book. She walks the earth and "cries aloud in the streets, in the markets she raises her voice" (v. 20). Wisdom's voice is true. It is the voice of the message of God in a world filled with noise. The world's busyness and noise, distract unwise people from the reality that life is unpredictable and deadly serious. Wisdom continues to call; she is the messenger of God's Word, will, and ways. Wisdom calls us and we can hear her. Her voice echoes through the pages of God's Word. As we read and heed Wisdom's voice, we become wise ourselves. And we become "wisdom speakers," inviting people to listen and apply God's Word so they too "will dwell secure and will be at ease, without dread of disaster" (v. 33).

PSALM 1
January 6

"Two Roads Diverged"

Psalms is the hymnbook of the Bible. In its pages, David and a few other inspired composers lead the people of God in worship. This amazing hymnal opens with a song contrasting two ways of living: the way of the wicked and the way of the righteous. The life of the wicked person is a life of wandering away from God, walking with worldly counsel, enjoying worldly company, engaging in worldly scorn of the ways of other people who are not as "enlightened." The other road is the way of the righteous. There is no wandering in this life journey. In fact, it is "planted." It is a life nourished by the living water of God and His Word. What a life it is!

- A productive life: "...that yields its fruit in its season."
- A protected life: "...its leaf does not wither."
- A prosperous life: "In all he does, he prospers."

These two roads diverge. The way of the righteous is the one less taken, but its destination is out of this world! Is your path "the road less taken"?

"Upside Down, Right Side Up"

Make no mistake about it; Jesus was a radical. He turned the money-changers' tables in the temple upside down, and He turned the established religions' order of the day upside down hundreds of times. Jesus turned things upside down by turning everything right side up. He said His mission was not "to abolish" the Law or the Prophets but "to fulfill" them. Jesus had the highest possible view of the Law (v. 18) but He knew that, over the centuries, the man-made rules and regulations added to God's law. It had made the free and glorious revelation of covenant God into a hollow and legalistic code of bondage. Jesus turned that all *upside down* by turning life *inside out*.

In His Sermon on the Mount, Jesus filled the Law full of its ultimate purpose which is *love*—loving God and loving those created in His image. Nothing illuminates our dark hearts like the love of God, and nothing brightens, impacts, and attracts in this gloomy world like love to others. Love changes everything. When we persistently pursue knowing and following Jesus, He turns our hearts inside out and then we can join Him as the early disciples did in turning the world upside down (Acts 1:6), which is really turning lives *right side up*!

Apply & Pray

- When were you part of turning a personal relationship with someone right side up? Is there a relationship in your life that is upside down right now? How are you seeking to make that right side up?

- Ask God to reveal and help you address any relational problems that are hindering your worship (vv. 23-24).

MATTHEW 6
January 8

" *Father* "

No one had ever said such a thing. No one. Ever. But Jesus did say it. In fact, He said it 17 times in the Sermon on the Mount, and He taught his disciples to say it as well. He called God "father." Before this time, Jehovah had often been referred to as the father of Israel, but Jesus knew Him as "father." Someone once said that the difference between the Old Testament and the New Testament is in the word "father." Jesus came to make the eternal infinite God known, and to make Him known as *father*. "But to all who did receive him, who believed in his name, he gave the right to become children of God" (John 1:12).

God as our *father* knows this, cares for us, provides for us, protects us, supplies us, values us, hears us. Yes, He is *father*. How often do we take time to truly address Him and focus on Him as our *father* who is in heaven, our constant and ever-present *dad*? Sure, it might feel weird for some of us to talk and think about God that way, but we need to get over it and get used to it. Jesus said so. He said, "God is my father and, if you believe in me, He is your father too."

Take some time right now to have a long talk with your father.

"*Life's Compass*"

We rarely need a compass. For most of us, our sense of direction is governed by very familiar and predictable landmarks: a street sign, a school, a store, a large tree, etc. We don't usually need a compass to go to work or church. When the familiar surroundings of our daily lives are unavailable, that's when we need a compass. A compass guides us to our destination when the road is unclear.

In Chapter 7 of Matthew, the Lord has provided a compass that He says will guide our steps on a lifetime journey through a maze of human relationships. "So whatever you wish that others would do to you, do also to them, for this is the Law and the Prophets" (v. 12).

The "Law and the Prophets" refers to all the direction given in the Old Testament Scriptures. God's guiding principle of life decision making is this—"treat others the way you want to be treated." Ultimately, that means there is one GPS for navigating life—love. Love means we treat others as we would want to be treated. When we do that, we are following our Lord's directions and that is always the best route!

"Jesus is Willing"

One of our biggest challenges in life is overcoming one of the biggest doubts in life—doubting the Lord. Not doubting that the Lord is able to help us, but that He is truly *willing* to help us. This should not surprise us really, because the first temptation that Satan brought to Adam and Eve was to doubt God, to question whether the Heavenly Father really had their best interest at heart.

This struggle to trust that God's desire is for His children's good has continued for the thousands of years since Eden. It continues today in each of our lives in thousands of different expressions. What is the answer to this depressing doubt? The answer is Jesus. We learn from our reading today, Jesus is "willing." What a thrill of hope must have flooded the heart of the poor, suffering leper described in verse 2. Having pleaded with Jesus, "Lord, if you will, you can make me clean." He then heard Jesus' comforting reply, "I am willing, be clean."

The entire chapter in our reading today is a collection of situations in which people were experiencing a variety of crises, and to each one Jesus responded with an attitude or action that communicated, "I am willing." Don't allow doubt to rob you of the priceless treasure of resting in God's goodwill toward you. Take your doubts to Jesus. Pour out the struggles of your life and the struggles of your faith to Him. Then, listen for the comforting promise of His response, "I am willing."

" Look Around the Room "

During the early days of His ministry, Jesus is building His leadership team of disciples. So far in Matthew's gospel, we are told about the first four members: two sets of brothers, Simon and Andrew along with James and John. They are hard-working, respectable individuals involved in the fishing business. It is the calling of the fifth disciple that amazes (and probably offends) the first four. Jesus calls Matthew, a tax collector to be a disciple. Tax collectors were hated by the Jewish people because they were considered traitors to the Romans, and this tax collector taxed fishermen! Yes, Simon, Andrew, James, and John had been taxed and no doubt swindled by Matthew. Now, Jesus is calling him to join their team! If that were not awkward enough, that evening Jesus and His team attended a party with "many tax collectors and sinners." This simply was not done by observant Jews, especially a rabbi!

What was Jesus' reply to the insinuating and condemning question from the Pharisees? A simple, but profound ministry philosophy: "Those who are well have no need of a physician, but those who are sick... I came not to call the righteous, but sinners."

Take a look around the "room of your personal relationships." Are all the people with whom you associate "healthy"? Is the circle of your friendships as big as the love of Jesus? We who are healthy are healthy because we have been "infected" by the love of Christ. Our mission is to live "contagious lives" among those who need the cure from the Great Physician.

PROVERBS 2
January 12

"*Priceless Protection*"

Perhaps some of you reading this page grew up in a community in which everyone had locks on their doors but rarely ever used them. It was a secure neighborhood. Sadly, mine was not that. Every home had doors with well-used locks, and most yards had a mean dog just to make sure. Security is necessary because the world is not a safe place.

However, even in a world that is often dangerous and deceptive, the Lord has provided the ultimate protection system we need, and that is to protect us from ourselves. Each of us is programmed in our nature toward dangerous and deadly pursuits. But by God's grace, we are offered a security and guidance system that is priceless—pursuing Him. Solomon challenges us in this chapter to pursue "wisdom" and seek after "insight," "understanding," and "knowledge." These are the ultimate qualities of security, and they are found in God Himself. "Then you will understand the fear of the Lord and find the knowledge of God" (v. 5). God Himself is wisdom, knowledge, discernment, insight, and every other resource for security we need. God Himself is our security. Seek Him and be safe.

PSALM 2
January 13

" *Rejoice with Trembling* "

We associate fear with many things: heights, crowds, dogs, needles, public speaking, etc. But how often, if ever, do we associate fear with joy? I can hear the answer. Never! That makes perfect sense. Fear is not generally a pleasant emotion. However, in Psalm 2 David challenges us to, "Serve the Lord with fear, and rejoice with trembling" (v. 11). That makes absolutely no sense at all unless you really know God. The fear of the Lord is the beginning of wisdom (Prov. 1:7). Jesus called on His disciples to fear God (Matt. 10:28).

The fear of God is a radically different kind of fear because it is a fear that is rooted in *awe-struck love.* "Awe-struck" in the understanding of God's glory and majesty. "Love" that is based in the amazing love God has for us—a love demonstrated in sacrificing His beloved Son to rescue us from His wrath.

When we behold in worshiping our glorious and gracious God, we rejoice, we tremble, we serve. Sinful fear is dispelled and godly fear delights.

"There is no fear in love, but perfect love casts out fear."
(John 4:18)

MATTHEW 10
January 14

" The Sword of Peace "

Jesus chose twelve special disciples to be His "apostles." They were the first "sent ones" to begin building His church by sharing the good news of the King and His kingdom. No ambassadors were ever sent with a commission of greater contradictions. Jesus told them they were loved and they would continue to be loved, and Jesus told them they were hated and they would continue to be hated.

They were loved, and they had no need to fear because they were speaking with His authority. Their message would change lives and the Heavenly Father who loved them so would provide for them in every way.

But they would also be hated. Their ministry and message in the King's name would bring them to arrest, trial, imprisonment, and worse. Their message of peace for all people would bring the sword of division wherever they went. In fact, their allegiance to Him would divide and separate them from some of the people they most dearly loved. So why would these disciples take up such a cross-like burden in following Jesus? Why would *we*? There is only one answer to that question, and it makes perfect sense to every person whose heart has been enlightened by grace. Why follow Jesus? Because it is Jesus we get to follow. Enough said.

MATTHEW 11
January 15

" *Rest for the Stressed* "

I once heard a well-known pastor be asked if he struggled with stress. His answer was amazing and enlightening. "How should I know?" He had gotten so used to the relentless pace of his life that he couldn't imagine how to measure its stress. Jesus recognizes stress as part of our human condition. He takes it for granted that people are stressed out, but it makes Him sad. He knows that we were not created for stress-filled labor but for rest-filled service. That's the way He served His Father, and He invites us to join Him. "Come to me, all who labor and are heavy laden, and I will give you rest. Take my yoke upon you, and learn from me, for I am gentle and lowly in heart, and you will find rest for your souls. For my yoke is easy, and my burden is light" (vv. 28-30).

Jesus invites us to exchange our stress for rest by:

- Coming to Him
- Joining with Him
- Learning from Him
- Serving with Him

In effect, Jesus invites us to a life partnership with Him. And what a sweet deal that is!

> *"Thou hast made us for thyself, O Lord, and our heart*
> *is restless until it finds its rest in thee."*

> – Augustine, 4th Century

MATTHEW 12
January 16

" *Minding Our Business* "

In the classic story by Charles Dickens, *A Christmas Carol*, Ebenezer Scrooge is visited by the spirit of his former partner, Jacob Marley. In an attempt to appease this chain-laden apparition, Ebenezer says to Marley, "You always were a good man of business, Jacob." Marley's ghost explodes in response, "Mankind was my business! The common welfare was my business; charity, mercy, forbearance, benevolence, were all my business!" Marley was declaring that he had in fact lived as a successful failure. He had succeeded in business but failed in the purpose of his very life.

Jesus expressed eternal warning and wisdom for us when He asked the piercing question, "Of how much more value is a man than a sheep?" (v. 12) It is so easy to "fulfill" our religious obligations and "succeed" in our career involvement, and yet utterly fail in carrying out the mission of our Master—loving mankind. May the Lord in His great grace help us to value what is invaluable—the lives of human beings who are made in His image; and may we be delivered from living a successful life that is an eternal failure.

MATTHEW 13
January 17

"The Secrets of the Kingdom"

Matthew Chapter 13 has been mostly called "The Kingdom Chapter" of the gospels. It is a chapter filled with word pictures used by Jesus to describe the operation of the kingdom of God for His followers. Most of Jesus' teaching in this passage is shared in parables. When asked by His disciples why He taught so much in parables, Jesus responded, "To you it has been given to know the secrets of the kingdom of heaven, but to them it has not been given" (v. 11).

Jesus' meaning is that spiritual understanding is a grace gift to those who truly follow Him. It is the gift of valuing and evaluating life with a kingdom perspective. Followers of Jesus are gifted to know what *really* matters, what has *real* value. By God's grace, we who follow Jesus can live a life that has lasting value and incredible joy. We can be the man who finds the hidden treasure in a field and joyfully sells all to buy that field (v. 44). What is the hidden treasure? It is life with the King. It is the incredible treasure of a life of following Jesus now, and the treasure of life with Him in eternity.

"Then the righteous will shine like the sun in the Kingdom of their Father." In light of Jesus' words in this chapter, "evaluate your values" today. Is King Jesus your hidden treasure, your pearl of great value? Would you willingly give up all for the surpassing joy of the treasure of Christ?

"Sharing in the Miracle"

The only miracle of our Lord mentioned in all four of the gospels is the feeding of the five thousand. In fact, John includes it in one of the seven miracles he records as "signs" that prove Jesus was the Son of God. Truly, only God could transform two pieces of fish and five small rolls of bread into a feast for thousands. But did you notice how Jesus permitted His disciples to share in this divine work? The miracle was completely an act of God, but the miracle took place in their hands. As the twelve disciples were each obedient to share 1/12 of the boy's lunch, the Lord accomplished His purpose.

The disciples would never forget this moment; and because the event would be included in all four gospels, all Jesus' disciples of all the ages would never forget the lesson—Jesus is enough. Nothing the Lord ever asks His followers to do is greater than their resources. Jesus is enough. Our Lord has not promised his resources for *our* plans, but He will personally supply whatever is needed to accomplish *His* will.

Jesus asks a lot from us as His followers. He *really* does. However, Jesus never asks of us anything that is beyond His resources: spiritually, emotionally, or physically. It may seem that Jesus is asking the impossible. He certainly asked His disciples to do the impossible that day in feeding the multitude. But when we respond like them, in obedient faith to our master's command, we learn what they learned. Jesus is enough!

" God's GPS "

The invention of the GPS system has been an unbelievable advancement in providing directions for travel. I'm still amazed (and just a little frightened) that there is a system that can track my exact position with pinpoint accuracy anywhere on the globe. What makes this technology even more helpful is that not only can it tell me where I am, it can also show me where I want to go and the best way to get there. Amazing.

However, that guidance system for geography is nothing compared to our Lord's guidance system for every aspect of our life's journey. To me, Proverbs 3:5-6 is the ultimate positioning system: "Trust in the Lord with all your heart, and do not lean on your own understanding. In all your ways acknowledge him, and he will make straight your paths." This is an amazing promise from God on how clearly He will guide us in His will. There are four coordinates, however, that we must enter if we desire His guidance.

REST
"Trust in the Lord with all your heart." Believe in and depend on God's good intentions for you.

REFUSE
"Do not lean on your own understanding." Don't permit yourself to believe you can make the best decision on your own.

RECOGNIZE
"In all your ways acknowledge him." If you desire to know God's unrevealed will, then obey Him in all ways in which He has already revealed His will.

RESPOND
"And he will make straight your paths." Don't be an initiator and determine to "make it happen," but walk with the Lord as He opens and makes smooth the way for your next steps.

PSALM 3
January 20

"A Song in the Night"

I do not remember who said it, or even where I was when I first heard it. But it is a simple reminder that has guided and encouraged me so often over the years, and I have been able to share this simple truth with so many others. "Don't forget in the darkness what you learned in the light." Times of darkness not only can make us fearful, but they can also make us forgetful. We have to choose to remember the light of truth in the night of fear.

David was a man walking in the darkness. His own son had betrayed him, and many of his closest friends had deserted him. It seemed there was only a step between him and death. He was afraid; anyone would be. But, David made a decision in his darkness of heartache and fear. He encouraged himself by what he had learned in the light, "But you, O Lord, are a shield about me, my glory, and the lifter of my head" (v. 3).

David was not in denial. He realized he was surrounded by his enemies, but he chose to remember a greater truth. Yes, he was surrounded; he was surrounded by God Himself as his shield. That was the truth that brightened his darkness. He cried out to God and David's darkness blazed with the light of renewed confidence and peace. His position was not changed but his disposition was transformed. David, in the midst of terrible conflict, experienced supernatural peace. That peace is available for you today from the greatest warrior of all—the Prince of Peace. "Peace I leave with you; my peace I give to you. Not as the world gives do I give to you. Let not your hearts be troubled, neither let them be afraid" (John 14:27). *Don't forget in the darkness what you learned in the light.*

MATTHEW 15
January 21

" The Heart of the Matter "

Religion and relationship are not the same, but the practice of our religion as Christians is very important. So important, that the Lord has given very clear and specific guidelines in the New Testament regarding what should and should not be included in the observance of our public gatherings of worship. However, our faith is not centered on external practices but is anchored to a personal living relationship with our Father God through our Savior Christ Jesus. Without a passionate love for our God, our religion will evolve into idolatry.

This happened to the religious leaders in Jesus' day. They were offended that Jesus' disciples ate without ceremonially washing their hands, but they permitted grown children to rob and dishonor their parents by saying they had "given to God" all the profit of their labor. Their religious traditions were violating one of the first commandments of God. Their hands were very "religiously clean," but their hearts were filthy and defiled.

What a contrast we have in the example of the Canaanite women. No person could have "outwardly" seemed farther from the religious leaders of Israel. She would have been considered a dog. Yet, her heart cried out in faith to the Lord, the Son of David, and her pleading prayers were answered. Yes, we must carefully follow the guidelines of faith and practice what the Lord has given in His Word. But we must avoid, at all costs, the danger of *religion without relationship*, for the heart of the matter is always the matter of the heart.

"Beware of Bad Bread"

There is a big difference between "hearing" and "understanding." The disciples heard Jesus when He told them, "Beware of the leaven of the Pharisees and the Sadducees" (v. 6). However, they completely failed to understand what their master was saying. When Jesus warned about "the leaven of the Pharisees and the Sadducees," they immediately thought about food and that perhaps He was rebuking them because they brought no bread. They could not perceive that the Lord was not concerned that they had not provided enough food for their journey. He had certainly recently demonstrated that He could provide all the food they needed!

Jesus was talking about the food for their souls. He was warning them about the "dangerous food" of the Pharisees and Sadducees, meaning their dangerous teaching. What made the teaching of these two groups dangerous? The dangerous way they handled God's Word. The Pharisees *added* to God's Word with their man-made traditions. The Sadducees *took away* from God's Word by denying key doctrinal truths.

Jesus' message to His disciples then is so vital for us to perceive today. Only the Word of God can give us spiritual health. *Partial* truth is total poison. That *partial* truth may be popular, appealing, and even shared with us by people we love, but *partial* truth is poison. We must fill our minds with God's *entire* truth in order to feed our souls with healthy food. Dig in!

" *Jesus Only* "

Just a few days earlier, Peter had made his great confession. He was asked by Jesus, "Who do you say that I am?" Peter boldly responded, "You are the Christ, the Son of the living God" (Matt. 16:16). The Lord told Peter he was asked because what he had confessed was evidence of a revelation given to him by God about the identity of Jesus. But an even greater revelation was in store for Peter and James and John as well. For the ministry that was coming in the difficult weeks and years ahead, they needed to see who Jesus *really* was. That incredible glorious display was provided for them on the mountain top when Jesus was transfigured before their eyes.

They were dumbfounded by Christ's majesty and in that experience, Peter said a dumb thing. He made a request to build three tents—one for Moses, one for Elijah, and one for Jesus. At that moment, God gave Peter another revelation. "This is my beloved Son, with whom I am well pleased; listen to him" (v. 5). At the voice of God, all those men face planted themselves to the ground. When they finally opened their eyes at the gentle touch and comforting assurance of their master, "they saw no one, but Jesus only." No longer did they see three; they saw only one—the one who is absolutely unique, the Son like no other, the Lord like no other, the friend like no other. The one, the only... Jesus.

MATTHEW 18
January 24

" *The 200,000 Year Debt* "

Imagine a debt so large that it would take your salary for the next 200,000 years to pay! That is how much the man owed his master, the king, in the story told by Jesus. One talent of gold was equal to twenty years of wages for a common laborer. The servant owed the king ten thousand talents—200,000 years worth of wages. You can do the math, but my calculation reveals a total of over three billion dollars based on our minimum wage.

Guess what? The good king forgave the debt! Unparalleled kindness and mercy! And what did this infinitely forgiven man do? He went looking to find a person who owed him some money, about $6,400. When the indebted man begged for more time, the forgiven servant had him thrown in prison until he paid the debt.

This story is Jesus' answer to Peter's question about how forgiving we should be. Do we know the answer? Let's do the math. First, estimate the number of sins that Jesus has forgiven you. Next, calculate how much your worst enemy has sinned against you. Now, compare the two totals. Apply the results. Class dismissed.

MATTHEW 19
January 25

" A Camel - Sized Miracle "

The man was very serious about the condition of his soul. He came to Jesus asking about the way to eternal life, but he left sorrowful without peace in his soul. He was rich, but his wealth was not the problem. It is not money that keeps a person from heaven because money inherently is not evil or good. It's just money. What made it impossible for this wealthy man to inherit eternal life? He had a heart problem. He loved himself and his comfort more than he loved Jesus.

His money was not the issue; it was the value he placed on things above the value he placed on the Lord. Until his heart was changed, he could no more pass into the Kingdom than a camel (the largest animal in Israel) could pass through the eye of a needle (the smallest opening familiar to people in that area). His value system had to be transformed. His wealth had to shrink to a tiny size in his estimation, and Jesus had to become invaluable as his treasure. Until that happened, This man could not be saved. Neither can anyone else. It is only the "poor in spirit" who can become as rich as citizens of the Kingdom. This is humanly impossible, "but with God all things are possible."

How about you? Will you ask the Lord to work that miracle in your life so that you value knowing Jesus as the greatest treasure of your life? Then, and only then, will you truly be rich.

PSALM 4
January 26

"The Pillow of the Lord"

One of the amazing moments in the life of Jesus took place as His disciples were terror-struck by a fierce storm that, at any moment, threatened to send them all to the bottom of the Sea of Galilee. Where was Jesus? He was fast asleep, taking a nap in the back of the boat.

No doubt you recall how in response to their cries of help, Jesus rose and calmed the wind and the waves in one command, "Peace, be still." Amazing. Just as amazing, perhaps, is that Jesus was able to sleep in such a crisis. How could He do that? He had a perfect pillow. The pillow about which David sang in this Psalm, "In peace I will both lie down and sleep, for you alone, O Lord make me dwell in safety." Jesus was resting on, and David was singing about *the pillow of the Lord*.

David and the Son of David rested their minds on the reality of the all-powerful and unfailing love of God. That is how they both could lie down in perfect peace and sleep when surrounded by turmoil. God was their pillow.

What pillow do you take to bed? Stress? Worry? Anger? Bitterness? We have all placed our heads on stony pillows like that many times. Change your pillow tonight or maybe even during a nap today. Imagine you are John during that final supper in the upper room. You are not quite sure what Jesus is saying. You may feel doubt and fear. Don't toss and turn like a boat in a storm. Place your head on the most peaceful pillow—the chest of Jesus.

PSALM 5
January 27

" *The Shield of the Lord* "

David was an amazing musician. He was also a brave and battle-tested warrior. He began his military career facing the terrible giant Goliath with weapons of his sling and stones. For years after that confrontation and victory, David experienced a life of combat. He was familiar with a variety of weapons and how to use them.

David also knew the value of a shield. On many occasions, he had seen the sky literally darkened by a pouring torrent of arrows launched by the enemy archers. And on those days, David, with his many men, found safety from the arrows of death by sheltering themselves beneath their united shields. No doubt, many times David wryly smiled as he heard the deadly arrows thump against the impenetrable canopy of shields.

David knew the value of a shield and he knew the provision of the *ultimate shield.* "For you bless the righteous, O Lord, you cover him with favor as with a shield."

There is no denying the reality of arrows being fired at us, at times by both physical and spiritual enemies. But what are those arrows compared to the steadfast love of our God? God Himself is our defense, and we are safe as we rest under the cover of His care. His favor is our faithful shield. God blesses and covers His children. Stand in His favor and stand firm.

MATTHEW 20
January 28

"Five O'clock Grace"

Jesus' parable makes no sense at all. It's not even fair. How can the kingdom of heaven possibly be like the master who hired day laborers to work in his vineyard at 6 am, 9 am, noon, 3 pm, and 5 pm, then at the end of the day the master paid them all equally? Anyone can recognize that isn't fair. Why, at the very least, it would be grounds for a formal complaint to the Fair Labor Board, or perhaps even a lawsuit!

But this is absolutely right. The kingdom of God isn't fair. If the kingdom of God were based on "fairness," then nobody would get in. In fact, every person would receive, in fairness, what he or she deserves from the King.

Think about it. Does anybody really want to receive what he or she deserves from the King? Absolutely not! We don't want fairness from God; we want grace. We don't want what we really deserve; we want what we don't deserve. In the service of the King, we are all five o'clock workers. We are recipients of what we *don't* deserve—free grace. When that truth dawns on us, we stop counting how many hours we or others have served, and we throw away the timecard. The Master owes us *nothing*, but He has given us *everything*. When that gracious truth reigns in our heart, we stop punching a timecard and we stop counting other workers' hours. That's so much better than being fair. That is being free!

MATTHEW 21
January 29

"Bothered by Blessing"

It has well been said that the blindest of all eyes are those that will not see. The darkest of all hearts are likewise—those who cannot feel the joy of God's gracious spirit at work right before them.

The Pharisees and Sadducees of Jesus' day were the epitomai of spiritual blindness and darkness. Before their very eyes, the glory of God was on display in the marvelous works of Jesus. The praises of God from the children echoed in the temple as their hearts leaped in response to God's good news. Rather than being inspired, these religious leaders were indignant. They actually resented the enthusiastic joy of these little followers of Jesus. How could that be? They were more devoted to their own interests rather than the interests of the King. They were practicing religion in the King's house, but they were oblivious to the King's presence.

This is a real danger for followers of the King today. We are prone to selfishness and self-focus, and without dependence on His spirit, we will value the practice of our religion above the presence of our ruler. Our King is faithful, but He is *not* predictable. He is constantly at work in fresh and surprising ways, and we must beware lest we become "old wineskins" that cannot contain the fresh wine our Lord is creating. If we stay or become inflexible, the loss will be our own and our spirits will stop soaring with childlike praise, "Hosanna to the Son of David!"

"Two Kingdoms, One King"

The Pharisees were convinced they had finally trapped Jesus. They had caught Him, they thought, on the horns of a dilemma by asking Him an unanswerable question, "Is it lawful to pay taxes or not?" They had brought together in one question the four "hot topics" of the day: politics, religion, money, and taxes. No matter how He answered, Jesus would be in trouble, either with the Jewish people or the Roman authorities.

Of course, the one who is Master of all things is also the master of wisdom, and He is not about to be entrapped by the perverted logic of wicked men. Jesus' answer was as simple as it is astounding. He requested a coin and then asked whose image was on it. Of course, the image was that of Caesar. Then came His amazing answer that destroyed their trap, "Therefore render to Caesar the things that are Caesar's, and to God the things that are God's." Brilliant and illuminating. Brilliant in the way Jesus escaped the trap of His enemies. Illuminating in the way His answer guides His disciples to this very day.

We who are citizens of the Kingdom of God are at the same time citizens of the kingdom of Caesar—human government. Our King Jesus has not commissioned us to be rebellious citizens in this world. We are commanded by our King to honor the king (1 Peter 2). We are to expand His kingdom, which is spiritual and eternal, in living for and testifying for our King in the kingdom of this world, which is physical and temporary. We are called as Christ-followers to be the best possible citizens. We pledge our allegiance to the flag, while we pledge our ultimate allegiance to our King.

MATTHEW 23
January 31

" The Weightier Matters "

I remember one of my teacher's "trick questions" when I was in elementary school, "Which is heavier—a pound of feathers or a pound of steel?" Of course, without thinking carefully, I immediately fell for it and responded enthusiastically, "A pound of steel!" Wrong answer, but a great learning moment. A pound is a pound as a measurement of weight. Weight is not a measurement of density. A pound of feathers is not as dense as a pound of steel. In measuring density, steel is "weightier" than feathers.

Jesus condemned the hypocritical Pharisees for their perverted scales of spiritual measurement. "You tithe mint and dill and cumin (spices for food) and have neglected the weightier matters of the law: justice and mercy and faithfulness. These you ought to have done, without neglecting the other." Jesus was saying all laws are important, but they are not equally important. Jesus placed the emphasis on the qualities that matter most to God. Not the outward obedience to the practice of the law, but the inward qualities of God's love. We must never let the Lord's scale of measurement be substituted in our lives. What are the things I should continue to do; but even more importantly, what are the qualities of love I must stop neglecting? I may be measuring myself with the wrong scale. God's first measurement is always to weigh my heart.

FEBRUARY

"*The greatest of these is love.*"

MATTHEW 24
February 1

"*Before He Comes*"

Our reading in Matthew 24 today is what is often referred to as the *Olivet Discourse*. It is called that because Jesus is sharing these truths as He and His disciples are seated on the Mount of Olives looking out over one of the wonders of the ancient world, the temple in Jerusalem. As the disciples pointed out to Jesus the beautiful aspects of this sacred shrine of Judaism, Jesus bluntly told them it would be torn down stone by stone. The disciples recognized their master was referring to a future judgment, so they asked Him, "When will these things be, and what will be the sign of your coming and of the end of the age?" (v. 3) Our Lord then told them what would happen: wars, strife, famine, earthquakes, false prophets, false Christ, false believers, and faithlessness. Not a pretty picture, but a very accurate one to any person acquainted with the history of the world and the church. Our Lord did not tell them when the end of the age would come because that was a day only known to the Father (v. 36).

But what the Lord did reveal to His disciples, then and now, is what He wants done before the end of the age comes. "And this gospel will be proclaimed throughout the whole world as a testimony to all nations, and then the end will come" (v. 14). Jesus is not coming back until this purpose is fulfilled. If the gospel is to be proclaimed to the whole world before He returns, then that should be our focus until He returns—not making predictions but making disciples. The King is coming. That is ultimately all we need to know. With that wonderful promise, let's focus on helping others know Him too.

PSALM 6
February 2

" *Jehovah - Shama* "

"The Lord has heard my plea; the Lord accepts my prayer."
(Psalm 6:9)

It does not require a deep and careful reading of the Bible to be struck by the fact that within its pages a number of different names and titles are used to refer to the one and only God. What makes this even more significant is that it was His people who assigned almost all these names and titles to God. On one very notable occasion, however, God deliberately assigned a name to Himself. This occurred the day God revealed Himself to Moses from the burning bush on Mount Sinai, and commissioned him to be the human deliverer of His people. Moses asked God how he should answer the Israelite slaves when they wanted to know who had sent him to lead them to freedom. God responded by saying that Moses should tell them "I AM" had sent him. (Exodus 3:14)

God called Himself, "I AM." The English letters for "I AM" in Hebrew are "YHWH," and when the vowel markings are included it is pronounced "Yahweh." Most often "Yahweh" is transliterated into the name "Jehovah" in English. As you may know, when we see the word LORD in our English Bibles, it is to inform us that this name "Yahweh" is being used in the Hebrew text. God instructed Moses to tell the Israelites "I AM" had sent him to them, and in doing this He communicated so very much about Himself to His people. "Yahweh" or "Jehovah" means that God is the ever-existing, ever-present maker and sustainer of life itself. He is the One *Who Is,* always present and always present tense. Throughout history the people of God have found such comfort in this incredible reality of God's changeless presence.

Our reading today in Psalms is a song of David that celebrates what God's presence meant to him personally in a time of crisis. The song records a time in David's life when he was bedridden by illness. It was also a season of deep emotional distress because David sensed that the Lord had brought this ordeal on him. In his physical weakness and emotional depression, David despaired of life itself. Yet, in his darkness David cried out to Yahweh, Jehovah, the One who is present and always present tense. In his darkness, 'The LORD" gave David light and David knew that his prayers had been heard and accepted. (v.6) David did not give God this name, but he experienced Him that day as "Jehovah-Shama," "the LORD who hears." "Jehovah-Shama" is the greatest prayer promise that could ever be given, for how futile is prayer if there is not a "God who listens," but how powerful is prayer when the ever present One is listening closely!

As you begin your prayer time today, why not begin with the name of the One who is always listening? Go ahead. "Jehovah-Shama..."

PSALM 7
February 3

" Praise in the Persecution "

Jesus told us it would happen. He said, "If they persecuted me, they will also persecute you" (John 15:20). The apostle Paul said that persecution was inevitable for every serious Christian. " Indeed, all who desire to live a godly life in Christ Jesus will be persecuted..." (2 Tim. 3:12). It's not easy to be treated badly when trying to live a good life! We know so little about persecution in our culture when compared to what our brothers and sisters are experiencing in other parts of the world, but we will experience it. What is more important than experiencing persecution is how we respond to it.

Persecution for our truth and values can make us better or make us bitter. Guess which one our Lord desires? That's right—our sovereign God ordains times of persecution in our lives, not that we might be pressured into depression but be pressed deeper into Him. It is in times that we feel like God is all we have in which we discover, in fresh ways, that He is all we need. Yes, the Lord plans for our persecution to lead us to praise for who we find Him to be. Listen to the song of David, a man in the pressure cooker of persecution.

> *"I will give to the Lord the thanks due to His righteousness,*
> *and I will sing praise to the name of the Lord, the Most High."*
> (Psalm 7:17)

Right now, take a moment to consider those words again. Now, offer them as your own in praise to God. Keep doing that during any experience of persecution, and you will always be protected. You won't get bitter; you will get better. Praise wins.

MATTHEW 25
February 4

" Don't Waste Your Life "

Much of Jesus' teaching was based on parables. A parable has often been described as "an earthly story with a heavenly meaning." Jesus used parables to teach kingdom truth by means of deep, simple, earthly stories. Most of the time these stories taught truth using comparison—what the Kingdom is *like*. But sometimes the story was used to teach what the Kingdom in many ways is *not like*.

In Matthew 25, Jesus shared the parable of the talents, the story of a wealthy, hard man who wanted to invest eight talents of money through three of his slaves. In today's economy, a talent would be worth about $350,000. Two of the slaves doubled the amount of capital given to them to invest. But one of the servants, because he was terrified of losing his cruel master's money, hid the money instead of investing it. The two faithful slaves were commended by their master and invited to share in their master's joy and generosity. However, the fearful and faithless slave was condemned because he produced nothing and was cast into a dark and terrible prison of torture.

In many ways, the Kingdom is like this parable. We who are servants of the King have been given so much spiritual treasure to invest for our King. If we are faithful, we will be amazingly rewarded by our King and will be given incredible opportunities to joyfully serve Him more in the coming, eternal Kingdom. However, the Kingdom is *not* like this parable in some very important ways. Our King is not a hard and cruel Lord! He is infinitely loving and full of grace. He has redeemed us from destruction by His own agony and death. We are bound to Him by the chains of love and gratitude. We serve Him because we love Him, and we love Him because He first loved us. Love is the greatest motivation of all.

" *The Wisdom of Worship* "

Someone has said with a great deal of insight, "Today in America we know the price of everything and the value of nothing." That may very well be true, but it is not just a problem in our nation. It is also a problem among the closest of Jesus' disciples. It always has been a problem.

Verses 6-13 describe one of the most remarkable scenes from the ministry of Jesus. The events unfold in a location just as remarkable. Jesus and His disciples are having a meal in the house of "Simon the Leper." Read that again, "Simon the Leper." No one ate in the home of a leper, let alone a Jewish rabbi and his disciples. But this was now the home of a "former leper" because Jesus had completely healed him. This meal in effect is a thanksgiving dinner as the rescued host offers his home for lodging and a delicious meal. But the thanksgiving is taken to a whole new level as a woman, in the most expressive act of loving worship, kneels behind Jesus and anoints Him with the incredibly expensive perfume. That alabaster container itself was extremely valuable. The room was infused with the amazing fragrance.

But what did the disciples smell? They smelled waste. Then they complained the price of the perfume could have better been given to the poor. They didn't get it. This wealthy worshiper did. Jesus is going to His death in Jerusalem. Somehow, through her worshipful listening to her master in recent days, she knows it is for her sake. In adoring worship and thanks, she seizes this moment to anoint Jesus for His burial in advance of His sacrificial death. So moving! Just as Jesus said it would be wherever this story was told. When we worship Jesus we learn, we are liberated, we have our value system transformed, and we leave a legacy that blesses lives long after ours is over.

MATTHEW 27
February 6

"The Ultimate Question"

There are questions and then there are *questions*. Some questions, when answered, have the most significant of consequences. The way in which the question is answered has huge implications.

Our reading today in Matthew 27 contains the *ultimate question* because how the question is answered determines everything. It is a deeply spiritual question asked by one of the most secular and calloused of men—Pontius Pilate. Listen to his question, "Then what shall I do with Jesus who is called Christ?" Amazing.

Pilate is sitting on the judgment seat and standing before him is the judge of all mankind. Then the question on which all people must make their own judgment is asked, "Then what shall I do with Jesus who is called Christ?" Pilate thought he could wash his hands of the responsibility for answering his own question. And he did answer it when he delivered Jesus to His enemies for execution.

We cannot wash our hands of the "Christ question" either. We have already answered the question by either accepting or rejecting Him as our Savior and King. We also answer the question every day as we live our lives: "Then what shall I do with Jesus who is called Christ?" The answer reveals itself in a thousand different expressions during our everyday lives. What am I going to do with Jesus? Do we leave Him in the pages of the Bible? Do we leave Him in the church building as we leave services on Sunday? It is the question for eternity, and it is the question for this day.

"Then what shall I do with Jesus who is called Christ?"

MATTHEW 28
February 7

"Jesus Said 'All'"

I heard a pastor refer to the use of the word "all" in a particular verse of the Bible, and the pastor said, "all means all and that's all that all means." I'm not sure his statement was that insightful, but it was certainly memorable because that was over 35 years ago!

In our passage today, Jesus shares His Great Commission for His followers, and in it, He really emphasizes "all" (vv. 18-20).

All Authority: Jesus declares that He possesses all inherent authority in creation and that out of His authority, the ministry of His disciples will be carried out. It is not *our* ability but Jesus' authority that accomplishes His ministry.

All Nations: Jesus has determined that by His authority, all the people groups of the world are to hear His gospel. God's forever family is to reach across all man-made boundaries and include people from all the families of mankind.

All His Commandments: A disciple is a "learner," and Jesus wants people to know and follow all His teachings. Making disciples is more than making converts. It involves sharing all the teachings of our Master so that His pupils do not just know more about Him, but are actually becoming more like Him.

All the Time: Jesus will always be with His followers. Always. We are never alone. Ever. We can do this with Jesus' power and His principles and His presence; we can make disciples from among all people. I guess that just about says it *all*, doesn't it?

MARK 1
February 8

"*Immediately*"

The Gospel of Mark is the gospel of action. It is decisive. The sixteen chapters contain much less narrative than the other three gospels, but Mark compresses into his account of Jesus' life, much more information about what Jesus actually did. For this reason, many Bible scholars believe that Mark wrote with the mindset of the Roman people. The Roman psyche was one that valued strength and action. Perhaps this explains why one of Mark's favorite words is "immediately." In fact, Mark uses the word seven times in the first chapter alone (v. 10, 12, 18, 20, 23, 29, 42). Jesus' ministry is described as suddenly bursting forth with His baptism and then being filled with action thereafter. Any reader of this gospel quickly gets the idea that events were moving quickly in Jesus' life, under the direction of the Holy Spirit, and that Jesus was responding quickly to what the Holy Spirit was revealing.

Jesus' first disciples responded to His call the same way. Simon and Andrew "immediately left their nets and followed him" (v. 18). Note that. They *immediately* left and *immediately* followed. Perhaps imperfectly they understood; but they knew they had a new Master, a new motivation, a new mandate, and a new mission. They now were identified by more than an *occupation*—fishermen. They were identified by their *vocation*—followers. They were followers of Jesus. That is a very important question for each of us. Do I identify myself first by my occupation or by my vocation? Each day, am I guided first by "whose I am" or "what I do?" That is a question that requires an answer...*immediately*.

PROVERBS 4
February 9

"Ever Brighter"

It is an incredible thing to watch. The pitch black of night ever so slowly begins to give way on the horizon. At first, only a grey curtain seems to rise in the East. But then the sky begins to glow with an amazing mixture of purple, blue, and orange hues. At last, the beautiful yellow sphere begins to emerge, and ever to slowly rise in the sky.

If you are blessed with a schedule that permits a few hours of dedicated focus, you can watch the sun rise higher and higher until the whole sky is blazing with its glory, and you must shield your eyes to its brightness. A new day. Darkness once again giving way to the relentless journey of the sun.

Solomon meditated on this scene and made an inspired application, "But the path of the righteous is like the light of dawn, which shines brighter and brighter until full day" (v. 18). Paul tells us "at one time you were darkness, but now you are light in the Lord. Walk as children of light" (Eph. 5:8).

Our Lord and Savior illuminated our *spiritual darkness* with the *light of His salvation*. We have no light of our own, but we are bearers of God's light in Christ. Jesus said we are the light of the world. Our journey through this world, by His grace, can brighten the lives of those who live in the shadows. We can warm, with His love, those who are shivering in darkness. As we daily follow the Son, our path can shine brighter and brighter until we step into the perfect day... "and night will be no more" (Rev. 22:5).

PROBERBS 5
February 10

" *Out of Bounds* "

We griped all the time. We really did. Years ago, when I was actively involved in sports, we complained on a regular basis. We would gripe and complain about the heat, the length of practices, the limited number of balls or bats, the constant exercises and sprints, or tacky uniforms, etc., etc., etc.

However, with all of our complaining, I never once remember anyone being upset about the lines on the field or on the court. No one ever complained about boundaries. We didn't think lines that defined inbounds and out of bounds were legalistic. The game *required* boundaries. Boundaries made the game fun and kept it from descending into chaos.

Proverbs Chapter 5 is about the blessing of boundaries, in particular, *moral* boundaries. When we live within these God-given boundaries, we experience freedom. Our lives are liberated by "wisdom," "understanding," and "discretion" (vv. 1-2). When we believe Satan's original lie, that real freedom is found in a life without boundaries, what do we experience? Bondage. "The inequities of the wicked ensnare him, and he is held fast in the cords of his sin" (v. 22). What is freedom? Freedom is not the right to do your own thing; it is the privilege to do the *best* thing.

" The Friend of Sinners "

Being offensive is not a strategy for advancing the Kingdom. Sadly, there are some who profess faith in Christ who seem to think that being dogmatic and argumentative about their beliefs is the way to spread the gospel. Now, this certainly does not mean that the gospel is not radical, for it is completely radical. However, what is most radical in the gospel is the "good news" of God's love to those who are farthest from deserving of it. It is the radical message of a holy Lord who is a friend to sinners.

Jesus offended people by His friendships. He actively pursued friendships with those who were considered by the religious people of the day to be outside of "polite company." Thank God Jesus reached out then and reaches out now to bring outsiders inside a loving relationship with Himself, or we would be doomed forever. Nothing is more certain than this—both the writer and the reader of this devotion would be separated from any hope were it not for Jesus' proactive friendship. Yes, we were *outsiders*, but Jesus made us *insiders* by His loving, proactive friendship.

Now, we, as followers of the Lord, have the same commission to win people to Jesus by winning them to ourselves in friendship. Take some time right now to prayerfully evaluate how you are doing on this mission. Think through your list of friends. How many of the names are those who are yet outside of the Kingdom? Who else should be on your list of evangelistic friendships? Talk to the Lord about this is in prayer. Ask Him to guide you on the mission to "make friends of sinners." He knows exactly how to do it, and He will show you the way.

MARK 3
February 12

"Our First Calling"

Our passage today records one of the most momentous decisions Jesus made in His entire ministry. Verses 13-19 tell us that Jesus went up on a mountain and called twelve men to the special ministry of serving as His apostles. The word "apostle" literally means a "sent one." It conveys the idea of a unique calling to represent a person or government in an official capacity. We are told in another gospel account that Jesus prayed all night about this decision. What an incredible calling it was to be one of His apostles!

But, did you notice what the first calling of these twelve men was to be? Even though they had been chosen to be "sent ones," their first responsibility was to be "staying ones." Yes, verse 14 says, "And he appointed twelve (whom he also named apostles) that they might be *with him* and he might send them out to preach." Note that. The first responsibility of the apostles was to "be with him."

How important it is for all of us whom Jesus sends with the gospel to remember that priority. Before we are called to do anything for the Lord, we are called to be *with* the Lord. Our identity is not first that of being *workers* for Christ but as *worshipers* of Christ. The Bible says later of the apostles that people took note of them that they had been with Jesus (Acts 4:13). Yes, it is being *with* Jesus that we have the greatest impact *for* Jesus. Let's not forget our first calling—not to go to the world *for* Jesus, but to go to the world *from* Jesus. What we receive from the Lord in His presence, we take with us as His representatives, His "sent ones." What a calling!

MARK 4
February 13

"The Security of a Sleeping Savior"

Jesus was bone tired. So tired that the loud and noisy crew in a rather small boat did not keep Him from taking a nice nap. In fact, so soundly was Jesus sleeping that He was completely oblivious to the pitching of the boat, the howling of the wind, and the fearful cries of His disciples. It was not until they physically roused Him from His deep sleep that Jesus was even aware of the storm. But even when He was fully awakened, Jesus was not frightened. What fear could the waves cause Him? As the old song says, "No water can swallow the ship where lies the Master of ocean and earth and sky."

The storm did not concern Jesus, for He quickly calmed that. But what did concern Jesus was the response of His disciples, "Why are you so afraid? Have you no faith?" His followers were overwhelmed. Now they were afraid! More afraid of the one inside the boat than the storm outside the boat!

That was exactly the lesson they needed. They learned that if you are in a storm with Jesus, the storm itself only allows you to experience the power and presence of the Master more fully. Our Lord has promised each of us as His followers, "I will never leave you or forsake you." Since this is true, no storm of any kind can ever be out of His control. *He is with us, and He is as peaceful in our storm as He was during that nap on the boat with his disciples.* Whatever storm you may be facing today, it is nothing to the peaceful Master who journeys with you. He may not immediately calm the storm around you, but He will calm the storm within you as you rest on the soft pillow of His almighty power and infinite love. Meditate on the one who sails with you in your storms. Then, consider doing something very faith-filled. Take a nap!

> *"In peace I will both lie down and sleep; for you alone, O Lord, make me dwell in safety."*
> (Psalm 4:8)

MARK 5
February 14

"Hope for the Hopeless"

What a day is recorded in Mark Chapter 5! Jesus got out of a boat, which a short time earlier had been a scene of hopelessness for His disciples who knew they were only a few moments from drowning in a terrible storm. Hopelessness turned to wonder as Jesus calmed the storm.

As soon as Jesus steps from the boat, He is confronted by a hopeless man filled with innumerable demons. In a moment of command, the pitiful man is delivered and becomes quiet in peace and worship at the feet of Jesus. Later in the same day, at His feet another miracle takes place. A woman, suffering continual hemorrhaging of blood for twelve long years, in desperate faith reaches out to touch the hem of Jesus' garment. Immediately, her hopeless condition is transformed by His power, and she becomes a lifelong witness of Jesus' healing power. This miracle occurred at the moment news arrived of another hopeless situation—a sick child Jesus is going to visit has passed away. Hopeless? Yes. As hopeless as death. But Jesus, the Prince of Life, brings celebration to that house of mourning by raising the little girl to life. What a day. Filled with hope for the hopeless.

My friend, that day has never ended. The world is filled with hopeless situations, and sometimes we find ourselves living in that atmosphere. But with Jesus, every day is a day of hope. In each of these stories recorded in Mark Chapter 5, hopeless people came to Jesus. A man tortured by demons, a woman tortured by sickness, a father tortured in concern... They all came to Jesus as their only hope in their hopelessness. What hopeless situation surrounds you or someone you love today? What are you going to do with that hopelessness? It is definitely beyond your abilities, but it is definitely *not* beyond His! All three of these helpless and hopeless situations recorded in our passage today were transformed at the same place—the feet of Jesus. That is the place where hope for hopelessness is found. Today in prayer let's take our needs and the needs of others to the place of hope—to the feet of Jesus.

MARK 6
February 15

"A Familiar Blindness"

Rejection is never a pleasant thing, but the rejection of family and friends is probably the most painful form of rejection a person can experience. Jesus knew this pain well. For over 30 years he lived a virtuous life in his hometown of Nazareth. He was well known, not only for his trade as a carpenter but also for his giftedness as a powerful teacher of God's Word. He was respected as a Rabbi and often read and taught the Scriptures in the synagogue. They knew him, but they did not *really* know him. In fact, as his fame grew regarding his marvelous works, they were offended because of his notoriety.

In another passage, we are told that even his own brothers did not believe in him. If the expression "familiarity breeds contempt" has ever been personified, it is in the response of Jesus' family and neighbors to his identity. Their blindness even amazed Jesus. Verse 6 says, "he marveled because of their unbelief."

Of course, it is very easy for us to pass judgment on those ancient residents of Galilee, but perhaps we should be slow to do that. How often do we fail to see the presence and power of the Lord because of the familiar events and surroundings of our daily life? Our evangelical theology correctly teaches us that God is present and active in his creation. But do we *really* see him? *Really*? How often do we see the work of the Lord in His beautiful creation that shouts His glory? How often do we hear His voice in the laughter of a child or the melody of a song? Did we *worship* this Sunday, or did we "go to church?" Did we *listen* to the Lord or just read verses from the Bible a few minutes ago? When we don't expect to encounter the Lord throughout the day, we miss him in the blindness of the familiar.

> *"Open our eyes, Lord, we want to see Jesus,*
> *To reach out and touch him, and say that we love him.*
> *Open our ears, Lord, and help us to listen.*
> *Open our eyes, Lord, we want to see Jesus."*

("Open Our Eyes, Lord," written by Robert Cull)

PSALMS 8 & 9
February 16

"The Power of His Name"

"And those who know your name put their trust in you, for you,
O Lord, have not forsaken those who seek you."
(Psalm 9:10)

We cannot trust someone we do not know, certainly not in the deepest meaning of the word, "Trust." We may have quite a bit of confidence that the other driver is going to stop at the red traffic light, but that is not the same as trust. Trust is based on knowledge of another person's character. That requires time and experience.

We often refer to a person who is worthy of trust as having "a good name." We mean that over a period of time and experience, he or she has proven to be a person who can be trusted. Trust requires knowledge, *personal* knowledge.

The Lord has a good name. His character has been proven and tested innumerable times throughout the ages. As people have come to experience God's character over the centuries, they have actually given Him names that communicate His nature. They know Him, name Him, and trust Him. They know His name, His faithfulness, justice, righteousness, salvation, peace, comfort, holiness, helpfulness, strength, joy, provision, goodness, kindness, etc. They know His name, so they trust Him. They become people who know their God.

Take a few moments to reflect on who you know God to be through your personal experience. Express your trust in Him today by praising Him in prayer for some of the ways you have experienced Him in your life. Now, claim one of His names for today:

"Lord, I praise you because you are _____."

PSALMS 10 & 11
February 17

"It Will Be Worth It All"

I have heard him sing the same song several times. Each time my eyes fill with tears. I am overcome with the profound, guiding truth being shared with such a stammering, halting voice. His name is Stephen, and he suffers significant mental and physical impairment from a brain injury at birth. Life is not easy for Stephen. Every step is a challenge. Each conversation requires incredible concentration to frame the thoughts and to form the words. Stephen cannot provide for his own basic needs. He cannot drive, live independently, work a typical job, or balance a checkbook. The world is a difficult place, and life is tough for Stephen, but Stephen knows Jesus. In an incredibly simple and yet brilliant way, he views life in the light of the reality of glory to come.

He learned a song years ago that he claimed as his personal testimony. He has sung it hundreds of times to thousands and thousands of people. Stephen has changed the lives of countless people by reorienting their view of *problems*, in light of the *promises* to come. Mine included. Listen to Stephen sing this transforming truth:

"It will be worth it all when we see Jesus!
Life's trials will seem so small when we see Christ.
One glimpse of His dear face all sorrow will erase.
So, bravely run the race, till we see Christ."

Amen.

("When We See Christ," lyrics by Esther Kerr Rusthoi)

MARK 7
February 18

" *Inside Out* "

The teaching of the apostles was so powerful that the response of the amazed population was well expressed by the citizens of Thessalonica, "The people who have turned the world upside down have come here also!" (Acts 17:6) The gospel truly did turn the world upside down, or we might more accurately say, right side up. The message of Christ turned people's hearts toward God, which is always the right direction. The heart is the GPS system of every life.

That is the reason the Lord always directs His work toward our hearts, because it is from within, that change comes to every area of our lives. One of the greatest dangers to God's people is permitting a subtle but devastating drift of focus that shifts our attention from the internal matters of our relationship with God to the external observance of religious forms and activities. In time, we become like the Pharisees whose entire lives were built around religious practices, yet whose hearts were so far from God.

The way we protect ourselves from that deadly drift is to keep our focus on the only One who can change our hearts. Our activities of religion don't necessarily need to change, but our focus in those activities definitely does. For example, we still go to church but we go to worship. We still read our Bibles, but we listen to God. We still pray, but we talk to the Lord. We still give, but we give to our Savior. We still go to work, but we go in service to our King. We still interact with people, but we treat them as image-bearers of God. When our life-focus is upward to God, he changes us...from the inside out.

"Thinking Like the Devil"

What an emotional roller coaster for Peter! He had just made the greatest confession and received the greatest commendation from the Lord. Now, a short time later, he is involved in a confrontation with Jesus and receives the greatest condemnation. What is going on?

Peter does not realize it, but he is double-minded. He is thinking and speaking God's truth, "You are the Christ," and he is also thinking and speaking Satan's lies, rebuking Jesus when the Lord speaks of His coming crucifixion and resurrection. What a terrible rebuke Peter received when Jesus said, "Get behind me, Satan! For you are not setting your mind on the things of God, but on the things of man." Peter was uttering, in effect, the same lies of temptation Satan had spoken to Jesus in the wilderness three years earlier.

At that moment, Peter was not speaking like an apostle of Jesus; he was talking like an adversary of Jesus. Our Lord took this tense moment as an opportunity to speak to all His disciples, then and now. Jesus' message is very clear. You cannot be His follower and attempt to be His leader. If we want to be the leader, then we lose everything. However, if we are willing to be Christ's follower, whatever the cost, then we will gain everything. "For whoever would save his life will lose it, but whoever loses his life for my sake and the gospel's will save it" (v. 35).

Take a "Selah moment" (a silent moment) right now to reflect on what Jesus said to Peter, for he is saying it to you. Then, make the decision to follow Jesus' wisdom by following Him closely today. Now that is good thinking!

MARK 9
February 20

" *A Cry for Faith* "

Today's passage contains one of the most moving scenes in the ministry of Jesus. A man has brought his demon-plagued son to the disciples, but they are unable to cast the demon out. When Jesus arrives on the scene, the father asks Him, if he can, to please help his son. Jesus replied, "'If you can!' All things are possible to the one who believes." Out of his heartache, the father cries out, "I believe; help my unbelief!" Jesus responded to the man's imperfect faith with a perfect miracle of deliverance for his son.

We all struggle with faith at times. The greatest struggles are often over those things for which we have prayed so long and yet seen no answer. What should we do when we struggle with doubt? The simple answer is to take those doubts to Jesus and confess them to Him. It's not that he needs to be made aware of our doubts, but rather we need to find encouragement and renewed faith by going to the "founder and completer of our faith," Jesus Christ. Taking our doubts to Jesus is an act of faith in itself. Our faith is increased as we come to realize a situation is beyond our control, and then that desperation takes us to the Lord, not only for help in the insurmountable obstacle but to also help us in the struggle of developing confidence in Him.

What are your doubts today? Don't sit with them in gloom and worry. Take them to Jesus. Make that father's prayer your own, "I believe; help my unbelief!"

MARK 10
February 21

" *Descending into Greatness* "

Talk about an awkward situation! Two of Jesus' closest disciples, the brothers James and John, came to Him on the journey to Jerusalem with an astoundingly brash request, "Grant to us to sit, one at your right hand and one at your left, in your glory." We learn from another gospel account that it was their mother who had put them up to doing this. Mrs. Zebedee wanted her sons to have the highest positions in the kingdom, and they were more than willing to express her desires.

The scene became even more tense as the other 10 disciples heard what the brothers had requested. Jesus decided it was time for all the disciples, and all the disciples for all time, to learn the path to leadership in the kingdom. Jesus declared that in His kingdom people don't climb the ladder to greatness; they descend the ladder into greatness, "...whoever would be first among you must be slave of all" (v. 44).

In the kingdom of Christ, disciples do not rise to leadership; they kneel to leadership by serving others. This leadership model is based on following the leader. "For even the Son of Man came not to be served but to serve, and to give his life as a ransom for many" (v. 45). Leadership is service, and beyond that, discipleship is service. This means *serving people*. It is not incidental to the Christian life; it is fundamentally what being a Christian really is—serving the Lord by serving others.

A question we should seriously ask ourselves today is not, "What am I doing?" But more specifically, "Who am I serving?" Why not take inventory right now? Take a few minutes and make a list of the names of people you are truly serving. Thank God and pray for every person on that list, and also thank Him for the privilege of doing something that is *truly great* in His eyes.

MARK 11
February 22

" *Cleaning House* "

Jesus was not an angry man. On the contrary, His words and actions throughout His life revealed Him to be a man of humility, meekness, and peace. So, when we read of Him overturning the tables of businessmen and thrashing them with a whip of cords, it seems to be totally out of character for Him.

As we consider Christ's surprising actions in today's passage, it is important to recognize that this is, in fact, the second time that Jesus, filled with anger, beat the moneychangers out of the temple. We are told in John Chapter 2 that at the beginning of His ministry Jesus cleansed the temple of these swindlers. Both times we are told Jesus routed these men while quoting from Isaiah 56 and Jeremiah 7, "My house shall be called a house of prayer for all nations. But you have made it a den of robbers." It is crystal clear that Jesus forcefully declared and expressed the judgment of God against those who use the place of His worship as a vehicle for selfish greed.

Of course, we can all see the application of this passage to the awful, but prevalent, sin of using the ministry of the gospel as a profit-making machine. Truly horrible. However, we also need to make a personal application and evaluation of this sin with regard to our own lives. For *we* are God's temple. Our bodies are His sanctuary. Our purpose is to be "living sacrifices, holy and acceptable to God, which is your spiritual worship" (Rom. 12:1).

We may not be moneychangers in the temple, but we may be just as guilty of selfishly using His temple and His sacrifice (our lives) for our own self-centered goals. It may just be that in prayerful reflection, we will be led to do some "house cleaning" of our own today.

PROVERBS 6
February 23

"A Mountain from an Anthill"

If you have ever attempted to learn another language, you know it is not an easy undertaking. When the Lord confused the languages at the Tower of Babel, he did a really good job of it! People from other countries have often told me that learning American English is quite difficult because it is a language full of so many idioms—figures of speech that convey a concept in a *word picture* that the literal words themselves do not communicate. For example, in America, the phrase, "Don't make a mountain out of a molehill," is a typical, well-known expression. Can you imagine how confusing that could be to a person trying to learn American English! However, for most people raised in America, they clearly understand this expression means, "Don't make a big issue out of a minor event or situation." That is a good idiom, and it is also great advice.

In Proverbs 6: 6-11, our Lord, in effect, reverses the message of the molehill idiom by telling us to make a big deal out of a very little hill—the anthill. In fact, God urges us to carefully study the ants on the anthill in order to gain a mountain of wisdom.

What do we learn from the ants? We learn that the answer to financial want and emotional worry is to diligently work. The ant does not work under *slavish* obligation to a master but in wise response to the opportunity to prepare now for the future needs in the winter season. The ant works in the summer in preparation for the next season of life. That's pretty smart! Let's learn from these little "wise guys," the ants. Life is short. Opportunities abound. Death is certain. Eternity is long. Rewards are promised.

"Go to the ant, O sluggard; consider her ways, and be wise."
(Proverbs 6:6)

PSALMS 12 & 13
February 24

"Singing in the Dark"

One reason the Psalms are so dearly beloved is because David often says things we know to be true and we feel in our soul, but we would never say them in church. Psalm 13 is a perfect example of one of those brutally honest moments. David is in a dark season, not only because of treachery from some of his closest companions and dearest loved ones but also because he feels abandoned by God and utterly alone. So much so that he cries out in despair, "How long, O Lord? Will you forget me forever? How long will you hide your face from me?" (v. 1)

You know the feeling, don't you? Maybe that is where you are and what you are feeling right now. So, what should we do when we feel the darkness around us and within us, but we don't feel *Him?* Take heart, for that is exactly the reason this Psalm is included in God's Word. How gracious our dear Lord is to record this song so we can sing it with David!

First of all, confess your feelings. This means to confess to God how you feel. Denial is not a spiritual virtue. Get honest with God, just like David. God will not be surprised, and he will not be offended. Tell God what you are feeling and ask Him the questions that are grieving your soul, but don't stop there. After you have confessed your feelings, just like David, *confess your faith.* Give voice to what you know is true even if you are not feeling it right now. Make the choice to rejoice. Sing out the truth of your faith in the midst of your darkness and doubt. Sing with David in the dark:

"But I have trusted in your steadfast love; my heart shall rejoice in your salvation. I will sing to the Lord, because he has dealt bountifully with me."
(Psalm 13:5-6)

" A Widow's Might "

Over the years of ministry, I have had a few of them given to me as gifts, "widow's mite" coins. They are indeed tiny coins, and their value was tiny as well. Jesus observed a woman who was a widow placing two of them in the offering box in the temple (hence, the name "widow's mite" given to these coins). These two small coins were worth a Roman "quadrans," which was a coin worth 1/64th of a denarius. A denarius was the average amount of a day's wages in the first century. So, this dear lady was only contributing the equivalent of less than $1.00 in today's currency. How humble and small her gift must have seemed in comparison to the vast sums being donated by the wealthy people into the offering box! But, not to Jesus. In fact, the Lord startled His disciples by declaring that she had given more than all the combined contributions of the wealthy that day. How is that possible? It is not just possible; it is actual.

This is the true valuation in the only economy that really matters, the King's economy. What the King values is a *faith that is produced by love* (1 Tim. 1:5). This widow was totally trusting God to provide for her, and she was trusting Him because she loved Him and knew that He loved her. How rich she truly was! Also, how much richer the lives of millions of believers have been made over the centuries by the testimony of this lady's tiny gift and huge, devoted faith! The lesson she teaches us is not that the Lord demands we give *all we earn* to Him but that we give *all we are* to Him. God's economy values *faith* more than *finances*. May we pray today to be much more wealthy in *that* currency!

"Stay Awake!"

Mark Chapter 13 shares what has come to be known as "The Olivet Discourse." It is also included in the gospel accounts of Matthew and Luke. It is given this title because Jesus climbed the Mount of Olives on the East side of Jerusalem in order for the disciples to take in the whole panorama of Jerusalem as he answered the question posed by Peter, James, John, and Andrew.

A few minutes earlier, in response to the disciples' exclamation about the grandeur and beauty of the temple, Jesus said, "Do you see these great buildings? There will not be left here one stone upon another that will not be thrown down." Now, these four men wanted to know when all these things would be accomplished (vv. 1-4). Jesus took the opportunity from their question, not only to predict the destruction of the temple, which was fulfilled in 70 AD by the Roman armies but also to give an overview of the centuries of conflict to come to the earth and the persecution His followers would experience for their faith (vv. 5-13).

Finally, Jesus shared about the terrible and final Great Tribulation, which would precede His return in glory to bring His Kingdom to Earth (vv. 14-27). Jesus declared that everything He predicted about those final days would occur, and they would take place quickly (vv. 28-31).

Since the day of His message, there have been so many who have attempted (and always failed) to set dates as to when Jesus will fulfill His promise. Sadly, they mislead people and cause so many to miss the entire point of Jesus' message. It is so obvious. He shares it four times in verses 32-37, "Stay awake!" Jesus does not want us to spend our time trying to determine what is the Father's secret (v. 32). He wants us to spend our days doing the Father's will—staying awake, being alert, being ready to meet the Lord when he returns on that great day, by serving Him faithfully *every day*. No day is a good day to "sleep in" when it comes to serving Jesus!

MARK 14
February 27

"Sacred Surrender"

We cannot begin to comprehend it. No human being who knows his or her own sin all too well can fathom the horror of what it would mean for the One who knew no sin to become sin. That is the awful, inexpressible reality that was overwhelming Jesus that night in the garden. It was altogether fitting that this place should be called "Gethsemane," a place where olives were crushed, for there Jesus would be devastated by the terror of what would take place on the cross the next day.

It was simply too much for Jesus. In anguish, he pleaded three times with His Father that if it were possible, the dreadful cup of suffering for sin might be taken from Him. His sweat was as great drops of blood glistening in the Passover moonlight. So immeasurable was His suffering that had angels not come to minister to Him, He might not have physically survived the ordeal.

But, greater than the fear and doubt Jesus was experiencing in His agony beneath the limbs of the olive trees, was His absolute confidence that His Father could not be mistaken. He knew His Father was too good to be unkind, and too wise to be mistaken. With that supreme assurance, He could surrender, "Yet not what I will, but what you will" (v. 36). Jesus won our victory on the cross the next day because He won His victory that night through *sacred surrender* in the garden.

If we desire to follow Jesus, our paths will lead to Gethsemane experiences as well. There will be times when we are overwhelmed with a crushing burden and we cry out to our Heavenly Father for deliverance but it does not come. Maybe you are there right now.

Sometimes as Christians, we suffer not because we are *out* of the Lord's will, but because we are *in* His will. Yes, if we want to truly know Jesus and to be like our Master, he has lovingly ordained that we must experience the "fellowship of His sufferings" (Phil. 3:10) in order that we might be "conformed to His image" (Rom. 8:29). Truly, it is a prayer of *sacred surrender*, "Yet not what I will, but what you will." May we be given grace to make it our own.

MARK 15
February 28

"Come on In!"

Anyone reading the Bible from the beginning page will not read very long until he or she is struck by the fact that God is very separate from human beings. After the terrible betrayal and rebellion by our first ancestors, Adam and Eve, no one was allowed to come into God's holy presence as before. In fact, everything about the sacrificial system that God instituted by Moses was specifically intended to reinforce the truth of God's absolute holiness and separateness from sinners. People could worship Him; they could approach Him through the divinely ordained practices established by the Law given through Moses. However, no one could come into God's presence except the High Priest, and he only one day each year, bringing a sacrifice for his own sins and the sins of God's people.

These rituals were burdensome, but they were a mercy, for no one could come before all-holy God without immediate and total destruction. This awful isolation of God continued for ages and ages, but it all changed in an instant and changed forever. With Jesus' final cry, surrendering His spirit back to His Father, we are told, "The curtain of the temple was torn in two, from top to bottom" (v. 38). How important that it was torn from the top to the bottom, meaning that God Himself was tearing back the curtain that separated Him from anyone who desired to come. The way was opened for all. It was opened by the one who is "the way, the truth and the life," the Lord Jesus Christ. His suffering on the cross for sinners opened the way back to paradise, which is the presence of the life-giving God. In fact, the tearing of the curtain was the holy God's declaration, "Come on in! You are welcome in my presence if you come trusting in the merits of my Son for your acceptance."

Amazing. Truly, "Amazing Grace." God invites you into His presence today. He desires your company. So, today my friend, in Jesus' name, "Let us then with confidence draw near to the throne of grace, that we may receive mercy and find grace to help in time of need" (Heb. 4:16).

MARCH

"Consider the lilies of the field, how they grow: they neither toil nor spin."

" *And Peter* "

The Gospel of Mark has been called by some Bible teachers "The Gospel of Peter." It has been called this because the early church fathers mentioned Mark as being an associate of Peter in ministry in the years following the formation of the church in Jerusalem. Mark is also called "The Gospel of Peter" because we are given more information about Peter's involvement with Jesus than in any of the other three gospels.

Especially, it is Mark who gives us the most personal insights into Peter's actions after our Lord's arrest and crucifixion. Mark is the one who tells us in detail how Peter followed Jesus "afar off" as He was led to the house of the High Priest. Mark takes us into the courtyard and allows us to listen to Peter as he curses and swears that he does not know the Lord. It is Mark who tells us that after his denial, Peter found a solitary place and "broke down" and wept over the reality of his sin. It is also Mark who, in two small words, shares an insight into the undying devotion of Jesus when he records that the angel at the empty tomb told the women, "Go, tell his disciples *and Peter*" that the Lord has risen. "*And Peter*."

We gather from the angel's statement that evidently Peter no longer considered himself a disciple because of his terrible sin, and more than all the others he needed to know his master still included him among His disciples. How wonderful to recognize that no sin was greater than the love in the heart of Jesus, a heart beating again for all eternal ages. Perhaps today you need to claim as your own the deathless love of Jesus for you. Confess your sin and failure to the Lord, then by faith take your place with Peter as a trophy of grace and a messenger of your resurrected King.

" *Two Voices* "

Proverbs Chapter 7 begins and ends with two startling contrasts:

> (v. 2) "Keep my commandments and live."
> (v. 27) "Her house is the way to Sheol, going down to the chambers of death."

This is a message about the pleading calls of two women. One woman is "Wisdom," who often in Proverbs is symbolized as a beautiful woman that calls on people to follow the commandments of God. The other woman is often referred to as the "Adulteress," who pleads with men to forsake God's path and come to her house and fulfill their desires in sensual pleasure. Certainly, the warning in these passages is directed toward young men. However, the deeper principle and application is shared with *all* people whether men or women.

There are constantly two voices calling out to be heeded and followed, the voice of Wisdom and the voice of the World. In reality, the voice of Wisdom is the voice of the Lord, calling us to keep His commandments, to follow His ways and experience life. The other voice (and it is alluring indeed) is the voice of the World. This lively voice promises self-fulfillment and pleasures of every kind, but in terrible reality, ultimately only produces misery and destruction.

How do we hear Wisdom and her voice more clearly, and how can we make the World's voice grow more faint? One word, "Devotion." Devote yourself to Wisdom, pledge your allegiance to her. Make her your closest companion. "Say to Wisdom, 'You are my sister,' and call insight your intimate friend" (v. 4). How do we develop this love relationship with Wisdom? The Father of Wisdom tells us how:

> *"My son, keep my words and treasure up my commandments with you; keep my commandments and live; keep my teaching as the apple of your eye; bind them on your fingers; write them on the tablet of your heart."* (Proverbs 7:1-3)

Amen.

PSALMS 14 & 15
March 3

<h1 style="text-align:center">" God's Neighbors "</h1>

Psalm 15 opens with David gazing upon Mount Zion in Jerusalem and on the *Tent of Meeting* where God dwelt with His people. David's home was on the same ridge in Jerusalem; he was God's neighbor. This amazing truth led David to meditate on who could truly be "God's neighbor," not just in physical residence but in spiritual reality. David lists five "zoning requirements" for people who desire to be "God's neighbors." Let's take some time to note those requirements today:

1. (v. 2) "He who walks blamelessly and does what is right." That is, he or she is guided by truth, refusing to do what is wrong and focused on doing what is right.
2. (v. 2) The person who "speaks truth in his heart" means a person who first applies God's truth to his or her own soul. They meditate on God's Word for their own benefit.
3. (v. 3) "Who does not slander with his tongue and does no evil to his neighbor, nor takes up a reproach against his friend." This person considers a neighbor's reputation and character sacred and protects it.
4. (v. 4) "In whose eyes a vile person is despised, but who honors those who fear the Lord." He or she values the character of others on how they value the character of God.
5. (vs. 4, 5) "Who swears to his own hurt and does not change; who does not put out his money at interest and does not take a bribe against the innocent." These people don't live for money. They live for God and others.

Living according to God's zoning laws gives us an eternal title deed to the best neighborhood!

> *"He who does these things shall never be moved."*
> (Psalm 15:5)

LUKE 1
March 4

"Questions of the Righteous"

Luke's gospel opens with a very lengthy chapter, 80 verses, one of the longest chapters in the New Testament. Of course, the chapter has to be lengthy because Luke intends to make his record of the life and ministry of Jesus, a story which is built around the personal encounters of people with the greatest events to ever unfold in all of human history. Luke writes as a historian, but also one who is determined to tell the story through experiences of the people involved (vv. 1-4). Luke knows that what he is writing is intended to bring people to faith. So, it is very appropriate that he begins his gospel by sharing how, from the beginning of Jesus' life, people were called by God to trust in Him.

In this opening chapter, two individuals have some very deep questions in regard to faith when they hear the promise of God shared by the Angel Gabriel. Zachariah, the father of John the Baptist, has a question, "How shall I know this? For I am an old man, and my wife is advanced in years" (v. 18). Mary, the mother of Jesus, has a question for Gabriel as well, "How will this be, since I am a virgin?" (v. 34) The questions are similar, but they are met with very different reactions from Gabriel. Why does Zachariah receive a rebuke, but Mary receives more information and encouragement? What is going on?

Notice the questions again carefully. Zachariah said, *"How shall I know?"* Mary said, *"How will this be?"* Zachariah was a righteous man, but he needed *proof* to believe. Mary, a virtuous teenager, believed but wanted to know how it would happen. These are two very different attitudes. Likewise, we can be people of faith in God's promises. Like Zachariah, our faith can be tainted by desire for selfish proof, or like Mary, our faith can be full of selfless submission. Which example will you follow? This would be a good thing for us to pray about today!

LUKE 2
March 5

"Sovereign Submission"

The chapter for our Scripture reading today is one of the most beloved in all the Bible, and rightly so. It contains the beautiful story of the night of nights when the Son of God was born. The words of the message and song of the angels, first shared with those shepherds, have thrilled the souls of untold millions throughout the ages. The events of that night are so powerful that we can easily overlook the fact that Luke Chapter 2 spans a timeframe of 30 years. These verses give us the only insight we really have into 30 of Jesus' 33 years here on earth.

What do we learn about Jesus in these few verses covering the majority of His life? Two things—His *wisdom* and His *submission.*

We are told that He was "filled with wisdom" (v. 40). In fact, by the age of twelve, Jesus was so wise in the truths of Scripture that He astounded the greatest theologians of the day (v. 47). We learn from these verses that Jesus not only knew the Word of God, but He also knew He was the Son of God (v. 49).

What did Jesus do with this incredible wisdom? He practiced submission. Read that again—*He practiced submission.* "And he went down with them and came to Nazareth and was submissive to them" (v. 51). Jesus, filled with wisdom, expressed that wisdom in submission. Submission to God's authority and the authority of those who have God-ordained positions of authority in our lives, is not bondage. It is *Godly wisdom.* From His childhood through His youth and young adulthood, Jesus showed us the wisest way to live—in submission to God by honoring others. Our sovereign Lord possessed a submissive spirit during His life. Let's take some time to evaluate our submissive spirit today.

LUKE 3
March 6

" Time to Get Serious "

We know from the writings of Paul that Luke was a physician (Col. 4:14). It is also clear from reading his gospel account that Luke was also a very precise historian. In verses one and two of our reading today, Luke mentions the specific year during the reign of Tiberius Caesar. He also further qualifies the timeframe by mentioning the public service of seven other individuals connected to that year. All of that specific information is shared to help pinpoint the exact year that "the word of God came to John" (v. 2).

Luke wanted to be certain that anyone reading his account of the life of Jesus would know very well that it was not a compilation of fables, but rather a reporting of documented facts that occurred in recent history. Luke makes it clear that the calendar of human events has been intersected by the timeframe of God. It is a season of revelation from God about the importance of repenting of sin and receiving the good news of forgiveness and restoration.

"The word of God" came once again after three hundred years of silence since the time of the prophet Malachi, and the message was one of urgency and opportunity—repent and prepare your heart for a living encounter with the holy and merciful Lord of the ages.

In reality, that day so carefully defined by Luke has never ended. This is the Lord's day. This is the day of salvation. And this is the time acceptable to God for helpless sinners such as you and me, to open our hearts to Him. No day is ordinary when it is dedicated to God. This very day is filled with eternity and is, in fact, timeless when we respond to the "word of the Lord" which He graciously gave us. So today, let's "listen up" because our Master is speaking! When we obey His message, this "ordinary day" becomes priceless and eternal.

LUKE 4
March 7

"Deliverance at the Synagogue"

I will never forget the day. It is one of the most memorable in my entire life. I was standing in the synagogue in Capernaum that had been erected in the second century on top of the original structure where Jesus had taught the Scriptures. As I walked around its pillars, I reflected on what it must have been like on that day when the demon-possessed man burst into the building crying out in terror at the presence of the Son of God. I also tried to imagine the stunned silence in that room as Jesus commanded the raging demon to be silent and leave the tormented man. And that is when I heard him.

At first, I thought it was my imagination, but I distinctly heard a man softly weeping. As I walked around the corner of the synagogue, I saw a member of our group kneeling on the ancient stones overcome with deep emotion. After a few moments, I knelt beside him with my arm around his shoulders and asked him what was wrong. Through his tears, he answered, "It's all become *so real*. Jesus really did this, and He did it *all for me*."

Now it was my turn to weep. We knelt there, where Jesus delivered the demon-possessed man and thanked Him for delivering us. My friend's life was completely changed that day. He has never been the same, and I know it will always be a sacred moment for me. Perhaps you need a "sacred moment" today. You do not have to travel to Israel and visit the synagogue in Capernaum. The same powerful and merciful Master is with you right now. Ask Him to make it all become *so real*. *"Jesus, you really did this, and you did it all for me."*

LUKE 5
March 8

"Something Old, Something New"

Jesus said some things just do not go together. Like fasting at a wedding, patching new cloth on an old garment, and pouring fresh wine into an old wineskin (vv. 33-39). In these examples, Jesus was comparing the empty religious traditions of the Pharisees with the abundant life He offered those who followed Him.

Now we need to be clear. Jesus was not condemning traditions of faith. He was condemning the empty observance of religious traditions that are not rooted in *true love* for God but are, in reality, expressions of self-righteous pride.

The Pharisees wanted Jesus to conform His teaching to their legalistic observances of religious traditions. Jesus declared this was impossible because the life of love and faith is not compatible with the old practice of legalism. Trying to do so would be like attempting to put a patch of new cloth on an old piece of clothing, or trying to store fresh, new wine in old, stiff wineskins.

The new cannot be added to the old, and the old cannot contain the new. What Jesus gives us never becomes worn out, and it never becomes stiff. He gives life, eternal life, which is always a present-tense reality. The gift of life we have in Jesus is not something we are called to observe, but something we are called to experience.

This would be a good time to evaluate. How fresh is your faith? Our faith may be old in years, but it should never become stale in experience. Ask the Lord today to do some new things in your life, and while you are praying, ask Him to make you a fresh and flexible container of His daily, amazing grace.

PROVERBS 8 & PSALM 16
March 9

" *Fullness of Joy* "

God is joyful. Please read those words again. *God is joyful.* Honestly, there are many qualities and attributes we associate with God, but how often do we think of His *joyfulness*? But it is true, God is the most joyful being that exists because the joy of perfection permeates all He is! God is *completely joyful.* The only true and lasting joy any person can experience is through knowing and sharing in *God's joy.* In fact, it is God's joy to share His joy with His people.

King David knew God's joy by experience, and he sang about it in Psalm 16:11, "You make known to me the path of life; in your presence there is fullness of joy; at your right hand are pleasures forevermore." David looks back over his life and recognizes that God, in His grace, revealed the path David should take. It is the "path of life." God has been David's companion on this journey, and David has found God's friendship to be the "fullness of joy." Then, David's heart exults to think that this joy will never end; he will experience "pleasures forevermore" with his God. Wow! What an eternal companion—the God who is contagious with joy!

Dear friend, this song was written by David, but it was recorded for us to sing. Life is not always easy. It might be filled with challenges for you right now. But the song is ever true. God's path is life. His presence is joy. His promise is pleasures forevermore. Now that is something to sing about today!

" *En Gedi* "

*"I love you, O Lord my strength. The Lord is my rock and my
fortress and my deliverer, My God, my rock,
in whom I take refuge."* (Psalm 18:1)

The area east of the Dead Sea is a barren and desolate landscape, practically without vegetation. And then there is En Gedi. A series of cascading waterfalls brings a flowing river of freshwater through a canyon that is surrounded by sheer cliffs and pockmarked with innumerable caves. En Gedi is like a garden teeming with life, surrounded by a landscape resembling the surface of the moon.

It is a perfect place of provision and refuge. And that is exactly why David led his men there to escape King Saul. Time and time again, David would find shelter and safety within this craggy oasis in the wilderness. En Gedi became such a place of shelter to David that it stood as a metaphor in his mind of the refuge he found in God. Like En Gedi, God was his rock, his fortress, his hiding place, his shelter, and his strong tower.

God is En Gedi to His people. God is En Gedi for you when your soul feels like a desert and your spirit feels pursued by your enemy. Today your En Gedi, your God of refuge, is near. Don't make Him your last resort; make Him your first response in time of trouble. Spend some time in your safe and soothing En Gedi today.

*"The Lord lives, and blessed be my rock,
and exalted be the God of my salvation."*
(Psalm 18:46)

LUKE 6
March 11

"An Eye Exam"

In Jesus' day vision problems were part of life, but not easily corrected. Doctors could prescribe a variety of eye salves for eye infections or inflammation. However, when it came to poor eyesight or failing eyesight, there was very little that could be done. This added to the importance of several miracles Jesus performed in restoring eyesight to the blind. In verses 39-42 of our reading today, Jesus addresses eyesight in a very different way. Like a spiritual ophthalmologist, our Lord warns us as His disciples about the dreadful but deceptive eye disease of a hypocritical and judgmental focus on others. "Why do you see the speck that is in your brother's eye but do not notice the log that is in your own eye?" (v. 41) Ouch! That eye exam hurts a bit, doesn't it?

Evidently, both the speck and the log are made of the same substance—wood. But there is a lot more wood in a log than in a splinter! The image of a man with a *log* in his own eye trying to deal with a *splinter* in another man's eye is quite humorous. However, Jesus' subject is very serious. He is addressing sin, the awful sin of hypocritically judging others.

Jesus is aware of the danger his disciples face. Apart from humble self-examination, we can develop a proud, hyper-critical focus on the faults of others. It is not wrong to detect a spiritual problem in someone's life and desire to help them address it. In fact, Jesus encourages that. (v. 42) But our first focus needs to be an exam on our own spiritual condition, and then, by God's precious forgiveness, we can have the genuine spirit and spiritual vision to help others. Today might be a good time for us to see the Great Physician for an updated vision test.

" *Extravagant Love* "

It was a little awkward, and Simon was more than a little offended. Simon, the Pharisee, had invited Jesus to dinner, but he certainly had not invited her, and he had not expected this! The most notorious women in town suddenly appeared in the middle of dinner, and kneeling at the feet of Jesus, anointed His feet with expensive perfume, washed them with her tears, and wiped them with her hair.

Even more than what this woman did was what Jesus *did not do* that offended Simon even more. Jesus *did not* rebuke this sinful woman. So, how could He possibly be a prophet of God? Simon so quickly reached his judgmental decision, but he was completely clueless to the motives of the heart of this woman and the heart of Jesus. Even more tragic, Simon was oblivious to the condition of his *own* heart. Simon had never sensed the weight of his own sins or felt the need of redeeming grace, so how could he possibly understand the expression of extravagant, grateful love being displayed at his dinner table? Simon was an incredibly religious man, but he knew nothing of the heart of God toward repentant sinners. All of us must beware of the tendency to drift toward the *religion of Simon.*

How long has it been since you knelt in tears at the feet of Jesus and poured out the perfume of worship upon Him for His grace to you? How long has it been since you did not ask for anything in prayer, but only offered grateful praise to Him? How long since you basked in the joy of Jesus' words to you, "Your faith has saved you, go in peace?" This would be a good day.

LUKE 8
March 13

"The Fringe of His Garment"

In his account of the life and ministry of Jesus, Luke focuses more than any of the other gospel authors on Jesus' perfect humanity. More than the other three gospels combined, Luke shares with us the encounters of individual people with Jesus.

In our reading today, we see Jesus surrounded by a sea of humanity pressing to catch a glimpse of the rabbi from Nazareth. But Luke shares the *personal* encounter in that crowd that one woman had with Jesus. Her case is truly pathetic. She is sick and has been suffering from a blood disorder for over 12 years. She is bankrupt, having spent all her resources on medical treatments, but to no avail. Most heart-wrenching of all, she is disqualified from public worship of God, since, according to Jewish ceremonial law, her blood disorder makes her unclean and therefore forbidden from entering the temple or any synagogue. Her only hope is Jesus; she believes that if she can just secretly touch the hem of the Lord's garment, she will be healed. Her desperate faith was totally rewarded for, in an instant, the power of healing flowed from Jesus through her fingertips and throughout her entire body.

There are so many lessons from this story, but one is very clear. Jesus is the Lord of all creation, but He is completely available and *personal* to every individual. Jesus is aware of all of us as if there were only *one* of us on earth. He is a *personal* Savior who is *personally* concerned for each human being. Best of all, we can reach Him. By faith, we can cross time and space and touch the hem of Jesus' garment today. His answer is still the same to all who do. *"Your faith has made you well; go in peace."*

LUKE 9
March 14

" *The Biggest Loser* "

We keep score on everything from sports, to grades, to investments, etc., etc. We do this in order to determine who is succeeding and who is failing. The scorecard tells us who wins. However, there is a huge fallacy in our reasoning about the scorecard. What if our way of taking score is wrong? What if the way we determine success and failure, the way we decide who wins and loses, is ultimately and fundamentally mistaken? That would mean our entire life would, in the end, be a total failure.

What I have just shared may seem depressing but that is exactly the message Jesus shares in verses 23-25 of today's reading. He does this not to depress our spirit but to make a success of our lives. Jesus truly wants us to be winners, but first He has to fundamentally change our understanding of what winning and losing really is.

"If anyone would come after me, let him deny himself and take up his cross daily and follow me. For whoever would save his life will lose it, but whoever loses his life for my sake will save it. For what does it profit a man if he gains the whole world and loses or forfeits himself?"

This is a radically different scorecard. However, it is the only one that truly matters because it is shared by the one who ultimately determines winning and losing. How gracious our Lord is to define winning and losing for us! And how important it is for us to start keeping score *His* way. He tells us in this passage how to do this "daily," to decide each day that denying ourselves and following Him is the path to winning now and forever! What a wise thing that is to do! How right the missionary Jim Elliot was:

> *"He is no fool who gives what he cannot keep*
> *to gain what he cannot lose."*

LUKE 10
March 15

"Working and Worshiping"

Luke Chapter 10 could be called "the chapter of ultimate priorities." These 42 verses share stories that define the ultimate priorities of life— the priority of our personal salvation (vv. 17-20), the priority of love (vv. 25-37), and the priority of worship (vv. 38-42). Each of these could require a series of messages. But today, notice how simple, yet completely, our Lord addresses the importance He places on our worship. He does this by contrasting the two choices made by two of His most beloved disciples, Martha and Mary.

The women, along with their brother Lazarus, have welcomed Jesus into their home. Martha immediately gets busy preparing a meal for Jesus and His disciples, but Mary takes a seat at the Lord's feet and completely focuses on what He is teaching. The more Martha works at preparing the meal, the more frustrated she becomes with her sister. Finally, Martha is so exasperated that she interrupts and blames Jesus, "Lord do you not care that my sister has left me to serve alone? Tell her then to help me." Wow, what an awkward moment! But Jesus is grateful for Martha's hard work, and He lovingly refocuses her priorities. "Martha, Martha, you are anxious and troubled about many things, but one thing is necessary. Mary has chosen the good portion, which will not be taken away from her" (vv. 41-42).

Martha put the priority on working but Mary chose to worship. Both working and worshiping are important, but work without worship leads to worry. Mary recognized that the meal that was truly most important was the spiritual nourishment provided by Jesus' teaching. Mary's choice still instructs us today. At the feet of Jesus is where worship takes place, and that is where our best work begins. Let's start there.

Work without worship leads to worry.

"The Treasure of God's Word"

In Psalm 19, David sings a song celebrating God's revelation. David exalts the grace the Lord has demonstrated in making Himself known. David especially praises in verses 7-11 the infinite value of God's Word to His people. Today let's focus on the 9 qualities of God's Word that are priceless to each of our lives.

1. The Word of God provides *spiritual renewal.* "The law of the Lord is perfect, reviving the soul" (v. 7).
2. The Word of God provides *wisdom.* "The testimony of the Lord is sure, making wise the simple" (v. 7).
3. The Word of God provides *deep joy.* "The precepts of the Lord are right, rejoicing the heart" (v. 8).
4. The Word of God provides *insight.* "The commandment of the Lord is pure, enlightening the eyes" (v. 8).
5. The Word of God produces *holy awe.* "The fear of the Lord is clean, enduring forever" (v. 9).
6. The Word of God is *true and righteous.* "The rules of the Lord are true, and righteous altogether" (v. 9).
7. The Word of God is *invaluable.* "More to be desired are they than gold, even much fine gold" (v. 10).
8. The Word of God is *delicious.* "Sweeter also than honey and drippings of the honeycomb" (v. 10).
9. The Word of God provides great *reward.* "Moreover, by them is your servant warned, in keeping them there is great reward" (v. 11).

What a priceless treasure!

PSALMS 21 & 22
March 17

"*The Psalm of the Cross*"

All of the Psalms of David rise out of his own experience. Each of his songs are his own expression of his life's journey. However, sometimes David writes as a prophet. His words have a fulfillment in the years to come. Psalm 22 is certainly a word of prophecy, for it was not fulfilled in David's experience, but in the life of his greater Son, Jesus Christ. Psalm 22 takes us to Calvary, to the sufferings of the Savior.

Jesus quotes from this Psalm during His agony on the cross. In fact, verse 1 expresses the ultimate horror Jesus experienced, "My God, my God, why have you forsaken Me?" The only time Jesus referred to Him by any other title than "Father" was as He suffered. Why did Jesus refer to His Heavenly Father as "God" on the cross? You and I are the reason. On the cross of Calvary, the Lord Jesus bore our sin as He offered Himself to God as the atoning sacrifice for our forgiveness.

There is a mystery in this Psalm that the most brilliant of theologians cannot fully comprehend. Martin Luther, as he meditated on this verse, declared, "God forsaken by God, who can understand it?" Thank God we do not have to understand it, but we can trust in the gospel message. "For our sake he made him to be sin who knew no sin, so that in him we might become the righteousness of God" (2 Cor. 5:21). Yes, Psalm 22 is a terrible song, but it is the wonderful theme of our salvation in the redeeming love of our Messiah and our God, Jesus of Nazareth.

Hallelujah, what a Savior!

LUKE 11
March 18

" The Biggest Request "

John Newton is famous for writing a song. This song is the most recorded song in the history of the world. Of course, I am referring to his beloved hymn, "Amazing Grace." But John Newton wrote hundreds of hymns in his lifetime. One which is not sung in our day was probably inspired by Jesus' words of encouragement regarding prayer from today's passage. Newton's song has a title that sounds strange to us today, "Come, My Soul, Thy Suit Prepare." However, the second stanza contains a timeless challenge for our boldness in prayer:

> *"Thou art coming to a King,*
> *Large petitions with thee bring;*
> *For His grace and power are such,*
> *None can ever ask too much;*
> *None can ever ask too much."*

To put John Newton's challenge in the vernacular of our day, Newton's challenge might simply be, "Pray Big." God is a big God and His Son, the Lord Jesus, challenges His disciples to pray with boldness and expectancy. He is not at all like the reluctant friend of verse 7 who has to be pressured to answer the door. God delights in His children's requests and joyfully answers. In fact, Jesus encouraged us to make the biggest of all requests, "...how much more will the Heavenly Father give the Holy Spirit to those who ask him!" (v. 13) Wow, what a prayer encouragement to ask God for the biggest request of all—Himself! The Lord desires us to know by experience the power of His presence. There is not a bigger request or a better answer than that, so accept the Master's challenge and "Pray Big!"

LUKE 12
March 19

"More Than Sparrows"

Recently, while enjoying a morning cup of coffee, I happened to look out the window and saw the fulfillment of one of the verses in this chapter, and I felt the application fresh and new in my heart. A tiny sparrow was enjoying the refreshment in our birdbath, just splashing away and flapping his tiny wings for all he was worth! The Spirit immediately brought to my mind the words of comfort Jesus shared with His disciples recorded in verses 6-7, "Are not five sparrows sold for two pennies? And not one of them is forgotten before God. Why, even the hairs of your head are all numbered. Fear not; you are of more value than many sparrows." Our Savior turned bird watching into a devotional exercise.

It is clear that our Heavenly Father is able to provide for the needs of the smallest birds and also all the untold millions of birds of all sizes around the earth. If God cares for the needs of the birds, will He not much more provide for His own dear children that have been purchased by the precious blood of His beloved Son? The answer to the question is so clear, it does not even need to be expressed. God is good. He is infinitely good, and His goodness is perfectly united with an infinite awareness of our every need. There is nothing that concerns *us* that does not concern *Him*. I felt that assurance in my heart that morning as I watched the sparrow merrily splashing in the birdbath. I think a little more bird watching might be helpful for my faith. How about you?

LUKE 13
March 20

"A Tale of Two Towers"

On September 16, 2001, more Americans attended church than on any Sunday in decades. People flocked to services in record numbers because of the personal impact on their lives from the terrible events on September 11. Our nation was viciously attacked by terrorists, and thousands of lives were lost. The nation was in shock and grief. People were seeking answers and an understanding of how to process the events.

As I prayed about what to share on that Sunday, I tried to recall if any similar event had been addressed by Jesus in His ministry. My search brought me to verses 1-5 of today's passage. Jesus' answer was not what people expected when they told Him about the vicious attack by the Roman governor, Pontius Pilate, on Jesus' fellow citizens from Galilee. Jesus used the event to address the one great certainty in life and the importance of preparing for what it would bring. Jesus said, "Unless you repent, you will all likewise perish." Then, Jesus referred to the falling of the tower in Siloam that killed 18 people and repeated his declaration, "Unless you repent, you will all likewise perish."

Jesus surprised His listeners by His answer, and I probably surprised some people by using Jesus' words for the message on that Sunday following 9/11. However, the reality of death, regardless of how or when it comes, needs to be the ultimate preparation of every person. There is only one place of safety where we can run for our ultimate protection, the tower which will never fall.

"The name of the Lord is a strong tower;
the righteous man runs into it and is safe."
(Proverbs 18:10)

"Counting the Cost"

There are few things more frustrating than false advertising. It is sometimes referred to as the "bait and switch," making a very inviting offer but hiding the details of *other* cost and fees.

Jesus called all people to follow Him, but He could never be accused of using false advertising. Jesus was loving but also absolutely truthful as He invited people to be His disciples. Salvation is completely free! Totally paid for by Jesus Himself, but the cost of being a disciple is absolute. Following Jesus means total surrender, "So therefore, any one of you who does not renounce all that he has cannot be my disciple" (v. 33). Jesus did not pull the "bait and switch;" he did not make this requirement *after* people became His disciples. He declared it to all the "great crowds that accompanied him" (v. 25).

There is in vogue today, a ministry philosophy that says the message shared with the "seekers" of truth should be communicated in a very "sensitive" way so as not to put roadblocks in their way of pursuing a decision to follow Jesus. That ministry philosophy may be popular, but it is certainly not biblical and is definitely not the practice of Jesus.

Our Lord is completely honest and forthright; He will have no one follow Him under false pretenses. If we follow Him, He must be master of all, or He is not master at all. However, Jesus also promises that if we surrender to Him, we will know the greatest life imaginable here on earth, and a life with Him in heaven that is beyond our wildest dreams. Praise the Lord, there is no false advertising in that!

LUKE 15
March 22

" *Lost and Found* "

The fifteenth Chapter of Luke is the "Lost and Found" chapter of the New Testament. Jesus tells three stories about lost things that were found—a lost sheep, a lost coin, and a lost son. This series of stories was told by our Lord to respond to the accusation brought against Him by the Pharisees and the scribes, "This man receives sinners and eats with them" (v. 2). Jesus told these stories to reveal the heart of God for the lost and also to reveal how far from the heart of God the religious leaders of Israel truly were.

Everyone can identify with the emotions of the shepherd, the woman, and the father as they desperately long for the lost sheep, the lost coin, and the lost son. Each story includes the joy of what was lost being found and the invitation for all to celebrate in the joy of the return. Everyone joins in the celebration—everyone except the eldest son.

The son who stayed and lived in the father's house did not share his father's heart. That was exactly the attitude being displayed by the religious leaders. They claimed to be the spokesmen for the Lord, but they demonstrated how little they really knew Him by how little they cared for the tax collectors and sinners who were becoming followers of Jesus.

Jesus declared His mission was to "seek and to save those who are lost," and how every one of us who knows Christ as Savior, praises Him for that mission! However, we must always be careful that as we serve and worship the Lord in His house each week, we also share His heart for the lost, and share in His joy over every sinner that repents. There is joy in heaven when lost people come to Christ. Let's share in that party!

PROVERBS 9
March 23

"God's Curriculum"

God, by His very definition and His attributes, is the source of all knowledge. What we refer to as the past is the present moment to Him, and what we call the future is to our Lord as certain as things that have already happened. All that can be discovered has always been known to Him. He possesses all knowledge. Therefore, whatever we want to call "education" can only be genuine as it relates information correctly to Him, the God of all truth. To gain information without connecting it to Him is, in reality, a journey into foolishness. That is why the wisest man to ever live, King Solomon, rightly declares "The fear of the Lord is the beginning of wisdom, and the knowledge of the Holy One is insight" (v. 10).

True education, Solomon says, is always spiritual in nature. It involves aligning ourselves and all of life with Him. Apart from Him, human education is only folly.

Being a truly enlightened person is a journey into the Lord. The journey begins with the "fear of the Lord," which means an awe-inspired respect and love that becomes the guiding star of our life. This journey does not end with a graduation or degree, but it continues into the increasing understanding of who God is and how all of our existence relates to Him. The "knowledge of the Holy One" provides us with insights into life that cannot be provided by the finest of universities. How wonderful that his education is not available for just a few but for all who will hear God's gracious invitation, "Leave your simple ways, and live, and walk in the way of insight" (v. 6).

For all of us, class is in session today!

PSALMS 23 & 24
March 24

"The Gates Will Open"

Standing on the crest of the Mount of Olives and gazing upon the city of Jerusalem is one of the most spectacular sights a believer can ever look upon. Just beneath your location is the Garden of Gethsemane and the ancient olive trees beneath whose limbs the Lord prayed in the moonlight. Further beyond is the Kidron Valley, across which He was led in chains by His captors. Then your eyes reach the hillside across the valley, and you look on the walls of Jerusalem atop Mount Zion.

As your eyes follow this wall, you notice the outline of a large set of gates. The gates open directly onto the temple mount, but you can see that these gates were bricked shut long ago to limit access to the area of the Al-Aqsa Mosque that now sits on the temple mount as one of Islam's most holy sites. A few years ago, an archaeologist discovered that directly under the currently closed gates, lie the remains of ancient gates that existed in the time of Jesus.

The ancient eastern gates are covered by mounds of dirt. The modern eastern gates are bricked shut, but one day those gates will be opened again. Jesus will return to the Mount of Olives and will once more ride down the slopes of the hill, not as the humble servant, but as the victorious Lord. On that day, the shout from Psalm 24 will resound across the Kidron Valley:

> *"Lift up your heads, O gates!*
> *And be lifted up, O ancient doors,*
> *that the King of glory may come in.*
> *Who is this King of glory?*
> *The Lord, strong and mighty,*
> *the Lord, mighty in battle!"*
> (Psalm 24:7-8)

Even so, come Lord Jesus.

LUKE 16
March 25

" *A Bad Man's Good Example* "

There are times when bad people provide good examples, not regarding their character, but their shrewdness. Jesus often used these types of people as main characters in His stories to teach His followers wisdom from their worldly ways.

One of the best (or worst) of these individuals is described in our reading today. The man is a manager of all the possessions for a very wealthy lord. For years he has been "skimming money off the top" and embezzling his master's money. However, the scheme has come to light, and the master calls for an audit of his affairs. The crooked manager knows that his days of employment are numbered, but he has one more crafty idea to prepare for the inevitable. He quickly goes to several of his master's creditors and reduces the amount each owes on their debts to his master.

In the story Jesus told, the master commended his manager, not for his honesty, but for his shrewdness. He gained the affection of these people so that they might help him after he lost his position. In applying the lesson, Jesus said, "And I tell you, make friends for yourselves by means of unrighteous wealth, so that when it (or 'you') fails they may receive you into the eternal dwellings."

Jesus is telling us to prepare in this life for the life to come. In this world, we can use our "worldly" resources to "make friends," that is, to provide for the physical and spiritual needs of others. When we fail, that is, when life is over, those whom we have ministered to on earth will gladly receive us in the eternal kingdom. The smartest investment is one that has the least risk, with the highest return, for the longest period. When we invest our resources in the souls of men and women, that is a brilliant, eternal investment. The dividends are out of this world!

89

"Be That One"

One of the most dreaded diseases around the world for thousands of years has been that of leprosy. Although it is practically unknown in the developed countries of the world today, it still ravages the lives of thousands of people in parts of Africa and Asia. Leprosy has been called the "living death" because the illness slowly destroys the cells in the body's extremities and face before spreading inward to the major organs. It progressively destroys the body; but, just as terribly, it robs the people of the meaningful social relationships with family and other humans.

In Jesus' day, added to these horrors of leprosy was the rejection from the community, isolation, and loss of acceptance in gatherings of worship. You can imagine the first glimmer of hope that reached the camps of these pitiful sufferers when they heard of one called Jesus of Nazareth who was able to heal all manner of diseases.

Our reading today tells us of ten lepers who set out to find this wonder-worker. He was their only hope. No doubt, they were forced to travel at night and hide during the day to avoid being stoned. At last, they saw the crowd following Jesus on His way to Jerusalem. With their croaking, rasping voices they cried out, "Jesus, Master, have mercy on us!" Jesus did not come to them, He simply spoke, "Go and show yourselves to the priests." At Jesus' command, the lepers shuffled off; but amazingly, their steps quickened, their legs strengthened, and looking at each other, they saw their faces fresh and restored.

Imagine the rejoicing! What a caravan of praise they became as they marched on...but not all. One leper, overwhelmed with love and gratitude for Jesus, ran back and fell at His feet in adoration. He was a Samaritan, an outcast spiritually and physically, now completely delivered. There were ten healed, but there was only one who knelt and worshiped Jesus with thanksgiving. Today, be that one.

LUKE 18
March 27

"A Tale of Two Religions"

No one ever had the ability to tell a timeless story with such simplicity and clarity as did Jesus. In our reading today, we have perhaps the finest example of Jesus' ability to do this. He shares the story of two men who entered the temple to pray. They are alike in only one way—both of them are approaching God and seeking His acceptance.

In every other way, they are complete opposites. The one, a Pharisee, is respected, religious, and rigorous in his observance of the rituals of Judaism in his day. The other man, a tax collector, is a traitor to his people, an employee of an occupying government. He has made his money by robbing his fellow man. His life is a waste. Both of these men have come to pray to God, but their prayers, like their lives, are completely different. The Pharisee prays a prayer of self-confidence and comparison: "'God, I thank you that I am not like other men, extortioners, unjust, adulterers, or even like this tax collector. I fast twice a week; I give tithes of all that I get.'"

How radically different was the prayer of the tax collector. He sobbed out a prayer of self-condemnation and contrition: "But the tax collector, standing far off, would not even lift up his eyes to heaven, but beat his breast, saying, 'God, be merciful to me, a sinner!'"

Two men, two prayers, representing two forms of religion. The Pharisee approached God on the basis of his own merit; the tax collector approached God on the basis of divine mercy. Merit or mercy, which prayer does the God of heaven receive? Jesus shares the gospel answer, "I tell you, this man (the tax collector) went down to his house justified." The prayer for mercy is the prayer that the Lord hears. May our prayer today be based on God's mercy. May the Lord help us to be people of mercy as we live this day for Him.

LUKE 19
March 28

"A Little Man's Big Change"

Just outside the city of Jericho, next to the main road, stands a huge and ancient tree. It is called the "Zacchaeus Tree." Of course, it is not the same tree that the "vertically challenged" tax collector climbed nearly 2000 years ago. However, it does manage every day to draw tour buses with busloads of people who stop to take pictures, buy trinkets, and ride camels. So, it is appropriately called the "Zacchaeus Tree," for it certainly generates a lot of tax revenue for the city of Jericho!

Zacchaeus was a little man, and his quality of character was smaller still. He is referred to as the "chief tax collector," which means he oversaw, for the Roman government, all the tax collectors in the area of Jericho. The tax collected from this entry point for Judea was huge, and Zacchaeus had become incredibly wealthy by means of all the excess taxes collected by all the tax collectors in the region of Jericho. He had heard about Jesus, probably through the communication of other tax collectors, since so many had become his followers. He may have known Matthew, one of the twelve disciples, who was also a tax collector in Galilee.

Zacchaeus was determined to see Jesus—so determined that he climbed a tree to catch a glimpse of Him. What Zacchaeus didn't know was that Jesus also wanted to see *him* and intentionally stopped beneath the sycamore tree to invite Himself to dinner at his house! We are not told what transpired between Jesus and Zacchaeus at the meal; but in the midst of it, Zacchaeus stood to his feet, proclaimed Jesus as his "Lord," and declared that half his riches would go to the poor and he would pay back everyone he had cheated "fourfold."

This little man had undergone a big conversion, and Jesus rejoiced to see the work of His Father's grace. That night before His entry to Jerusalem, Jesus saw in Zacchaeus's changed heart the purpose for His journey to the cross. "For the son of man came to seek and to save the lost." And all of God's people said, "Amen!"

LUKE 20
March 29

"The God of the Living"

During our Lord's final week of ministry, He was encircled by groups of His enemies, who were constantly attempting to entrap Him through religious arguments so they might bring charges against Him.

One of the leading groups were the Sadducees. They were the power brokers in Jerusalem. They were the religious liberals of the day in that they denied the reality of miracles and angels and, most of all, denied the doctrine of the resurrection. Fittingly, these men tried to trick Jesus into a religious argument by telling, in verses 27-33, the contrived story of a woman who was married and widowed to seven brothers. They believed the follow-up question, about to whom she would be married in the resurrection, would put Jesus in a situation so that any answer He gave would cause Him to be condemned by many leaders in Israel. They were not prepared for His answer.

Jesus declared that marriage is an institution for *this* world, not the world to come. In this, resurrected people will be like the angels (whom the Sadducees denied existed) who do not marry. Then, Jesus boldly declared the truth of the resurrection, which the Sadducees also denied. Finally, Jesus astounded those who listened, and He blessed His disciples for all ages, in His revelation about God and His people: "But that the dead are raised, even Moses showed, in the passage about the bush, where he calls the Lord the God of Abraham and the God of Isaac and the God of Jacob. Now He is not God of the dead, but of the living, for all live to him" (vv. 37-38).

What a revelation! God is not the God of the dead but of the *living*. Because God lives, all His people also live. What a light in the darkness of grief and the gloom of impending death. God lives forever, and His people live with Him! That is a promise to live by!

" *The Secrets of the Lord* "

"The friendship of the Lord is for those who fear him,
and he makes known to them his covenant."
(Psalm 25:14)

All of us have different levels of relationship and personal intimacy in our interactions with others. There are things we are willing to share with acquaintances, and then there are matters we share only with friends. Then there are those things about our lives that we only share with those with whom we have the deepest of relationships.

These levels of intimacy are also true of our God. There are things about Himself that He makes known through the general revelation of creation. "The heavens declare the glory of God, and the sky above proclaims his handiwork" (Ps. 19:1). There are those truths the Lord reveals to people who will seek Him through His special revelation of Scripture. "And beginning with Moses and all the Prophets, he interpreted to them in all the Scriptures the things concerning himself" (Luke 24:27). And then, there are, as our text above tells us, personal and intimate insights into God's heart and ways that He shares with those who worship Him in fear, that is, in awe-inspired love. David called this "the friendship of the Lord," or as it can also be translated "the secret counsel of the Lord."

This is an amazing truth and an incredible invitation! The amazing truth? *God is not hiding.* The incredible invitation? *He desires to make Himself known.* Our Creator-God desires a relationship with us that is conscious, personal, and intimate! The question for us is how much do *we* desire that kind of relationship? Why not have a "confidential talk" with Him about that today?

PSALMS 27 & 28
March 31

"A Song in My Heart"

"The Lord is my strength and my shield; in him my heart trusts,
and I am helped; my heart exults, and with my song
I give thanks to him."
(Psalm 28:7)

There has never been discovered a people group in all the world that does not do two things—laugh and sing. Laughter and singing are somehow imprinted into all the people groups of the world. This is part of the image of God and His nature that we human beings bear, even in our sinful state.

When people come by the grace of God to know Him and trust Him, these qualities of joy and song are sanctified. The responses of a human being redeemed and reconciled to his or her creator is to exult with joyful singing. Of course, this does not mean that believers in the Lord are automatically given the ability to sing. However, as one country pastor once said, "The Lord, when He saved me, did not put a song in my mouth, but He sure put one in my heart!" This is the song of joyful praise that David described, "...my heart exults, and with my song I give thanks to him." Praise should be the overflow of our hearts as we reflect on who our God is and what He has done for us. There is also spiritual power in the expression of praise to God, so praise should be a regular part of our prayer time to Him.

We must be careful that our prayer time with God not become a reciting of only our problems and our needs. This could result in depressing ourselves! The devil delights when people only talk to God about their problems. But how He hates to hear the praises to the Almighty rise from the voices of troubled saints. May we make sure to take time to praise God today. It will bless Him, help us, and irritate the devil; and that's a good thing!

APRIL

"He is not here, for he has risen,
as he said."

LUKE 21
April 1

"The Times of the Gentiles"

Just as is recorded in Matthew and Mark, during his final days in Jerusalem, Jesus was asked to take note of the beautiful and priceless stones that adorned the temple. It was truly a wonder in both size and beauty. In fact, it was numbered as among the wonders of the ancient world. Jesus' answer to the remarks about the building was beyond startling, "As for these things that you see, the days will come when there will not be left here one stone upon another..." (v. 6). Jesus said that this terrible destruction of Jerusalem and the temple would usher in a period of time He described as the "times of the Gentiles." "Jerusalem will be trampled underfoot by the Gentiles, until the times of the Gentiles are fulfilled" (v. 24b).

These "times of the Gentiles" began with the destruction of Jerusalem by the Romans in 70 AD and has lasted until this present day. Yes, Israel miraculously became an independent state in 1948; however, even now much of Jerusalem and the temple mount itself is controlled by Gentile nations.

These "times of the Gentiles" are also referred to by the Apostle Paul as the "fullness of the Gentiles" in Romans 11:25. Both Jesus and Paul are saying that the Gospel of Messiah will go out to all the non-Jewish people groups of the world, and a multitude (no one can number from among the nations of the world) will be brought into the covenant family of God.

But God has not forgotten the people of Israel or the promises He made to Abraham thousands of years ago. To this day, there is a remnant of the Jewish people who are believers in Messiah Jesus. And that number is growing as never before. Jesus said the final days would be marked with distress and tribulation as never before; but in these times, the greatest evangelism of both Jews and Gentiles would occur. Then will come the great moment of all the ages, "They will see the Son of Man coming in a cloud with power and great glory. Now when these things begin to take place, straighten up and raise your heads, because your redemption is drawing near" (Luke 21:27-28).

Maranatha!

LUKE 22
April 2

" The Look of the Lord "

What a night swirled around Peter! In the span of a few hours, he heard the Master say that one of the twelve would betray Him. Peter experienced the humbling rebuke of Jesus as He knelt to wash his feet. Peter brashly boasted that though all people might forsake the Lord, he never would. To this, Jesus responded that before morning Peter would deny Him three times. Then he failed the battle with overwhelming fatigue as he tried to pray near the Master in the Garden of Gethsemane. Again, Peter experienced Jesus' gentle rebuke and loving admonition about understanding the weakness of the flesh.

Then came the armed soldiers to arrest Jesus, which started the confusion and fighting in the darkness. Peter grabbed a sword and attempted to kill one of the guards. Again, Jesus rebuked him and told him he was resisting the Heavenly Father's will. Fleeing arrest, Peter ran into the darkness of the olive grove, and yet he had to see what would happen, so he followed the soldiers and Jesus to the house of the high priest. He wasn't prepared for what followed.

Not once, but three times individuals identified him as a disciple. Terror seized him. Oaths mixed with curses mingled with his denials that he *even knew* Jesus. That is when it happened. The rooster crowed just as Jesus had predicted, and with that sound "the Lord turned and looked at Peter" (v. 61). Human language cannot express what was communicated in that gaze of Jesus to Peter's heart, but it broke it and Peter broke beneath it. Little did Peter know that his *breaking* was the beginning of his *remaking*.

The gaze of our Lord sees all about us. It is always a gaze of love. Let's not foolishly try to hide from it but rather bow under it and be healed.

Amen.

LUKE 23
April 3

"*I am Barabbas*"

As we have noted earlier, the Gospel of Luke is unique among the four gospels in regard to the depth of the human encounters related to Jesus. Luke is almost a compilation of short stories regarding lives that intersected with Jesus. This is true most of all regarding the arrest, crucifixion, burial, and resurrection of our Lord. Of these personal encounters, none is more poignant and impactful as that of Barabbas. In many ways, Barabbas is representative of every believer's life in relationship to Jesus. Think about it; each of us can, in the most meaningful of ways, say, "I am Barabbas."

1. *Barabbas was convicted of terrible violations of the law.* Each of us "has sinned and fallen short of the glory of God" (Rom. 3:23).
2. *Barabbas was under the sentence of death.* Like him, "... the wages of [our] sin is death" (Rom. 6:23).
3. *Jesus died in Barabbas' place.* "Christ died for our sins according to the scriptures" (1 Cor. 15:3).
4. *By taking his place and paying his debt, Jesus set Barabbas free.* "So if the Son sets you free, you will be free indeed" (John 8:36).

Yes, what Jesus did for Barabbas, He did for us. So much so, that when we trust in Jesus, we become Barabbas.

Do you know what the name Barabbas means? It means "*son of the father.*" Wow. How amazing is the infinite plan of God's grace! The true "Son of the Father," Jesus, died for guilty sinners like Barabbas and us, so we can become "sons of the father."

Take a good look in the mirror today and praise God that because of Jesus, the Son of the Father, you can say, "*I Am Barabbas.*"

LUKE 24
April 4

"Road Trip with Jesus"

*"Did not our hearts burn within us while He talked to us
on the road, while He opened to us the scriptures?"*
(Luke 24:32)

Luke concludes his gospel by recounting perhaps the most unusual conversation Jesus shared following His resurrection from the tomb. The conversation takes place as Jesus, having disguised Himself as a traveler, joins two of His disciples as they journey to the little village of Emmaus.

After the disciples express their confusion regarding the events and reports of the previous three days, the Lord gently rebukes the bewildered men, "And beginning with Moses and all the Prophets, he interpreted to them in all the Scriptures the things concerning himself" (v. 27). Then, during a late afternoon meal as Jesus once again broke the bread with them, their eyes were opened to His true identity. They then understood why their hearts burned within as He had shared the Scriptures with them on the way.

There is a beautiful picture of the privilege each of us, as disciples, has as we walk with the Lord on our life's journey. First, our life is more than an existence; it is a journey with Jesus. Secondly, our Lord Himself, by His Spirit, will open His own Word to our hearts. Thirdly, the Lord, as He walks with us and teaches us, will provide us with life-changing experiences of personal encounters with Him. Fourthly, what the Lord shares with us and allows us to experience, becomes our living witness to share with others.

What a "story for Christ" our life can be when our journey to heaven is a daily walk on the road to Emmaus!

JOHN 1
April 5

"The Word Made Flesh"

It only requires reading the first few verses of the Gospel of John to recognize this book is a radically different account of the life of Jesus than Matthew, Mark, or Luke. That is the reason the first three gospels are referred to by theologians as the "synoptic gospels." That is, they share the "same view" of the life of Jesus.

John certainly shares much of the same information about Jesus as the other writers, but John gives more than *information* about Jesus. He also gives an *interpretation* of Jesus. John's focus is more about the *essence* of Jesus' life than the *events* of Jesus' life. This is the reason John does not open his gospel at the beginning of Jesus' life or the beginning of His ministry, rather he starts the account of Christ from the beginning of eternity.

John calls Jesus "The Word," that is, "The Logos." This was a term used by the Greek philosophers, and also Jewish writers influenced by them, to define the creative and sustaining power of the Divine mind. It was a term to describe the life force in all creation. However, according to this philosophy, this power, "The Word," communicated itself in all of life, but the power itself could never truly be known.

John, led by the Spirit, takes up a quill and ink, and, in a few inspired sentences, obliterates that philosophy. Yes, there exists "The Word," but The Word is the one true God—The God of Abraham, Isaac, and Jacob. The Jehovah of the Old Testament has become "flesh and dwelt [pitched His tent] among us, and we have seen his glory, glory as of the only Son from the Father, full of grace and truth" (v. 14).

What an astounding truth! The invisible, eternal God clothed Himself in human flesh so that He can be known, understood and experienced, and experienced in the deepest, most gracious way. "But to all who did receive him, who believed in his name, he gave the right to become children of God" (v. 12). God the Word came as God the Son so that we might become sons and daughters of God. Amazing grace, how sweet the sound that the Word has spoken.

PROVERBS 10
April 6

" *Priceless* "

"The blessing of the Lord makes rich,
and He adds no sorrow to it."
(Proverbs 10:22)

The two afternoon strolls were separated by only three days, but they seemed to be taken on two different planets. While traveling to a mission ministry in Asia recently, my wife and I were able to include in our travel schedule a two-day layover in Paris. On the second afternoon, we hopped off the tour bus in order to take pictures of the Arc de Triomphe and then walk down the famous avenue Champs Elysees. This street is considered to be the fashion and culture capital of the world, and the prices proved it! The sidewalks were crowded with people from around the world carrying the shopping bags proudly displaying the logo emblems of the most elite design houses.

Our afternoon stroll, seventy-two hours later, had a slightly different ambiance. Along with our ministry partner in India, we visited members of his congregation living in one of the slums of Delhi. Words fail in trying to describe the sights, sounds, and smells of countless thousands of people living in what amounts in America to a garbage dump. No one carrying designer bags, no fragrances of Chanel wafting from doorways, no lighted display cases, no diamond-encrusted jewelry, and no designer clothes.

But guess what we did experience there? Children with beaming faces singing praise songs to Jesus, joy-filled believers gladly welcoming us into their dirt-floor shanties, former idol-worshiping people of the pariah caste, now members of the family of God through faith in Jesus. My wife and I walked both of these streets in Paris and Delhi, and in our minds we remembered God's real estate appraisal, "Listen, my beloved brothers, has not God chosen those who are poor in the world to be rich in faith and heirs of the kingdom, which he has promised to those who love him" (Jas. 2:5)?

Amen.

PSALMS 29 & 30
April 7

"Dancing in the Tomb"

"You have turned for me my mourning into dancing;
You have loosed my sackcloth and clothed me with gladness
that my glory may sing Your praise and not be silent
O Lord my God. I will give thanks to You forever!"
(Psalm 30:11-12)

It was certainly not what I expected. For so many years, I had wanted to visit a site in Jerusalem that had eluded me on previous visits—the tomb of David. When I stepped into the entry room of the structure, the first thing that surprised me was the music; not the sad and mournful chants I would have expected in a mausoleum, but bright joyful singing and clapping. Even more amazing was the scene that awaited me in the burial chamber itself, which was the source of the celebration. In the far wall of the room was a stone sarcophagus draped by a beautiful blue tapestry with a gold emblazoned star of David. Around the final resting place of David, a group of Jewish rabbis dressed in their black garments and were joyfully dancing and singing, their curled ringlets of hair bouncing as they danced. Even we who were non-Jewish visitors were invited to join the celebration of praise.

Afterward, our guide explained that since David wrote many psalms of joy and often danced before the Lord, it was the tradition of orthodox rabbis to honor David's life by dancing before his tomb every day.

As we left that praise-filled tomb that afternoon, I thought of another tomb just a short distance away. Over that tomb, a large structure has likewise been built, but that building is a place of silence, incense, and solemn chanting. It is the tomb of King David's descendant, Jesus of Nazareth. For a moment I was discouraged that at His tomb there was no joyful singing. But as I reflected on these two very different scenes, I remembered the biggest contrast of all between the two sites—the tomb of Jesus is empty, and then my heart began to dance.

JOHN 2
April 8

"Jesus' First Sign"

In this second chapter, we see that John introduces the miraculous power of Jesus in a very different manner. John does not even use the term "miracles" to describe the mighty wonders Jesus performed. He calls them "signs" (v. 11). This word does more than describe what Jesus did; it also communicates what the miraculous acts mean.

John says that these "signs" of Jesus "manifested His glory" and "His disciples believed in Him" (v. 11). John, in writing his gospel, is led by the Holy Spirit to choose wonders that Jesus performed that prove He truly is the "Logos," the creator in human form. These signs were used to create faith in His disciples to trust Him as their master.

How fitting it was that John chose the turning of water into wine at a wedding feast as the first miraculous sign he shared. This was clearly an act of God. By His own will, Jesus changed the molecular structure of H_2O into wine. No dramatic action, just divine *re-creation*. The empty pots became vessels of wine fit for a King.

This was a perfect "sign" of Jesus' entire ministry. What Jesus did with those empty vessels, He does for all who believe in Him. We come to Jesus completely empty, as jars of clay; and by the miracle of His grace, He fills us with the wine of His joyful salvation to share the sweetness of His love with people who have tasted all the world has to offer but found no satisfaction.

"But we have this treasure in jars of clay,
to show that the surpassing power
belongs to God and not to us."
(2 Corinthians 4:7)

JOHN 3
April 9

"The Measure of God's Love"

Nicodemus had questions. He also had a lot of pride. He came to Jesus seeking to get his questions answered, but he also came *at night* seeking to keep his respect in the community.

In his day, Nicodemus represented the highest and best of the Jewish culture. He was a ruler, a member of the supreme court of Israel called the Sanhedrin. He was greatly respected—"the teacher of Israel" (v. 10).

Yes, Nicodemus was a ruler and respected, but he was also restless. His religiousness had not brought him rest in his soul. This young Rabbi from Nazareth, Jesus, clearly a prophet from God, was teaching about a new and living relationship with Jehovah and Nicodemus was clueless. Things just didn't add up. How can anyone experience this new birth of which Jesus spoke?

In the interview recorded in our reading today, the Lord had to kindly, but plainly, explain to Nicodemus that the message of salvation would never add up for him until he learned a new kind of math. Not the math of a religion based on the law, but a relationship based on the love of God. The peace that Nicodemus sought (or any person seeks), cannot be found in measuring ourselves to God's law, but in measuring the love of God to us.

In one simple statement, Jesus summed up the good news of salvation in measuring the love of God.

The *height* of God's love: *"For God so loved the world,*
The *depth* of God's love: *that he gave his only Son,*
The *width* of God's love: *that whoever believes in him*
The *length* of God's love: *should not perish but have eternal life."*

Now, that is a math we can never comprehend, but it is a math we can live by, now and forever!

JOHN 4
April 10

" *Do You See What I See*? "

What a study in contrasts John provides for us in John Chapter three and four! In the previous chapter, John records an interview that Jesus conducted with one who would be considered the pinnacle of society, Nicodemus, a leader of the Jews. In Chapter four, Jesus conducts another interview with a Samaritan woman whose life has been a series of relationships gone bad.

What is so amazing about this interview is that Jesus deliberately scheduled it. He intentionally went to a village where He and His disciples would not be welcome and His followers definitely did not want to be. But Jesus "had" to go there (v. 4). He was compelled to go to Samaria because of what He could see and because of what His disciples needed to see.

Our Lord could see beyond the immense differences between Him and the Samaritan woman. The cultural mores of the day, not only erected these differences but they were expected to be kept. He could see a skeptical but thirsty soul seeking some lasting satisfaction. This woman, coming to the well with her empty vessel, represented the whole reason that the Father had sent His Son into the world. Jesus could see that and His disciples needed to see it as well. This spiritually thirsty woman was His *mission*; and after Jesus revealed Himself to her, she became His *missionary*!

It wasn't long until, at her testimony, all the men of the village came running down the hill to meet Jesus. As our Lord saw their white-turbaned heads bobbing up and down, He knew His disciples had to *really* see this: "Do you not say, 'There are yet four months, then comes the harvest'? Look, I tell you, lift up your eyes, and see that the fields are white for harvest" (v. 35). The harvest surrounds each of us as believers every day. Do we see it? We won't until we ask the Lord to open our eyes to see that His harvest is not an "it." The harvest is "her," "him," and "them." The harvest is people. Do we see them as Jesus does? Talk to Him about that today.

JOHN 5
April 11

"Honor the Son"

*"The Father judges no one, but has given all judgment to the Son,
that all may honor the Son, just as they honor the Father.
Whoever does not honor the Son does not honor
the Father who sent Him."*
(John 5:22-23)

There is no one whose teaching is more cited and endorsed in our culture than that of Jesus. However, we can wonder which Jesus is being so positively referenced, for it is very clear that the historic Jesus said things that would be the farthest thing from "culturally correct."

The statement from John Chapter five referenced above is one of the most glaring examples. Jesus said that it was God's will that all people would honor Jesus, just as much as they honor God, and that all who *do* not honor Him, to this extent, do *not* honor God at all. Wow. Either Jesus was speaking God's truth, or He was expressing the most egotistic blasphemy that could be imagined.

Yes, He *was* speaking God's truth and God's will. A challenge for us as His followers is if *we* are willing to speak this way about Jesus. It is very culturally acceptable, in fact even commendable, to talk about "God." "God" is in vogue from political conversations to poolside conversations. But, not so much with "Jesus."

"Jesus" can be considered a word that is a little too narrow and even divisive. The reason for that is *Jesus* is divisive, as in BC and AD. Time itself is divided by Jesus, so we should not be ashamed as His people to speak *for* Him and *of* Him in our day. We need to honor Him by speaking of Him...often.

Our God has a name, and it begins with a "J" as in "Jesus." We should let the "J word" be a natural part of our conversations. After all, we are talking about our master and our dearest of all friends, "Jesus."

JOHN 6
April 12

"When Jesus Lost His Crowd"

Jesus' miracle with the bread gained Him a huge following, but His message *about* the bread cost Him most of it. Multitudes of people were following Jesus as a result of the astounding miracles He performed. Those crowds grew even larger after His amazing feat of multiplying a boy's lunch of a few pieces of fish and some biscuits, into a banquet for thousands.

However, Jesus would have no one follow Him out of false motivations. "Truly, truly, I say to you, you are seeking me, not because you saw signs, but because you ate your fill of the loaves" (v. 26). Not to be dissuaded, the "self-focused seekers" pressed their case, "Our fathers ate the manna in the wilderness; as it is written, 'He gave them bread from heaven to eat'" (v. 31). Their pseudo-religious arguments gave Jesus the platform needed to share His message of the true, life-giving bread He offered. "For my flesh is true food, and my blood is true drink. Whoever feeds on my flesh and drinks my blood abides in me, and I in him (vv. 55-56). This was certainly not the menu most of the crowd wanted! As a result, "After this many of his disciples turned back and no longer walked with him" (v. 66). So many walked away, that Jesus asked His twelve disciples, "Do you want to go away as well?" (v. 67) Peter answered from his own heart, but also for everyone who has found the ultimate satisfaction in Jesus, "Lord, to whom shall we go? You have the words of eternal life" (v. 68).

Peter had tasted in his soul the sweetest of all delicacies, the precious grace of life in Christ. The food provided by his master satisfied the longing of Peter, yet over 30 years later he was still hungry for more:

> *"Like newborn infants, long for the pure spiritual milk,*
> *that by it you may grow up into salvation—if indeed*
> *you have tasted that the Lord is good."*
> (1 Peter 2:2-3)

Stay very hungry, my friend!

PSALMS 31 & 32
April 13

"God's Heavy, Healing Hand"

It has been said that the deepest theology is the theology of the heart, not the head. There is all the difference in the world in knowing truth about God through *education* and knowing Him through *experience*. The Psalms of David are filled with some of the deepest truths of God in all the Bible, but what gives these songs such power is that they flow from the *personal experience* of David in knowing and serving his God. These experiences span every segment of David's life, and sometimes they bring together in song, both physical and spiritual encounters with God.

There are some people who believe there is no connection whatsoever between our physical and spiritual well-being, but David knew better than that...by experience. "For when I kept silent, my bones wasted away through my groaning all day long. For day and night your hand was heavy upon me; my strength was dried up as by heat of summer. I acknowledged my sin to you, and I did not cover my iniquity; I said, 'I will confess my transgressions to the Lord,' and you forgave the iniquity of my sin" (Ps. 32: 3-5).

David literally felt in his body the spiritual and physical pressure of God's conviction for his sin. Truly God was "heavy-handed" in His dealing with David's sin. Why would the Lord treat His beloved servant this way? Why does He treat *us* this way? Because as the Westminster Catechism says, He wants us to glorify Him and enjoy Him forever. God knows that in honoring Him, we experience the joy found only in Him. Unconfessed sin short-circuits our joy. Confession restores our joy connection with God, so God presses us to confess. He literally squeezes our life back into us! He wants us to sing again!

> *"Blessed is the one whose transgression is forgiven,*
> *whose sin is covered. Blessed is the man against*
> *whom the Lord counts no iniquity, and in whose spirit*
> *there is no deceit."* (Psalm 32:1-2)

PSALMS 33 & 34
April 14

"The Fear That Frees Us"

We keep score on everything from sports, to grades, to investments. President Franklin Roosevelt, as he began his administration in the heart of the Great Depression, famously declared, "We have nothing to fear, but fear itself." In many ways, he was certainly right. When fear grips the hearts of any people, many can begin to respond in desperation and the very fabric of civil society can begin to tear apart. That type of fear is definitely dangerous.

However, there is a different kind of fear that does not cause people to lose control but rather brings us *under* a control that is the ultimate expression of true freedom. I am talking about the fear of God, the same kind of fear that David praised in Psalm 34. When we fear the Lord, we are freed from all other fears, because the true fear of the Lord does not cause us to run *from* Him but to run *to* Him. "I sought the Lord, and he answered me and delivered me from all my fears" (v. 4).

I grew up in a neighborhood that was known to be a rough one in many ways. I learned very early in life that some "not so nice" individuals lived on those streets and I had to keep my eyes open for them. However, I also remember that when I walked through those streets and alleys, as I often did accompanied by my father, I had no fear whatsoever. I had a deep respect for my dad that was rooted in the security I sensed in his love. I also possessed a loving fear for my father, and the knowledge of his love for me and his presence *with* me "delivered me from all my fears."

Our Heavenly Father is an awesome, holy God, but He is our *Father*. We fear him, yet with a fear that flows from reverential love. It is a fear that draws us to Him and frees us from all other fears.

"The Angel of the Lord encamps around those who fear Him, and delivers them. Oh, taste and see that the Lord is good! Blessed is the man who takes refuge in Him! Oh, fear the Lord, you His saints, for those who fear Him have no lack!" (Psalm 34:7-9)

" The Agnostic's Answer "

Once while flying to a speaking engagement, I had the opportunity to share my faith with a gentleman seated next to me on the plane. During our conversation, he said, "Well, I guess you could say I am an agnostic."

I responded, "Okay. Are you an honest agnostic or a dishonest agnostic?"

Startled, he replied, "What's the difference?"

"Well," I said, "the word agnostic means 'I don't know.' An honest agnostic admits he doesn't know for sure, but he is willing to investigate. A dishonest agnostic says he doesn't know, but he won't even investigate." I went on, "A dishonest agnostic can't find the truth for the same reason a thief can't find a policeman; he's not looking for one!"

The man chuckled and said, "Well, then. I guess I am an honest agnostic."

"Wonderful!" I replied. "Did you know Jesus made you an unconditional promise?"

"How do you figure that?" he asked.

I then quoted verse 17 from today's Scripture to him, "If anyone's will is to do God's will, he will know whether the teaching is from God or whether I am speaking in my own authority." I explained to my travel companion that the two key words in Jesus' statement are "will" and "know." If a person truly is *willing* to do God's will, he will *know* if Jesus is speaking the truth and, in fact, *is* the truth. I encouraged the man to read the Gospel of John and just offer a sincere prayer, "Jesus, if you truly are the truth, please reveal that to me, for I am willing to do your will." The man promised me he would do that. I haven't heard from him again, but I have prayed for him many times.

What I shared with that man on the plane is a promise not just for agnostics but for all who sincerely want to know God's will. Knowing God's will begins with *our* will. Are we *willing* to do God's will? If we are, we will know the direction we need from Him. God wants us to do His will more than we ever could. God is not playing hide and seek, but neither will He play games with us if we are not seriously desiring to do His will. The key to knowing the *unrevealed* will of God is doing today the *revealed* will of God. If we are willing to do God's will, then we will know God's will in His time and in His way. We have Jesus' word on that, and there is no doubt when Jesus makes a promise.

" *Free Indeed* "

It would almost have been funny if it were not so tragic. Jesus was teaching in the courts of the temple. One of his great themes in his message was that of "freedom." "If you abide in my word, you are truly my disciples, and you will know the truth, and the truth will set you free" (vv. 31-32). This offended many of the people in the crowd, "We are offspring of Abraham and have never been enslaved to anyone. How is it that you say, 'You will become free'?" (v. 33)

Really? The Jews had never been enslaved to anyone? The whole history of the nation had been a story of centuries of slavery. Even as the people made this proud statement, they were standing in a courtyard overshadowed by the Fortress of Antonia, under the watchful eyes of an occupying force, with the banner of the Roman Empire fluttering from the battlements. What deception! Declaring their freedom while living in bondage. Yes, that happens a lot.

You see, our freedom is determined by our Master. Jesus' logic is inescapable, "Truly, truly, I say to you, everyone who practices sin is a slave to sin" (v. 34). "So, if the Son sets you free, you will be free indeed" (v. 36). Freedom begins when the deception ends. Freedom was available to the enslaved people that day, but only if they would acknowledge their slavery. Jesus came as the Great Emancipator; he came to free slaves but only those slaves who acknowledge their bondage.

The shackles of deception are the worst form of bondage because the chains are invisible to the deceived soul. Our liberator's work of freedom begins by shattering the bonds of deception. He does that by revealing "the truth" to us; the truth sets us free (v. 32).

Let's not take our freedom for granted. Let's ask Jesus to reveal the reality of any bondage that might be in our lives. We should not be afraid of the truth, for the purpose of His truth is to bring us liberty. Jesus will reveal those invisible, ignored chains and, bringing us to brokenness over our bondage, He will set us "free indeed." Jesus desires us to be the freest of all people, slaves of the Great Emancipator, "... slaves of righteousness" (Rom. 6:18).

JOHN 9
April 17

"*The Blind and the Blinded*"

*"For judgment I came into this world, that those who do not see
may see, and those who see may become blinded."*
(John 9:39)

John, in writing his gospel, captures for us the major teaching themes of Jesus during his ministry. Much more than the other gospel writers, John records the lengthy section of Jesus' teaching as He discussed His mission in terms of "light," "darkness," "water," "food," "life," "truth," etc. Also, it is John who captures the personal encounters of Jesus with people who illustrate these themes. Our reading today contains one of the longest, most personal, most humorous, and most touching of those encounters.

In one of the signs of His deity, Jesus heals a man who has been blind since birth. This healing provokes quite a controversy among the crowds in Jerusalem if this blind man really *is the* blind man. The poor fellow practically has to prove his identity. The religious leaders even called in his parents to affirm that the man who had been healed was their son.

Having confirmed the man's identity and his healing, the religious leaders interrogate him to the point of challenging him, "Give glory to God. We know that this man is a sinner" (v. 24).

Now it is the formerly blind man's opportunity to share some light, and he does it with a little bit of "attitude." "Why this is an amazing thing! You do not know where he comes from and yet he opened my eyes.... If this man were not from God, he could do nothing" (vs. 30, 33).

The logic of the formerly blind man blazes with light, but the blind-hearted, religious leaders love their darkness, and they angrily cast him out of the temple. In effect, they excommunicated him from God's house. He had been cast out from God's house, but not God's heart, for Jesus sought him out. Jesus gave the man his sight again—spiritual sight—by revealing Himself to him as the Son of Man. Now, the man could *truly* see. "'Lord, I believe,' and he worshiped him" (v. 38). Jesus saw in the events of this day a living allegory of his mission. "For judgment I came into this world, that those who do not see may see, and those who see may become blind" (v. 39). If you are one of the blind who now can see because of Jesus, then give Him praise today.

*"Amazing Grace, how sweet the sound that saved a wretch like me.
I once was lost, but now am found, was blind, but now I see!"*

JOHN 10
April 18

"Safe Forever"

One time, a country preacher was speaking on verses 27-30 of John Chapter 10, and he especially wanted to emphasize how believers in Jesus were completely safe, even from the devil himself. As he tried to emphasize this truth, he declared, "Before the devil could steal me from the Lord, he would have to pull off the hands of Jesus. Then, he would have to pry back the fingers of God the Father. And then, the devil would have to break the seal of the Holy Spirit because my life is inside the Spirit of God. And when the devil came inside the seal of the Spirit, praise God, he would be a saved devil!"

Well, we might question the earnest preacher's theological interpretation, but he certainly understood and conveyed the extent of the security Jesus promised to His sheep. "My sheep hear my voice, and I know them, and they follow me. I give them eternal life, and they will never perish, and no one will snatch them out of my hand" (vv. 27-28). Eternal life is a gift from Jesus. It is not just a future hope; it is a present reality. Believers *have* everlasting life *right now*. It is secured by the precious blood of Christ and by His omnipotence. In fact, Jesus not only guards each of His people on the journey to their heavenly inheritance, He also guards their heavenly inheritance until each one of them arrives.

Peter, who heard Jesus' words that day, expressed them this way, "Blessed be the God and Father of our Lord Jesus Christ! According to his great mercy, he has caused us to be born again to a living hope through the resurrection of Jesus Christ from the dead, to an inheritance that is imperishable, undefiled, and unfading, kept in heaven for you, who by God's power are being guarded through faith for a salvation ready to be revealed in the last time" (1 Pet. 1:3-5).

Yes, there are times when we feel the harsh reality that, as followers of Jesus, we have been sent out as "lambs among wolves," but may we rejoice today that regardless of the number and ferocity of all wolves, human or demonic, all the sheep of the Good Shepherd are completely safe in Him. Every one, forever. Amen.

JOHN 11
April 19

" The Delays of Jesus "

Our reading today includes the greatest and final miraculous "sign" recorded by John that proved Jesus to truly be the Son of God—the resurrection of Lazarus from the dead. This greatest wonder performed by our Lord took place in an environment of terrible disappointment— disappointment in Jesus.

Mary and Martha had sent word immediately to Jesus when their brother Lazarus became suddenly ill. These two sisters were some of Jesus' most devoted followers, and they were certain of his deep love for them and their brother. We can only imagine their growing concern and their despair as, hour after hour, then day after day, they watched the road for Jesus. Where could he be? The messengers had gotten word to the Master; why had He not quickly come?

Before long, the concern and disappointment of the sisters were mingled with the grief of their brother's death. When Jesus finally did arrive, the pain of both the sisters poured out in the first words each of them sobbed out to Him, "Lord, if you had been here, my brother would not have died." Those words conveyed an unquestioned belief in His ability, but a bitter questioning of His *inactivity*. It just didn't make sense. That's the painful reality every follower of Jesus sometimes experiences—the Lord's seeming unconcern and inaction does not make sense, especially in light of what we know about His infinite love and concern for all of His people.

You might be there right now, experiencing a heartache that at times even hurts more because you have poured out your breaking heart to the Lord many times over the situation, and He has not responded. Take heart today from the heartache of these two sisters in Christ; *the Lord's delays are not His disapproval* and *His silence is not absence*. God's ways can be mysterious, but they are always for the good of His people and the glory of His name. Before a resurrection must come a funeral. "Weeping may tarry for the night, but joy comes with the morning" (Ps. 30:5b). The present darkness will not last forever; He is your "bright and morning star." He will come. "Even so, come Lord Jesus."

PSALMS 35 & 36
April 20

" The Fountain of Life"

The World's Fair Exposition held in New York City in 1893 highlighted many of the advances that were being made in what we would now describe as the Industrial Revolution. One of the most effective, but somewhat deceptive, displays that intrigued the patrons at the exposition was that of the amazing mechanical man. Approaching the display, a person's attention would go to a life-size man made out of metal who was furiously pumping a water pump that poured out gallons and gallons of refreshing water. It truly seemed like a miraculous scientific breakthrough until the viewer finally recognized what was taking place. The purpose of the display was to show possibilities of hydraulic power. The mechanical man was not pumping water; the water was pumping him!

Psalms 35 and 36 are written by David in a time of personal hardship. He laments the deviousness of a false friend who has betrayed and attacked him. Evidently, this traitor has been joined by others who have been relentless in their lies and attacks against David. It is all too much for David, way too much, so David decides to tell somebody. He tells his anger and anguish to the Friend who has always proven faithful, the Lord his God.

In going to the Lord in his distress, something miraculous takes place; David's pleas turn into praise. His broken-hearted and bitter song in Psalm 35 becomes an anthem of praise in Psalm 36. The wilderness experience in David's life becomes a river of God's flowing grace, and the praise pours out of his soul.

> *"For with You is the foundation of life; in Your light do we see light.*
> *Oh, continue Your steadfast love to those who know You,*
> *and Your righteousness to the upright of heart!"*
> (Psalm 36:9-10)

Our Fountain of Life still flows; may we drink deeply from Him today.

"Do What You Love"

Every person of a "certain age" reading today's devotion can remember (or wish you could forget) the lighthearted tune made famous by Bobby McFerrin in 1988, "Don't Worry Be Happy."

Okay, I apologize to many of you for planting that song in your head again where it will repeat itself many times for the next few days! Believe it or not, I actually used those words as a sermon title for a message on Psalm 37:1-4 many years ago. It seemed like a very "cool" idea at the time. Though I would not use that 80's title in this "millennial" culture, the words do serve as bookends for the message conveyed in those verses. "Fret not yourself because of evildoers..." Don't worry. "Delight yourself in the Lord..." Be happy.

David says in this song that you cannot do the first—fret over wicked people, and experience the last—be happy in the Lord. Of course, like most things in the Christian life, this is easier said than done. Most of us have struggled at times with an inability to understand how wicked people can seem to prosper in every way. Also, it is difficult to hear and see the stories of terrible violence around the world and in our own communities, and not be overwhelmed with concern.

What is the answer? Faith and faithfulness. "Trust in the Lord, and do good; dwell in the land and befriend faithfulness" (v. 3). The antidote for the fear of man is faith in God and pursuing Him. Does that mean the world and its evil will change? No, but it does mean *we* will change. When we delight ourselves in knowing God, the Lord actually begins to change our desires. Our lives begin to find ultimate joy in who He is and what He is doing.

Eventually, as the Lord becomes our chief desire, then the ultimate freedom comes to us—we want what God wants! We can pursue any goal or any interest we have because our values are anchored in God. Bobby McFerrin and his catchy tune, "Don't Worry Be Happy" can then become a catechism for our daily lives.

"Delight yourself in the Lord,
and He will give you the desires of your heart."
(Psalm 37:4)

" *Dying to Live* "

*"Truly, truly, I say to you, unless a grain of wheat falls
into the earth and dies, it remains alone;
but if it dies, it bears much fruit."*
(John 12:24)

Jesus made the statement above as a strange answer to what seemed a very simple request. Some men wanted to see Him. They were Greek men, meaning either that they were from the area of Greece, or, more probably, John refers to them as "Greeks" because they were non-Jewish men, Gentiles.

Jesus responded in this fashion because as He looked on these men, He saw His mission. He had spoken on many occasions that, as the Good Shepherd, there were "other sheep" not of this fold (Jewish) that He must also bring safely home (John 10:16). Jesus saw in these Greek men the "first-fruits" of hundreds of millions from the nations of the world whom He would bring to God by being "lifted up" on the cross (v. 32). Jesus would be "lifted up" in His death, "planted" in His burial and then "bear much fruit" in His life-giving resurrection. This is the sacred law of "sowing and reaping," and it not only applies to our Lord, but to *us* as His followers as well.

It is only as we die to our self-focused lives through faith and surrender to Jesus that we can ever truly experience life. "Whoever finds his life will lose it, and whoever loses his life for my sake will find it" (Matthew 10:39).

In Christ, the "losers are the keepers." When we lose our life in surrender to Jesus, then and only then, do we truly keep it for all eternity. It is in sowing the seeds of our life in death to self, that our seed of life can be multiplied beyond imagination in the lives of others.

I have conducted many, many funerals, but I have yet to hear a single eulogy or testimony about anyone's life that ever mentioned the size of his house or the contents of his bank account or the variety of her jewelry or the collections in her closets. However, I have often heard people, with tears in their eyes and quivering voices, express the priceless impact that someone's life has made on theirs. Now that is living...timeless and priceless.

JOHN 13
April 23

" *Surprised by Joy* "

"Truly, truly, I say to you, a servant is not greater than his master,
nor is a messenger greater than the one who sent him.
If you know these things, blessed are you if you do them."
(John 13:16-17)

Several years ago, I enjoyed listening to a lady named Laurie, share a story about one of the most life-changing experiences of her life. Laurie had heard about the work of Mother Teresa among the lepers in India. She decided that what was needed was to take her narcissistic teenage girls in the youth group of her suburban church, to Calcutta.

It took nearly a year to raise the funds for the long trip, but miraculously she and the girls found themselves standing before the entrance to Mother Teresa's hospital. Surprisingly, Mother Teresa was not there to meet them. She was out of the country on a ministry trip. Rather, the group was met by a very stern nun who handed each of them a basin and a towel and abruptly said, "Come, it is time to bathe the lepers." In a few moments, Laurie and her mortified girls found their manicured hands washing the limbs (covered with open wounds) of the pathetic, suffering lepers. According to Laurie, everyone in the group was gagging, and some of them had stomach-churning responses that *exceeded* gagging. The girls were begging to go home, and every natural emotion within Laurie wanted to do the same. But deep in her heart, Laurie knew God had brought them there and that they must stay.

The days passed and something truly miraculous started to take place. Laurie and the girls slowly began to *feel* for the lepers. The physical contact, with hideously deformed people, was somehow awakening a bond between the young girls and those they served. Within a few days, all the group had smiles on their faces as they cared for the lepers, and their chores of ugly mercy began to be carried out with songs of praise.

They felt the week was over too soon, and found themselves in the Calcutta airport awaiting the return flight to the United States. That is when Laurie saw her—a tiny elderly lady dressed in white, trimmed with blue, and surrounded by others wearing the same uniforms. Yes, it was Mother Teresa!

Before she realized what she was doing, Laurie ran to the diminutive nun and began to blurt out all they had experienced that week. For the rest of her life, Laurie said she would never forget Mother Teresa's response: "Laurie, when you cared for the lepers, did you feel *His* joy?" With a bursting heart, Laurie responded, "Yes, oh yes! I felt *His* joy!"

JOHN 14
April 24

" *Our Home and God's* "

It does not take long for the newest believer, as he or she begins to read Scripture, to find passages that touch their heart. Without a doubt, John 14 is one of those passages. It has ministered to believers since the night our Lord first uttered these words. Jesus spoke of His imminent departure, but He comforted His disciples that night by telling them *where* He was going and *what* He would be doing, and most of all, that He was coming back. Jesus promised that He was going back to the Father's house to prepare for each of His followers, a dwelling place and that one day, He would return to usher them home, "...that where I am you may be also" (v. 3b). What an amazing, comforting promise!

But, Jesus also made another promise, a promise about another home. This home is God's home, and it is not in heaven but is here on earth; it is God's home in us. "If anyone loves me, he will keep my word, and my Father will love him, and we will come to him and make our home with him" (v. 23). Wow! It is amazing to think that God has a home *in heaven* for us, but to consider that God has a home on earth *in us* is truly astounding.

This is why Jesus said it was "better for us" (John 16:7) that He leave because only then could He, the Father and the Spirit, take up residence *within* each believer. This is a real experience of the eternal life which Jesus provides, "And this is eternal life, that they know you, the only true God, and Jesus Christ whom you have sent" (John 17:3). Eternal life is knowing God in Jesus. It is so much more than a knowledge of *information*; it is a knowledge of *revelation*. We truly and personally know God.

How do you really know someone? By sharing life with that person. The mutual experiences over a period of time bring you a deep understanding of who that person is. You could say you really feel "at home" with them. That is exactly the gift of His amazing grace that our Lord gives to those who faithfully follow Him: "And he who loves me will be loved by My Father, and I will love him and manifest myself to him... we will come to him and make our home with him" (vs. 21b, 23b). What a home! What a life!

JOHN 15
April 25

" *Abiding and Abounding* "

Based on the last verse of John Chapter 14, it appears that Jesus shared the message recorded in today's Scripture reading, as he was walking with His disciples. It was only a short journey from the upper room, where they had just celebrated the Passover and where Jesus had instituted the observance of communion, across the Kidron Valley and up the slopes of the Mount of Olives. Their destination was an enclosed vineyard that contained a garden. The name of the place would become famous as "Gethsemane."

As Jesus and His disciples passed the beautiful temple, shimmering in the light of the huge lampstands that stood in the courtyard and also bathed in the light of the Passover moon, their attention would have been captured by the enormous golden vine and grape clusters that were attached to the marble walls of the temple facing eastward. No doubt, it was this symbol on the temple walls that represented Israel as the "Vine of the Lord" that was the inspiration for the introduction of Jesus' final teaching to His disciples, "I am the true vine, and my Father is the vinedresser... I am the vine; you are the branches" (vs. 1, 5a). Jesus emphasized again the union they shared with Him and with the Father. It was this *life-giving fruit* that would allow them to produce "fruit," "more fruit" and "much fruit" (vv. 2-8). Their responsibility in this process would be to "abide in the vine," that is, to stay in a bonded union with Jesus. The Father would take care of the rest.

It seems simple, doesn't it? And it is, but it requires the humility of absolute dependence on Jesus. This is a comforting and challenging thought for us today. Jesus and the Father desire our lives to produce fruit *more* than we do, but it requires resting and it requires surrendering control to our Lord. Stressing is fruitless. Resting is fruitful. Here endeth the lesson. {Selah}

JOHN 16
April 26

"*Peace, Persecution, and Victory*"

"I have said these things to you, that in Me you may have peace.
In the world you will have tribulation. But take heart;
I have overcome the world." (John 16:33)

As Jesus brought His teaching ministry to a close, the night before His sacrifice on the cross, He left His disciples with a provision, a prediction, and a promise. His promise to His disciples (then and now) was that He would provide them with peace. Jesus is the Prince of Peace, and peace reigns wherever His presence exists. This is a gift of Jesus to His followers that nothing can take away because nothing can take Jesus away from His people. Jesus was leaving, but He would be with His people as never before. He would be in them by His Spirit. He is with you right now.

Jesus also gave His disciples a prediction that they would have persecution in the world. The world system hates Jesus and hates the ones who follow Him and bear His name (John 15:18). We are destined for persecution. "Indeed, all who desire to live a godly life in Christ Jesus will be persecuted" (2 Tim. 3:12). We should *expect* to be persecuted at some level. In fact, it is when we experience *no* persecution that we should become concerned. We need to ask ourselves, "Am I living godly in Christ Jesus?"

If then, persecution is inevitable, how is it possible for Christians to live in peace in the midst of this persecution? Because of Jesus' great promise, "But take heart; I have overcome the world" (v. 33). We can have peace in the struggle because the outcome is already accomplished. Jesus has overcome the world; past tense, it is already an accomplished fact. *His* victory is *our* victory. Now that is something to praise Him for today! Right now would be a good time.

" *Tempus Fugit* "

"O Lord, make me know my end and what is the measure of my days;
let me know how fleeting I am!"
(Psalm 39:4)

The ancient Greeks and Romans had an interesting image for time. They often portrayed time in the figure of a running man whose long forelock of hair was flowing in the wind. The concept behind this image was the idea that time was quickly passing, and you had to catch it by the hair of its head. The Latin phrase "tempus fugit"—"time is fleeting"—expresses this.

In our reading from Psalm 39 today, David not only recognized the brevity of time but also prayed that the Lord would cause him to feel it. "Let me know how fleeting I am!" (v. 4) What an important prayer this is. Our time on earth is so brief, and it is also so unpredictable. None of us has the promise of a long life. Rather than discouraging us, this reality should motivate us. In the New Testament, the Apostle Paul challenges us to be "making the best use of time" (Eph. 5:16). His challenge is so instructive; we should not measure our days in their *quantity* but in their *quality*.

Only the Lord is in control of how many days we will live, but we share, through His grace, in deciding *how* we will live those days. Since our time on earth is so limited, it only makes sense that we should invest our time in what is eternal. That narrows the focus considerably because only God and people are eternal. When we prioritize our days around them, then our days take on an *eternal significance*.

It should come as no surprise that this is exactly how the Lord has instructed us to live our days on this planet. "You shall love the Lord your God with all your heart and with all your soul and with all your strength and with all your mind, and your neighbor as yourself" (Luke 10:27). It is through worshiping God and working on His behalf for others that the days of our life become more than time, they become timeless. Today is a treasure; let's not squander it, but invest it!

PSALMS 40 & 41
April 28

"Rising Above the Clouds"

Several years ago, a major airline expressed a theme in its commercials that I have always thought was not only effective but also inspiring. In each of the commercials, the closing statement shared, in a very encouraging voice, "Where the sun is always shining, just above the clouds."

I really liked that motto because I have experienced it when traveling by air on so many occasions. The weather would be dark and cloudy early in the flight, but when the plane finally popped through the grey, overcast skies, there was a moment when the sunshine and beautiful blue of the upper atmosphere would surround me.

Both Psalm 40 and 41 express a season in David's life when he was surrounded by enemies, to the point of where he despaired of life itself. In fact, much of Psalm 40 is Messianic in nature as it expresses the thoughts and emotions of the Lord Jesus as He carried out His Father's will.

Faithfully serving God does not mean we will never struggle with emotional and spiritual gloom and the feeling of being surrounded by it. Believers do not constantly live on the mountaintops emotionally just because they are believers. However, neither do our emotionally dark times define the ultimate reality or our true identity.

We are children of the light, and the Son is always shining above the clouds *around us* and the clouds *within us*. Through determining that we will worship God in spite of our emotional and spiritual fog, we are able to take in the "high view" and the "long view" of life. That is what David did in both of these Psalms: "But may all who seek You rejoice and be glad in You: may those who love Your salvation say continually, 'Great is the Lord!'" Psalm 40:16. "Blessed be the Lord, the God of Israel, from everlasting to everlasting! Amen and Amen" Psalm 41:13.

Now, that is a shining light to walk in no matter how dark our day!

"When Jesus Prayed for You"

"I do not ask for these only, but also for those who will believe in Me through their word, that they may all be one, just as You, Father, are in Me, and I in You, that they also may be in Us, so that the world may believe that You have sent Me."
(John 17:20-21)

John Chapter 17 is unique among all the passages in the Word of God. We are invited to listen to Jesus pray to His Father as He knelt in the Garden of Gethsemane. In these 26 verses, we hear one member of the Trinity praying to another member of the Trinity. Astounding! What is even more amazing is the fact that Jesus was praying, more than anything else, for His disciples. Not just the 11 men huddled together and fighting with sleepiness a few feet away, but for all His disciples across the centuries. He was praying for you and me. What was it that Jesus desired for us, so much that in His final hours he would pray for us to experience it? In a word—unity. Jesus prayed that the reality of the union He and His Father shared and that we, by His love and sacrifice, would share with them, might be known and expressed by us as His people.

What Jesus desired was not a shallow and superficial unity that is only communicated in theology books or a pastor's devotionals! No. He prayed for an authentic unity between believers, that He would die and rise to provide... That this authentic unity might be displayed in a love and devotion so sincere "that the world may believe that you have sent me" (v. 21b). Yes, Jesus knew the power of love as a witness.

We affirm the reality of our Lord when we express love in our relationships with each other. A good question for us to consider today: If love is the powerful expression of the gospel of Jesus, what kind of witness am I?

" *A Different Kind of Kingdom* "

"My kingdom is not of this world. If My kingdom were of this world,
My servants would have been fighting, that I might not be delivered
over to the Jews. But My kingdom is not from the world."
(John 18:36)

Jesus was very clear when He stood to give testimony before the High Priest and before Pontius Pilate. He was the Son of God and He was a king. His testimony sealed His fate. Pilate was especially interested in knowing whether Jesus considered Himself to be a king. Pilate could care less about the concerns of the religious leaders regarding their faith, but for a man to affirm that he was a king, that was a totally different matter to the Roman governor. Insurrection against Rome was something that would not be tolerated whatsoever.

Jesus affirmed His kingship, but He also affirmed that His kingdom was not from this world. It was a kingdom from above, from heaven, and it did not operate with the power of armies on the earth. Jesus came to establish His kingdom in the hearts of people. Jesus' answer bewildered Pilate, but it also relieved him. After all, what threat could some "delusional" king and his "spiritual" kingdom be to the might of imperial Rome? How little Pilate understood the power of such a kingdom! I wonder, do we understand? The greatest force on the earth is not in the power of armies or elections, but it is in the power to change hearts.

It is so easy to forget that in sharing the love of Christ in word and deed, we are releasing the mightiest force the world has ever known. How is the world changed? How is it "conquered?" It happens one life at a time through the power of God's love. Within a few generations of Jesus' interview with Pilate, the Roman Emperor himself would declare Jesus as the ultimate king. Our Lord's kingdom is spiritual, but it is *real*. We are expanding that kingdom today, as we serve our Lord by releasing His love...one person at a time.

MAY

"*He remembers his covenant forever...*"

" *Secret Saints No Longer* "

Crucifixion was not only a *hideous* way to die, it was also a *humiliating* way to die. Every possible expression of dignity was denied the victim, from the public procession, to the stripping away of all clothing and exposure to jeering mockery of the soldiers and the crowd. Also, the Romans carried out this torture as close to a main road as possible as a way of warning as many people as possible that a similar fate awaited anyone who would dare challenge the authority of the Roman empire.

The gospel narratives indicate that the site of Jesus' execution was situated near a public crossroads since we are told that people passing by mocked and disparaged Him. Certainly, to stand with Jesus at the moment of His agony was a bold thing to do. It was not a small thing to be identified in the community as a person who in some way sympathized with a criminal and traitor. For a few faithful followers of Jesus, His cross was also their "crossroad moment" as they accompanied Him to the very end. In doing so, they publicly professed their loyalty. So, it is very revealing that it was at the death of Jesus that two very influential men came forward to make their devotion to Jesus known—Joseph of Arimathea and Nicodemus. Both these men were members of the Sanhedrin, the religious ruling council of Judea, and they had much to lose—their honor, their status, their wealth, perhaps even their lives.

However, Jesus' death brought to life their love and devotion for Him. Boldly, Joseph requested Jesus' body from Pilate and dedicated his own new tomb as a final resting place. Nicodemus joined in honoring Jesus by providing 75 pounds of spices for preparing Jesus' body for burial and helping Joseph lay Him in the tomb. As they sealed the Lord's body in the tomb, they did not know whether they had sealed their own fate, but that did not hinder their bold allegiance. They would be secret disciples no longer.

An appropriate question for us to consider today is whether we are "going public for Jesus." Joseph and Nicodemus risked their lives for Him in His death. What are we willing to risk for Him in the blazing light of His glorious life and resurrection? Will we be "secret saints," or will we boldly identify ourselves today with the One who was not ashamed to identify Himself with us?

JOHN 20
May 2

" *A Doubter's Deliverance* "

It has been well said that some people are so negative that they can brighten any room just by leaving it! I wonder if any of the disciples ever had that impression of Thomas? He has come down to us in history as "Doubting Thomas," but it might be more accurate to call him "Downer Thomas."

Every time we read of Thomas speaking in the gospels, it is to say something discouraging, "Let us also go, that we may die with him" (John 11:16); "Lord, we do not know where you are going. How can we know the way?" (John 14:5); and here, "Unless I see in his hands the marks of the nails, and place my finger into the mark of the nails, and place my hand into his side, I will never believe" (v. 25). Wow. We are told Thomas was a twin, so we can only hope his brother did not have an identical spirit!

How wonderful it is, though, that the doubt and discouragement of Thomas was not greater than his Lord's devotion. Jesus met Thomas in his doubts and overcame them by His revelation. "Put your finger here, and see my hands; and put out your hand, and place it in my side. Do not disbelieve, but believe" (v. 27). Thomas's doubts were destroyed in a moment of grace, and then from the lips of this life-long doubter came the greatest confession of faith recorded in Scripture, "My Lord and my God!" This formerly doubting Jewish man declared Jesus of Nazareth as Jehovah, his Master and his God! Just amazing. And beyond that, the Lord used Thomas's confession to confer a blessing on us, "Have you believed because you have seen me? Blessed are those who have not seen and yet have believed" (v. 29).

For Thomas, seeing was believing, but for us believing is seeing. By the same marvelous grace, our Savior meets us not just in our doubt, but also in our spiritual death and unbelief. He opens our eyes by His Word so that we might truly "see Him," and come to faith and live. "But these are written so that you may believe that Jesus is the Christ, the Son of God, and that by believing you may have life in his name" (v. 31). In that verse, John shares his purpose in writing the gospel we have been reading for the past twenty days. I wonder, has His purpose been accomplished in your life? To be *convinced* is not to be *converted*. Believing *about* Jesus is not the same as believing *on* Jesus.

Whether Thomas had ever been converted before, we do not know, but he was definitely converted now. At the feet of Jesus, he confessed Jesus as his Lord and his God. That is where real life begins, and that is where it is sustained for everyone. May we all sincerely proclaim at His feet today, "My Lord and my God!"

JOHN 21
May 3

" *A Renewed Focus* "

Jesus asked Peter to do the most difficult thing, at the most difficult time, and in the most difficult place. Jesus asked Peter, along with the other disciples, to wait. And not just to wait anywhere, but to wait for Him in Galilee during the springtime. Everything about the season and the place called Peter back, back to the familiar life he had lived for so many years on the shores of Galilee before all the astounding and confusing events of the past three years took place. Finally, Peter could stand it no more, "I'm going fishing!" he declared. Immediately, several of his fellow disciples said, "We will go with you." How little Peter realized that this was not a day to return to the days gone by, but rather it was to be a day of renewal for all the days ahead. In fact, the Lord orchestrated all the events to bring Peter face-to-face with some very important issues in his life.

First of all, the Lord brought Peter face-to-face with his frustrations. All night he and the other disciples worked at their "bright idea" with all their might, but they caught not a single fish. The Lord, unrecognized on the shore, even called out to them, "Children do you have any fish?" How they hated that question, and how reluctantly they obeyed the stranger's advice when He said to cast the net on the other side of the boat. The huge teeming catch of fish not only revealed who the stranger was but also revealed how fulfilling it is to follow the Lord's instructions.

Secondly, the Lord brought Peter face-to-face with His failures. Not once, but three times beside the charcoal fire the Lord asked Peter the same question, "Simon, son of John, do you love me?" The questions immediately took Peter back to that terrible night when, by another charcoal fire, he denied his Master three times. Broken before the Lord, Peter finally cried out, "Lord, you know everything; you know I love you." Beside that fire, Peter was firmly but gently restored to fellowship with his blessed Lord. The issue of his denial was never spoken, but his heart was broken and also mended. The Master wanted and needed nothing from Peter beyond his devoted love.

Finally, Jesus brought Peter face-to-face with his future. Jesus gave Peter a glimpse of what the future would hold in addressing his martyrdom, but He also gave Peter a rebuking about focusing on what was in store for the others like John, "If it is my will that he remain until I come, what is that to you?"

Frustration, failure, and the future. The Lord addressed them all in one extended conversation with Peter. Perhaps they should be a topic of conversation between you and the Lord today. The result will be "A Renewed Focus."

PROVERBS 12
May 4

" Take a Load Off "

"Anxiety in a man's heart weighs him down,
but a good word makes him glad."
(Proverbs 12:25)

Many years ago, I heard a speaker say, "If someone ever tells you that he never gets depressed, I have some advice for you—don't buy a used car from him, because a man who will tell a whopper like that cannot be trusted!" Well, that may have been just a little overstated, but probably not very much. The truth is, life can be depressing at times, and it tends to be contagious. We catch it occasionally. A depressed spirit is not in itself sinful. We are told in the Scripture that some of the greatest people of faith struggled with depression at times. Moses, Elijah, David, and Jeremiah experienced the "dark night of the soul." Even the One who was filled with perfect faith knew the weight of a depressed spirit.

Our Lord was in many ways a "man of sorrows and acquainted with grief" (Isa. 53:3) and in the garden of Gethsemane, His soul was burdened down so terribly that He asked His closest friends to stay close by and pray with Him. The disciples were so exhausted, physically and emotionally, that they were unable to provide their Master with the encouragement He desperately needed. Yes, we all struggle with depression and anxiety at times, but this spirit does not have to dominate our lives. We can walk in the light because we are children of the light.

One of the ways we can lighten our own spirit is by speaking light into someone else's. "Anxiety in a man's heart weighs him down, but a good word makes him glad" (v. 25). Our words have power, and other than worship, the best use to which our words can be given is encouragement. Encouraging words lighten a heavy heart and give life to a sagging spirit. Mark Twain once quipped, "I can live two months on a good compliment." Most of us are not blessed with great abilities, but we all have the ability to encourage. This is a true ministry and very needed in the church and the world as well.

Take a few moments to give this vital calling some thought right now. Who could you visit, call, email, text or write today and give them a "good word?" It will only take a few moments, but your investment of encouragement will be a treasure in the heart of the person in which it is deposited. "For I have derived much joy and comfort from your love, my brother, because the hearts of the saints have been refreshed through you" (Phlm. 1:7).

PSALMS 42 & 43
May 5

"Sacred Self-Talk"

"My soul is cast down within me; therefore I remember you..."
(Psalm 42:6)

Few people would readily admit that they occasionally talk to themselves, but in reality most of us do. It has been said that talking to yourself is entirely normal but answering yourself... Now that's a problem! Self-talk can actually become an expression of healthy self-awareness when it is practiced with grounding in truth.

David was a big-time self-talker. In many of his psalms, he enters a conversation with himself as he seeks to work out the inner conflict he feels in his soul. Psalms 42 and 43 are perfect examples of David's practice of this spiritual discipline as he asks himself the same question three times. "Why are you cast down, O my soul, and why are you in turmoil within me?" (vs. 42:5a, 11a; 43:5a) Reading these two psalms together, it is clear that David is going through a season of deep emotional trauma. It appears to be rooted in vicious attacks by people he once considered to be his friends and companions in worship, but who have now become unrelenting in their lying assaults. David is heartbroken by their betrayal and tearfully pours out his grief to God, "My tears have been my food day and night, while they say to me all the day long, 'Where is your God?' These things I remember, as I pour out my soul..." (vv. 3-4a).

Truly David is in the middle of an emotional and spiritual crucible, and that is when he does a very wise thing. He starts talking to himself. Yes, he is in the dark, but he recalls and repeats the truths he learned in the light, "Hope in God; for I shall again praise him, my salvation and my God" (vs. 42:5b, 11b; 43:5b). Three times David speaks to himself and speaks against the turmoil within him by declaring the rock of his confidence—the reality of God, his Savior.

External events and internal emotions can change quickly and can also endure persistently, but one thing that cannot change for any of us who trust in the Lord, is the steadfast love our God pledges to us. He is our ultimate reality, the fixed center of our very existence. When all sources of human security fall away, He remains unchanged and we still abide in His unconditional love through Christ our Lord. So, go ahead and engage in a brilliant conversation...talk to yourself about the greatness of your God.

ACTS 1
May 6

"The Adventure Begins"

With our reading today, we leave the gospel accounts of the life and ministry of Jesus. In reality, however, the ministry of Jesus has never ended; it has only entered a new phase as He carries out His mission through the power of the Holy Spirit in the lives of His disciples.

This second book, written by Luke, has often been titled, "The Acts of the Apostles." Perhaps it could better be described as "The Acts of the Holy Spirit," for the Lord made it very clear that His followers should attempt to do nothing until the Spirit baptized them, "But you will receive power after the Holy Spirit has come upon you..." (v. 8). We cannot imagine how those eleven men must have felt as they gazed at their departing Lord being transported to heaven in the clouds. Certainly, they were filled with awe, but they must have also felt the awful weight of the responsibility that had been given to them to take the gospel to the ends of the earth. How could they possibly accomplish such a task, and how could they do it without their Master?

The reality of the situation was two-fold; first, they definitely could not accomplish the mission by themselves, and secondly, they would not be without Jesus. Jesus had promised, many times over the past few weeks, that He was sending them another companion just like Himself—the Holy Spirit. He would be with each of them and all of them, all of the time. The Holy Spirit would comfort them, guide them, empower them and speak through them. In their acts and words, He would convince people around the world of the reality of their witness regarding Jesus.

The mission the Lord had given to his disciples was actually not theirs at all. He was sharing with them the mission of the Trinity—Father, Son, and the Holy Spirit. The mission would be accomplished. It would not fail, and *they* would not fail as long as their reliance was in the power of God and not their own.

My friend, that mission continues to this very day. If we are Christians, then we are missionaries. Each of us has a life planned by God from eternity past, not only for our salvation but also for our involvement in God's mission. Serving on mission does not involve a special call beyond the special call to salvation by God's grace. We are a chosen people with a chosen purpose. "You did not choose me, but I chose you and appointed you that you should go and bear fruit...." (John 15:16a).

Life is never the same for any believer when it finally dawns on him or her that life is a mission and they are truly missionaries for Jesus. Regardless of what time of day or night you are reading these words, may it be the dawn of that amazing reality for you. Now, go...

ACTS 2
May 7

" *The New Community* "

It did not take long for the people in Jerusalem to know that something very new and radical was taking place. It all began at 9:00 on a Sunday morning, when crowds of amazed people watched and listened as a group of national Jews began to proclaim the glory of Jehovah and His Messiah, not just in their native Aramaic, but in languages of people groups around the world.

At first, they considered them madmen or drunkards. But Simon Peter, their leader and key speaker, explained what was happening with a powerful message filled with the promises of the prophets about a coming age of the Spirit, and also filled with bold witness regarding the resurrection of Jesus of Nazareth, recently crucified by the Romans.

Even more astounding was the result of his message, as over three thousand people marched with Jesus' disciples in a procession to the temple complex where each one publicly professed faith in Jesus of Nazareth as their Lord and Savior and then were baptized in His Name. What a day that was!

Of course, many attributed the events of that day to mass religious hysteria. However, it was what took place over the coming weeks that was completely astounding and radically new. These followers of Jesus did not behave as a bizarre mob of wandering fanatics; on the contrary, they settled into a rhythm of life the likes of which the world had never known. They were utterly devoted in love to their Master and one another. They gathered in the temple courts to praise and worship God, and they gave liberally to those in need when they, themselves, were mostly poor people. In fact, those who owned lands or valuable items were delighted, when learning of a need, to sell their possessions in order to provide for the common welfare.

They were the most faithful employees in the entire region, and those among them who were employers treated their workers with fairness and generosity. Not only did these people congregate in the temple, but they would also gather in their homes to discuss the teachings of their leaders called apostles, and there they would pray and share a meal that included an unusual ceremony of breaking bread and drinking from a cup of wine offered in the name of Jesus. They were so filled with gladness and joy that people were being added to their number day by day. What a season it was! The only question was this, "How long will this last?" Good question.

ACTS 3
May 8

" *A Walking Witness* "

There once was a man who lived in downtown Chicago who was known as someone whose life was completely destroyed and controlled by the addiction to alcohol. It was a common site to see him on the street corners begging for some coins to purchase his next bottle of oblivion.

One day, the man was invited into the Union Rescue Mission for a meal and a good night's sleep off the streets. That evening the man heard the good news of a Savior who refuses none and will receive and change all who come to Him by faith. The addict was gloriously converted by the grace of God, and he soon became a shining witness on the same streets where he used to beg.

One day a man who knew the former addict's history, skeptically and sarcastically asked him, "Do you mean to tell me you believe Jesus turned water into wine?" To which the delivered alcoholic replied, "Mister, that is nothing. If you come to my apartment, I will show you how He turned whiskey into furniture!" Things drastically change when the power of Christ is released into a person's life.

Our reading today is a timeless example of the testimony of a life touched by the Lord. Day after day, a poor man crippled from his birth was laid at the Beautiful Gate of the temple. He survived off the pity of pilgrims coming to worship. That is what he expected on the morning he lifted his cup for coins toward the two men approaching the gate. The bigger of the two, fixing his eyes on the beggar said, "I have no silver or gold, but what I do have I give to you. In the name of Jesus of Nazareth, rise up and walk!" As the big man took him by the right hand and lifted him up, the beggar felt an energy he had never known course through his crippled legs. Immediately, he began to do something he had only done in his dreams; he walked and ran and hopped and leaped. With his arms around the two men, he also began to do something else he had never done; he praised and exalted the God at whose temple he had sat outside so long. He became a walking worshiper of God. Clinging to Peter, he was now the living embodiment of the power of Jesus. He was a living sermon illustration of God's grace.

You are too. Your testimony is probably not nearly as dramatic as that of this lame man, but it is just as real if you are a believer. You were once spiritually crippled, outside of God's house and unable to enter His presence, but now things are radically different. You can walk in His healing power and bear witness with praise for His amazing grace. Your healing is real and total. You have a story to tell. People will listen. *They will.*

ACTS 4
May 9

"*Prayers of the Persecuted*"

One of the biggest challenges to believers in the United States is that our experience in following Jesus has been so abnormal in a very significant way. We have known so little persecution. That is not normal. The normal experience of Christians since the earliest days of the faith has been the presence of persecution.

On the day that I write these lines, and on the date that you read them, untold millions of our brothers and sisters in Christ are subject to varying levels of opposition simply because they have pledged their faith and their loyalty to Jesus. Let me quickly say that we who live as believers in America should not feel guilty because of the freedom we have enjoyed to freely worship according to our conscience. However, because we have known so little persecution, we often do not have experience in how to honor our Lord in the midst of it. The understanding of how to respond under pressure may come to us more quickly than we expect either personally or collectively, but it *will come* for all sincere followers of Jesus. "Indeed, all who desire to live a Godly life in Christ Jesus will be persecuted" (2 Tim. 3:12).

Pressure and opposition come to Christians for one underlying issue —the insistence that we conform to an authority contrary to that of our Master. Like the apostles, at some time we will be urged or challenged to yield our convictions to another culture; we will have to choose whether we obey God or someone else (v. 19). That is when the real test will come, not only of our *allegiances to Christ* but just as important, our *attitude in Christ*.

How should we respond when it comes? The early followers of Jesus show us the way. "And now, Lord, look upon their threats and grant to your servants to continue to speak your word with all boldness" (v. 29). Their prayer showed they saw persecution as *a fulfillment of Scripture* and *identification with Jesus*, and also as an opportunity for an even *greater witness for the gospel*. Persecution did not *embitter* these believers; *it empowered* them and *emboldened* them. Persecution will either make us or break us. The choice will be ours.

ACTS 5
May 10

"Friends in High and Low Places"

For the Apostles in the early days of the church, daily life was a continual contradiction in terms. On the one hand, they were held in such high esteem and reverence by the people. Many would bring the sick into the streets so that at least the shadow of Peter might fall on them.

However, at the same time, the political and religious leaders in Jerusalem despised them. Neither esteem by the public nor hatred by the leaders guided the Apostles; they had already committed that they must live for God's pleasure above anyone else's (Acts 4:19). As a result of their desire to honor God, the Apostles were truly free men. Also, because they were men who honored Him, the Lord made sure they had friends wherever they were. When they were locked in the lowest dungeon, God sent them a friend in an angel who set them free. When they were arrested by the soldiers (for the second day in a row!), the Lord placed friends in the crowd to restrain any possible abuse (v. 26).

Then in an incredible turn of events, the Lord raised up an advocate for them in the midst of the council of the Sanhedrin, and what an advocate he was—none other than Gamaliel, the most respected Rabbi in all of Judaism! (vv. 34-40) Of course, their greatest friend was the Heavenly Companion, who just as Jesus had promised, was always with them, supporting them and empowering their message. "We are witnesses to these things, and so is the Holy Spirit, whom God has given to those who obey him" (v. 32). The Apostles had terrible enemies for sure, but they were also surrounded at all times by friends, both visible and invisible.

There are times in our lives as believers that we do feel very lonely, but the truth is that no follower of the Lord can ever truly be alone. The Father has promised that He will never leave us or forsake, and Jesus promised, "I am with you always, even to the end of the age" (Matt. 28:20). Our Lord also said that the Comforter, the Holy Spirit, would abide with us forever (John 14:16). That is an amazing thought; every Member of the Trinity is pledged to be with us at all times. That is the truth that we must claim by faith, even when we do not feel it.

One of the most important aspects of prayer is not only to confess our sins, but also to confess the truth. It is never a foolish thing to say in prayer what God says in His Word. Hearing our own voice proclaiming the truth of God over the deceptiveness of our *feelings* is one of the most powerful sources of encouragement. Today, the truth is that in spite of how lonely we might feel, we have friends everywhere—within us, around us, and above us. In praise, thank the Lord for that today, and encourage your own heart.

PSALM 44 & PROVERBS 13
May 11

"A Guarded Mouth and Guarded Life"

"Whoever guards his mouth preserves his life;
he who opens wide his lips comes to ruin."
(Proverbs 13:3)

It has well been said there is great significance in the fact that God created us with one mouth and two ears; it may very well be that He intends us to listen twice as much as we speak. Regardless of whether there is anatomical support for that statement or not, there is certainly much instruction in God's Word regarding the importance of being very careful about our speech. To apply these Bible principles adequately, it is important that we think of our "words" and our "speech" as more than just verbal communication.

In our technologically advanced world, communication is now not just from our mouths but also our fingertips on a keyboard, and also from the lens of the camera on our smartphone. Today we communicate in many different ways. So perhaps, more than ever, the incredible importance the Lord places on the control of our communication should be emphasized.

In our text above from Proverbs 13:3, we are challenged by Solomon to guard our lives by guarding our words and warned that when we are quick to "say what we think," we are exposing ourselves to ruin. When we are quick to enter into issues that do not directly involve us, we are partners in strife (Prov. 13:10). When we answer a matter before we fully understand the issues, it is folly and shame to us (Prov. 18:13). Ungoverned speech leads God's people into transgression (Prov. 10:19). When a person is hasty in his words, there is no hope that he can avoid bringing guilt upon himself (Prov. 29:20). Uncontrolled speech is indeed so dangerous. However, it is clear that the Lord gave us mouths and wants us to use them for the noblest of purposes, and that is for the encouragement and strengthening of others. "Let your speech always be gracious, seasoned with salt, so that you may know how you ought to answer each person" (Col. 4:6).

Paul also challenges us, "Let no corrupting talk come out of your mouths, but only such as is good for building up, as it fits the occasion, that it may give grace to those who hear" (Eph. 4:29).

The best way to guard and guide our communication is to use the **T.H.I.N.K.** test.

T - Is it True?
H - Does it Honor God?
I - Does it Inspire?
N - Is it Necessary?
K - Is it Kind?

PSALMS 45 & 46
May 12

"Knowledge in the Stillness"

"Be still, and know that I am God.
I will be exalted among the nations,
I will be exalted in the earth!"
(Psalm 46:10)

Psalm 46 is one of several of the psalms in which David intentionally creates tension by contrasting radically conflicting experiences. He does this to share a message of worship regarding the Lord's character and provision. In this psalm, David writes about events in the world that are described as *a raging among the nations*. The convulsions are so fearful, he likens them to *earthquakes that topple the mountains* and *floods sweeping over the face of the earth*. The *nations totter* and the *earth melts*. The earth is in chaos. Sound familiar?

This psalm also says that in the midst of all this international upheaval, there is a peaceful stream flowing for God's people that brings joy to their hearts. That stream is the living presence of God Himself. The earth is in turmoil, but He is not and neither should His people. The simple truth is, God has got this! "Come, behold the works of the Lord, how he has brought desolations to the earth. He makes wars cease to the ends of the earth; he breaks the bow and shatters the spear; he burns the chariots with fire" (vv. 8-9). God is in sovereign control of all things. His purposes will be accomplished. We need not fear, "The Lord of hosts is with us; the God of Jacob is our fortress" (v. 7).

Yes, we as believers know this; the question is how do we experience this calm in the midst of the clamor of the world? Ready for the answer on what to do? Do nothing. Seriously, don't do anything, but rather *be* something. *Be quiet*. The reason many of us can't hear the murmuring of the "streams that make glad the city of God" (v. 4) is that we won't sit on the bank and be still. The Lord says, "Be still and know that I am God." If we won't be still, then we really won't know.

In the Lord's purpose for our lives as believers, *being* always comes before *doing*. We are told that when Jesus selected the Apostles, He chose twelve "so that they might be with him and he might send them out to preach" (Mark 3:14). Their first calling was to "be with him;" it is our first priority as well. Being "still" is the most proactive thing we can do, for it is being still in God's presence that we come to *know* God more intimately, and that is the ultimate purpose of our lives. "And this is eternal life, that they know you, the only true God, and Jesus Christ whom you have sent" (John 17:3). The world may rage, but God will be exalted among the nations. When we are still, He is exalted in our hearts.

ACTS 6
May 13

"No One Left Behind"

Our reading today describes the first fracture that occurred in an incredibly united church in Jerusalem. As we read the passage today, it might not seem to be that big of a deal, but it was a serious problem that revealed a much deeper and dangerous issue.

The chapter opens with this statement: "Now in those days when the disciples were increasing in number a complaint by the Hellenists arose against the Hebrews because their widows were being neglected in the daily distribution." It is important to understand who is being identified in verse one. The "Grecians" refers to Jewish believers in Jesus who were not native-born in the land of Judea. The "Hebrews" means the members of the congregation who were also Jewish, but they were also born in the land of Judea.

It seems that a form of favoritism was being displayed, with widows who were "Hebrews" being cared for more devotedly than those who were "Grecians." The danger was that this perceived favoritism would produce a divided church, and a divided church cannot provide a united testimony for Jesus Christ to a watching world. Jesus told His disciples, "By this all people will know that you are my disciples, if you have love for one another" (John 13:35).

Much was at stake for the early church and its mission in Jerusalem, and thank God love and wisdom won the day. Spirit-filled men (several of them with Greek names!) were appointed to oversee this important ministry. As a result of the continued unity of the church, "...the number of disciples multiplied greatly in Jerusalem, and a great many of the priests became obedient to the faith" (v. 7). This is a great lesson for each of us today. Love is caring and caring for all in tangible ways. Love is healing to wounded hearts. Love is a powerful witness that all of us can share.

"Little children, let us not love in word or talk
but in deed and in truth."
(1 John 3:18)

" The Insanity of God "

Several years ago I read one of the most remarkable books of my entire life, *The Insanity of God*. The book was written by Nik Ripken (a pseudonym for his protection and the protection of others), a missionary who served in some of the most gospel-resistant areas of the world. Over an extended period of time, Nik was able to document that one of the most important factors in seeing evangelistic breakthrough around the world was persecution. Yes! Persecution! Hence, the startling title, *The Insanity of God*, for against all reasonable expectation, it was clearly demonstrated that persecution actually spurs evangelism and church planting in the most oppressive of environments. The findings seem completely illogical, but on closer consideration, it is seen that this outcome of persecution is totally Biblical. In fact, this is the model we see worked out from the earliest days of the church.

Our reading in Acts 7 recounts the events leading to the death of the first recorded Christian martyr, Stephen, a deacon and evangelist of the Church of Jerusalem. Stephen was arrested under false charges and lying witnesses because of his powerful preaching of the gospel of Christ. Just like his Master, Stephen was hauled before the Sanhedrin, the religious/ civil council of the Jewish people. There, with his face beaming like an angel, this gracious and good man preached one of the most amazing sermons ever recorded—a veritable history of God's redemption and mercy to Israel and the nations hard-hearted rebellion.

The hate-filled hypocrites could not tolerate Stephen's convicting message any longer, and, losing all pretense of justice, they dragged him outside the city and beat him to death with stones. In his dying agonies, Stephen saw the glory of heaven and his Savior standing to greet him. With his final breaths he called on Jesus to forgive his executioners. How could this senseless and tragic injustice possibly have any connection to God whatsoever?

Well, first of all, there was a young man who heard Stephen's sermon and watched how he died. He may have even been the prosecuting witness since the executioners laid their cloaks at his feet. His name? Saul of Tarsus. Saul could never get this scene out of his mind, and in spite of his continuing hatred of believers, the death of Stephen was a constant goad that wounded his conscience (Acts 26:14).

Also, this terrible persecution that began with Stephen's martyrdom caused the disciples to scatter from Jerusalem and travel all over Judea and Samaria. Guess what they took with them—the good news of Jesus Christ! God knows what He is doing. What seems like insanity to us is never out of His sovereign control and is often part of His divine plan for our lives accomplishing a greater testimony for Jesus. As the anonymous poet has said so well, "God knows what He is about."

ACTS 8
May 15

" *Into Africa* "

Perhaps you will be as surprised as I was. I recently read an article in a leading Christian periodical that said the continent in the world with the most Christian residents is Africa. I did not see that coming, did you? Many of us might tend to believe that Islam holds sway over all of Africa, but that is not the case. There are now 600 million people in Africa that profess to be Christians. In fact, it is estimated that 45% of all the believers in the world live in that "dark" continent. 600 million believers in Africa and our reading today in Acts 8 tells us the story of the first one.

We do not know his name, but we do know that he was a high court official, the treasurer of Queen Candace of Ethiopia. He had made a long pilgrimage to worship Jehovah in the temple in Jerusalem. While there, he purchased a scroll that contained some or all of the Prophecy of Isaiah, an incredibly expensive document. This man was a serious seeker of the Lord, but in truth, it was the *Lord* who was seeking *him*. So much so, that He commanded the evangelist Philip to cut short an amazingly successful gospel mission in Samaria and journey, literally, into the middle of nowhere—the Gaza desert bordering Egypt. There, after long journeys in the broiling sun, these two men had a "chance encounter" in the desert. And it took place as, "it just so happened," the Ethiopian treasurer was reading from Isaiah Chapter 53, "The Gospel of Messiah" in the Old Testament. There, sitting with him in the chariot, Philip explained the fulfillment of Isaiah's prophecy through the life, death, and resurrection of Jesus of Nazareth. And there, as the man listened in the chariot, the Holy Spirit worked the gift of repentance and faith in the heart of this Ethiopian, and the first recorded person from the continent of Africa was born again.

Coming up on a desert oasis, the Ethiopian requested baptism, and there, with Philip, he professed his faith and identified himself with Christ in the beautiful ordinance. The first of 600 million to come was led to Christ by an obedient but somewhat confused witness, who was called away from "an evangelistic harvest" to plant the seed of the gospel in one man's life in the middle of the desert. Philip was immediately caught away by the Spirit, so he probably never knew what became of the Ethiopian, but he knows now.

Because Philip was ready to share his faith, wherever he was, with whomever he was with, a Queen's servant journeyed on through the desert "Into Africa" rejoicing that he was now, also, a servant of the King of Kings and a son of the God of Abraham, Isaac, and Jacob. He was the first one of 600 million more to come. We just never know, do we? That's right, and may we never forget it, we just never know.

ACTS 9
May 16

" *Risk Takers* "

In Acts Chapter 9, we read the account of one of the most significant events in the history of the world. An incident so impactful, that even agnostic historians consider it to be world-changing in its importance. Of course, I am talking about the conversion of Saul of Tarsus, who would be known in a few years and for all the centuries to come as Paul, the apostle. This "most unlikely to be converted" enemy of Christ and His people became perhaps the most influential evangelist and defender of the faith the world has ever known.

No one would have anticipated Saul's conversion; in fact, as we shall see, many faithful Christians did not believe it even after it took place. However, by God's grace, there are always those whose obedience to Christ is greater than their lack of faith, and it is people like that who change the world. People like Ananias and Barnabas. The Lord Jesus is the *Divine Hero* of Acts Chapter 9, but these two men are the *human heroes*. They were willing to take a risk, a very big risk indeed, to share the love of Jesus Christ with the man who might very well be their worst enemy on the face of the earth.

In obedience to Christ, Ananias was the first Christian to place his hands on Saul, bless him, and call him "brother." No doubt, it was Ananias who, later that night, held Saul as he was baptized in the name of his former archenemy, Jesus of Nazareth. Ananias was a risk-taker; so was Barnabas. It was Barnabas, "...the son of encouragement" (for that was the name the apostles had given to Joseph), who took a risk and took Saul by the hand and brought him into the fellowship of the church in Jerusalem. Barnabas, the risk-taker, by his example brought this ultimate outcast into the fellowship of the saints. Before Paul would ever write one of his many epistles to local churches, through the risk-taking love of Barnabas, Saul of Tarsus experienced the unfathomable forgiveness and acceptance that can only be found in the church. These two men, Ananias and Barnabas, by being *loving risk-takers,* did not know that they were being *world changers*. Neither do we.

When we step out of our comfort zones to invest in people who are not like us, and in fact, may not *like* us, we are releasing the most powerful force in the entire universe, love. Love changes things because love changes people. The love of God has been poured out in our hearts by the Holy Spirit for one purpose—to be shared.

Love is not a treasure to be hoarded; it is a gift to be invested. Yes, love is to be invested in the nice safe fields of family and friends, but love is *also* to be invested in the soil of strangers and the hardened soil of enemies. Sound risky? Yes, love is risky. Love is also eternal. So is its influence. And so is its reward.

ACTS 10
May 17

" Tear Down This Wall !"

It was an iconic moment in the 20th century. The President of the United States, Ronald Reagan, stood next to the Berlin Wall that divided the city between communist and democratic sectors and proclaimed his challenge to the Soviet Premier, "Mr. Gorbachev, tear down this wall!" The President's words were a call for unity for the citizens of Berlin but also a call for freedom to all people in the Soviet Bloc. Of course, the wall did not come down immediately, but a process was set in motion that would change the political and geographical map of Europe.

Acts Chapter 10 similarly shares a transformational moment in the history of the church. Things were never the same after the events that transpired on the rooftop of the house of Simon the Tanner and in the parlor of the home of Cornelius the Centurion. On that rooftop, Peter received a vision that was repugnant to everything in his nature, a command from the Lord came to him demanding that he eat from a cloth filled with all sorts of unclean animals that were forbidden to an observant Jew. Peter's objections were met by the Lord's stern reply, "What God has made clean, do not call common" (v. 15).

Immediately after experiencing this same vision three times, three men appeared at the gate of Simon's house encouraging Peter to come with them to the home of the pious Roman centurion, Cornelius. What a sight awaited Peter when a few days later he entered Cornelius' home and found assembled a room full of Gentiles waiting to hear his message from the Lord. The meaning of his strange vision on the rooftop became instantly clear to Peter as he heard Cornelius's testimony, "I understand that God shows no partiality, but in every nation, anyone who fears him and does what is right is acceptable to him." If God had accepted these Gentiles, how could Peter not? God made that doubly clear when, as Peter shared about Jesus Christ, the Holy Spirit came upon those Gentile listeners just as He had to the Jewish audience in the upper room a few years earlier.

No man could or would ever tear down the wall that separated Jews and Gentiles for centuries, but God did through the sacrifice of His Son and the baptism by His Holy Spirit. In one incredible moment, God demonstrated for the ages that the walls that separate people have come down, and that there now exists in Jesus Christ, a new humanity of one blood and by one blood. If we are Christians, we have experienced this. Now the question we must ask and answer for ourselves every day is— do we embrace this? The Lord will help us. If we truly desire to hear His voice, He will be very direct and very clear, "Tear Down This Wall!"

PSALMS 47 & 48
May 18

"*Greatly Feared, Greatly Praised*"

The Psalms of David were the songbook of Israel and also of the early church. We do not know what these songs sounded like; it may be that the words could be sung to a variety of chord structures or often sung a cappella. What we do know is that sometimes the singing was loud, very loud.

Some of the Psalms, such as those we read today, were specifically written by David to be sung by the Sons of Korah, a choir of priests numbering in the hundreds as they stood upon the walls of the temple. Can you imagine several hundred men's voices singing lyrics like these with all their might?

"Clap your hands, all peoples! Shout to God with loud songs of joy! For the Lord, the Most High, is to be feared, A great king over all the earth." (Ps. 47:1-2)

"Great is the Lord and greatly to be praised in the city of our God! His holy mountain, beautiful in situation, is the joy of all the earth, Mount Zion, in the far north, the city of the Great King." (Ps. 48:1-2)

Wow. Visualize that scene and hear those sounds in your mind. Can you imagine the people just muttering along with these words? Could you see the congregation standing with blank, expressionless faces as these songs were sung? Hardly. Why? Because the greatness of the Lord, the God of Israel, was being proclaimed! "This is God, our God forever and ever!" (Ps. 48:14)

Jesus told the woman at the well in John 4 that God is seeking worshipers who will worship Him "in spirit and in truth." That means God delights in people worshiping Him with all they are, for all He is. If you have been faithfully reading the words of the Scriptures and the words of these devotionals for several weeks, I think I can safely assume that you have a sincere desire to worship God in truth, but allow me to challenge you today about worshiping God with your spirit—all you are. Worship is to be emotional; worship means we are moved in our spirit by God's Spirit. This does not mean that we are to disengage our *minds* in worship, but it also does not mean we are to disengage our *emotions* in worship.

How long has it been since you *joyfully*, and yes, *loudly* expressed your raptured soul in praise to God? Yes, there are times we are to be quiet before the Lord (Ps. 46:10), but there are also times we are to be loud. Yes, that might be emotional, but it is also Biblical.

"Clap your hands, all peoples!
Shout to God with loud songs of joy!"
(Psalm 47:1)

148

PSALMS 49 & 50
May 19

"Worship, Walk, Wisdom"

"The one who offers thanksgiving as his sacrifice glorifies me;
to the one who orders his way rightly I will show
the salvation of God." (Psalm 50:23)

Psalm 50 is a song of worship about worship. In this song, David speaks as a worshiper expressing why the God of Israel is so worthy of the worship. But in this song, David also takes his place as a worshiping listener. David's pen becomes the voice of God calling the people to an understanding of the requirements and rewards of acceptable worship. God affirms that the nation is offering plenty of burnt offerings, and doing so in the prescribed manner, but their sacrifices are not acceptable to God. God did not need the animals they were offering, for "the cattle on a thousand hills" are His, as is the world and all it contains.

What God desires in worship is the *worshiper*—the heart devotion of His people expressed in thanksgiving. The utmost offering is one of thanksgiving, for who God is and what He has done for all of His people and each of His people. God is a jealous God. He cannot be bought off with ritualistic religious activities. His people are His people; they belong to no one else and nothing else. God desires to be loved and *deserves* to be loved because He is love and has fixed His love on His people. God is glorified in our loving worship, and He is also glorified in our loyal walk. He is honored as we live our lives in His presence and walk before Him rightly (v. 23).

Worship is a walk, a way of living as to the Lord. As Paul would say a thousand years after David, our lives are "living sacrifices" and to be presented "holy and without blemish to the Lord" as our spiritual act of worship (Rom. 12:1-2). When the Lord calls us to thanksgiving in worship and dedication in our walk, it is not motivated by what we can give to Him but by what He can give to us. "I will show the salvation of God" (v. 23). This promise involves more than the guarantee of eternal salvation. It is the promise of understanding the salvation of God, which means to know God intimately and personally. This is the promise of the "abundant life" that Jesus said He came to give. It means to live life with the highest form of wisdom, which is the knowledge of the Holy One Himself.

"The fear of the Lord is the beginning of wisdom, and the knowledge of the Holy One is insight" (Prov. 9:10). Psalm 50 is a call from the Lord to measure our worship and our walk, and it is an offer from God to immeasurable wisdom, a life ever-growing in the knowledge and experience of God. What better way of living could there possibly be?! Let's not miss it.

" The First Christians "

A few months ago, while strolling through a city, I was attracted to a large imposing statue depicting a general from the Revolutionary War. On closer inspection, I was amazed to see that it was a statue of George Washington. It might not seem very surprising to you, but I was walking on a street in Paris, France! I didn't see that (I mean, "George") coming. Not being able to speak or read French, I was unable to find out why a statue of the "Father of *Our* Country" was publicly displayed in another nation. Our chapter today tells us that one of the most famous terms in the history of the world was coined in one of the most unlikely of places. "And in Antioch the disciples were first called Christians" (v. 26b). Nobody would have seen this coming either. Antioch was nearly 500 miles away from where the church began in Jerusalem, and it was light years away from Jerusalem in culture and religion.

At that time, Antioch was the third largest city in the empire. It was also the crossroads between Europe and Asia and was a clash of religions and cultures. It was also a moral cesspool and considered the most debauched city in all the empire. A place like this would be the origin of the word "Christian?" How was that even possible? A careful reading of the chapter explains the reason and why Antioch was the perfect place for believers to first be called Christians. The word "Christian" had nothing to do with the location of the city, but it had everything to do with what was taking place for the first time in history within this city.

Jews and Gentiles who had hated each other for centuries were now suddenly gathering together for teaching and singing and praying and sharing meals. They called each other "brother" and "sister." They didn't look alike, they didn't dress alike, they didn't eat alike, but it did not seem to make any difference. They did not just *tolerate* each other; they actually seemed to *love* each other. They came from different countries and cultures, they had different hair color and facial features, but instead of being *divided*, they were *united*. The amazed investigators could only find one thing they shared in common, and that was the love and allegiance they expressed about their leader—a Jewish Rabbi crucified by the Romans a few years ago but whom they affirmed had risen to life again, ascended to heaven, and who gave salvation and forgiveness of sins to all who believed in Him. They called him "Christ," the anointed one.

Jesus was the one thing they had in common. He was their leader and master, so they were "Christ ones,"—"Christians." The title was given because people, so radically different in how they loved one another and lived their lives for each other, just had to be explained, and Christ was the only explanation. How would people explain the way *we* live today? How would they identify us? Would Christ come to their minds?

ACTS 12
May 21

" *Evil Overwhelmed* "

Acts Chapter 12 records so many important, amazing events that reading it is like watching the curtain rise for a dramatic play. Scene 1 is brief but poignant. James, the brother of John, one of Jesus' beloved "sons of thunder" and an early disciple from Galilee, is arrested and executed by the tyrant, King Herod. He is the first of the Apostles to give his life for His Master's cause. Then, to further please the Jewish leaders, Herod had Peter arrested and kept in prison, planning to have him publicly executed after the Passover. However, King Herod's fiendish plans cannot hinder the sovereign plans of the King of the Universe.

In Scene 2, God sends an angel who awakens Peter from a sound sleep, releases his chains, opens the locked doors of the citadel, and leads him safely outside. The curtain falls, and when it rises for Scene 3, Peter is standing outside the house of Mary, the mother of John Mark, where a prayer meeting is being held on his behalf. In a comical moment, the servant girl, Rhoda, comes to answer the door and in hearing Peter's voice, runs overjoyed to tell the others. Poor Peter is left continuing to knock on the gate while the people gathered in the prayer meeting for his deliverance begin to dialogue about who the person at the door can possibly be! Finally, Peter gains entrance into his own prayer meeting and informs the disciples of all that has taken place in answer to their prayers.

Scene 4 is one of confusion and condemnation as the guards cannot find their carefully guarded prisoner anywhere and, unable to convince King Herod of their innocence, are executed for their involvement in the treachery. Scene 5 opens with Herod giving an oration to the people of Tyre and Sidon, following which he is proclaimed by them as a god. For his evil and blasphemy, this vile man, who killed James, attempted to kill Peter, and exalted himself as divine, is struck by the Lord with terrible judgment and dies in agony as a plague of worms slowly eat his intestines. The final scene shows the witness of the Word of God that Herod attempted to crush, multiplying the number of the disciples in the region, and the dramatic chapter concludes with a significant transition. The focus of the Book of Acts shifts to Paul and his ministry team returning to share the gospel to the Gentiles. Traveling with them is a young man, John Mark, the son of Mary, in whose house the prayer meeting for Peter had been held.

As we read Acts, we are reading history; but it is a *living* history, for the same God is continuing to act in the lives of His servants to advance the Kingdom of His Son. He is working in your life today. You are part of His story. James, Peter, Rhoda, Mary, John Mark, Paul, and Barnabas all had their part, and so do you. Whether your scenes are many or whether your lines are few, your part is significant. Now for today's performance, give it your very best!

ACTS 13
May 22

" A Timeless Epitaph "

As we read through the Book of Acts, we have several different occasions to hear the exact words that the apostles and missionary-evangelists used in sharing the gospel of Jesus Christ. As we read these sermons, it becomes evident that there are a couple of points that are raised, quite often, by the preachers to affirm the message of Jesus.

The earliest recorded messages of the apostles and evangelists centered on the fact of Jesus' resurrection as proof that He was, in truth, the Son of God—the Messiah. Connected to this emphasis on Christ's resurrection were frequent quotations from the Psalms of David as Scriptural support that the Messiah would be buried, yes, but that His body would *not* experience decay. He would be resurrected *before* that decay would take place in His body.

This was a focus of Peter's message on the Day of Pentecost, and Stephen also bore witness of Jesus' resurrection in his sermon before the council of the Sanhedrin in Jerusalem. Paul too cited these references to David's psalms of prophecy in his messages to Jewish audiences. As a result of these messages, there are references to David throughout the sermons recorded in the New Testament and also in the writings of the early church fathers. As a man of faith in Messiah, David impacted people with his songs of gospel hope for over a 1000 years after his death. Truly "through his faith, though he died, he still speaks" (Heb. 11:5).

In one of his messages, Paul gives a wonderful epitaph to David and the impact of his life. "For David after he had served the purpose of God in his own generation, fell asleep and was laid with his fathers..." (v. 36). That is an epitaph any servant of God would be honored to have written on his tombstone! It shares the simplicity and the totality of a life lived for God, "serving the purpose of God in our generation." That is not a wasted life! What could be a better use of our limited time on this planet than to serve the Lord in our own generation?

Our life is not our own; it belongs to God and should be invested in the people of our generation. When we do that our life takes on a quality that is eternal because investing our life for God, in our generation, makes an impact on the generations to come through the lives we touch *in our lifetime*. How beautifully Paul describes the death of David—he "fell asleep and was laid with his fathers." David fell asleep in death and entered the rest, known by his ancestors who had served God before him. David entered the eternal rest of the righteous, but the testimony and influence of his life powerfully works to this day. Now, that's a great epitaph and a great legacy!

ACTS 14
May 23

" Friends and Enemies "

Our Lord and Master is truly "The Prince of Peace." His birth was heralded by the angels who sang, "Glory to God in the highest, and on earth peace among those with whom he is pleased" (Luke 2:14)! Jesus came to this world so that through Him we might be justified by faith and have peace with God (Rom. 5:8). Jesus promised His disciples then and he guarantees His disciples today, "Peace I leave with you; my peace I give to you" (John 14:27). Jesus provides for us the peace "...which surpasses all understanding, will guard your hearts and your minds..." (Phil. 4:7) All believers look forward to the day when peace will reign over all the earth in the Kingdom to come.

All of these promises are true, but it is also true that following the Lord does not bring peace in *all* situations. Jesus told us, "Do not think that I have come to bring peace to the earth. I have not come to bring peace, but a sword" (Matt. 10:34). Jesus is the Great Peacemaker, but He is also the Great Divider. He divides time itself into BC and AD, and He has divided people through all the centuries. Jesus brings division among people groups, friends, and even families. This happens because with Jesus there is no neutrality. Jesus is either a liar, a lunatic, or the Lord.

One day all humanity will be divided at the judgment and placed on Jesus' right hand or His left. But that division already exists. Each person is already on one side of Jesus or the other, so what does that mean for us now? It means something similar to what we read about in Acts Chapter 14. Paul and Barnabas shared the good news of the gospel of Jesus Christ wherever they traveled and to some, it was good news indeed! Some rejoiced in the message of salvation and gladly received the Lord by faith. Some loved Paul and Barnabas and stood united with them. But only some. Not everyone.

Many were offended by the message of a crucified Messiah, whose horrible death was necessary for the depth of their sins to be forgiven. People do not like being reminded that they are rebellious, lost sinners desperately in need of salvation. Paul and Barnabas were ridiculed, attacked, and driven from the city; not because they brought a message of hate, but a message of love and peace experienced in Jesus Christ. They experienced what Jesus had predicted, "If they have persecuted me, they will also persecute you. If they have hated me, they will hate you also" (John 15:18-20).

Rather than consider it a strange thing that we do not suffer some rejection because of Jesus, we *should* think it odd, and frankly, very concerning, if we *do not*. Are we ready to consider it an honor to suffer for the sake of His Name? How can we possibly be prepared? One way is by remembering that *we too* were once enemies of Christ, but the Prince of Peace conquered us and gave us peace through the blood of His cross. Remember, and be kind, and be bold.

ACTS 15
May 24

"*Brothers Divided*"

There has rarely, if ever, been a more impactful team for the gospel than Paul and Barnabas. What they accomplished for God in their missionary endeavors literally changed the world by beginning the global mission of world evangelization. The churches they planted and pastored became centers of gospel witness in the midst of urban areas of the darkest paganism. Together they discipled and trained missionary evangelists who multiplied the church planting movement they initiated.

Paul and Barnabas were devoted to each other. Barnabas had reached out to welcome Paul into the community of believers when no one else trusted his profession of faith. The two of them established the Church in Antioch where Jews and Gentiles first embraced each other in the faith, and where the disciples were first called "Christians." These men had stood, side-by-side, facing the most demonized of mobs bent on their destruction.

Yes, Paul and Barnabas were true brothers, but something terrible happened. Their incredible unity was broken by a very deep and personal disagreement. Paul did not think it wise to take John Mark with them on their next journey since his courage had given way previously in Pamphylia and "had not gone with them to the work" (v. 38). Barnabas, "The Son of Encouragement," and the relative of John Mark (Col. 4:10) thought that Mark was deserving of another opportunity to prove his worth. Both Paul and Barnabas were inflexible in their positions, and the tension escalated to such a "sharp disagreement, so that they separated from each other" (v. 39). Barnabas took Mark and sailed away to Cyprus, and Paul chose Silas and journeyed on through Syria and Cilicia.

This was a tragic event in so many ways. It is impossible for us to say which of the two men was in the wrong. In some ways, they both had good reasons for the positions they took regarding Mark. It is obvious that the Lord blessed the ministry of Paul and Silas as they continued the mission outreach in Asia Minor and then into Europe. However, it is also clear from the overall message of the New Testament, that Barnabas' ministry was very important in training Mark for future ministry. After all, he did write one of the four gospels! Even Paul, several years later, told Timothy to "Get Mark and bring him with you, for he is very useful to me for ministry" (2 Tim. 4:11).

There are so many lessons we can glean from this division between Paul and Barnabas. Probably one of the most important for us to apply is to make sure that disagreements do not lead to the animosity that infects others. Our relational problems do not need to become personal poison in the lives of others. We cannot afford to let division defile our spirit or deter us from the service of our Lord. Life is too short and eternity is too long to waste our energy on proving we are right.

" A Light to Guide Us Home "

What would it sound like if a man on death row finally decided to fully confess? Not just to a pastor or priest, but to God? What would the confession of a traitor, murderer, and adulterer sound like? It would sound like Psalm 51. This Psalm is the darkest song David ever wrote; it is utterly personal and penitential as David sobs out his confession to the Lord.

This song has been months in delay as David has tried to hide his terrible secret. But all that changed when Nathan the prophet pointed his finger in David's face and powerfully condemned his hiding and hypocrisy, "You are the man!" (2 Samuel 12:7). Finally, David was brought face-to-face with the enormity of his sin against Bathsheba, against her husband Uriah whom he had murdered, against his people whose trust he had betrayed, and most of all against his God who never failed him or withheld anything from him. David fled to the tent where the Ark of the Covenant rested, and there the tears of repentance came in torrents of grief and the words of confession flowed from his lips:

> *"Have mercy on me, O God,*
> *according to your steadfast love;*
> *according to your abundant mercy*
> *blot out my transgressions.*
> *Wash me thoroughly from my iniquity,*
> *and cleanse me from my sin!*
>
> *For I know my transgressions,*
> *and my sin is ever before me.*
> *Against you, you only, have I sinned*
> *and done what is evil in your sight,*
> *so that you may be justified in your words*
> *and blameless in your judgment."*
> (Psalm 51:1-4)

Nothing could undo what David had done by his sin. But his sin could be pardoned and forgiven, not because he deserved it, but because of the love and mercy in the heart of God. David cast himself completely on God's redeeming grace and pleaded for forgiveness, and God granted it to him. God still hears the repentant prayers of His people.

Psalm 51 is recorded in the Bible not just to let us know what David said, but to guide us in what to say when we confess our sins to our Heavenly Father. Yes, it is a dark song, but it is bright with promise. The Lord put the psalm in His Word for the darkest hours of our lives to guide us back home to Him.

PSALMS 53 & 54
May 26

"Severe Mercy"

"Behold, God is my helper;
the Lord is the upholder of my life."
(Psalm 54:4)

On several occasions, David writes in his Psalms about how the Lord blesses him with "songs in the night." Several of David's most moving lyrics were written during the "deep nights of the soul." Reading the Psalms is to read a personal journal of almost the entire range of human emotion. David is not writing fiction or history. No, David is writing out of his own personal experiences; and in doing so, he is sharing his experiences with God. This is especially true of his experiences with deep, personal pain.

The author C.S. Lewis once described pain as "God's megaphone." By that, Lewis meant that in times of plenty and prosperity, we typically *do not* listen to God's voice. But in times of pain, we are alert to hear from the Lord and the message He has to share with us. Trouble is a wonderful mentor for our soul's pursuit of God.

In Psalm 54, David is struggling again with heartache and fear because he has been betrayed by people who made a covenant pledge of protection with him. He feels helpless and life seems hopeless. That is when the Lord speaks to his heart, in his darkness and pain. The light of God shelters his darkness. "Behold, God is my helper; the Lord is the upholder of my life." (v. 4)

Today we might say it this way, "God's got this, and God's got me!" David, even in his swirling emotional distress, was safe in God's hands. No one was in charge of his life but God. God was the "upholder of his life." My friend, what was true of David 3,000 years ago is true for you today. Whatever you are facing today, "God's got this, and God's got you!"

Selah.

Trouble is a wonderful mentor for our soul's pursuit of God.

156

" *Divine Detours* "

Have you ever had the experience of reading a passage of Scripture many times only to discover that in reading it again you see something for the first time? It isn't that the words were missing all along, but because of your familiarity with the passage, you overlooked a fresh message that had been "hiding in plain sight."

That was my experience recently regarding this chapter. One day, I noticed in verses 6-7 that Paul and his team were forbidden by the Spirit from speaking the Word in Galatia. Then, in the next verse, they are forbidden by the Spirit of Jesus from going into the area of Bithynia. It struck me as strange that someone like the Apostle Paul would not have *a golden compass* so that every step of his ministry was so clearly guided by God in the utmost detail. But that is not the case, because Paul faced many detours in life. He was doing the will of God to the best of his knowledge, but things somehow were not working out. It was as if he were being "hindered by the Lord" in what he was attempting to do for Him. If the Apostle Paul faced confusing detours in his life, then maybe we are not as spiritually insensitive as we might think we are. Following Jesus does not mean we will *not* face detours on our journey, but it *does* mean that those detours will be "divine detours."

Look closer at the detour in Paul's life described in verses 6-7 and you will see it was truly divine. Paul was trying to take the gospel message into the East, but he was hindered. Then he tried to take his mission into the North, and again he was not permitted to do so. It was as if the Lord was clearly saying, "No." Well, if Paul is traveling from the South and he is not allowed to go east or north, what other direction is there? That's right—West. Paul and his team turned to the West and they continued going west until they ran out of land at Troas! The waters of the Mediterranean Sea stretched before them. What now? That is when the detour made sense.

That night, Paul saw in a vision a man of Macedonia standing and urging him, "Come over to Macedonia and help us." Now God's plan was clear; Paul and his friends were to take the gospel into the continent of Europe. That's right. The evangelization of Europe and eventually the Western Hemisphere started here at Troas, and it started because of a confusing detour in the life of a faithful servant seeking to follow the Lord. But there was not just a *global* purpose in this detour; there was a *personal* purpose as well. If you read carefully, you notice a change that takes place in verse 10. The pronouns change from "they" to "we." Luke joined the team. The Lord needed Paul to get to Troas so Luke, a physician (Paul would be needing one!) and also a historian (the author of The Gospel of Luke and The Book of Acts) could join the team. The Lord knows exactly *where* He needs us to be, and where it is *best* for us to be. His detours for us are always there to keep us on the right road.

" Same Kind of Different "

In following the life of Paul on his journeys for the gospel, it is amazing to consider the variety of environments in which he found himself. At times they were nothing less than completely opposite in nature. Consider where Paul was just a few weeks before the events described in Acts Chapter 17. He and Silas were sitting in filth with hardened criminals in the prison at Philippi. However awful we may imagine that place to have been, it was worse. Now, where do we find Paul? He is standing at the very epicenter of culture and education in the entire world—the Areopagus in Athens. Here the greatest philosophers of the day would come to listen and debate.

Some of the members of this elite group had overheard Paul sharing "new teaching," and they invited Paul to share his philosophy with them. If ever there existed a situation in which a person might be tempted to "adjust" the message of Jesus, it would be in such a cultured and academic environment as that which existed on Mars Hill in Athens. But not for Paul. He did not stand among those philosophers and orators with any different calling than he had in the Philippian jail. His message to the jailer was the same message to the scholars. He was a witness of Jesus, and his message was all about the One who would judge all mankind, the Resurrected Son of God (vv. 29-31).

Paul was always faithful to share the gospel, and then he left the results to God. The results are always the same for all of us who share a witness of Jesus. Some "mocked," some said, "We will hear you again about this," and "...some men joined him and believed" (v. 32, 34).

These are the three primary responses to the message of the gospel: some will mock, some will wait, and some will believe. None of us are in control of the response to our witness. Each of us is responsible to sow the seed, and to only sow the *pure* seed. The seed is the gospel, the good news of Jesus Christ—His death and His glorious resurrection to save all who will repent and believe. The soil is the heart of the hearers. Sometimes the soil is rock-hard, sometimes it is not yet fully prepared and then sometimes the soil of a person's heart is perfectly prepared by God to receive His Word.

Again, our responsibility is simply to sow; to sow where we are and with whomever we are. Rich or poor, educated or illiterate, young or old, famous or infamous, we are to share the seed of the gospel. But we must make sure it is the *pure* seed we sow. The seed itself never changes...ever. Paul had one gospel message to proclaim wherever he went, for it was "the power of God for salvation to everyone who believes" (Rom. 1:16). As the hymn writer Fanny Crosby penned years ago, our message is always and simply, "The Old, Old Story."

"I love the old, old story, It did so much for me; And that is just the reason, I tell it now to thee."

Tell it. Always. Everywhere. To everyone.

ACTS 18
May 29

" *Watch God Work* "

When I first came to be the pastor of West Park Baptist Church, I felt completely overwhelmed by the responsibility and very difficult situation, spiritually and financially, that the church was facing at that time. I was young and inexperienced, and my wife, Susan, and I knew no one in Knoxville, Tennessee. We were lonely and afraid. Then one day I remembered a statement that Dr. Richard Snavely, the pastor of Calvary Baptist Church in Findlay, Ohio, where I served on staff for seven years, often used to encourage us as a congregation when faced with adversity. He simply told us, "Watch God Work." In remembering these words, I was so encouraged that I decided to make it a theme for *our* church family. We created a number of laminated cards containing that statement for people to post around their homes and places of employment. It reaffirmed to us that the ministry of the church was God's work and that if we were faithful to Him, we would see Him accomplish great things for His glory. Praise God, we have been blessed to "Watch God Work" for over 32 years!

Acts Chapter 18 shares about a season in Paul's ministry when he felt especially overwhelmed. By his own testimony, he came to Corinth in "weakness and in fear and much trembling" (1 Cor. 2:3). Paul was alone, overwhelmed, and out of money, but he was in God's will. Faithful in spite of his fears, Paul was blessed to "Watch God Work" on his behalf. The Lord gave him a job making tents with two refugees from Rome, Aquila and Priscilla. These two became Paul's first converts in Corinth and went on to become some of the most noted church planters and disciple-makers recorded in the New Testament. Paul was encouraged by the Lord in a night vision, "Do not be afraid but go on speaking and do not be silent, for I am with you, and no one will attack you to harm you, for I have many in this city who are my people" (vv. 9b-10). Paul "Watched God Work" in bringing many people to faith in Jesus. One of these converts included Crispus, who was the ruler of the synagogue. When Paul was expelled from the synagogue, a Gentile man named Titius Justice welcomed him into his home to hold church services, and his house just happened to be next door to the synagogue! The next ruler of the synagogue, Sosthenes, brought charges against Paul before the proconsul, Gallio, but God intervened on Paul's behalf. Gallio refused to hear the case, and the city mob listening to the public hearing turned on Sosthenes and attacked him rather than Paul.

Now with protection from the Roman government, Paul spent 18 months teaching in Corinth and experiencing amazing results as he "Watched God Work." When Paul finally left Corinth to continue his mission work in Asia Minor, he took a new disciple with him to assist him. "Paul, called by the will of God to be an apostle of Christ Jesus, and our brother Sosthenes" (1 Cor. 1:1). Paul's greatest enemy and chief persecutor in Corinth, Sosthenes, became his dear brother and fellow church planter!

Feeling discouraged, weak, or fearful today? Don't be ashamed of that, and don't quit. Be faithful, and "Watch God Work!"

ACTS 19
May 30

"*Unstoppable*"

As I sat in the ancient theater that day, I tried to imagine the view in the middle of the first century AD. Below me lay the ruins of ancient Ephesus, one of the largest cities in the Roman world and capital of the province of Asia Minor. Very early in the expansion of the gospel, missionaries came to this city to share the message of Jesus. Within a few years, a small congregation was gathering in this city, given over to the worship of many gods, but above all, Ephesus was a city dedicated to her patron goddess, Artemis.

Artemis' temple was one of the seven wonders of the ancient world. This temple covered an area nearly twice the size of a football field and almost 80 feet in height. More than 180 beautiful columns held up the roof of this gleaming marble structure. That was only one of the many beautiful temples in the city, not to mention the libraries, universities, gardens, forums, and civic buildings.

I tried to visualize all of this as I sat in the top row of the theater that once held over 25,000 people. Most of all, though, I tried to imagine what it would have been like on the day described in Acts 19, when the building in which I was seated echoed over and over again for hours with the chant of tens of thousands of voices proclaiming, "Great is Artemis of the Ephesians!" What was the cause of such a frenzy of loyalty among the populace? Greed and fear. The financial well-being of the silversmiths who made a fortune selling coins and medallions of the goddess Artemis was being threatened. How? By the gospel. That's right, so powerful had been the transformation in people's lives by the good news of salvation in Jesus Christ, that the market for the silver testaments to Artemis was being greatly reduced!

The leaders of the silver business stirred the populace into an uproar by lies and accusations, but it was too late. The message of Jesus had already swept through the entire province of Asia Minor, and more and more people were coming to faith every day. Jesus was building His church, and the gates of Hades could not stand against its assault. The mob could chant, "Great is Artemis of the Ephesians!" but the invisible, irresistible power of the Son of God, Jesus Christ was unstoppable. It still is.

Today, we hear much that would lead us to think that the demise of the church is at hand, but don't believe it for a minute. It may be true that in some areas we do not see the church advancing as before; but on a global scale, the Kingdom of Christ has never been expanding more rapidly. In Africa, Asia, South America, and the Middle East, thousands are coming to Christ every day. The technical revolution of the past thirty years has only served to exponentially increase the sharing of the gospel worldwide. Yes, the television cameras may show the chanting mobs threatening death to "the infidels," but my brothers and sisters, never doubt for a moment that the mission of our Lord will succeed. He is unstoppable! Amen.

ACTS 20
May 31

" *A Driven Disciple* "

"But I do not account my life of any value nor as precious to myself, if only I may finish my course and the ministry that I received from the Lord Jesus, to testify to the gospel of the grace of God."
(Acts 20:24)

We often use the terminology "a driven person" to describe someone who is unusually focused on accomplishing goals or achieving results. Most often, this is used in a somewhat negative connotation to describe an individual who seems to have no outside interests, or time for deep relationships with people because he or she is fixated on other priorities.

Of course, a life lived like that would not be considered a model life, especially for those who are followers of Christ. Jesus said, "Take my yoke upon you, and learn from me, for I am gentle and lowly in heart, and you will find rest for your souls. For my yoke is easy, and my burden is light" (Matt. 11:29-30). Following Jesus is the best possible life anyone can ever live. However, it is important to recognize that while serving Christ is not a call to living a stressed-out life, it is also not a life to be lived with aimlessness.

We were not called by the Lord to just "chill out" while we wait for heaven. There must be some purpose that *drives* the engine of our lives. There is a difference in being a *focused* disciple and a *driven* disciple. Some people would consider the Apostle Paul to be the epitome of a driven man. He certainly was not lazy! However, Paul was not some ultra-independent, isolated "ministry machine." On the contrary, Paul was incredibly relational!

In his letters, Paul specifically names almost 100 people who were his associates in ministry. That doesn't sound like an isolated life. Paul was extremely focused on his calling, but he also had time for people. Paul recognized and modeled the core value of ministry—it's all about people. That is why he said in verse 24 that his life was completely focused on the goal "to testify to the gospel of the grace of God." The gospel is "good news" for people, and to "testify" is to share that good news *with* people. The reality of Paul's "driven-ness" is that he was a servant of Jesus Christ and a "debtor to all men" (Rom. 1:14) because of the gospel of God's grace that he had personally experienced. For Paul, his life was "all about Him and all about them." He lived for Christ and others. That is the philosophy of a "driven life" that will never allow us to "run *over* people," but rather "run *to* people" and "run *with* people" as we run our race and finish our course for Jesus Christ. Drive on!

JUNE

"The marriage of the Lamb has come,
and his bride has made
herself ready."

PROVERBS 14
June 1

"The Wisest Wrong Road"

Several years ago, our family vehicle had an early edition of a GPS system that we named "Edna." I'm not sure how we came up with that name, but we did so because the system gave directions in the most crisp and articulate female voice, so we decided to call her Edna. Edna was incredibly helpful on many of the trips we took as a family. She guided us over a good part of the eastern United States. Edna almost became an invisible part of the family as we traveled together. We would often journey many miles without a word from Edna, but then suddenly she would speak out in her lovely voice to guide us on our way.

Edna was amazingly accurate *most* of the time, and therein lies the problem. She did not give you correct directions *all* of the time. As a matter of fact, the longer we had Edna, the less dependable she became. More and more often we would follow her directions given in the lovely voice, only to find she had taken us on a wrong road. Finally, we discovered the problem; Edna's guidance system was based on data that was not being updated as changes were made to the highway infrastructure around the country. Edna was using *outdated* information and, as a result, she often gave faulty directions. Oh, Edna's crisp, articulate voice sounded just as convincing as ever, but we couldn't trust her anymore.

This is a very similar and sinister issue for us as well when we are guided by our IGS—*Internal Guidance System*. King Solomon, the wisest man who ever lived, warns us in the strongest terms, not to trust the guidance we receive from our own understanding and insight: "There is a way that seems right to man, but its end is the way to death" (v. 12). Our internal guidance system is faulty and cannot be trusted because the data on which it operates is corrupted. The impact of our sinful nature on our decision-making system makes it fatally flawed. The guidance we give ourselves at times can seem so sound and wise, but it cannot be trusted; in fact, it can be terribly deadly. How can we avoid the danger of a flawed internal guidance system? By making our decisions on a guidance system that never relies on corrupted or out-of-date information—the infallible "GPS," *God's Positioning System*.

Our Lord's guidance system, based on His eternal Word and indwelling Spirit, can always be trusted. The road on which He guides us may not always be the easiest or most direct route, but it is always the *best* route! What is your guidance system? Honestly, thoughtfully consider that. Do you trust in the IGS or GPS? Always "Go with God, my friend." Always.

" Making It Personal "

If every member of the congregation did it, it would be a problem. However, sometimes I find it to be personally helpful. On occasion, as the church family sings a song where the word "we" is used, I will change it to "I." Many times I have experienced added power to the words of exaltation, testimony, or confession as I have made it more personal. Sometimes we just need to hear our own voices personally expressing to the Lord the deep issues that we feel in our hearts.

This is definitely a Biblical practice as we often hear David speak to himself as he declares his praise or plea to God. Psalms 55 and 56 are a perfect example of this. David is struggling to cope with the traitorous actions of someone he held as a beloved and trusted friend. The pain was just too much for David to carry, but he knew it wasn't too much for God, so David decided to give it to Him.

> *"Cast your burden on the Lord, and he will sustain you;*
> *he will never permit the righteous to be moved."* (Psalm 55:22)

Having made this personal decision, David followed it up with a personal declaration; in fact, he declares it twice. "In God, whose word I praise, in God I trust; I shall not be afraid. What can flesh do to me?" (Ps 56:4, 10, 11) David is so right. We may have been victimized, but we don't have to be victims; we can be victors. The burden may be too great for *us*, but it is not too great for *God*. Roll it onto His broad shoulders and raise up your voice in a declaration of trust in Him. Go ahead, do it out loud. It may not be pretty, but God will enjoy it.

ACTS 21
June 3

"God's Will Be Done"

"Let the will of the Lord be done."
(Acts 21:14b)

The previous chapter in the Book of Acts ended with one of the moving scenes recorded in the entire New Testament. Paul called the elders of the churches in Asia Minor to the coastal city of Miletus, located about 85 miles to the south. There Paul shared with these beloved colleagues that they would never see him again because he was journeying to Jerusalem under the compulsion of the Holy Spirit (Acts 20:22). Very clearly, Paul considered it a distinct possibility that he might be executed in Jerusalem, and he had already been clearly informed by the Holy Spirit that his ministry would result in persecution and imprisonment. A few days later, this reality was again confirmed by the Spirit, as the prophet Agabus prophesied in Caesarea that Paul would be arrested and delivered to the Gentiles. Hearing this, Paul's own ministry team pleaded with him not to go on to Jerusalem (Acts 21:12).

However, Paul was adamant, "What are you doing, weeping and breaking my heart? For I am ready not only to be imprisoned but even to die in Jerusalem for the name of the Lord Jesus" (v.13).

What are some takeaways for us from these moving conversations? One important thing for us to note is that doing the will of God must be the "true north" on the compass of our lives. Our lives are not our own, and so our will is not our own.

As Christians, we are the freest of all people, but we are slaves to the will of our Master. The call to follow Jesus is a call to die to self and to follow Him.

A second important takeaway is the reminder that God's will in the lives of those we love, may not always *please* us, or even at times, *make sense* to us. Our faith is tested at times in releasing those dearest to us to the will of God. Whether we believe they are correct or mistaken in their discernment; we must commit them to Christ. Perhaps today there is someone for whom you are greatly concerned. Your Heavenly Father is concerned for them, too. "Let the will of the Lord be done" (v. 14).

" *Dual Citizenship* "

"Anxiety in a man's heart weighs him down,
but a good word makes him glad."
(Proverbs 12:25)

On one occasion, the enemies of our Lord believed they had cornered Him into issuing a statement that would either make Him seem to be a traitor to His people or to appear to be a rebel to the Roman authorities. Jesus was asked whether it was lawful to pay taxes to Caesar or not. His answer was brilliant and inspired, "Render to Caesar the things that are Caesar's, and to God the things that are God's" (Matt. 22:21). Jesus' answer that day not only avoided the trap set by His enemies, it also established a principle to guide His disciples for all time.

We are *two-kingdom* people. As believers, we are citizens of earthly countries and kingdoms; but we are also citizens of the Kingdom of our Lord Jesus Christ. These kingdoms, at times, come into conflict, and we must always devote our first allegiance to King Jesus. However, as we learn from our reading today, there are times when we can use our "dual citizenship" to protect our lives and liberties on earth so that we might continue to advance the Kingdom of Heaven.

Paul was attacked by a mob in Jerusalem; that was not a surprise to him, but it was illegal. He was arrested by Roman soldiers, imprisoned, and ordered to be flogged. That was also not a surprise to Paul, but it was definitely illegal to treat a Roman citizen in that fashion. Paul exercised his rights as a citizen to preserve his life and promote his witness for Jesus. Likewise, we need to use our "dual citizenship" privileges for Kingdom purposes. Being a disciple does not mean being a doormat. We have every right to speak against injustice in all of its forms, even when that injustice may be directed against us, personally. The key is our *motive*. Do we want to be *proven right*, or do we want to *promote righteousness*? In all things, "It's not about us; it's about Him."

ACTS 23
June 5

" *An Enemy Escort* "

*"When a man's ways please the Lord, he makes
even his enemies to be at peace with him."*
(Proverbs 16:7)

I have always wondered what happened to those men. Our text today tells us that more than 40 men bound themselves by a sacred oath that they would neither eat nor drink until they had killed Paul (vv. 12-13). I'm sure it wasn't many days until some of them started to realize that this might not have been a brilliant idea! Paul was not only moved from Jerusalem to Caesarea, but he was also guarded by 470 Roman soldiers on the journey! Paul's enemies certainly had not counted on that turn of events.

This was just another display of God's sovereignty that is like a thread weaving together the events recorded in the book of Acts. In fact, God's ways are often humorous. The Lord Jesus visited Paul in his prison cell and promised him, "Take courage, for as you have testified to the facts about me in Jerusalem, so you must testify also in Rome" (v. 11). Not only did the Lord determine that Paul would be a witness in the capital of the empire, but He also decided that the Roman government would pay for Paul's travel expenses and security detail on the mission trip! Now that just makes us smile. We can smile because our God laughs. Yes, God laughs when the authorities of this world believe they can hinder the reign of His Son. "He who sits in the heavens laughs; the Lord holds them in derision" (Ps. 2:4).

Our God is unstoppable, and so is His mission. That means His "missionaries" are unstoppable as well, and that means you and me. No one can keep us from doing God's will. If it is our desire to faithfully serve our King, then His will, which is "good and perfect" (Rom. 12:2), will be accomplished in our lives. He may even have the government pay for it. Now think about that and smile!

ACTS 24
June 6

"Clear Conscience the Best Pillow"

"So I take pains to have a clear conscience
toward both God and man."
(Acts 24:16)

As we make this journey through the New Testament, we are going to learn something about the Apostle Paul. A careful reading of his messages and epistles gives us a unique insight into the workings of his mind, and what a mind it was! Paul was a scholar, theologian, philosopher, and orator of the highest caliber, and he was also a sports junkie. Oh yeah, the Apostle Paul loved his sports! His sermons and letters are filled with allusions to track, boxing, wrestling, and even gladiatorial games.

In our reading today, Paul makes a sports reference that does not come across clearly in English, and he uses it in a most unique association. As Paul shares his personal testimony to Felix, the Roman governor, he says, "So I always take pains to have a clear conscience toward both God and man" (v. 16). The word Paul uses for "take pains" is "askeó," which is used to describe the exertion athletes put forth in giving their full strength during a competition. It is sometimes used of sprinters running and stretching their bodies toward the finish line. And what was the goal line for Paul to which he gave all his strength? A clear conscience. Paul told the Roman governor that the supreme motivation in his life was to know that, as much as was possible, he wanted to live each day with a clear conscience with God and all people.

My friends, what would it mean to us if our "daily workout" was focused on exercising our lives to have a clear conscience with God and people? It would mean each day unwasted, and a soft pillow awaiting us each night. Priceless.

ACTS 25
June 7

" The Heart of Kings "

One of the most beautiful statements made in the Scriptures describing God's sovereign power in controlling all things is found in Proverbs 21:1. "The king's heart is a stream of water in the hand of the Lord; he turns it wherever he will." This statement is even more impactful when we realize that it was written by the richest and one of the most powerful kings of all time, King Solomon. Solomon recognized that, in spite of all his wisdom, riches, and might, he was not in control of anything. In fact, even his decision-making process was under God's control.

In our reading of Acts 25 today, three rulers are mentioned: Governor Festus, King Herod Agrippa, and Nero Caesar of Rome. Not one of these three rulers had any personal spiritual knowledge of God, whatsoever. Festus was a brutal and dishonest soldier-politician; King Agrippa was a pompous, incestuous beast; Nero was a deranged monster. These wicked rulers were not unique. Rather, their morals and behaviors were characteristic of leaders across the empire. In the midst of this immoral swamp, God was guiding the decisions of ungodly people to carry out His mission of world evangelization. They were keeping Paul in prison so he would have time to think and write a good part of the New Testament, and they were sending the most unique and powerful witness on the face of the earth to share the gospel of King Jesus in the epicenter of the greatest empire the world had ever known.

Yes, friend, even if it appears that elections succeed in "draining the swamp," never fear. A river, guided by a sovereign God, runs through it.

" *The Shadow of the Almighty* "

She was a young widow not yet 32 years old, and mother to a little girl nearing two years of age. She and her husband had spent less than three years together with the brightest of hopes in how God was going to use their lives for sharing the gospel of Jesus and His love. That all changed in a horrible way one day in January 1956. Her ever-moving, ever-smiling husband Jim, and four of his friends and missionary colleagues, were brutally ambushed and killed by Auca warriors on a jungle riverbank in Ecuador. Elisabeth was devastated beyond words, as were the other young wives and families of these martyred servants of God. In her grief and depression, Elisabeth Elliot sought comfort where all through her young life she had found it in prayer to God and in His Word. One verse from our reading today in Psalm 57, became her comforting prayer and renewing reality:

> *"Be merciful to me, O God, be merciful to me, for in you my soul takes refuge, in the shadow of your wings I will take refuge,*
> *till the storms of destruction pass by."*
> (Psalm 57:1)

"The shadow of your wings" is where Elisabeth found comfort for her breaking heart. And in time, she also found meaning regarding the sacrifice of her husband's life and those of his friends.

Elisabeth committed into writing the things God gave her in His presence. What she wrote became one of the greatest classics of Christian literature, *The Shadow of the Almighty*. Since 1958, millions of copies of this book have been published worldwide. Only God knows how it has been used to call and inspire multitudes in service for Jesus. You and I will probably never write or say anything that will be read by millions of people for decades to come. However, God is writing a story in each of our lives, and He also has messages for each of us. We hear His voice most clearly when we are alone, quiet, and in the shadow of the Almighty.

PSALMS 58 & 59
June 9

"Howling Dogs, Happy Hearts"

Many years ago, when my wife and I traveled to Romania to adopt our son Stephen, we experienced one of the most unique hotel amenities imaginable. At the main entrance of our hotel was a fashionable container that resembled an umbrella stand. However, this container was not holding umbrellas but large sticks. We noticed that most people who walked out of the hotel picked up a large stick to carry along with them. This seemed just a little strange to us, but on finding out the purpose for the container of sticks, we were even more surprised and quite frankly, a little alarmed.

The sticks were made available to people who were going for a walk so that they could use them against the packs of dogs that sometimes prowled the streets! That was a definite first for us in our international travels. We have been blessed to return to Romania several times, and thankfully, any walking sticks provided now are just for walking!

In Psalm 59, David refers to those threatening his life as howling packs of dogs—the human kind. They are the "hired dogs" of King Saul who is set on David's destruction. Against these growling enemies, David picks up a "walking stick" to support him during their attacks. It is the walking stick of praise, and David uses it to "beat back" panic that the hate-filled enemies of God can produce in his heart. "But you, O Lord, laugh at them: you hold all the nations in derision. O my strength, I will watch for you, for you, O God, are my fortress. My God in his steadfast love will meet me; God will let me look in triumph on my enemies" (Ps. 59:8-10).

Now, that is a big stick we can pick up anytime we need it!

ACTS 26
June 10

" *The Heavenly Vision* "

*"Therefore, O King Agrippa, I was not disobedient
to the heavenly vision." (Acts 26:19)*

Several years ago, I read a somewhat scholarly article concerning historic proofs for the resurrection of Jesus Christ from the dead. The article was not an easy read for me, scholarly articles rarely are. But there was one proof for the resurrection of Jesus that the author set forth that I certainly had never considered before, and I have never forgotten since. The author stated that one of the greatest evidences of Christ's resurrection was...the Apostle Paul. I did not see that coming, but neither did anyone else about the year 39 AD. How was it possible that Saul of Tarsus, fanatical hater and persecutor of all things and people connected with Jesus of Nazareth, became obsessed with fervor, love, and devotion to Christ, His cause and His people?

The answer is as simple as it is profound—*Saul of Tarsus met Jesus.* He experienced the ultimate "close encounter of the divine kind." Paul described it to King Agrippa as "the heavenly vision" (v. 19), but it was completely real and infinitely powerful.

It has been said that *visionary leaders* are people who, on some occasion, have come under the control of a compelling idea. Christian philosophy is a little different. I like to think of it as becoming a "visionary servant." The great reality of our lives as believers is to come under the control of a compelling truth—*Jesus is alive, and by His grace, we have met Him through faith.*

If you are a Christian today, you have personally experienced the resurrected Jesus. Now today, let us not be disobedient to this heavenly vision.

ACTS 27
June 11

"Communion in the Tempest"

Chapter 27 of the Book of Acts is one of the most unique chapters in all of the New Testament. Almost the entire chapter is given over to recounting fourteen of the most harrowing days that can be imagined. Compliments of the Roman government, Paul is being transported as a political prisoner to stand before the emperor Nero in Rome. Against the advice of Paul and the awareness of how treacherous an east-west crossing of the Mediterranean Sea was in late autumn, the centurion in charge of the detail decided to take the chance. Bad decision. Within a few days, a sudden and terrible northeaster drove the vessel back and forth around the eastern and central sections of the Mediterranean Sea.

In this chapter, Luke's language is so colorful and descriptive that you can almost feel the vengeance of the storm. Also, Luke's references to various locations during the storm go a long way to affirming just how historically accurate the New Testament really is in describing the geography of the first-century Roman world.

The scenes in this chapter are truly gripping in their growing tension, but one stands out for its amazing image of faith and peace. When the storm is at its fiercest level and the vessel is in imminent danger of breaking apart, Paul decides this would be a perfect time to hold a Communion service. That's right, verse 35 tells us that Paul shared a meal with everyone on the ship and then, in everyone's presence, he gave thanks to God, broke bread, and began to eat. Imagine that...sharing holy Communion in howling chaos!

What a powerful witness that was. What a pacifying experience that was. God was in the storm. God was in the ship. God was in their lives. So they worshiped the Master in the worst moment of their lives.

Amen.

ACTS 28
June 12

"To Be Continued"

Don't you hate it? You are watching a television program that has absolutely gripped your attention and kept you riveted to the screen, and then suddenly there pops on the screen those three hated words, "To Be Continued." You, along with everyone else watching the program, unite in a single word of protest, "No!" How can they possibly do this to you? Take you to such a climactic moment of suspense and leave you there with no resolution of the tension or the story? Terrible rudeness. Brilliant marketing.

At first, the "ending" of the book of Acts can feel that way. There is no resolution. Paul has been brought as a prisoner to Rome, but since no official charges have yet reached the capital concerning him, he is allowed to rent a dwelling and live under "house arrest." Luke ends his narrative with these words, "He lived there two whole years at his own expense, and welcomed all who came to him, proclaiming the kingdom of God and teaching about the Lord Jesus Christ with all boldness and without hindrance" (vv. 30-31).

That's it? Yes, that's it. Luke is led by the Holy Spirit to lay down his quill and roll up the scroll. Why does the book of Acts end this way? On a very practical level, Paul was no longer traveling. He had entered into an extended phase of teaching, preaching, mentoring, and writing in one location. He was waiting, and he was working. But on a higher and timeless level, the book of Acts *stops* here, but it does not *end* here. There is a very real sense in which the book of Acts is still being written, in the church and in us as individual believers.

The church is the living united witness of the continuing "Acts of the Holy Spirit," and each of us is a living epistle being written by God and being read by the world around us (2 Cor. 3:1-3). May each of us pray that the pages of our life be worthy of His story that is always, "To Be Continued."

" *The Most Powerful Debt* "

It has often been said in jest, "Any day you wake up and don't read your name in the obituary column is a good day." Well, you can imagine how Alfred felt, one morning in 1888 when reading the morning paper, he *did* read his own obituary in the local newspaper! However, I'm sure none of us can understand how Alfred felt when he read the caption at the top of his premature obituary, "The Merchant of Death is Dead." What terrible crimes had Alfred Nobel committed to being thought, by that paper and many people, to be deserving of such an epitaph? He invented dynamite.

Alfred Nobel, years before, had almost *accidentally* discovered the incredible explosive power of the ingredients forming what he named "dynamite." With that knowledge, he used the chemistry from his discovery to make an application for the armaments and munitions industry, and as a result, he became incredibly rich, and also became a significant contributor to the weapons of modern warfare. Hence, his sad nickname, "The Merchant of Death."

Emotionally traumatized by the experience regarding his obituary, Nobel pledged his remaining years to work for world peace, and at his death bequeathed his entire fortune to promoting endeavors directed toward peace between peoples of the world.

The Nobel Peace Prize has, for over 100 years, been awarded in recognition of his legacy. The word for Nobel's "dynamite" discovery comes from the Greek word "dunamis," which means "inherent power." The Apostle Paul uses that word in verse 16 as he expresses the power of the gospel. Paul "discovered" personally the power of the gospel in his life and, from that moment on, considered himself a "debtor" to share his undeserved "wealth" with all people.

Each of us as believers owe a never-ending debt to our Lord and an obligation to share His "gospel dynamite" to bring His peace to all people.

ROMANS 2
June 14

" *Impartial* "

"For God shows no partiality."
(Romans 2:11)

Perhaps you are familiar with the statue that adorns many courthouses in the towns and cities across America. She holds a balance scale in her hand and has a blindfold covering her eyes; she is known as "Blind Justice." She represents what is the ideal and the best expression of our justice system when it functions properly—equal and impartial treatment before the law for all people. Sadly, we are very aware that the ideal of "Blind Justice" is often just that, an ideal, and not the reality of our judicial system.

In Romans Chapter 2 we are given a graphic description of God's justice; it is fearful to read about because it is not *blind justice* but *omniscient justice*. Every thought and deed of every human being is totally exposed to the all-seeing, all-knowing Judge of the universe. His justice is perfect because it is based on absolute knowledge, absolute truth, and absolute impartiality. Again, this is a fearful thing to consider, but it is also incredibly helpful to us. How can that be?

First of all, if we recognize we will be judged by God based on the perfect justice of a perfectly holy and impartial God, then we will recognize there is no possibility that we can be saved by trying to keep the law of God we violate daily in so many ways. That realization will make us candidates for salvation found only in pleading for mercy and grace from this God we have offended. No one is ever saved without first knowing he or she is completely lost. God's perfect and impartial justice causes us to be delivered from our self-righteous deception.

Secondly, knowing our God is completely impartial, challenges us to treat others with mercy-filled impartiality. We, as believers, have experienced this in Christ, so today let's express it to every person with whom we interact today. Our God is watching.

PSALMS 60 & 61
June 15

"*Higher and Closer*"

The Psalms of David are unmatched in all literature in the way they unite the most contradictory emotions. Our reading today of Psalm 60 and 61 perfectly highlights these sweeping changes in emotions. In these two Psalms, David moves from *protesting* to God, to *praising* God—from *pleading* with God, to *pledging* himself to God.

Sound familiar? Maybe that is why we love David so much. We just don't say things as eloquently and beautifully as he does! It is because David is so human, so contradictory, so real that we are bonded to him, and that is exactly why the Lord has recorded these songs in His Holy Word.

But we are not to just *read* these songs. We are to *enter* these songs with David and *join* Him in singing them to the Lord. When we join in on these songs, we are no longer just *listening* to them, but we are *experiencing* them ourselves and *expressing* them to God. Let me encourage you to read the Psalms this way on a regular basis.

Why not start today? Take a moment to quiet your heart, and then read these words, vocally, as joining David in a song to the Lord. It may feel strange at first, but you will get over that, and you will hear your voice joining with David.

> *"Lead me to the rock that is higher than I, for you have been my refuge, a strong tower against the enemy. Let me dwell in your tent forever! Let me take refuge under the shelter of your wings!"*
> (Psalm 61:2b-4)

You did well. Now, keep it up!

PSALMS 62 & 63
June 16

" Preaching to Ourselves "

On a Sunday nearly 150 years ago, the famous pastor of the Metropolitan Tabernacle in London England, Charles Spurgeon, slipped into the back row of a small, rural church located near the place he and his family were vacationing. That Sunday morning Spurgeon felt himself to be anything but great. In fact, the purpose for the "vacation" was actually to find some relief from the relentless stress of his many and widespread ministry responsibilities as well as some emotional sunlight for the darkness of depression that covered his spirit.

As the pastor of the little chapel began to preach, Spurgeon sensed he recognized the minister's message. As the sermon continued to be shared, it dawned on Spurgeon that he was listening to one of his own sermons! At the conclusion of the service, the most famous preacher in the world shook the hand of the understandably embarrassed pastor of the chapel who said, "Oh, Dr. Spurgeon, it was one of your own sermons I preached this morning," to which the famous preacher replied, "Indeed it was; and was it not so gracious of our Lord to use my own words to so encourage my heart as he did today?"

That's a great story. Yes, the best sermon is the one we preach to ourselves. That is exactly what David is doing in Psalm 62. He is preaching to himself the truth he has been declaring to others for years, "For God alone, O my soul, wait in silence, for my hope is from him" (v. 5). This is exactly the testimony he shared in verse 1, except that now he directs the challenge to himself. David is preaching to himself what he has shared with others about the Lord.

Let's do that today. Right now, reflect on some things you have learned about God and then preach that sermon to the congregation of "you." It will be a powerful worship service!

ROMANS 3
June 17

" *Propitiation* "

*"For all have sinned and fall short of the glory of God,
and are justified by his grace as a gift, through the
redemption that is in Christ Jesus, whom God put forward
as a propitiation by his blood, to be received by faith."*
(Romans 3:23-25a)

It's a big word, "pro-pi-ti-a-tion," and it has an even bigger and deeper meaning. The Greek word itself means "a sacrifice that makes atonement." What gives the word an even deeper significance is that the translators of the Jewish Scriptures used this word to convey the meaning of the Hebrew term for the "mercy seat" described as covering the lid of the Ark of the Covenant.

Under the lid of the Ark were the tablets of the Ten Commandments given by God to Moses. Above the mercy seat was where the presence of the Lord resided, in the tabernacle and later the temple. Upon the mercy seat the blood of the goat slain on the day of atonement was sprinkled by the High Priest. This signified that the sins of the people of Israel, in breaking God's laws, had been covered for another year.

However, lasting peace with God could not be made by this sacrifice, and therefore it had to be repeated each year. Paul, in the passage we read today, shares the incredible truth that Jesus, in suffering on the cross for our sins, *became* the mercy seat—the place of propitiation. And His sacrifice did more than just cover our sins. He took them upon Himself and bore them *away from us*. "But as it is, he has appeared once for all at the end of the ages to put away sin by the sacrifice of himself" (Heb.9:26b).

All who trust in Christ alone for their salvation are justified before God, that is, they are declared "not guilty" by God based on the merit of His beloved Son. Our minds can never comprehend a fraction of this infinite, gracious plan of God. But we don't have to understand a free gift; we just humbly receive it and give thanks! Take some time to do that right now.

" *Father Abraham* "

Have you ever traced your ancestry? It is becoming a much easier investigation than in the past, thanks to the internet search engines that can connect you with many relatives attempting to do the same thing. A couple of years ago, I decided to give it a try and began tracing my ancestry through my father. I was amazed at the amount of records that were readily available and the number of people who had already compiled a lot of information. Within a few evenings on the computer, I was able to trace my relatives back to Albermarle County, Virginia, and from there to Falkirk, Scotland. I did not dig deeper into the details of these ancestors, and I am not sure I want to!

All believers in Christ share a common ancestry back to an ancient patriarch. Paul states in verse 11 that Abraham is "the father of all believers." We are not his *physical* descendants on the basis of genetic code, but we are his *spiritual* descendants on the basis of saving faith. Abraham "believed God, and it was counted to him as righteousness" (v. 3).

When Abraham was a pagan idol worshiper in the Ur of the Chaldeans, he was counted as righteous on the basis of his faith alone. God justified an ungodly man (v. 5) on the basis of his faith. Abraham did not earn salvation because he was Jewish; he had not even become the first Jew yet! He believed God and he was declared righteous, and by his faith he became the spiritual "father of many nations" (v. 17).

What a wonderful encouragement this should be to all of us who trust in the Lord. We are part of an incredible *heritage* of faith, and we can share a *legacy* of faith. We all have a father in the faith in Abraham; now what about our spiritual descendants? Who are you influencing by your life of faith? Who will be able to call you a father or mother in their spiritual life? Abraham could not have possibly imagined the timeless impact of his faith, and neither can we.

ROMANS 5
June 19

"*Hope Springs Eternal*"

*"Through him we have also obtained access by faith into this grace
in which we stand, and we rejoice in the hope
of the glory of God."*
(Romans 5:2)

Alexander Pope, the famed British writer, in his work "An Essay on Man" made famous the statement, "Hope springs eternal in the human breast." His point was that there exists in human beings the limitless ability to always believe that their situation will improve.

Hope is truly a beautiful quality, and it is certainly a characteristic that brightens the lives in which it resides. When hope is lost, life itself fades away. The hope of a believer in Jesus is truly unquenchable because it is not based on what *might be*, but on what is *absolutely certain*. Christian hope is reality not yet experienced. It is a gift that is included in the grace of God that saved us and the same unchanging grace in which we stand (v. 2). By the unmerited grace of God we *are* forgiven, we *are* accepted, we are enrolled as citizens of heaven, we *are* adopted into God's family, and we *are* heirs and joint-heirs with Jesus Christ.

This really is a hope that springs eternal, because it *is* eternal. No suffering in this world can ever extinguish it. In fact, suffering only expands it because trials and afflictions only brighten the reality of our hope, like black velvet highlights the beauty of a precious jewel. As believers, we are never expected to rejoice *because* of our suffering, because that would be insanity. But we are exhorted to rejoice *in* our suffering because of the hope we have in Jesus Christ. That hope is the ultimate reality!

ROMANS 6
June 20

"*Dead and Alive*"

*"So, you also must consider yourselves dead to sin
and alive to God in Christ Jesus."* (Romans 6:11)

Perhaps you have watched this scene in a television program or movie about the old west. A man slowly walks up to a poster displayed on a building and sees his own likeness imprinted on it with the caption, "Wanted Dead or Alive." Regardless of whether the man is guilty or not, what is written on that poster defines and guides his actions; "Dead or Alive" changes the way he lives.

In Romans Chapter 6, Paul writes a poster that has the picture imprinted of every single believer, and here is what the caption says, "Dead *and* Alive." That at first seems startling and strange perhaps, but nonetheless, it is an absolute fact. Every believer in Jesus is dead in regard to the controlling power and eternal penalty of sin (vv. 1-3). In Christ, we died to sin and were raised to life and righteousness in Him as well. This really did happen; it is not imagination but the reality of the miracle of regeneration when we trust in Jesus.

The essential key to growing in grace is *considering* this to be true. "So, you also must consider yourselves dead to sin and alive to God in Christ" (v. 11). We must read God's poster about us, "Dead and Alive," and then *act* upon it. Faith is acting like God is telling the truth. The devil tells us it isn't so. God says it is. Now, who are we going to believe? It is not a prideful thing to say what God says about you. So, take some time in prayer today and then say it to yourself throughout the day, "I am dead to sin and alive to God in Christ Jesus." Your *confession* of your *conviction* will become your *conduct*.

" *Chained, but Not Forever* "

"Wretched man that I am! Who will deliver me from this body of death? Thanks be to God through Jesus Christ our Lord!"
(Romans 7:24-25a)

Some of the people groups, conquered by the Romans, were notorious for the forms of torture they devised for their enemies. One of the more sadistic practices was carried out by the Parthians. They would chain a captured soldier to the dead body of one of his comrades. The result was the unimaginable horror of slow death due to shared decomposition and decay. What a horrible experience! And yet, it is exactly what comes to Paul's mind as he ponders his own experience *spiritually* in his struggle against sin.

He is redeemed in his spirit; he is a new man. But the old man, that is the corrupting presence of sin that remains in his mind, is still rebelling against the law of the God he loves and serves. His new spirit is willing, but his old flesh is weak (vv. 18-24).

Every single believer in Jesus completely identifies with this warfare between the spirit and the flesh. It seems the more we pursue a life of faithful obedience, the more aware we become of how weak we are. What should this make us do? *Flee to Christ.* Our only strength and confidence is in Christ. If we look at the demands of the law, we only find defeat. If we look within ourselves, we find no confidence or consolation. But when we take our sin and failure to Christ, we find His grace is sufficient every time. He saved us, He is saving us, and thank God, one day He will completely save us from this body of death. Then, we shall live with Him to sin no more and completely experience what we sing, "Oh, victory in Jesus!"

PSALMS 64 & 65
June 22

"The Hope of All the Earth"

It is one of the most beautiful yet pathetic works of art that exists in the world today, and it is on prominent display in our nation's largest city. The work is truly beautiful; it is entitled "Let Us Beat Our Swords into Plowshares," and it depicts a man taking his sword and hammering it into an emblem of peace, a plowshare.

The sculpture is truly beautiful. It is based on one of the most touching promises in the Old Testament from the lips of the prophet Isaiah. "He shall judge among the nations, and shall rebuke many people; and they shall beat their swords into plowshares, and their spears into pruning hooks: nation shall not lift up sword against nation, neither shall they learn war anymore" (Isa. 2:4). That is a truly beautiful image of the peace that will come to the earth when the Messiah establishes His kingdom on the earth.

What makes this amazing work of art so pathetic is that the sculpture was presented to the United Nations by the USSR in December of 1959. That nation at that time was the epitome of anti-Christ philosophy and atheistic totalitarianism, and the sculpture was presented to the organization that is the epicenter of secular humanism in all the world. Just as the builders of the Tower of Babel declared, "Come, let us build a tower to heaven," so this sculpture declares, "Let us accomplish what God has promised He alone will accomplish."

Mankind cannot change mankind. Leaders of nations may speak words of peace, but war springs from the recesses of the heart, which no power on earth can change. But, praise God. He changes human hearts and by doing so, He changes the world. He does this one individual at a time by bringing His peace to rebel hearts. Our God is the God of salvation, "The hope of all the ends of the earth and of the farthest seas" (Ps. 65:5b). Yes, a new world order is coming, a kingdom in which peace will reign because Jesus will reign. Until then, may we pray that our King will make us instruments of His peace.

"Blessed to Be a Blessing"

*"May God be gracious to us and bless us
and make his face to shine upon us."*
(Psalm 67:1)

News flash. We are selfish. I hope that does not come as a surprise to you; it certainly does not to me regarding myself. In my basic nature, I am a very selfish man. The struggle with selfishness is that it is so deceptive. We often equate selfishness with being greedy or completely materialistic, and this is not what is at the heart of selfishness.

Selfishness is the natural tendency we all have to view and value life as it relates to us. We can even begin to form a faith that is about us. The incredible amazing truths of all that Jesus has done for us can lead us to believe that our salvation is ultimately about us. It isn't. The Bible is clear that the ultimate purpose in our salvation is for the display of God's glory in this life and the life to come. We have been redeemed to bless God and bless others. Paul tells us we were saved for the praise of God's glory (Eph. 1:6).

Two thousand years earlier, David expressed it this way, "...that your way may be known on earth, your saving power among all nations. Let the peoples praise you, O God; let all the peoples praise you!" (Ps. 67:2-3) It's not about *us*. It's about *Him*, and it's about *them*. We have been blessed to be a blessing, to God and to others.

This is not natural; it is supernatural and yet, it can become the actual guiding principle of our lives as we make it a matter of focused prayer. David shows us the way in Psalm 67. Take a few moments to read it out loud. Did you feel it in your spirit? This prayer of David lifts us up from the valley of self-focus and gives us a view of the greater purpose of our lives. Our lives really matter! God has blessed us to make His blessings known to people everywhere. Now, that's a blessing!

ROMANS 8
June 24

"The Chain of God's Grace"

"For those whom he foreknew he also predestined to be conformed to the image of his Son, in order that he might be the firstborn among many brothers. And those whom he predestined he also called, and those whom he called he also justified, and those whom he justified he also glorified." (Romans 8:29-30)

Romans Chapter 8 has been called by some Bible scholars and teachers "The Mount Everest" of the Bible. It is a fitting title to a passage that gives us a view of God's grace that stretches from eternity past to eternity future. Most of all, for God's people, this chapter is a mountain of security because it is revealed to us that God's thoughts, plans, and provision for our salvation began before the foundation of the world and will continue after the world passes away.

God is determined that each of His children will truly be an image-bearer of Christ and reflect His glory through the eternal ages. This is God's plan for every believer, and what God plans He accomplishes, and the work He began in each of us, who are redeemed, He will perform (Phil. 1:6). In verses 29 and 30 quoted above, the Lord describes the "golden chain of salvation" that secures His people to Himself forever. If you are a believer, God says these things are true of you, so true that they are written in the past tense. The Heavenly Father:

- ***Foreknew you***: entered a love relationship with you before time began.
- ***Predestined you***: marked you out as His own and chose you for Himself.
- ***Called you***: in a personal and powerful way, spoke to you in sin and darkness and brought you to light and life in Jesus.
- ***Justified you***: declared you not guilty based on your faith in the Lord Jesus.
- ***Glorified you***: restored you as His image-bearer and returned you to eternal perfect life in His presence.

Wow. Take a moment to sit and gaze from this "summit of Mount Everest" on the grandeur of God's grace to you. That's quite a view isn't it? Remember it as you serve Him on this, another day.

"*Grace Alone*"

If Romans Chapter 8 describes the *heights* of God's gracious *love,* then Romans Chapter 9 describes the *depths* of God's gracious *wisdom.* Both of these chapters share the theme of God's grace. Chapter 8 shares *what* God has done for us in His grace, while Romans Chapter 9 shares *why* God in His grace has done it. Both answers are beyond our comprehension because our finite minds cannot comprehend the infinite mind of God. Perhaps more than any other passage in the Bible, this chapter strips away every shred of merit any person might grasp about why he or she has been saved.

There is only one ultimate reason for our salvation—God. Salvation is of the Lord (Ps. 68:20). We did not choose Him, He chose us (John 15:19). We were not converted by our "free will," but God in His relentless grace subdued our "rebel will" and made us willing to come to Christ (John 1:13). We are saved by the totally unmerited grace of God. God could have allowed every single human being to receive the just penalty of their sins and experience His wrath forever, and still be the perfect God that He is. He was under no obligation to save *anyone,* let alone *everyone.* The fact that, in His mercy, God has chosen to redeem, at the cost of His own dear Son, a multitude of sinners beyond number, while allowing others to receive the punishment they deserve for their sinful deeds, does not make God unjust.

Rather than arrogantly trying to determine why God has chosen to save some and not others, we should humbly, and with stunned amazement, worship Him for His gracious determination to save wretched sinners like us. God's absolute sovereignty is a truth, blazing like the sun throughout Scripture. The proud who try to comprehend it will be blinded by its glory; the humble who humbly kneel before it will have their hearts warmed with assurance and inflamed with loving devotion to serve their gracious God.

" *The Gospel Heart* "

"Brothers, my heart's desire and prayer to God for them
is that they may be saved."
(Romans 10:1)

The Apostle Paul is a wonderful model for us of both theology and missiology. His great commitment to knowing and teaching deep doctrine never hindered his fervent passion to share the gospel. The section we have been reading in Romans reveals that. In Chapters 8 and 9, Paul shares the heights and depths of God's love and grace. And here in Chapter 10, he shares the passions of his heart to see his people, the Jewish nations, come to faith in Messiah, Jesus. He knew that the God who has purposed to save unbelievers has also purposed him to be a tool to bringing them to faith.

The same is true for you today. If you are a Christian, part of God's plan for your salvation is to use you in making his salvation known. That is truly an incredible responsibility, but it is also amazingly simple. He wants you to share the gospel, the message of salvation. He wants you to say what He says, "If you confess with your mouth that Jesus is Lord and believe in your heart that God raised him from the dead, you will be saved" (Rom. 10:9). That is the gospel. In it is the power of God to salvation (Rom. 1:16).

The power is not in your presentation or persuasiveness; the power is the message itself. You don't have to be a prophet or a preacher; you don't have to be bold or be an extrovert. You just have to be sincere and obedient, and that is the result of prayer. Sometimes we wait for a burden for the lost and then we pray. That is backwards. Pray for the lost and you will receive a burden that leads to sincere obedience. Who in your circle of relationships do you know or believe to be unsaved? Pray for them, then pray for them, then pray for them. Your heart will respond to your prayers; and then, in sincere love, you will tell them. Then, the continuing gospel conversations will have just begun.

ROMANS 11
June 27

" Promise Keeper "

"For the gifts and the calling of God are irrevocable."
(Romans 11:29)

God cannot lie. It is impossible. Why? Because if God were to lie, then by the very nature of His perfection, He would be less than He is. He would not be God. So, when God makes a promise, it is not just His reputation that is on the line, so to speak. It is His very nature and identity that are also committed with that promise. God made a promise to Abraham nearly 4,000 years ago, telling him that He would make of his descendants a people who would always be His special people, and that through Abraham's descendants, he would become the father of many nations.

In Paul's day, and over the centuries since, it has seemed as if this promise, made by God, has failed. This is exactly the question Paul rhetorically asks in verse 1, "Has God rejected his people?" Since the Jewish rulers have rejected the Messiah, since most of the descendants of Abraham do not believe in Jesus of Nazareth, has the promise of God failed? These questions lead Paul to reveal two truths: first, though most of the descendants of Abraham have not believed, *some have*. This is God's remnant of grace who share Abraham's faith; they are his *spiritual* descendants, the true Israel of God.

Secondly, God in His infinite wisdom has determined to use the rejection of Messiah by most of the Jewish people to bring the message of free salvation in Messiah to all the peoples of the world. This process of blindness and blessing will continue until "the fullness of the Gentiles has come in" (v. 25b), that is until the gospel reaches to all the ends of the earth. Then, in the end of this age, God will visit the people of Israel with loving deliverance and salvation (vv. 26-27).

God keeps His promises. They ever live before Him. He makes His promises so we claim them, rely on them and, in worship, rehearse them to Him. Remind God of His promises today, and in doing so, remind yourself. God keeps His promises and He delights to hear His children remind Him of what He said, even though He never forgets!

"*Break Out of the Mold*"

*"Do not be conformed to this world, but be transformed by the
renewal of your mind, that by testing you may discern what is the will
of God, what is good and acceptable and perfect."*
(Romans 12:2)

It is often said that life is a pressure cooker, and it is. However, it
is actually more powerful and sinister than that when we refer to the
world in which we live, not the world as in the planet on which we live,
but the world as a system of values disconnected from the Creator. That
world is not just a pressure cooker. It is a "pressurized mold," and it is
relentless. However, this outward pressure of the world can be broken
by an inward pressure that is greater—the power of God's Spirit within
us. We can break out of the world's mold. But we are not neutral in this
process; we are involved participants. We must take part in the "stops"
and "starts." We must *stop* allowing the world to "press us into its
mold." This is the exact translation of Paul's challenge in verse 2, "Do
not be conformed to this world."

Also, we must *start* being transformed. This process of
transformation is the Greek word "metamorphosis," which means a
change from the inside out. We cannot produce this metamorphosis,
but we can cooperate with this work of the Holy Spirit by "release" and
"renewal." We must "release" control of our bodies by deliberately
presenting them to God as an act of worship in response to His merciful
salvation (v. 1). We can also cooperate by "renewing" our minds by
aligning our lives and His revealed will (v. 2). As we "press against the
world" and "press into the Word of truth," we will discover "the will of
God." To our joy, we will find that God's will is good and perfect, and
that we really would rather have Jesus than anything this world could
offer us.

PROVERBS 16
June 29

" *The Greatest Victory* "

*"Whoever is slow to anger is better than the mighty, and he who rules
his spirit than he who takes a city."*
(Proverbs 16:32)

One time a young couple was in a marriage counseling session. When asked about how the couple handled conflict, the young man said, "Well, when I get angry, I may blow up, but it is over in just a few seconds." To this the counselor replied, "Yes, just like dynamite." Boom.

Getting angry is not necessarily a sin. The Bible says, "Be angry and do not sin" (Ps. 4:4a). Jesus Himself on occasion displayed very deep anger. However, anger that is self-focused and not self-controlled is always sinful, and oh is it ever destructive.

Recently, an angry meeting of some of our nation's leaders in Washington lasted less than two minutes before it concluded in outbursts of anger. That two-minute angry meeting tore down a two trillion-dollar plan for national infrastructure improvements. Expensive meeting.

Solomon was the most powerful man of his age, but he tells us the strongest person is the one who controls himself or herself. In one sense, we are not capable of bringing under control our emotions. However, the fruit of the Holy Spirit working in our lives is growing in self-control (Gal. 5:23). Ultimately, we cannot live under self-control until we lose control; that is, we surrender control to our Master Jesus Christ. We need Master control if we expect to experience self-control.

Anger is usually selfish; it is a learned technique of trying to control others. We can unlearn what we have learned. How does that happen? Talk to Jesus about it continually, and then ask others to tell you how you are doing. Invite the Lord to make you strong in self-control, and then be strong enough to ask others for help. Now that is a powerful step toward victory!

" *A Home for the Lonely* "

"Father of the fatherless and protector of widows is God in his holy habitation. God settles the solitary in a home...."
(Psalm 69:5-6a)

The verses above have a star next to them in my Bible and the date 1995. The notation is there because in the spring of that year, God used these verses to give my wife, Susan, and I the confirmation we needed for one of the biggest decisions of our life. At that time, we were in the process of adopting a child from Romania. All of the many steps in working on the necessary applications, background checks, etc., had been taken, and then it arrived. We received a packet in the mail with the picture of a 2-year old boy and some personal information regarding him. The adoption agency needed a decision; do you want to proceed or not? The enormity of the impact of our answer settled heavily on us. Is this the child for us or not? How do we decide?

Susan and I committed to pray about it separately and then talk later that day. That afternoon as I prayed, I was prompted to look again at the passage I had read earlier in the morning. When I opened my Bible to Psalm 68, my eyes fell on verses 5 and 6. In the version I was reading at that time, I saw these words I had read a few hours before, "Father of the fatherless and protector of widows is God in his holy habitation, God makes a home for the lonely." Wow. Okay, start packing for the trip! That was the word we needed that day, but it is also guidance for *every* day. God has made room for us in *His house* and in *His family*, and we need to make room for others in ours. We may not be led to the ministry of adoption, but we are all called to share the Father's love for the displaced, the outcast, and the lonely. Hospitality is the gospel in action. Yes, make a meal for others on occasion, but make room in your life for others *every* day.

JULY

"Where the Spirit of the Lord is, there is freedom."

" *The Unpayable Debt* "

*"Owe no one anything, except to love each other,
for the one who loves another has fulfilled the law."*
(Romans 13:8)

It is said that someone once asked Albert Einstein what was the greatest discovery he ever made, to which he replied, "Compound interest." By that, the famed mathematician meant that he was amazed at the compounding effect of interest being paid on the interest already earned on an investment. Compounding interest is astounding in its multiplying effect. Of course, compound interest has the same effect *negatively* on borrowed money! The Bible warns about excessive debt because it leads to bondage.

However, as Paul makes clear in our reading today, there is a debt that leads to freedom; that is the debt of love (v. 8). We have a debt to others that is unpayable and unending in our responsibility to love. The fact that we cannot pay this debt does not mean we are ever free from it. As a matter of fact, it is in working on this debt that we are actually set free. Through the debt of love we are not obligated to others as a *burden* but as a *blessing*, not as a *penalty* but as a *privilege*. "The one who loves another has fulfilled the law" (v. 8).

The responsibilities we have to other people are all wrapped up in one responsibility—*loving them.* This unending debt clarifies and simplifies life; just "love your neighbor as you love yourself" and you can stop fretting about the specific responsibilities that you may be trying to check off your list. "Love does no wrong to a neighbor; therefore, love is the fulfilling of the law" (v. 10).

Who is your neighbor? Anyone who comes within your circle of influence. That means your neighbor is anyone with whom you come in contact. Wow, that is a lot of creditors, and that is a big debt! Yes, and living to pay that debt is the path to freedom and a whole lot of joy, too!

ROMANS 14
July 2

"My Brother's Keeper"

The first recorded question by any human being in Scripture is the response Cain gave to God when asked about his brother Abel. "Am I my brother's keeper?" was the lying response of Cain. He was well aware that he had, earlier that day, murdered his brother. Still, though, Cain's question is incredibly significant for us to consider as followers of Jesus. "Am I my brother's keeper?" Paul tells us the answer to that in Romans Chapter 14, and it is a resounding, "Yes!"

The issues Paul discusses in this context are far removed from most of us today, but the principle he shares is timeless. Paul is discussing the issue of kosher foods and the observance of special days in regard to worship. People in that first century culture had very strongly held personal views in regard to these practices. How should these potentially divisive "hot topics" be handled? Paul does not lay down specific laws to address these issues. Rather, he lifts up a guiding principle—do not pass personal judgment on someone else's convictions or press your own personal convictions on someone else. The position of judge is already filled, and it belongs to the Lord (vv. 7-12). We are accountable to the Lord individually, and we are not given the authority to pass judgment on others.

What we are accountable for is the well-being of our brothers and sisters (vv. 13-14). In fact, we should be willing to sacrifice our *freedom* on a personal conviction if it would prevent "a stumbling block or hindrance in the way of a brother" (v. 13). There is something much more important than any of us getting our way, and that is not putting our *freedom* in the way of others. We cannot claim to be free in Christ and not also be willing to surrender our rights for the sake of others. As followers of Jesus, there is only one answer to the question, "Am I my brother's keeper?" and that is an emphatic, "Yes, I am!"

"Godly Goals, God's Way"

It has been well said, "If you want to make God laugh, just tell Him your plans." All of us can smile at that quote because all of us have had the experience of our plans not quite being God's plans, and then experience how He has made that very clear in powerful ways! However, it is very important that we not conclude from those experiences that it is somehow wrong to make plans and work toward accomplishing them.

Paul was a planner. That is obvious from reading Romans Chapter 15. He planned to take an offering to Jerusalem (v. 25). He planned to focus his remaining ministry in completely unreached areas (v. 20). He planned to go to Spain (vv. 24-28). He planned to visit Rome and build a partnership with them for his ministry in Spain (v. 24). Paul was actively making plans, and some of his plans were accomplished, as we discover from the book of Acts. However, those plans were not accomplished in the way Paul anticipated!

Paul did travel to Rome, but it was as a prisoner of the Roman government. He experienced a journey that included being swept across the Mediterranean Sea in a typhoon, marooned on the Island of Malta, and bitten by a venomous snake! Not quite what Paul had planned. Paul did not just visit Rome; he lived there under house arrest two years, and eventually shared the faith before Emperor Nero (2 Tim. 4:16-17). Did Paul ever make it to Spain? We don't know for certain, although early church tradition says that he did.

Regardless of whether Paul reached his goals or not, he was successful because success is not the *accomplishment* of goals. Success is the *pursuit of worthy goals*. Paul's goals were to share the gospel with the lost and to share in strengthening the faith of believers. Worthy goals indeed! What are yours? Have you placed your plans in His hands?

"Names, Names, Names"

"Anxiety in a man's heart weighs him down,
but a good word makes him glad."
(Proverbs 12:25)

Thirty-five names. You can check my math, but that is how many personal names I count in this final chapter of Romans. That number does not include the references Paul makes to other unnamed individuals in these final verses of arguably the greatest work of theology ever penned. What do we learn from this about Paul and his ministry? More importantly, what do we learn about ourselves and our own methods of serving the Lord?

In relation to Paul, we learn several things. Certainly, we learn that Paul was the farthest thing from a "lone ranger" when it came to the ministry for God. Paul did not just view himself as serving people but also as serving *with* people. Clearly from his writings, we recognize that Paul was in a "league of his own" when it came to his understanding of the faith and the revelation of God. However, Paul was not isolated and remote; he was completely relational and warmly personal in his personality. He could *write* these names because he *knew* these people. They were his friends, his family, and his colleagues in ministry. Imagine how much time Paul invested in these people! How did he find time for these friendships in such a busy ministry? It is because *people were his ministry.*

Of these thirty-five names, Paul is commending one person by name, greeting twenty-six people by name, and sending greetings from eight people by name...and this is just the letter to the Romans! Imagine how many friends Paul must have made all around the world! Now, let me be clear. I am not saying that Paul is our standard in this area, but I am saying that he is a great model.

The story of a life of service for God is written in the lives of people —people with names. People we could name, and they could name us as friends. Our list may never be as large as Paul's, but one thing is certain; it needs to be larger than it is. I'm committing to growing mine. How about you?

1 CORINTHIANS 1
July 5

"Stop the Partying!"

"I appeal to you, brothers, by the name of our Lord Jesus Christ, that all of you agree, and that there be no divisions among you..."
(1 Corinthians 1:10a)

The founder was fed up. Paul was the spiritual father of the believers in the city of Corinth. Several years earlier, Paul had started this congregation in a tent-making business in the city. Paul was alone and financially unsupported, so he took a job making tents. There in "the factory," Paul met and discipled two refugees from Rome, a Jewish couple named Aquila and Priscilla. From those first converts, over the next 18 months, one of the greatest stories of evangelism and community impact took place as huge numbers of Jews and Gentiles come to faith in Christ. It was a true missions miracle, but it was messy!

Corinth was a city notorious for its pagan, party atmosphere, and for the partisan spirit that permeated civic affairs. After Paul's departure, these influences crept into the church, and word had reached him of just how pervasive the problems had become. Paul's spirit is roused by this state of affairs, and the Holy Spirit moves him to write this corrective letter confronting, with his apostolic authority, these many issues. He writes addressing one problem after another to correct the wrongs and protect the witness of the church.

The first thing Paul confronts is the proud, party spirit in the church, as people identify themselves with their "favorite preacher" such as Paul or Apollos or Peter. Some of the hyper-spiritual categorize themselves as the "Jesus party" (vv. 11-12). Paul is appalled at such divisive attitudes. You can almost hear him thunder, "Is Christ divided? Was *Paul* crucified for you? Or were you baptized in the *name of Paul*?" (v. 13)

Division is disastrous for the church, and how terrible it is when it occurs by rallying around the names of God's *servants*. This dreadful practice still plagues the church today. Identifying ourselves and building loyalties around any name, label, or movement is a terrible wrong that we must not tolerate in our hearts. Our unqualified loyalty belongs to one name alone—Jesus of Nazareth. Amen.

" *Near-sighted Wisdom* "

*"The discerning sets his face toward wisdom, but the eyes of a fool
are on the ends of the earth."*
(Proverbs 17:24)

It has been said that the clearest vision is that which causes you to see the beauty that is right in front of you. William Randolph Hearst was a household name in America for decades in the early and mid-20th century. He founded the nation's largest newspaper and went on to establish the international Hearst Media empire. He was known as a total narcissist who lived only to own all the people and things he could.

Once, Hurst read of a famous work of art that he was determined to possess, so he sent his personal assistant on the worldwide search to find it and purchase it regardless of the cost. Weeks later, the assistant met with Hearst to inform him that he had located the treasure but that he was unable to purchase it. Hearst cursed in anger and demanded to know why not. To which Hearst's employee replied, "I could not buy it, sir, because you already own it."

Solomon was far richer than William Randolph Hearst and far wiser, too. Solomon had imported from around the world treasures beyond calculating, but he came to realize that the greatest treasure was always at hand and could be stored in his heart—the free and priceless gift of wisdom. Wisdom is seeing life on earth from an eternal and heavenly perspective. How foolish and incredibly sad to wander everywhere seeking something elusive to bring satisfaction when the greatest and most fulfilling existence is to peacefully journey with the Lord, treasuring what He shows you day by day. What a treasure we can find without having to look for it anywhere but up!

PSALMS 70 & 71
July 7

" *A Lifelong Purpose* "

"O God, from my youth You have taught me, and I still proclaim Your wondrous deeds. So even to old age and gray hairs, O God, do not forsake me, until I proclaim Your might to another generation, Your power to all those to come."
(Psalm 71:17-18)

Look at the date for today's devotional reading—July 7. Even as I see the date on the page, I am amazed at how quickly this year is passing by! Some of you who are reading these words can join me in saying that is true, not only about days on the calendar, but also the years of calendars themselves! We often use the image of grains of sand in an hourglass to express the passing of the years, but David, in the verses above, reminds us that our years are not grains of sand to be *counted*, but nuggets of gold to be *invested*.

Each year given to us contains experiences with God to "another generation" (v. 18). This was David's fervent prayer as a man of a "certain age"; he wanted to pass on a legacy of God's renown to the next generation and beyond. By doing this, we too can grow older and younger at the same time, through investing our lives in the lives of those who will remain on earth when we go to heaven.

As I write these words, I am impressed that there are many reading these words who need to pray verses 17 and 18 to the Lord today, and then look for ways to invest their golden nuggets of a long life with God into "another generation." Could you be one of them?

1 CORINTHIANS 2
July 8

"*Powerful Simplicity*"

"And my speech and my message were not in plausible words of wisdom, but in the demonstrations of the Spirit and of power, so that your faith might not rest in the wisdom of men but in the power of God." (1 Corinthians 2:4-5)

Paul was afraid when he came to Corinth, and he was not ashamed to admit it (v. 3). In Acts 18, we are informed that the spiritual warfare was so intense in Corinth, that the Lord Jesus visited Paul in a vision and challenged him not to stop sharing the gospel. The Lord also declared that He had many people in that city and that He had determined for Paul to reach them (Acts 18:10). But how would Paul accomplish that? What could he possibly share that could make an impact on a city so unbelievably wicked and steeped in such pagan philosophy? Paul came to a decision; he "decided" to share the "foolish message" of Jesus the crucified and risen Messiah (v. 2).

Paul was a scholar and orator of the first rank. He did not need to feel inferior to the most accomplished Greek philosophers or Jewish rabbis. Yet, Paul was determined that those who believed would have their faith rest only on the personally experienced power of God in the message of Christ. So Paul put his total confidence in the sufficiency of the gospel to conquer satanic strongholds and set enslaved sinners free. Paul was not disappointed. God showed up and honored the message of His Son. He always does.

What is your hope that you can possibly make a difference in such an anti-God culture in which you live? Do you actually think that in this day and age in which we live that just by prayer and gospel speaking and living you can make a difference? Good! I was worried there for a moment; you can and you *will* make a difference with that "old-time religion" for an end time world. Yes, you can and yes, He will.

1 CORINTHIANS 3
July 9

"Whose Fool Are You?"

*"Let no one deceive himself. If anyone among you thinks that he is
wise in this age, let him become a fool that he may become wise."*
(1 Corinthians 3:18)

In the days of the great depression in America, it was a common thing
for men who lived in the larger cities and in need of money, to hire
themselves out to work as "walking billboards." These men were
employed to walk up and down the busy streets wearing what were
known as "sandwich boards." These simple devices consisted of two
boards of wood connected by shoulder straps that the men would wear
like a vest. Each side of the sandwich board would advertise
information about shows, sales, events, etc. The men wearing these
became literal walking billboards.

One day, some volunteers at a large rescue mission got the idea that
using these walking billboards as a personal witness and advertisement
of the missions ministry, might be effective. So, a number of these
sandwich boards were constructed and then worn by volunteers
walking the city streets. The front of the billboard made a startling
statement in bright, bold letters, *"I am a fool for Christ."* As the men
walked past, an equally challenging question could be read on the board
on his back, *"Whose fool are you?"*

This unique witnessing campaign turned out to be quite effective in
its impact. The statement and the question on those boards is lifted
directly from Paul's challenge to the Corinthian believers, and by virtue
of God's inspiration of Paul's words, to every believer of every age—to
you and to me. The world system considers the gospel-centered life of a
Christ follower to be foolish. Likewise, God declares the "wisdom" of
this self-focused world to be foolish. Ultimately, by the guiding
principles that form our values and decisions, we decide to be one kind
of fool or another—a fool to the world or a fool for Christ. Whose fool
are you?

1 CORINTHIANS 4
July 10

" The Given, Not the Gifts "

It has been well said, "Humility is the display box of all the gifts of God." When we admire a beautiful ring or gem, our focus never goes to the container, but as it should, to the loveliness of the precious object it contains. Likewise, the gifts that the Lord gives through the lives of His servants are never intended to focus attention on them, the "human containers" of the gifts, but on the glory and grace of the Divine Giver of these graces.

Paul has addressed the spirit of pride that existed in the members of the Church at Corinth time and time again in the first four chapters of his letter. A spirit of sectarianism is dividing the church and being expressed in a culture of "super-hero fan clubs" rallying around their "favorite preacher." Paul denounces this self-centered and sinful spirit in the strongest terms. The purpose of the church is not ultimately about the ministers or the members, but about Messiah who is Master of all. Any gifts or abilities that believers possess are all gifts of grace, so how could or should any Christian boast about things that were given to him or her? (v. 7) All boasting should be boasting of the One who gave the gifts, not of the ones who undeservedly received them.

How do we avoid this tendency to self-focus, both in giving and receiving praise? Paul, who knew both unjust criticism and undesired adulation, shows us the way. "This is how one should regard us, as servants of Christ and stewards of the mysteries of God" (v. 1). "Servants" and "stewards" (managers) is how we should regard ourselves and others. We belong to the Master, and we manage what belongs to our Master that He places in our care. We are His. The gifts are His. The praise is His. When fruit comes of our labor, give it to Him. When praise comes for our service, give it to Him. Express gratitude to people but give the praise to Jesus. He alone is the Giver of every good gift (Jas. 1:17).

1 CORINTHIANS 5
July 11

" Clean House "

"For what have I to do with judging outsiders? Is it not those inside the church whom you are to judge?"
(1 Corinthians 5:12)

The White Glove test. No one enjoyed it, but almost everyone ended up appreciating it. When I was in college, one Saturday each semester was set aside for what was known as "white glove" inspection in the dormitories. That meant that on that day, every room in every dorm had to be completely and thoroughly cleaned. Quite frankly, it was a hassle. However, in those days with a crowded campus and 4-5 guys sharing an unairconditioned dorm room in South Carolina... Well, you get the idea. The cleaning was helpful and probably a health necessity!

In 1 Corinthians Chapter 5, Paul is calling for a spiritual house cleaning. There is a disgusting and filthy situation not being addressed. A man who claims to be a believer is living in an immoral relationship with his stepmother. As horrible as that situation is, even worse is the church's deliberate refusal to do anything about it. In fact, the church was deliberately ignoring a previous letter (v. 9) Paul wrote in which he demanded the believers withhold personal fellowship from anyone who "bears the name of brother" if he is known to be guilty of a flagrant, sinful lifestyle (v. 11).

Evidently, the members thought they were expressing love by continuing to associate with unrepentant believers like the man living in such an immoral relationship. Paul, in effect, denounces their self-deception by saying that by *condoning* the man's sin they are *condemning* him to a continued life of non-repentance. They are not loving *him*; they are loving *themselves* and losing their testimony before a pagan world. Paul commanded them and he commands us to judge sin in our own lives and also the lives of those we love (vv. 12-13). We are never to have a hypercritical spirit, but saying in love what the Judge says is never wrong or unkind; it is right and loving. We are called to help people get free and stay free. That is what truly loving, free-spirited people do.

1 CORINTHIANS 6
July 12

" *The Blessed Past Tense* "

"And such were some of you. But you were washed,
you were sanctified, you were justified in the name
of the Lord Jesus Christ and by the Spirit of our God."
(1 Corinthians 6:11)

Jesus changed everything. The impact of His life and mission has been so real in the world that for centuries we have even divided the calendar of human existence into AD and BC. The reality of Jesus not only radically changes human history but also radically changes the human lives He enters.

A believer's life is also divided into BC and AD. Our natures have been transformed by His presence, and our manner of life should bear witness to that transformation. We are not yet perfected, but we are not the people we were before He saved us. As one simple but sincere saint once said in a testimony service, "I ain't all I ought to be, but, thank God, I ain't all I used to be!"

We never want to be content with the progress we have made in Christ. Paul is certainly continuing to challenge the Christians at Corinth to bring their relationship with Christ into every area of their personal lives and personal relationships. Their lifestyles are to be different because they really are different. They are not living out a process of recovery but living out the experience of redemption and regeneration; they *are not* who they used to be.

In verse 11, Paul declares this change about them, and it is good for us to declare it about ourselves, "And such *were* some of you." Because of the reality of Jesus, we are not the "BC people" we used to be. It is no longer "I am a thief," or "I am a swindler," or "I am a drunkard," etc. The blessed truth is "I *was*" but now I have a new identity because in the Lord Jesus Christ, "I was washed, I was sanctified; I was justified" (v. 11). Today, give all the praise to Jesus and determine to live out your "AD identity!"

"*Good Things to Bad People*"

*"I was envious of the arrogant when I saw
the prosperity of the wicked."*
(Psalm 73:3)

It is an age-old issue, and it has troubled godly people for centuries, even before Priest Asaph wrote this 73rd Psalm about his struggle concerning good things happening to bad people. In these stanzas, Asaph is brutally honest about a crisis of faith he experienced. He was sickened by the continued prosperity of the ungodly and the ongoing oppression of God's people. It seemed to Asaph that the wicked did not have a care in the world. In fact, they appeared to get away with sinful living and face no consequences.

To Asaph, it seemed like all his diligence in obedient service to God was in vain (vv. 12-13). The only thing that kept him from declaring his feelings about God's unfairness was a concern of how he might impact the faith of others. Oh yes, he still had faith in God's justice, but he wasn't *seeing* it and he definitely wasn't *feeling* it. He had reached the crisis moment, and then everything changed. How did it happen? He *acted* on the faith he did not *feel*.

He went to church (the sanctuary of God), and he worshiped and listened (vv. 16-17). There in the presence of God, he received a fresh revelation of what he already knew—the wicked are destined for the terrors of eternal judgment (vv. 18-19). How could he possibly be envious of temporarily, carefree sinners who will experience God's righteous justice? (v. 19) Even more, how could he ever covet the lives of evil people when the real eternal treasures of the Lord Himself are his?

Asaph's self-focused bitterness was transformed into God-focused blessing: "Nevertheless, I am continually with you; you hold my right hand. You guide me with your counsel, and afterward you will receive me to glory. Whom have I in heaven but you? And there is nothing on earth that I desire besides you. My flesh and my heart may fail, but God is the strength of my heart and my portion forever" (vv. 23-26).

And the people of God said, "Amen!"

"God's Timetable"

"At the set time that I appoint I will judge with equity."
(Psalm 75:2)

The poet Henry Wadsworth Longfellow once wrote this short poem entitled, "Retribution."

> "Though the mills of God grind slowly;
> Yet they grind exceeding small;
> Though with patience he stands waiting,
> With exactness grinds he all."

Another poet, the priest Asaph, nearly 2900 years earlier often wrote on the same theme. Both Longfellow and Asaph were very aware of the injustice that was displayed in the highest levels of government and religion. It was discouraging for them in their day, and we are certainly aware of it in our own age. With the advances of communication in this generation, the images and messages of injustice are "constantly in our face."

Asaph in Psalm 75 reminds us that these things also happen in God's face as well. In fact, God is completely aware, not only of what is happening, but also the hidden agendas and motives of why it is happening. We must never allow ourselves to believe that God's silence is God's blindness. His promise is "at the set time that I appoint I will judge with equity (v. 2).

"The powers that be" are not "the powers that *will be*" forever. "All the horns of the wicked I will cut off, but the horns of the righteous shall be lifted up" (v. 10). Jesus pronounced a blessing on those who in meekness now are His humble servants, "...for they shall inherit the earth" (Matt. 5:5). The earth belongs to the One who created it. Yes, it groans and totters under sin (v. 3), but things are not out of control, for God declares, "...it is I who keep steady its pillars" (v. 3).

As Paul said, "the creation waits with eager longing for the revealing of the sons of God" (Rom. 8:19). The world waits and we wait too, but we wait in worship of the One who is working all things in His perfect way, and right on schedule!

1 CORINTHIANS 7
July 15

"Serving in Any Situation"

*"Only let each person lead the life that the Lord has assigned
to him, and to which God has called him.
This is my rule in all the churches."*
(1 Corinthians 7:17)

Paul begins today's chapter by saying, "Now concerning the matters about which you wrote...." It is clear that the elders of the Church in Corinth have sent Paul a letter requesting his guidance on a number of issues.

When the gospel first comes to a culture that has never been impacted greatly by God's Word before, there are often "messy situations" that must be addressed. Many times, there exists a conflict between the liberty that comes in Christ and the harsh realities of customs, or even laws, that do not reflect the principles of life in the kingdom of God.

Reading Chapter 7, it is clear that a number of believers in Jesus struggled to understand their responsibilities to Him in connection with duties to unsaved parents, spouses, master, or slaves. Clearly, each situation could not be addressed specifically by Paul, so what guidance could he give to leaders so they could provide godly counsel? Paul does address some specific issues related to marriages and advice for those who are single. However, the principle he shares that guides believers then and now is cited above in verse 17.

More important than a change in our station in this life is the change in motivation for the service we provide, or the responsibilities we carry in whatever position we fill. As believers, we are followers of Jesus wherever we find ourselves. Our life is His and whatever role or responsibility He has provided, or provides in the future, is a sacred calling. Life is not divided for us into secular or sacred, so as has been well said, "...every bush is a burning bush and all ground is holy ground." *No life is ordinary* when it is lived for Jesus. *No place is insignificant* when it is filled for Him.

1 CORINTHIANS 8
July 16

"The Greatest Liberty"

"But take care that this right of yours does not somehow become a stumbling block to the weak."
(1 Corinthians 8:9)

The most free people on the face of the earth are followers of Jesus Christ. Our Master once said, "So if the Son sets you free, you will be free indeed" (John 8:36). We thank God for that freedom, but we must never forget that the freedom our Lord provides is not a freedom to do our *own thing*, but a freedom to do the *right thing*. Ultimately it is a freedom to love. Acting in love to God and love to others is always the right thing to do. In fact, the love of Christ in our hearts sets us free from the worst form of slavery, and that is slavery to our own selfish interest.

This freedom is what Paul addresses in Chapter 8 of 1 Corinthians. It is the *knowledge* that does not puff up in pride but causes us, in love, to put the interest of others before our own (v. 1). Paul affirms that the "freed up" believers who recognize there is only one God and not many gods are technically correct in saying they can eat food from the marketplace that has been offered to idols. However, their exercise of spiritual freedom is not to be the guiding principle in their lifestyle choices. It is the loving consideration of how their "free choices" may impact weak believers. These brothers and sisters are "weak" because their consciences are grieved by the practices they used to be involved with in the worship of the false gods. Eating food for sale in the marketplace that has been offered to idols takes them back to the darkness they experienced before Christ. So, the issue for the "mature" believers is not the assertion of their liberty but the expression of their love.

Our liberty in Christ is never a license to grieve others. When we surrender our liberty for the sake of love, nobody loses and everyone wins.

1 CORINTHIANS 9
July 17

"The Free Slave of All"

*"For though I am free from all, I have made myself a
servant to all, that I might win more of them."*
(1 Corinthians 9:19)

In our reading today in Chapter 9, Paul continues the theme of freedom he began in Chapter 8. "Am I not free? Am I not an apostle? Have I not seen the Lord Jesus? Are not you my workmanship in the Lord?" (v. 1) Paul does not ask these questions in a boastful spirit, but he needed to make some things clear to those who are questioning his authority to give them spiritual direction (v. 3). Clearly, as he continues to write, he is addressing slanderous statements that had been made accusing him and Barnabas of being "ministers for money" or "prophets for profit."

These lies are without any basis, but Paul uses the accusations to make the assertion, based on Biblical principles, that servants of the Lord being supported financially by God's people is part of God's plan for the work of His church. However, the bigger issue for Paul is that the Corinthians know his motives, so that ultimately, they too can follow his example. It is the example of a free slave. No one had more rights than Paul in his position as an apostle and founder of the Church in Corinth. Yet, no one had more willingly surrendered such rights as he possessed in order to be a slave. A slave to whom? A slave to *all* for one ultimate purpose—that he might save *some* (vv. 19-22). "I have become all things to all people, that by all means I might save some."

This does not come naturally. Paul admits he has to work at this like an athlete, bringing his own body under the force of the will of his mind in Christ. Why would Paul do this, and more personally, why would we? One reason, "...for the sake of the gospel, that I may share with them in its blessing" (v. 23). Paul set aside his rights and privileges and became a servant of all for the pure joy of sharing in the gospel. He was a greedy man, greedy for the joy of experiencing other people set free. Gospel hedonism. What a rich way to live!

1 CORINTHIANS 10
July 18

" An Offensive Strategy "

"Give no offense to Jews or to Greeks or to the church of God."
(1 Corinthians 10:32)

One time many years ago, I heard a pastor refer to the verse above and say, "You see, Paul says other than the Jews, Greeks or church of God, you can offend anybody you want!" Of course, he made that statement with his tongue planted firmly in his cheek! The "Jews," "Greeks," and "Church" takes in just about everyone on the earth, doesn't it? And that is exactly the point Paul is making. As believers, we are to make it our goal to not offend people needlessly by the practice of our freedom in the Lord. Just because a certain practice might not be sinful does not mean it is necessarily helpful or beneficial to others.

Years ago, the founder of the Salvation Army, Edwin Booth, was too advanced in years and poor health to attend the convention of workers from all over the world. Of course, General Booth was the featured speaker, and everyone was anxious to hear a message from their beloved leader. So, even though he was physically unable to attend, General Booth decided to telegraph his message. The assembly of thousands waited expectantly as one of General Booth's associates walked up to the rostrum to deliver their leader's sermon. Never has there been a more brief message than that which General Booth shared. It was one word—"Others!" What a powerful mission statement! And, how well General Booth's one-word sermon echoes Paul's theme in 1 Corinthians.

"Others" is the compass of the Christian life because it was the focus and determination of our Master who came not to be served, but to serve and to give His life as a ransom for many (Mark 10:45). Serving others is a powerful "offensive strategy" to advance the Kingdom. "Just as I try to please everyone in everything I do, not seeking my own advantage, but that of many, that they may be saved" (v. 33).

1 CORINTHIANS 11
July 19

"*Out of Order!*"

"But in the following instructions I do not commend you, because
when you come together it is not for the better but for the worse."
(1 Corinthians 11:17)

Few things are more frustrating than a sign on a public snack or refreshment machine that says, "out of order," unless it happens to be the same sign on the door of a public restroom. Now that is frustrating!

Just imagine what it would mean for the door of a church to have an "out of order" sign on it! Yet, that is exactly what Paul says is the case with some of the worship gatherings of the Church in Corinth. Things were so *out of order* that the founder of the congregations says it would be better off if they did not meet at all (v. 17). How did the Church in Corinth come to such a terrible condition? In a word—*selfishness*. Yes, the issues were complex and some of them are not easily understandable to us in our culture 1900 years removed, but the Church in Corinth was in a mess because so many members thought only of themselves.

Selfishness is not an object we can leave at the door of the church like an umbrella. Selfishness is a sin of the spirit that is so contagious, a few people can infect the entire congregation. Then, it contaminates the witness of Christ to a lost and watching world. However, where sin abounds grace super-abounds (Romans 5:20), and this is certainly true of a gracious spirit.

When we go to church with a desire to exalt the Lord and encourage others, we bless the Lord, we bless others, and we bless ourselves. Selfishness sabotages the gathering of God's people, but going to Church in a Savior-focused spirit is never *out of order*.

PSALMS 76 & 77
July 20

" *Reminding God* "

"Then I said, 'I will appeal to this, to the years of the right hand of the Most High.'" (Psalm 77:10)

We do not know very much about Asaph. We do know that he was a priest serving in the temple. We know that, like David, he was an amazing poet. We think of the Psalms being written by David, but Asaph wrote many of them, and some are the most beautiful in the entire book of 150 Psalms. In Psalm 77, we listen to Asaph speak in another remarkable role, as a plaintiff to God.

Certainly, Asaph is a man of deep faith, but the silence of God in response to him and the people of Israel has troubled his soul very deeply. His crisis of faith comes to a climactic question in verse 9. Has God forgotten to be gracious? Has he in anger shut up his compassion? Asaph is pouring out his heart to God as if he were standing in the courtroom of heaven filing his complaint before the Judge of the Universe. At that moment, standing before Almighty God, an insight comes to Asaph, "I will remind God and I will remind myself of all the powerful deeds of His right hand" (v. 10). Asaph then begins to list many of the mighty acts God has done for His people with His mighty right hand (vv. 11-20).

Of course, God doesn't need this reminder, but Asaph does, and so do we. God has recorded His mighty deeds in His Word, and they are also recorded in our personal memories, so that we may bring them to God in worship and bring them to ourselves in encouragement. Asaph did not realize it, but in speaking of God's "right hand" he also spoke as a prophet. At the "right hand of God" is the most gracious and most glorious of all God's great deeds—the Beloved Son of His love, who is the eternal reminder of God's care.

If you are struggling with God's silence today, remember the works of His right hand and, most of all, remember the One *at* His right hand. No, He has not forgotten you!

PSALM 78 & 79
July 21

" *For Your Name's Sake* "

*"Why should the nations say, 'Where is their God?' Let the avenging of
the outpoured blood of Your servants be known among the nations
before our eyes!"* (Psalm 79:10)

Vengeance is an activity that is off-limits to every child of God. The Lord has made it very clear that vengeance is His private property and that repaying the wicked for their actions is His responsibility. Nevertheless, praying for the vengeance of God to come on His enemies is not wrong, as long as the prayer is offered with the right motive. The Bible contains numerous prayers to God for His vengeance to come on His enemies. Not only in the Psalms, but also in the Book of the Revelation, we hear the people of God crying out for vengeance (Rev. 6:10). When we pray the final prayer of the Bible, "Even so, come Lord Jesus" (Rev. 22:20), we are actually praying for vengeance. The Bible makes it very clear that when our Lord returns in glory, He will be coming in "flaming fire, inflicting vengeance on those who do not know God and those who do not obey the gospel of our Lord Jesus" (2 Thess. 1:8).

As you read this page today, multitudes of our brothers and sisters in Christ are languishing in prison, enduring torture for the cause of the gospel. God alone knows how many of His children, this day, will be martyred for their faith in Jesus. This grieves us. Yes, this angers us. We speak the words with our spirits if not with our lips, "How long, O Lord?" It is right to cry out to God for vengeance for His people and His cause. However, we must always be sure that our motives are right.

Our desire for God's vengeance must be for the glory of His Name and the vindication of His cause. And even in our prayers for God's vengeance to come, we must also praise Him for the unmerited grace and mercy He has shown to us.

*"But we your people, the sheep of your pasture will give thanks to you
forever; from generation to generation we will chant your
praise."* (Psalm 79:13)

"E Pluribus Unum"

"For just as the body is one and has many members, and all the members of the body, though many, are one body, so it is with Christ." (1 Corinthians 12:12)

The phrase "E Pluribus Unum" is recognized by many as the official motto of the United States. The words were often used in reference to the united colonies during the Revolutionary War. By an act of Congress in 1782, even before the formal ending of the war, the words were adapted as our nation's motto. The words mean "out of many, one" and were first known to be used during the days of the Roman Republic nearly 2200 years ago. Although Paul did not use this Latin phrase, it was certainly the message he was communicating in Greek as he wrote 1 Corinthians Chapter 12.

Paul was writing to a divided church. They were divided over personalities, practices of Christian liberty, and over the issues regarding marriage, hairstyles, and the observance of the Lord's supper. Most dreadful of all was the division Paul addressed in Chapters 12-14, concerning what spiritual gifts were most important and how they should operate in the church. What a divided church! Paul has one plan for unifying them—to remind them that they are each *different*, but they are not *divided*. Each of them is part of the unified body—the body of the Lord Jesus Christ. "Now you are the body of Christ and individually members of it" (v. 27).

A divided church is, in reality, a contradiction in terms. It is a terrible false reflection of the true identity of the church—*the body of Christ*. Each one of us has been uniquely created and gifted by the Holy Spirit who has made us one body (v. 12). None of us possess *all* of the gifts, but each of us possesses *a gift*. None of us is essential, but each of us is important. A unified church is a beautiful reflection of Jesus, and it is an awesome and powerful witness for Christ. "E Pluribus Unum" must always be our Christian motto!

1 CORINTHIANS 13
July 23

"The Greatest Thing in the World"

Over the many years of ministry, I have been privileged to see it modeled many times, and it never ceases to amaze me. It is a very special thing, indeed, to witness right before your eyes—the demonstrations of the most powerful force on the face of the earth.

It is not explosive. There is no deafening blast or blinding light. It does not need to be observed from miles away and through special lenses. It is usually experienced in a very ordinary location and often with a relatively small group of people. But it is powerful beyond measure, and its force impacts anyone in the vicinity.

What is this amazing and incalculable power? Love. That's right, love. I have witnessed, with my own eyes again and again, the miraculous and limitless power of love. Generations of fanatical hatred and hundreds of years of abuse and prejudice collapse before the might of love. Racial, ethnic, social, and economic divides that have separated people for ages are healed permanently by the gracious balm of love.

How is this possible in such a world as that in which we live? The answer is *love is not of this world*. Love existed before this world began and it will exist after this world ceases to be. Love is *in* this world, but it is not *of* this world. Love is divine. Love is of God because God is love (1 John 4:7-8). Love is the most *spiritual* force in all the world. It is also the most *practical* influence in the most common and human of interactions, like how members of a church should treat one another. God's love is in our hearts by the miracle of salvation, and that is to be demonstrated in our thoughts, our words, our facial expressions, our hands, our ears, and our feet. Love is either practical or it is not actual. Love either works or it is worthless. The only way we can live for time and eternity is to live for love, because only love is eternal. "Love never ends" (v. 8).

" Don't Blame God "

"And the spirits of the prophets are subject to the prophets.
For God is not a God of confusion but of peace."
(1 Corinthians 14:32-33)

Anyone growing up in America during the 1960's and 70's would be familiar with the name of the comedian Flip Wilson. He was a very funny man and was a regular guest on the many talk shows and variety shows of those years. Flip was best known for a character he created for his sketches, the loud and bossy Geraldine.

Geraldine was an active "church lady" who was nevertheless regularly saying and doing things that were not in keeping with her "church-going" practice. Whenever she was confronted about her wrong behavior, she would loudly and brashly proclaim, "The devil made me do it!" Even my mom, a somewhat strict "church lady" herself, couldn't keep from laughing when Geraldine pronounced her innocence. Of course, what made the scene humorous was that the behavior was practically all Geraldine and very little devil.

It would not, however, have been funny at all if Geraldine had exclaimed, "The Spirit made me do it!" Blaming God for wrong behavior is not a laughing matter. That is the reason Paul is not laughing as he rebukes the Corinthian Christians for the way they are behaving in the worship of the Lord and then saying the Holy Spirit forced them to act and speak that way. God was not to blame for the way so many believers were preaching, praying, singing, prophesying, etc., in an out-of-control manner.

God is a God of order and decency and the Holy Spirit, as God, would never subvert that. Loss of self-control is not a fruit of the Spirit. "But all things should be done decently and in order" (v. 40). This guiding principle of self-control and order should not only govern the worship services of the church but also the daily practices of all Christians. The Holy Spirit will always lead us to live well-ordered lives aligned with God's Word. The Lord will help us do that. May we never blame Him when we experience the consequences of our own selfish decisions. Amen.

" *Resurrection Reality* "

*"But in fact Christ has been raised from the dead,
the firstfruits of those who have fallen asleep."*
(1 Corinthians 15:20)

Our reading in the Scripture today is the greatest passage in all the New Testament dealing with the great truth of the resurrection—the resurrection of our Lord and the coming resurrection of every believer who dies prior to the return of Jesus. It might seem strange that Paul would devote the longest section in his entire letter to a subject that seems so fundamental to the Christian faith. That is exactly why he does take so much time to declare and defend this truth, because it is fundamental to our faith. Without the resurrection, there is no resurrection of Jesus; without the resurrection of Jesus, there is no gospel; and without the gospel, there is no hope. That means our hope is vain, and our faith is vain, and we are of all people most to be pitied. In fact, without the resurrection, we are not a help to the world but a harm to the world because we are just false witnesses of another deceptive cult.

The reason the teaching of the resurrection was under attack then and is still denied even within some churches today is because Satan knows the *priority* and the *power* of the resurrection. He knows that the resurrection of Jesus vindicated His sacrifice and His identity. To discredit Jesus, Satan attempts to discredit the resurrection. He knows Jesus is alive for he saw him rise, but unless the reality of the risen Christ reigns within the hearts of His disciples, they are no great threat to the kingdom of darkness.

Oh, Satan knows the followers of Jesus believe in His resurrection, but he just doesn't want them to be gripped by the glory of Christ's resurrection and their own resurrection in Him.

My brother or sister, does the resurrection of Jesus have a grip on you? Meditate on what the resurrection of our Savior means. Get a grip on it today! "Therefore, my beloved brothers be steadfast, immovable, always abounding in the work of the Lord, knowing that in the Lord your labor is not in vain" (v. 58).

1 CORINTHIANS 16
July 26

"You Just Never Know"

*"The Churches of Asia send you greetings. Aquila and Priscilla,
together with the church in their house, send you hearty greetings."*
(1 Corinthians 16:19)

Keith Bailey was a mailman. He seemed to have a perpetual smile on his ruddy, chubby face. Leonard Dice was a typesetter at the newspaper. He wore horn-rimmed glasses and sported a flat-top haircut that made him seem even shorter than he really was. His fingers were perpetually discolored from the ink on the pieces of type he handled each day. These two men and their wives were not what anyone would have called "cool" back in the late 1960's and early 1970's, but there are dozens of us scattered around the entire country today who give thanks that they were part of our lives.

We were a rough and rowdy bunch of teenagers from the working class neighborhoods of our factory-filled town. These two men had a hard time keeping law and order in our church youth group, but these were two things they always did—they let us know how much they loved us and each week they shared with us God's Word. These men loved the Bible and the author of it, and their eyes would often fill with tears when they talked about Jesus. I don't remember a lesson they ever taught, but I do remember *them*. And I remember how they made me and so many others want to know the Lord and His Word.

That has been almost 50 years ago, and their influence is still bearing fruit through some of the "least likely of disciples." You see, we just never know the influence our lives can make. Paul certainly did not know that the two Jewish refugees, Aquila and Priscilla, whom he met and discipled in the tent factory of Corinth, would become an incredible husband-wife, disciple-making, and church-planting team in Asia Minor (v. 19). We just never know.

That is why we must faithfully pray for grace to love and teach those whom God moves in our circle of influence. We may never see or know of the harvest, but the love of God and the Word of God will always bear fruit.

PSALM 80 & PROVERBS 18
July 27

"A Prayer in the Darkness"

"Restore us, O God; let your face shine, that we may be saved!"
(Psalm 80:3, 7, 19)

Many years ago, a group of coal miners were trapped when a sudden cave-in entombed them within the Appalachian mine in which they were working. It had been raining for a number of consecutive days in that area, and it was believed that the seeping water had eroded some of the hard soil serving as support for the wooden timbers. Day after day, the miners sat there in complete darkness as they waited to hear the digging of the workman frantically trying to reach them. After days without water and little sleep, one of the miners thought he must be hallucinating when he saw what appeared to be a pencil-thin stream of light shining into the back of the cave.

Waking his companions, they quickly discovered that it really was a faint stream of light. They did not realize that a few hours earlier, the days of rain and thick clouds had given way in the skies above to beautiful sunshine. Some of that glorious light had drilled its way through the rubble of the cave-in and was shining into their cavern of darkness. With a shout of joy, those miners scrambled to get their tools, and then in united teamwork they began digging. Where did they dig? Of course, they kept looking up and digging toward the light. The light meant life and freedom and salvation were just above them. After several hours of digging, the beautiful sunlight illuminated their faces and they knew they were saved.

Maybe this day finds you sitting in terrible darkness. Maybe you have experienced a spiritual or emotional cave-in; or perhaps you have been walking in dark places for a season, and darkness has just overtaken you. In your darkness, look for the light. The light is shining; it is the light of God Himself. Dig toward Him. Dig in persistent, repentant, faith-filled prayer. Freedom is found in His light. "Restore us, O Lord God of hosts! Let your face shine, that we may be saved!" (vs. 7, 19)

"Open and Enjoy"

It always seemed a little weird to me. However, the kids loved it. And I must admit, it was an effective motivation. Anyone who knows my wife Susan very well knows that she loves ice cream. Actually, that might be an understatement; the word "adores" comes to my mind, as I think about it! She *loves* ice cream, and she loves to cover a bowl full of whipping cream. All of our children also enjoyed ice cream but they *really* enjoyed the whipped cream! Susan always made sure that a can or two was kept in the refrigerator.

Often, when "Team Polson" had pulled together on some household chores, she would line the three of them up and, with mouths wide open, she would reward each one of them with a mouthful of delicious whipped cream! It could get messy, but like I said, it was a great motivation!

I have often thought of that image in connection with the Lord's pleas to Israel recorded in Psalm 81:10, "I am the Lord your God, who brought you out of the land of Egypt. Open your mouth wide, and I will fill it." With what did the Lord promise to fill the mouths of His children? "With the finest of wheat, and with honey from the rock I would satisfy you" (v. 16). What a picture!

The Lord desires to bless His children with the sweetest delicacies for the satisfaction of their lives and their souls. God does not want His children to simply *believe* in Him. He wants them to *experience* Him and know the sweetness of His loving provision.

However, God does not force-feed His children. He loves us too much to pry open our mouths against our will. Sadly, Israel proudly refused God's delightful provision, so he "gave them over to their stubborn hearts, to follow their own counsels" (v. 12). My friends, our Lord has some delicious things to place in our mouths. Are we going to open up or clam up?

2 CORINTHIANS 1
July 29

"Comforted to Comfort"

Bible scholars are not certain in regard to how much time elapses between Paul's letter we know as 1 Corinthians in our Bibles and the epistle that bears the ancient title of 2 Corinthians. A careful reading of the two letters seems to indicate that Paul wrote a letter that preceded 1 Corinthians and also another letter that preceded 2 Corinthians. Of course, the content of these letters is lost to us because the Lord did not preserve them, as they were not inspired to be included in the complete canon of Scripture.

What will be very clear on our journey through 2 Corinthians is that it is the most personal of all Paul's letters. In it, we learn more of Paul's motivations and experiences in his ministry than in any other of his letters. Most of all, we learn about the struggles and sufferings that Paul experienced to serve people and form them as followers of Jesus. Paul opens his heart to these people, and it is his broken heart that some of the people in Corinth have broken more than anyone else. However, Paul has come to know the Lord more intimately through his heartaches, and he has come to learn by experience that there is one essential quality above all others to make any Christian more effective in ministry, and that requirement is suffering. Yes, suffering. It is only in suffering that a person is pressed beyond their personal resources, and only then do they really begin to experience the limitless resources of God. Also, it is only in suffering that a follower of Christ experiences the comfort found in Christ and is thereby qualified to express that personally experienced comfort to those who are personally in need of comfort (vv. 3-6).

The Lord Jesus was a "wounded healer," and He leads us into woundedness so that we are qualified to share with others the healing balm Jesus applies to us. Suffering is not meaningless. Suffering is a severe mercy that brings us the comfort of Christ and qualifies us to be ministers of comfort to others. God really knows what He is doing, and it is special!

2 CORINTHIANS 2
July 30

" The Aroma of Christ "

"For we are the aroma of Christ to God among those who are being saved and among those who are perishing, to one a fragrance from death to death, to the other a fragrance from life to life. Who is sufficient for these things?"
(2 Corinthians 2:15-16)

An emotionally healthy person enjoys being liked and does not find pleasure in being disliked. Paul was a man who was filled with the love of Jesus and devoted himself to sharing that love. However, Paul also knew that to speak the message of the Lord in the Church and in the world was going to cause him to be received in extremely opposite ways. To some he would smell like a beautiful perfume; to others he would smell like the putrid odor of death (v. 15). He uses the image of a triumphal procession celebrating the great victory of a conquering general. To the soldiers, the smell of the incense and flowers would be the sweet fragrance of victory and reward. To the chained captives led behind the general's chariot, the incense and flowers would be the fragrance of their own impending deaths by execution.

Loved by some, hated by others; who is sufficient for these things? (v. 16) Yet, by God's grace and strength, Paul was committed to speaking the truth out of a motivation of love. In fact, Paul was so anxious to hear how the Corinthians had responded to his loving rebuke in his previous letter, that he sent Titus to see how the Corinthians were doing. When Titus did not return on schedule, Paul couldn't stand the wait any longer and traveled to Macedonia. There he met Titus, who was returning to see Paul with the wonderful news of the Corinthians' loving and obedient response. Paul was so relieved and comforted by the good report from Titus (2 Cor. 7:5-7).

My brothers and sisters, to *love deeply* is to be exposed to the possibility of being *hurt deeply*. But to live without loving is not to live at all. We are called to love at all costs, at all times, and sometimes that means to be rejected and hurt. However, to live sharing love and truth, is to express the aroma of Christ, and that always smells wonderful to His Heavenly Father!

2 CORINTHIANS 3
July 31

" *Light Reflectors* "

"And we all, with unveiled face, beholding the glory of the Lord, are being transformed into the same image from one degree of glory to another. For this comes from the Lord who is the Spirit."
(2 Corinthians 3:18)

Someone once said, "Never defend yourself. Your friends don't need you to do it, and your enemies won't believe you anyway." Good advice. Paul would have agreed with this recommendation, but in writing 2 Corinthians, he found it necessary to defend his ministry. It is a fine line of separation between defending *himself* and defending his *ministry*, but Paul believed it was vitally important to protect the motive of his ministry from slanderous attacks because the cause of the gospel and the souls of people were at stake.

Some of his harshest critics were fellow Jews who said his message and ministry were far inferior to the true ideal teacher, Moses. In Chapter 3, Paul takes much time to demonstrate that the ministry of the New Covenant that he shared was much greater than that of Moses, and he used an experience in the life of Moses to prove his point.

When Moses came down from Mount Sinai with the tablets of the Law, his face was shining with the glory of God, in whose presence he had been for 40 days. So brilliant was the radiance on Moses' countenance that the people asked that he put a veil over his face until the glory slowly departed. Paul uses this story to show the greater glory of the New Covenant in the lives of God's people. The ministry of the New Covenant far exceeds the old because our hearts are the tablet on which God writes his message of love, not by *external* letters of the Law but by the *internal* writing by His Spirit. We become "living epistles" that are seen and read by people as they observe our lives.

There is also a greater reflected glory of God produced in us as we worship the Lord with unveiled faces of faith. This glory of God actually changes us from the inside out, a spiritual metamorphosis that never fades but shines brighter and brighter by the sanctifying presence of God's Spirit. What an image Paul shares! None of us would compare ourselves to Moses in our devotion or service, but the glory of the New Covenant we carry in our hearts is far greater than the glory of the Old Covenant he carried in his arms. Shine on!

AUGUST

*"May his name endure forever,
his fame continue as long
as the sun!"*

" *Jars of Clay* "

*"But we have this treasure in jars of clay, to show that the
surpassing power belongs to God and not to us."*
(2 Corinthians 4:7)

In a message dealing with the subject of confidence in prayer, the famed evangelist D.L. Moody made this statement many years ago: "If the jeweler in New York City, Mr. Tiffany, gave me as a gift his most precious diamond, I would not be afraid to ask for a paper bag to put it in." By that, Mr. Moody meant that if God has given us His Son to save our souls, we should never lack the confidence to ask Him in prayer to meet our basic needs.

That is a profound and helpful message. The reality is that Mr. Tiffany, nor any of the finest jewelers or clothiers of New York, back in that day or even today, would never put their finest gifts in a very common looking container.

However, that is exactly what our Heavenly Father has chosen to do. Paul says it this way, "But we have this treasure in jars of clay" (v. 7). What is the treasure? It is the priceless gift of the glorious light of salvation in the knowledge of Jesus as Lord (v. 6). This incredible gift God has decided will be contained and shared with the world in "jars of clay." Who are the "jars of clay?" You and me.

One Bible teacher said this is a reminder that we are just "baked dirt." Another facetiously said, "God uses us as cracked pots to leak Jesus everywhere." I can certainly identify personally with both of those comments. However, the Lord has told us why He has placed the most priceless of all eternal treasures in "jars of clay" like us; it is "to show that the surpassing power belongs to God and not to us" (v. 7). By using the most common and ordinary of people, the Lord brings even greater glory to His amazing grace through His precious Son. I am sure you would agree with this thought: I would rather be a jar of clay filled with *Jesus* than be the most beautiful vase filled with *myself*!

2 CORINTHIANS 5
August 2

"Compelled by Fear and Love"

In Psalm 2, King David writes an amazing stanza to a song about God's sovereign power and plans for the earth through Messiah. "Serve the Lord with fear, and rejoice with trembling" (Ps. 2:11). At first, those phrases seemed to be completely disjointed and unrelated, "Serve the Lord with fear and rejoice with trembling." How do the feelings and responses of fear, joy, serving, and trembling possibly go together? Well, Paul gives us a great deal of insight into the union of the emotions of fear and love in our reading today from 2 Corinthians 5.

As believers we know the "sad news"; all human beings have violated God's holy laws and are rebels to His rule. As a result, all will one day stand before Him and receive the justice due for their selfish, sin-filled lives. This is horrible to contemplate, and the reality of this judgment to come compels us to persuade others to avoid it by repentance and faith in Jesus. We know what a dreadful thing it will be to "fall into the hands of the living God" (Heb. 10:31). The fear of the Lord compels us, yes, but there is an even greater motivation to faithfully serve this great God.

"For the Love of Christ controls us, because we have concluded this: that one has died for all, therefore all have died; and he died for all, that those who live might no longer live for themselves but for him who for their sake died and was raised" (vv. 14-15). As believers, we are "dead and alive." We are dead to our old lives of sin and guilt, and we are alive in Christ to an eternal and abundant life. The reality of this deliverance through "the love of Christ controls us." This is not *our love* for Christ, but *His love* for us.

Yes, fear and love grip our hearts, and both should compel and control us. People are lost and must stand before Jesus. We are saved and will meet and live with Jesus. "The fear of the Lord," and "the love of Christ," what greater motivation do we need?

PROVERBS 19
August 3

"Our Plans, His Purposes"

It has been well said that "failing to plan is planning to fail." Not only is it unwise to fail to make plans; it is actually unscriptural. The Bible is filled with admonitions to make plans. Solomon challenges us to make plans and to work diligently toward them. "Go to the ant, O sluggard; consider her ways, and be wise" (Prov. 6:6). Failing to make plans is closely connected with laziness, which Solomon mocks and strongly condemns in this chapter. "The sluggard buries his hand in the dish and will not even bring it back to his mouth" (v.24). In fact, the wisest thing any human being can do is to plan for the only thing that is completely certain in this life. "For as it is appointed for all once to die, and after this the judgment" (Heb. 9:27). Yes, it is very wise to plan, but it is folly to make our own plans separated from God's purposes.

Human plans only have wisdom and are only really good plans when they are aligned with God's purposes. Certainly, all of God's purposes have not been made clear to us, but God gave us His Word and His Spirit that we might be guided into all truth (John 16:13). Even when we feel that the plans we make are good and in accordance with God's wisdom, the ultimate act of faith is to submit them to His will. James challenges us, "Whereas we ought to say, 'If the Lord wills, we will live and do this or that'" (Jas. 4:15).

Perhaps it is true that we would always choose what God would choose if we were wise enough to choose it. It is always a wonderful thing to plan and to dream, but we must never forget that the One who loves us so much that He did not spare His own Son will always have as His purpose, the best plans.

PSALMS 83 & 84
August 4

"House Beautiful"

"How lovely is your dwelling place,
O Lord of hosts!"
(Psalm 84:1)

It is one of my wife's favorite magazines. Over the years, I have seen her read carefully through issue after issue. I'm talking about the magazine *House Beautiful*. Susan has to be one of its "hall of fame" subscribers! I have often teased her about it. But confidentially, I have picked up a copy, from time to time, when she is not around and enjoyed looking through it. Again, I'm telling you this in confidence!

All the members of the choir in Israel were men, the sons of Korah, yet they loved to sing the praises of the *ultimate* "House Beautiful," the temple of God. Psalm 84 is a lovely anthem of this priestly choir about the blessing and strength that comes to the people who dwell in God's house. Of course, the house itself, as incredibly beautiful as it was, had no special power to provide help to those who gathered there. It was the inhabitant of the house, the Lord God Almighty, who was the source of all the joy and strength that came to those who regularly entered the courts.

In the New Covenant, there is not a specific spot or particular building that is God's dwelling on earth. However, this does not mean there is *not* a place that is *not* in a very special way the "house of God."

The "house of God" is whatever location His people gather to worship in the name of His Son and their Savior, Jesus Christ. Paul refers to this gathering as the "house of God" when he gives instructions to one of the young pastors, Timothy (1 Tim. 3:15). The church is the house of God, and the gathering together of the body of believers is the beautiful dwelling place of the Lord, whether it is in a basement, a storefront, or stately sanctuary.

May the preciousness of the gathering of God's people always cause us to feel in our hearts, "My soul longs, yes, faints for the courts of the Lord; my heart and flesh sing for joy to the living God" (v. 2).

2 CORINTHIANS 6
August 5

"*Be Different*"

"Do not be unequally yoked with unbelievers.
For what partnership has righteousness with lawlessness?
Or what fellowship has light with darkness?"
(2 Corinthians 6:14)

As followers of Jesus, we are the last people on earth who should ever think we are better than anyone else. After all, the only reason we follow Jesus is because He sought us out, and we all know where He found us. He found us in sin and rebellion and called us to Himself and to life and freedom in His mercy and grace. The only thing that makes us different from unbelievers is Jesus; however, because of Jesus we *are* different.

We belong to the Lord; we are holy because He has set us apart as His special people. Therefore, although we are not *better* than other people, we are not to be *just like* other people. Jesus wants us to display that difference in the way we live, in what we value, in the things we do, and in the things we *don't* do.

Many of the believers in Corinth had forgotten this call to the distinctiveness of life. They continued to participate in the ungodly and pagan civic religious retreats in the temples. They united in close personal business partnerships with pagans; some of these contracts were confirmed in pagan rituals. Some of the Christians in Corinth were even entering into marriage covenants with people who rejected Jesus Christ and worshiped the false gods of the Greeks and Romans.

In response, Paul uses the words and the passion of the prophet Isaiah to call them to make a definite decision for holiness of heart and life to God (v. 17). God's plan is for us to be *in* the world, but not to be *of* the world. To be a friend to sinners just like our Master, but to be separate from sinners in our manner of life and motivations for life, also just like our Master. We are called to follow Jesus into the world as witnesses, but we must follow His call to live differently than the world in order to represent Him as lights shining in the darkness.

"Good Grief!"

*"For godly grief produces a repentance that leads to salvation
without regret, whereas worldly grief produces death."*
(2 Corinthians 7:10)

The comic strip and cartoon character Charlie Brown is famous for one statement above all others; that's right, "Good grief!" Usually, this statement was a cry of exasperation from Charlie as he dealt with the sarcastic criticisms of Lucy or the irritating antics of Snoopy. Now, I'm not sure Charlie Brown ever realized his cry of "good grief" was a statement of Biblical theology, but it truly was. "Good grief" is actually the testimony of joy from the Apostle Paul over what has taken place in the lives of so many believers at Corinth. They have experienced and expressed a grief that is good. It is good grief because it is the grief of repentance over the sin Paul had condemned in the "letter that grieved you." Paul's words hurt them deeply, and it broke Paul's heart that he had to do so (v. 9). However, his words of rebuke were used by the Spirit of God to reveal the deception and disobedience in the lives of those he so dearly loved.

Paul's condemnation of their ungodly attitudes and actions was a severe mercy from God to heal and restore His children. Good grief is never pleasant for either the one speaking the truth in love or the one who receives it, but it is always profitable if it leads to repentance. Repentance is good grief; remorse is bad grief. Repentance is a sorrow that turns a person back to God and produces the fruits of salvation. Remorse is a bad grief that leads a person to self-focused and angry bitterness that produces more spiritual darkness and death. It is not an easy thing to be either the source or the recipient of good grief. But as loving and truthful followers of Jesus, we are called to, at times, experience and express it. Ask the Lord in prayer if there is either a good grief mission or message for you today. It's all good because it's always of God.

2 CORINTHIANS 8
August 7

" *The Grace of Generosity* "

Generosity is fundamental to Christianity. It is not saying too much to say that generosity is the *root* and the *fruit* of genuine salvation. No doubt, that is the reason the Apostle Paul gives the subject of generosity the equivalent of two chapters in this epistle out of the entire thirteen chapters it contains. Paul is writing to the believers in Corinth a reminder of exhortation about a special offering he is taking among the churches of Macedonia (Northern Greece) and Achaia (Southern Greece) for the desperately poor and persecuted believers in Judaea.

The Christians in Corinth have known about this offering for over a year, and now Paul is writing in advance of his arrival to make sure they are prepared for contributing. In order to encourage them about this opportunity for generosity, Paul writes to inspire them by two examples: the example of their brothers and sisters in Achaia and the example of their Lord and Savior Jesus Christ. Their fellow Christians in Achaia have expressed "the grace of God" in giving generously, not out of their overflowing prosperity but out of their abject poverty (v. 2). Only the grace of God could cause such a selfless response.

It is very significant that Paul does not connect generosity with the *law* of God but rather with the *grace* of God. True generosity is always motivated by grace because it was grace that motivated the Author of grace, the Lord Jesus. The Corinthians have been the recipients of that overflowing grace from Jesus. "For you know the grace of our Lord Jesus Christ, that though he was rich, yet for your sake he became poor, so that you by his poverty might become rich" (v. 9).

The biography of a believer is a "riches to rags and rags to riches" story. Our Lord left the riches of His glory in heaven and became poor so that we, in our poverty, might become infinitely and eternally rich. Generosity, the generosity of Jesus, is truly the *root* of our salvation. Our generosity is the *fruit* of our salvation. Our generosity proves the genuineness of our love (v. 8). When we focus on our Master's incalculable generosity to us, we will need no other motivation for our own generosity, and we won't need a calculator either.

2 CORINTHIANS 9
August 8

" *The Seeds are in the Harvest* "

*"He who supplies seed to the sower and bread for food will supply and
multiply your seed for sowing and increase the harvest of your
righteousness. You will be enriched in every way to be generous in
every way, which through us will produce thanksgiving to God."*
(2 Corinthians 9: 10-11)

I once heard a well-known pastor-teacher share what he called the law
of sowing and reaping in relation to generosity. He said, "You reap *what*
you sow. You reap *later* than what you sow. You reap *more* than you
sow." That statement has stayed with me through the years, and I
believe it accurately communicates the basis of what the Apostle Paul
teaches us regarding the principle of financial generosity in our reading
today. Paul bases everything he shares concerning the practice of
generosity, on the law of sowing and reaping that God has ordained in
nature itself. It is the seeds sown in the spring that produce the harvest
in the fall. Then, it is the harvest in the fall that produces food for the
farmer and his family, food for others, and then the seeds to start the
process all over again next spring.

Do you see the infinitely wise and personally thrilling involvement
we are allowed to experience through generosity? God provides the
seeds (the finances), as ultimately all the seeds belong to God. God
allows us to scatter His seeds (generosity) that He has given us into the
lives of others. By doing this (giving generously) we are providing for
His physical and spiritual resources to be graciously shared with needy
people. The result will be a harvest (thanksgiving) to God for the
expression of His love and a harvest (joy) for us who participated in the
harvest cycle of God.

But the cycle comes back to us because the recipients of our
generosity then sow seeds (prayers) for us to God. God hears their
prayers then seeds and produces a fresh harvest (spiritual growth) in
our lives. All of this incredible cycle of generosity, love, and faith
ultimately brings praise to the Lord of the Harvest, Jesus Christ.
"Thanks be to God for his inexpressible gift!" (v. 15) Amen!

2 CORINTHIANS 10
August 9

" *This is War* "

"For the weapons of our warfare are not of the flesh but have divine power to destroy strongholds. We destroy arguments and every lofty opinion raised against the knowledge of God."
(2 Corinthians 10:4-5a)

In my office, I have two display cases that are very special to me. One of them holds the American flag that was presented to our family at the time of my father's burial in March of 1998. The other display case contains my father's "dog tags" from World War II, the shoulder patch from his uniform, and also a number of the medals he won for combat. Most special to me is the Purple Heart and two purple ribbons, which he received in recognition of the two times he was wounded in combat in the Philippines. I remember well, as a young boy, pleading with my dad, from time to time, to roll up his left sleeve to display the large indention in his tricep muscle that showed where the sniper's bullet had passed through his arm. As young boys, we thought that was "totally cool!" But when I grew older, and on occasion saw that same scar, it made me very proud of my father and also made me recognize that war is very real and deadly serious.

The Apostle Paul, in the closing chapters of 2 Corinthians, is forced to display his "war wounds" as he challenges the opponents of his ministry and the gospel in Corinth. Paul bears, in his body and his heart, the scars for faithfully providing and protecting the freedom of the gospel for his brothers and sisters in that region. *Spiritual warfare* is the price of *spiritual freedom* in Christ. The battles are constantly raging around the church, in the church, and within the hearts of the believers who compose the church. The warfare is *spiritual*, but it is *real*, and the weapons of the conflict are as well. The weapon against the arsenal of the enemy (lies), is the ammunition of the Lord (truth). The "arguments" and every "lofty opinion" that rises against the "knowledge of God" in our lives as Christians and in our midst as a church, must be "destroyed" and "taken captive" by the power of the Spirit of God through the Word of God. The battle is fierce and the spiritual forces around us and within us are real, but the victory is certain through obedience to Christ. We are on the Victor's side. Praise God!

PSALM 85 & PROVERBS 20
August 10

" *A Cry for Revival* "

*"Will you not revive us again, that your people
may rejoice in you?"* (Psalm 85:6)

Growing up as a boy in Immanuel Baptist Church, it seemed like our song leader, Bill Swift, led us in the same song about every other Sunday. I can still see him in my mind's eye with his flat-top haircut, horn-rimmed glasses, and a smiling face. He would beat his right arm up and down with his index finger extended as he enthusiastically led the congregation in singing. I wondered even then why we would sing such an old song; after all, it was published in 1863.

Of course, I did not know that the song was actually based on a hymn of praise sung by the choir in the Temple in Jerusalem nearly 3000 years ago. I just knew Bill Swift enjoyed it, and clearly, our small congregation did as well because they made the sanctuary ring with its words and melody. Over 50 years later, I can still hear it, and its memory and message still stir my heart to this day. I have often made it a prayer to God; perhaps you would like to join me in offering it today in a prayer for revival. *Revive Us Again* by William P. Mackay:

> *We praise Thee, O God! For the Son of thy Love,*
> *For Jesus who died, And is now gone above.*
> *We praise Thee, O God! For Thy Spirit of light,*
> *Who hath shown us our Savior, And scattered our night.*
> *All glory and praise To the Lamb that was slain,*
> *Who hath borne all our sins, And hath cleansed every stain.*
> *Revive us again; Fill each heart with Thy love;*
> *May each soul be rekindled With fire from above.*
>
> *Refrain:*
> *Hallelujah! Thine the glory. Hallelujah! Amen.*
> *Hallelujah! Thine the glory. Revive us again!*

That was beautiful. Bill Swift would be so happy! Now, may the Lord hear and answer our prayer. Amen

" *Deliverance and Dedication* "

"Give ear, O Lord, to my prayer; listen to my plea for grace. In the day of my trouble, I call upon you, for you answer me."
(Psalm 86:6-7)

Many of David's psalms were "written on the run." That is, he wrote a number of his songs as he was literally under pursuit by his enemies. Some of the deepest heartaches of his life was the fact that those who were pursuing him were often some of his closest companions and, in the latter years of his life, even members of his own family.

As you can read in these psalms, they were not the product of a peaceful and meditative season in David's life. You can literally sense the urgency and the desperation in his words as he prays to God. Yet, as I read the psalms like Psalm 86, I am struck by the fact that, in his cries for *deliverance* from his enemies, David also pleads for something more; he pleads for *direction*.

Of course, he prays for rescue, but he also asks for wisdom to learn what God desires to teach him through the ordeal. "Teach me your way, O Lord, that I may walk in your truth; unite my heart to fear your name" (v. 11). David asks that the Lord will use this season to draw him closer in obedience and deeper in understanding. He prays to *walk* in the Lord's truth and also to *know* the Lord's ways. This is the prayer of a "man after God's own heart." He understands that obeying the Lord in times of trial produces a deeper intimacy with Him.

David's "Greater Son," the Lord Jesus, promised all of us, as His disciples, that if we would *obey* Him, then we would really *know* Him. "Whoever has my commandments and keeps them, he it is who loves me. And he who loves me will be loved by my Father, and I will love him and manifest myself to him" (John 14:21). In the midst of the pressures of trials in our lives, we must pray as David showed us, and as Jesus taught us, that we "press on" in obedience and "press in" in worship. If we do that, we will not only know more clearly what our Lord *wants us to do*, but also more deeply *who our Lord is*.

2 CORINTHIANS 11
August 12

"Sacred Suffering"

"For I will show him how much he must suffer
for the sake of my name."
(Acts 9:16)

Throughout the letter of Second Corinthians, Paul has found it necessary to defend the integrity of his ministry. This is very hard to understand, given the fact that Paul was the founder of the church and that the incredible ministry of the gospel in Achaia was the result of his labors for Christ. However, over the space of a few years, the hearts of many in Corinth had been captured by the charisma and oratory of those whom Paul sarcastically referred to as "super-apostles" (v. 5). These men were incredibly captivating in their personalities, but their message was a false gospel that mixed law and grace. In reality, Paul said they were ministers of Satan who, just like their master, could transform themselves as messengers of light (v. 14).

In contrast to their attractiveness, Paul literally bore in his body the scars of his suffering for Jesus. He had received 195 lashes from the Jewish leaders. On three occasions the Roman authorities had beaten him with rods. Paul's body bore the scars of the terrible stoning he received in Lystra. Three times Paul was shipwrecked. His life, since meeting Jesus on the road to Damascus, had been one of relentless labor, danger, and personal suffering. As incredibly hard as all this had been for Paul to endure, even greater was the pain of personal rejection from those he so sincerely loved in Christ.

What sustained Paul through these unimaginable experiences and heartaches? Well, ultimately, of course, his strength was in the sustaining power of the Lord. On a personal level, there was one priceless quality that Paul possessed that no one could take from him—sincerity. Paul was genuine in his love for Jesus and his love for others, and his conscience was clear. Love is liberating. It frees us from the most insidious of all bondage—the slavery of concern for what others might think about us. When, by God's grace, we love and serve Him by serving others, then we are truly citizens of the freest realm of all—sincerity.

2 CORINTHIANS 12
August 13

"When God Says, 'No'"

"But he said to me, 'My grace is sufficient for you, for my power is made perfect in weakness...'" (2 Corinthians 12:9a)

For centuries, Bible teachers have theorized as to what Paul refers in this chapter as a "thorn" in the flesh (v. 7). Some have suggested that it was a terrible disease of his eyes, since Paul, on occasion, referred to the willingness of some brothers and sisters to pluck out their eyes for him (Gal. 4:15). Also, in closing the letter to the Galatians he says, "See with what large letters I am writing to you with my own hand" (Gal. 6:11). Other Bible teachers have believed that the "thorn" was a satanically inspired enemy who continually assaulted Paul. The truth is we simply do not know for what Paul was referring. My dad used to say he couldn't wait to ask Paul about it in heaven!

Whatever Paul endured, we do know a few things. It was definitely more painful than a thorn because the word translated "thorn" is more accurately rendered "a stake" in the flesh. We read that Satan was behind this awful anguish Paul endured. We know that it was a prolonged experience since Paul says he pleaded with the Lord on three occasions for deliverance. However, what we recognize above all things is what was "heard" from the Lord and "learned" from the Lord through this terrible ordeal.

Paul heard the Lord assuring Him that He was bigger than this trial. "My grace is sufficient for you, for my power is made perfect in weakness..." (v. 9). Paul also learned from the Lord that His power is experienced in even greater ways when Paul is weak. This led Paul to a place where he could "boast all the more gladly of my weaknesses" because "when I am weak, then I am strong" (vv. 9-10). Now, what Paul experienced was humanly illogical, but it was spiritually supernatural. When God says, "No" to us, it is only to say, "Yes" to something better. Charles Spurgeon once said, "God is too good to be unkind and He is too wise to be mistaken." Surely this is true.

That may be the place of faith God has you today. God may be saying, "No" in some area of your life. Can you trust Him for the greater and the better "yes?" You may not be able to "trace His hand," but you can always "trust His heart." Amen.

2 CORINTHIANS 13
August 14

" Together "

*"Finally, brothers, rejoice. Aim for restoration, comfort one another,
agree with one another, live in peace; and the God of
love and peace will be with you."*
(2 Corinthians 13:11)

In speaking of salvation, we often refer to it as having a "personal relationship" with Jesus Christ. This is not a specific phrase that is used in the New Testament, nevertheless, the idea of "personal relationship" with the Lord is a precious truth that the message of the gospel in Christ shares. Each of us by God's grace does enjoy a salvation that is very real and deeply personal.

However, we need to recognize that a "personal relationship" with Christ is not a "solitary relationship." The Word of God is very clear that when we enter into *faith* in Christ, we also enter a *family* in Christ. Our faith indeed is personal, but it is also completely relational. Paul, as he closes this letter to the church in Corinth, clearly recognizes that in addressing very difficult issues in the church the atmosphere can become very divisive.

So, in his final challenge, Paul calls the believers "together." Rejoice *together*. Restore *together*. Comfort together. Agree *together*. Love *together*. Maybe this is a good time for a question, "Are we all *together* on this?" By that, I mean that while I am sure we hear Paul's *expression* of peace and unity, do we work to *experience* this reality? It is very easy to adopt a spirit of neutrality regarding relationships in the Church, but neutrality has never won a battle against the flesh or the forces of the enemy, and neutrality has also never produced a lasting peace.

Paul uses strong verbs to challenge the Church of Corinth toward unity, and verbs are action items for us in our Church today. As you take time to pray to your *personal* Savior today, remember you are also praying to the *mutual* Savior of your brothers and sisters in His family. Our Heavenly Father doesn't want His family reunion taking place only in glory. He wants the reunion to be experienced and expressed on Earth. Let's make that happen.

GALATIANS 1
August 15

" Faith Alone "

To say that Martin Luther loved the Epistle to the Galatians would be more than just a slight understatement. He expressed his devotion to this letter from the Apostle Paul in this fashion, "The Epistle to the Galatians is my own epistle. I have betrothed myself to it. It is my Katie von Bora." We don't have a record of how Luther's wife, Katie von Bora, felt about that comparison!

Martin Luther preached from this book of the Bible hundreds of times and wrote a commentary on Galatians that is still in print today. Nearly 200 years after Luther's commentary on Galatians was first published, a gospel meeting was held in Aldersgate, England, for the public reading of Luther's work. While the preface to Luther's commentary was being read, a spiritually troubled Anglican priest felt his heart "strangely warmed" and at that moment knew that he truly did trust in *Christ alone* for his salvation. The name of the young priest? John Wesley.

Luther's commentary on Galatians is truly powerful, but the source of that power is in the epistle itself. The Book of Galatians has been called the "Magna Carta of Christianity" and the "Declaration of Independence of the Faith." The theme of this epistle we begin reading today is *"Faith Alone."* Paul wrote this letter as a declaration and defense of the gospel, the good news of salvation experienced by faith totally apart from works. Paul considered the purity of the gospel so important that he pronounced a curse on any man or angel who preached a different gospel, and then he pronounced the curse a second time! (vv. 8-9) Paul was serious about the gospel because the gospel is serious. It is the only hope of the world, with the souls of men and women in the balance and eternity at stake.

I wonder, how vital is the gospel to you? Is it your vital sign? Is it the beating of your heart? Has your heart ever been "strangely warmed" by the message of *faith alone in Christ* as the hope of your salvation? How important is faith to you and how often do you share it? As you read Galatians, ask God to confirm your own faith in Christ and ask Him for the grace to share your faith with others.

GALATIANS 2
August 16

"Kosher Conflict"

"But when Cephas (Peter) came to Antioch, I opposed him to his face, because he stood condemned." (Galatians 2:11)

One of the most significant blessings I am experiencing in the ministry is seeing the growing outreach to the internationals in our community, and also the growing diversity within our congregation as brothers and sisters from many national and ethnic backgrounds join the fellowship. This growing diversity also brings an increasing awareness and understanding of the sensitivities needed to break down unnecessary and unhelpful cultural barriers. It also requires a loving desire to not cause offenses that can hinder the gospel or impede the spiritual unity the gospel produces. This is not always easy, but it is vitally important.

The gospel that does not unite people in mutual love and submission is not the product of the message of Jesus Christ. It is, in the reality of its expression, "another gospel" (Gal. 1:8-9). Paul so strongly believed in the unity-producing power of the gospel that he was willing to oppose anyone who caused division, and that included the leader of the apostles, Peter. The Church at Antioch was a historic and completely unprecedented spiritual and cultural miracle. Jews and Gentiles worshiping the same God and Savior in love and unity. The result of this was a spectacular witness for Christ throughout the region of Galatia.

Peter at first responded with joy to the evidence of the further work of God's international grace that he had first witnessed at the home of Cornelius in Caesarea several years before. However, when racist and legalistic disciples came from Jerusalem, Peter withdrew from fellowshipping with believers who were Gentiles in their heritage and cultural practices. This was complete hypocrisy and a practical denial of the grace of God. The gospel was at stake, and Paul was willing to confront a dear friend and brother in Christ to oppose this sin (vv. 11-14). Are we willing to do the same? I believe this is one of the most important questions we can ask ourselves to confront the deceptive but deadly sin of racism in our hearts and the culture of our churches. There is one race, the human race, created by one God from one man and one blood. There is one body, with one Lord, united in one faith. This is our true heritage, and any heritage that erects cultural or racial barriers is sinful and must be personally addressed, renounced, and rejected by every gospel-loving Christian. I need to start with me. You need to start with you. Then, pass on the "tough love" to others.

PSALMS 88 & 89
August 17

" *Why* ? "

Not long ago, I sat with a brother in Christ and was just stunned. Then my tears began to flow, as did his, as he shared some of the things that were transpiring in his life and in the lives of those he dearly loved. I sensed myself literally *feeling* some of his pain and heartache connected with earthquakes and successive shock waves of suffering at that moment. I remembered Job and determined that I would not resemble Job's "friends" as they tried to respond to his suffering with challenges about the "hidden sins" that must be in his life. Then, I remembered David and the other authors of Psalms and how they expressed their own grief and complaints to God.

I reminded my friend, and I also spoke to myself, in saying that life is sometimes worse than hard; it is horrible, and it is not fair. I could not, nor would I even attempt to give my brother some glib and easy answers or some pseudo-philosophical reason for why terrible things happen. I also did not try to help him understand the "nature of evil" and the "practical implications of the doctrine of original sin." Those things are true, and they are appropriate in the classroom or the sanctuary, but not when you are sitting in a booth and weeping tears of bewildered pain. A couple of very Biblical responses were appropriate, and we both expressed them. First, "Why, God? Where in the world are you?" Yes, that response is Biblical: "O Lord, why do you cast my soul away? Why do you hide your face from me?" (Ps. 88:14)

It is spiritual, and it is healthy to grieve over the terrible agony of emotional pain and the even greater suffering of the *perceived* absence and indifference of God. My friend did that, and I agreed with him. But together we also did something else; while we cried together, we also claimed together what is true even when we do not "feel" it: the Lord God is good, and He is the God of our salvation (v. 1). The storms truly rage; they rage around us and they rage at times within us, but the anchor holds. God is real, and His steadfast love endures forever. Amen!

" *The Number of Our Days* "

*"So teach us to number our days that we may
get a heart of wisdom."*
(Psalm 90:12)

25,567.5. I'm sorry the strange working of my brain would not allow me to not do the math. However, that is a very Biblical number. 25,567.5 is the number of days in 70 years. Just in case you are curious, the .5 day comes from factoring in leap years! Moses in this psalm tells us to number our days, and then he also reminds us that the 70 years of a typical lifetime are soon gone and then we fly away (vs. 10, 12). Yes, we will soon be gone and then fly away, but how quickly do those days fly by even before we fly away! Got a calculator handy? How many days have you lived? Do the math and you may be amazed at how little is left of those "three score and ten years," or you may realize that in Moses' math, you are already living on "borrowed time!"

Regardless of where you stand in the number of days you have lived, it is never too late to begin devotedly serving the Lord. Take encouragement from Moses himself; the Bible says that Moses was 80 years old when he stood before Pharaoh and demanded, in the name of Jehovah, that he let God's people go. Moses lived for 40 more years and then passed away and was buried by God at the age of 120. What an impact he made in his "retirement years!" David tells us in Psalm 139 that "all of our days are written in God's book."

Only God knows the number of our allotted days; the Lord wants us to "number our days that we may get a heart of wisdom" (v. 12). The greatest wisdom is knowing that eternity is long and our days are few, but *eternity is in our days.* Yes, our lives are very brief indeed, but "whoever does the will of God abides forever" (1 John 2:17). The words of Moses gripped the heart of a young British athlete many years ago. C.T. Studd dedicated his life to live out a truth he wrote in a poem of exhortation, "Only one life will soon be past, only what's done for Christ will last."

GALATIANS 3
August 19

"Father Abraham"

I recall a conversation I was having once with another man, and it just so happened that his little girl, perhaps two years old, was sitting with him. I can't remember anything at all about the conversation, but I do clearly recall how that little girl communicated in no uncertain terms that in her view the conversation was over. She grabbed her father's arm tightly, glared at me, and loudly declared, "That's *my* daddy!" Well, I definitely got the message. In her mind, I had taken enough of her daddy's time and attention away from her and I needed to move on. As I recall, that is exactly what I did!

The Jewish people for nearly 2000 years proudly declared their connection to their ancestor Abraham, and rightly so, for he was a truly great man. They also did not appreciate sharing him with other people, especially those so-called "Christians" who wanted to claim him as *their* ancestor. Above all, the Jewish leaders despised their former hero, Saul of Tarsus, who now traitorously affirmed that the Gentile disciples of the crucified carpenter from Nazareth, Jesus, were now "children of Abraham." This was blasphemy at its worst.

The issue was, they misunderstood Saul's (Paul's) use of the term "father." Paul meant that Abraham was the "spiritual father" of not those who shared his genetic code, but those who shared his faith. "Know then that it is those of faith who are the sons of Abraham" (v. 7). Abraham was for Paul the "exhibit A" of the case for salvation by faith alone. "Abraham believed God, and it was counted to him as righteousness" (v. 6). It was through Abraham's greater son, Jesus, that God's promise to him would be fulfilled, "In you shall all the nations be blessed" (v. 8).

Jesus was the ultimate "Isaac" of Father Abraham, *physically*, and Father God, *spiritually*. God the Father, in His great redeeming love because He did not spare his Isaac, "but delivered him up for us all" (Rom. 8:32). Through faith alone in Jesus, He becomes for us our "Isaac," we become "sons and daughters" of Abraham, *and* we become children and heirs of Almighty God. May we never lose the wonder of this and may we worship Him for this today.

GALATIANS 4
August 20

"*A Tale of Two Mountains*"

Not long ago, I had a conversation with a couple who moved to a community in the mountains of North Carolina from their lifelong home in the mountains of Colorado. We exchanged some humorous comments about the comparison between our "mountains" in Appalachia to the towering Rockies of Colorado. They agreed that having lived above the 8,000-foot level for so many years did make the mountains of our region seem more like *large hills* in comparison. But then they both said something quite interesting to me. They shared that they had grown to love the Smoky Mountains even more than the Rockies in which they were raised and lived so long.

The reason for this, they explained, was that although the views from the heights of the Rockies were spectacular, they now recognized that the landscape was quite barren. They had both fallen in love with the lush and diverse vegetation of the Smoky Mountains and the beauty that now surrounded them.

I could not help but think of Paul's challenge to the believers in Galatia as I remembered what they shared, especially the comparison Paul makes in Chapter 4 to the two key mountains connected with the history of the Jewish people—Mount Sinai and Mount Zion. In his inspired allegory, Paul compares these two mountains to the Law and the gospel of grace. He also layers another allegory onto it as he compares those who seek to be saved by law-keeping, to children of Hagar (Sinai). That is, children of spiritual slavery, compared to the children of the Jerusalem above, that is, children of spiritual liberty who are born of faith.

Paul's allegory is foreign to our modern culture and experience, but the challenge is timeless. The Law, though it was holy and good, could save no one because sinful people are unable to meet its demands—total obedience. Those who try to earn their salvation by keeping the Law are doomed to failure, and to a life of spiritual bondage and an eternity of just penalty. However, those who look in faith to Christ, who fulfilled the Law's commands in His righteous life and the curse of the Law in His substitutionary death, are free now and forever. Paul's challenge to us is to live as children of freedom and not slavery. We need to hear and live Paul's call to liberty today, "For freedom Christ has set us free; stand firm therefore, and do not submit again to a yoke of slavery" (Gal. 5:1).

GALATIANS 5
August 21

" The Face of Liberty "

"But the fruit of the Spirit is love, joy, peace, patience, kindness, goodness, faithfulness, gentleness, self-control; against such things there is no law." (Galatians 5:22-23)

The Statue of Liberty was dedicated in the summer of 1886 and for over 130 years has stood in the harbor of New York City as, perhaps, the iconic image of freedom in America. The massive statue was the inspiration and creation of the famed French sculptor, Frederick Bartholdi. In the years since the dedication, incredible amounts of information have been recorded about the design and construction of the statue. However, there is one question that has been shrouded in mystery through the years regarding the identity of the woman who is the face of Lady Liberty.

While there has been much speculation, the theory with the most historical support, going back to the dedication of the statue, and one that has never been denied by Bartholdi is that the face of the Statue of Liberty is modeled after the likeness of his own mother, Augusta. If the face is indeed that of his mother, then Bartholdi did bestow on her one of the greatest of tributes, as the face representing freedom to the nations.

Paul, in writing Galatians, focused on the theme of liberty, the ultimate liberty enjoyed by all who trust in Christ. This freedom of God's children is truly a *spiritual* freedom provided by the Holy Spirit, as He brings eternal life in the miracle of the new birth.

What Paul makes clear to us in our reading today from Galatians Chapter 5, is that the work of God in our lives is *spiritual* in nature, but it is extremely *visible*. The work of the Holy Spirit bears fruit in the lives of believers, and this fruit is qualities of the spirit described in verses 22-23. These eight qualities are ultimately the character of Jesus Himself. Our Lord is the perfect example of "the fruit of the Spirit," and the work of the Spirit is to "conform us to the image" of Christ (Rom. 8:29).

Let that sink in for a moment. God's plan is for His children to be the "faces of liberty" in which people see the resemblance and likeness of Jesus. What an honor! What a responsibility! The biggest responsibility we have is to cooperate with the Sculptor as He molds us into that beautiful image day by day.

GALATIANS 6
August 22

"*Lifting Burdens and Bearing Loads*"

"Bear one another's burdens, and so fulfill the Law of Christ... For each will have to bear his own load." (Galatians 6: 2, 5)

There is a saying that is often used among churches and ministries that are involved in bringing the gospel of Jesus into the lives of those who have known the impact of the long-term generational consequences of sin. The statement is this: "Missional is Messy." As God's people, when we are committed to bringing the ministry and message of God's love to the lives and families that sin has ravaged, we can expect that the work can get complicated. One important ability that needs to be developed in serving in this way is "how to help without hurting." Sometimes providing assistance, while promoting personal responsibility to work toward change, can actually serve to enable bad behaviors rather than embracing personal steps toward change.

Paul touches on this balance of love and responsibility in the opening verses of Chapter 6. He challenges believers to fulfill the law of Christ in helping others bear their burdens (v. 2). This "law" is the law of love, and the "burdens" are situations that are too heavy for any person to carry by himself. God's law for us is to express His love in making personal sacrifices to help others when the burdens of life are beyond their ability or the responsibility to carry alone.

This help is not helpful, however, when it comes to a person's responsibility to "bear his own load" (v. 5). The word translated "load" is also capable of being translated as a "pack" or "bag." Paul is saying that each person should "carry his own pack," which means, pick up the responsibilities that he is responsible for and *capable* of fulfilling. In other words, it is not helpful to help a person who refuses to help himself.

Yes, if we want to live on mission, it is going to get messy. But love compels us to go into messy situations and help people carry huge and unpleasant burdens. However, love also compels us to speak words of challenge and exhortation to people about taking personal responsibility. Love does both and also love *receives* both, because sometimes we need helpful love in assisting us with overwhelming burdens, and sometimes we need helpful love in being challenged to take responsibility for our own stuff. Love gives and love receives whatever is best for others and ourselves.

EPHESIANS 1
August 23

"In the Heavenlies"

It only takes a few moments of reading the letter of Paul to the believers in Ephesus to recognize that you must read it very slowly. One reason this is necessary is because it is quite evident that Paul wrote it (or more likely, dictated it) very quickly. Paul did not do this because he was in a hurry, but rather because his heart was so full that his mind just overflowed with the glorious truths he shared. This is especially obvious when you see Paul's message in the Greek text. Other than the greeting in the first two verses, the entire first chapter of this letter is just two sentences! Verses 3-14 express one sentence, and verses 15-23 are the second sentence.

Paul communicates this way because earthly grammar cannot express the heavenly grace of the riches lavished on all believers through their exalted Master, Jesus Christ (v. 8). This entire chapter is, in reality, a "treasure chest" of the gifts of grace that are ours as a result of the Father's infinite love for each of us. I have found Ephesians Chapter 1 to be some of the most challenging material in all of God's Word to attempt to share. It is as if every phrase overflows with deep theological truth and priceless gifts of grace. That is the reason I want to encourage you, over the next few days, to take some extra time to linger over this *love letter* from the Lord. It is indeed a *love letter* containing God's devotion to you and also sharing the description of the inheritance He is providing for you as a member of His beloved family.

Look into the treasure chest of God's love again and calculate your wealth by claiming some of these riches as your own. A wonderful way to do that is by making some "I am" statements in claiming what God says about you. Let's do it together: "I am chosen" (v. 4). "I am predestined" (v. 5). "I am adopted" (v. 5). "I am redeemed" (v. 7). "I am forgiven" (v. 7). "I am an heir" (v. 11). "I am sealed" (v. 13). Now, think about what you have just said and recognize it is absolutely already true in Christ. How rich you are! Take time right now to praise God for this amazing grace.

PSALMS 92 & 93
August 24

" *Fruitful Forever* "

Several years ago, a member of our congregation showed me around his property. He was an elderly brother, and he and his dear wife had lived in the small frame house for nearly 50 years. My friend was especially grateful for several immense oak trees that grew in his front yard. He showed me the stump of the biggest oak of all, which had been damaged in a terrible storm a few years earlier and had to be cut down. When the tree was cut down, a professor from the school of agriculture at the University of Tennessee came by the property to determine the age of the mighty oak. The professor counted 232 annual growth rings in the base of the tree. That tree was already growing strong when the original thirteen colonies became the United States. In fact, it was over 25 years old when Knoxville was founded in 1791! It was humbling, in a special way, to think of the strength of that majestic tree in standing firm for over two centuries.

I thought of that ancient oak as I read about the tree that is described in our reading today from Psalm 92: "The righteous flourish like the palm tree and grow like a cedar in Lebanon. They are planted in the house of the Lord; they flourish in the courts of our God. They still bear fruit in old age; they are ever full of sap and green, to declare that the Lord is upright; he is my rock, and there is no unrighteousness in him" (vv. 12-15).

The ancient title for this psalm is "A Song for the Sabbath." It is a beautiful hymn of praise and worship for God's sustaining strength. These cedars have no special endurance in themselves, but they draw their life and strength from the blessed soil of the temple courts. The psalmist sees himself as one of those cedars who are blessed with strength as he draws his life from the God he worships.

3000 years have not changed the truth of this beautiful image for us today. We certainly will not live for 232 years like that oak did in our fellow worshiper's yard, but we can be full of life and bear fruit in each year we are given on Earth. Our worship is the root system that connects us with our source of strength, the God of Israel. He is the soil of our souls, and as we press deeply into Him, we flourish and bear fruit for His glory, year after year after year...

254

PSALMS 94 & 95
August 25

" *The Sheep of His Hand* "

"Oh come, let us worship and bow down; let us kneel before the Lord,
our Maker! For he is our God, and we are the people of his pasture,
and the sheep of his hand."
(Psalm 95:6-7)

As I read the verses above, I recalled a lesson shared by one of my professors in seminary regarding an experience he had one day while touring Israel. He told us that one afternoon as the tour bus traveled through a rural section of Israel, the group was forced to wait as a gathering of several flocks of sheep blocked the road. At first the professor, as the tour leader, was irritated because this delay could put them behind schedule. However, he did not realize that he was about to experience one of the most important Biblical insights that he would ever gain in his long career of teaching.

Hundreds of sheep clogged the roadway and the professor thought it impossible that these shepherds could ever separate the sheep into their individual flocks. Just then, the professor watched something incredible take place. Each of the shepherds, having ended their joint conversation, began to walk in separate directions, while at the same time humming or singing softly a song. Amazingly, as the shepherds slowly walked away, the sheep in their flocks lifted up their heads and began to follow their own shepherd. The professor told us he knew he was viewing the living illustration of Jesus' words, "My sheep hear my voice, and I know them, and they follow me" (John 10:27). We are truly the people of God's pasture and "the sheep of his hand" (Ps. 95:7).

What an amazing reality for us to meditate upon in our times of worship. We come before the Lord, the Creator and our Maker, but we have nothing to fear for we are the sheep of His hand. Our God's hands flung the stars into space, scooped out the seas, and pushed up the mountains. How mighty are the hands of our Creator! But our God's hands also have another quality; they are scarred. Our Maker's hands bear the marks of His redeeming love. We are God's lambs because He became *The Lamb of God*. Now it is the sheep's turn to sing! The Shepherd will listen.

EPHESIANS 2
August 26

" A Fence Offensive "

Many years ago my next door neighbor decided to build a fence for his yard, so one Saturday he had a few of his friends come over to help him with the project. I certainly had no issues with his plans to build a fence on his property, however it soon became obvious that the construction project was somewhat impacted by the amount of alcoholic beverages consumed as the fence was being built! Without a doubt that was the ugliest (not to mention most crooked) fence I have ever seen! Several years later I was able to purchase the home for my mother and I remember very well the incredible joy that was mine in tearing down that fence!

In our reading today from Ephesians Chapter 2, the Apostle Paul expresses his joy over the destruction of an ugly barrier that has divided people for ages. It is a spiritual wall that has been destroyed by the victory of the Prince of Peace. "For he himself is our peace, who has made us both one and has broken down in his flesh the dividing wall of hostility" (v. 14). Paul has in mind a literal wall that he had seen in the temple of Jerusalem. An ornate stone barrier separated the Court of the Gentiles from the inner courtyards where Jewish people could enter to worship Jehovah. This wall communicated that the Gentiles could worship the Lord, but they would never be His people as were the Jews. Paul's declaration is that the spiritual wall, that the physical wall represented, has been torn down in Christ. The Messiah of God is the Savior of all the people groups of the world, and all who trust in Him become members of the new family He has created.

Through His own blood, Jesus has brought peace and unity. This unity of which Paul speaks is not just a "possibility;" it is the "reality" for every believer in Jesus. In Christ, the walls have been torn down! Our responsibility is to keep tearing down the walls we selfishly and sinfully erect in our minds toward others who are not "like us." Take a few moments to do a "wall inspection" in your heart today. You will find there is a great joy in tearing down an ugly fence!

EPHESIANS 3
August 27

"A Determined Doxology"

*"Now to him who is able to do far more abundantly than all that we
ask or think, according to the power at work within us, to him be
glory in the church and in Christ Jesus throughout all generations,
forever and ever. Amen." (Ephesians 3:20-21)*

It is a regular experience for Paul, in many of his writings, to have his
theology lead him to doxology. As you read Chapters 1-3, you can
almost see Paul pacing the room. The incredible truths about the grace
of God pour from his mouth as he overflows in expressing *what* Christ
has done for us rebel sinners, for whom we now are in Him, and for
whom we have become together in His Body, the church.

If Paul is dictating this letter, you can imagine his scribe trying to
keep up with such a torrent of truth. If, on the other hand, Paul is
writing this letter to the Ephesians *himself*, you can, in your mind's eye,
see Paul's quill scribbling speedily across the sheets of papyrus as the
Holy Spirit fills his mind with the glorious gospel realities that he
shares. As Paul reaches the climactic conclusion of this doctrinal section
of the letter, he seems to break out in praise for the wonder to his own
spirit of the truths he has shared.

There is a great lesson here for every believer as a sincere student of
the Word of God and systematic theology. Our theology should always
lead us to doxology. The *Word* of God is intended to lead us to the
worship of God.

The Bible was not written so that we could only *know the book*.
More importantly, we should come to *know the Author*. Yes, the truths
of Scripture should fill our minds, but the God of the Scripture should
fill our very being and He should be exalted in praise and adoration, in
our personal times of worship, and our collective gatherings as a
church. We do this with a humble, confident faith that our Lord is
ready, willing, and able to do "more than we can ask or think" (v. 20).
That, in us and through us, both now and through the ages, God has
determined to reveal His glory in His people through His Son (v. 21).
Isn't it amazing? In His infinite grace, Our God has chosen, in sinners
like you and me, to display the glory of Jesus to watching angels and
humans. Let the doxology begin!

EPHESIANS 4
August 28

"Unity in Diversity"

Beginning in Chapter 4, Paul makes the transition that is so common in his letters; he moves from the *doctrinal* section to the *practical* section. That is not to say that Biblical doctrine is not personally practical. Indeed, just the opposite is true. Our doctrine must always be practiced, in our duty and our worship, in our walk. "Walk" is the verb that introduces the material Paul will cover in Chapters 4-6. "I, therefore, a prisoner for the Lord, urge you to walk in a manner worthy of the calling to which you have been called" (v. 1). That is Paul's primary challenge; the reality of our calling by Christ should produce a walk worthy of Christ.

This worthy walk is expressed in three primary virtues: a spirit of *humility*, a preservation of *unity,* and a celebration of *diversity*. No one can honestly embrace what Paul has shared in Chapters 1-3 with anything but a profound sense of humility. Who could possibly boast of being spiritually dead, depraved, and disobedient! Our only boast is in the cross of Christ Jesus our Lord. He, by grace alone, has called us to Himself and made us part of His Body, the Church.

Our Lord's unconditional grace is a *unifying* grace. The key word in verses 4-6 is "one." There is one body, one Spirit, one hope, one Lord, one faith, one baptism, and one God and Father. A seven-fold unity binds all believers together. We did not make this unity; only God could do that. However, we are to protect and preserve this unity. It is precious to God because it was purchased by the death of His beloved Son. We are called to walk in unity, but we must also never forget that unity is not uniformity.

Unity means that we are all different, but that those differences do not *divide* us. We are to celebrate those differences because they are not man-made but God-made. "But grace was given to each one of us according to the measure of Christ's gift" (v. 7). All of us have been gifted by the same Giver, but not with the same gifts. A worthy walk means we are following the *same leader*, but not necessarily following the *same path*, and it also means we are okay with that. Let's each remember our Lord's rebuke to Peter: "When Peter saw him, he said to Jesus, 'Lord, what about this man?' Jesus said to him, 'If it is my will that he remain until I come, what is that to you? You follow me!'" (John 21:21-22) Ouch and Amen!

EPHESIANS 5
August 29

"The Terrible 'S' Word"

"Submitting to one another out of reverence for Christ."
(Ephesians 5:21)

I have often said that some Christian men cannot quote John 3:16, but they have memorized, word perfectly, Ephesians 5:22: "Wives submit yourselves to your own husbands, as to the Lord." Some husbands mistakenly believe that the command of the Lord for wives to submit to their husbands is somehow an empowerment of men to command and demand complete obedience from their wives, at all times, in every situation. Clearly, those men do not understand what submission means, and they have also overlooked verse 21 that precedes their "life verse" of verse 22: "Submitting to one another out of reverence for Christ" (v. 21). Paul is describing the expression of the filling of the Spirit to which all believers are called (v. 18).

The *filling* of the Spirit is expressed in the *emptying* of ourselves and placing ourselves *under* others out of reverence for Christ. That is what "submit" means, to "place ourselves under." It is a military term that conveys the idea of "getting in proper rank." What Paul is saying to us is that our Commander-in-Chief wants us to take the same rank on earth that He did while He was here, the rank of a servant. In the army of the Lord, leadership is service. The way up is down. We don't *ascend* into greatness; we *descend* into greatness.

Jesus said that the one who would be a leader must become "as the one who serves" (Luke 22:26). Jesus is not describing slavery; He is describing freedom. The ultimate freedom is freedom from our own selfish, controlling spirit. It is the freedom of the *Lord's* Spirit, the freedom to love. Love does not seek its own interest but the interest of others. When we are filled with the Spirit, we overflow with loving submission to others. That is never "terrible." It is "wonderful!"

EPHESIANS 6
August 30

"Soldiers of Christ, Arise"

John and Charles Wesley were not physically imposing men; in fact, both of these "giants of evangelicalism" and founders of what became the Methodist denomination, were small and delicate. Their father was an Anglican rector. And their mother, who gave birth to them and 13 other brothers and sisters, was a highly educated and devout follower of Jesus. She taught all of them to fear the Lord and seek His ways.

John and Charles were devout men, but they were not converted until, as young adults, they were deeply impacted by the joyful witness of Moravian missionaries. Both of these men, upon their conversion, began to boldly proclaim salvation by a personal faith in Christ alone. Their preaching immediately met with much public attention and also vocal opposition. They were excluded from the Anglican Churches and were even locked out of their father's church. This did not deter their preaching; John actually climbed upon his father's tombstone in the church cemetery and used it as a pulpit to preach the gospel to the gathered crowds!

It was not long until the opposition became physical. Hired thugs and drunken rowdies would often break up the meetings by beating worshipers or hurling stones, garbage, and sewage at the congregation gathered in farm fields or clearings in the woods. The Wesleys knew this opposition was ultimately spiritual in nature, so they constantly exhorted the crowds to courage.

One day after reading Ephesians Chapter 6, Charles was inspired to give the faithful a challenge to be strong in a form that they could not just *hear* but also *sing*. The following words are part of that song, and though written over 275 years ago, they still inspire us with inspired truth. Here are just two of the sixteen stanzas Charles wrote:

> *Soldiers of Christ, arise,*
> *And put your armor on,*
> *Strong in the strength which God supplies*
> *Through His eternal Son.*
> *Strong in the Lord of hosts,*
> *And in His mighty pow'r,*
> *Who in the strength of Jesus trusts*
> *Is more than conqueror.*

Stand then in His great might,
With all His strength endued,
And take, to arm you for the fight,
The panoply of God;
That, having all things done,
And all your conflicts passed
Ye may o'ercome through Christ alone,
And stand entire at last.

("Soldiers of Christ, Arise," by Charles Wesley)

PSALM 96 & PROVERBS 21
August 31

"The Anvil of the Lord"

We seldom hear the sound in our day, but a few generations ago, practically everyone was familiar with the rhythmic singing coming from the shop of the local blacksmith. What hard work, but what amazing skill! Years of experience trained a young man how to heat metal in a blazing furnace and then, carefully and relentlessly, pound the moldable metal into the precise size and shape necessary. This trade is often mistakenly considered to have only been connected to the shoeing of horses, but in reality, an infinite number of necessary daily objects were framed by these master craftsmen.

We can hardly imagine the toll such work must have taken on the arms and joints of these strong men over the years, not to mention their hearing! The beating of the hammer on the anvil would produce a decibel level that could be heard for great distances. It was the ringing of the anvil that caught the attention of John Clifford. The chiming of the anvil sounded to him like the bells in the local church steeple calling people to vesper worship. The image of the beating of the hammer on the anvil reminded Clifford of the relentless hammering of the skeptics over the ages in the assaulting of God's Word. He used the imagery of that analogy to express the truth shared by the wisest man who ever lived, King Solomon, that we see today in Proverbs 21:30, "No wisdom, no understanding, no counsel can avail against the Lord." John Clifford captured the timeless truth beautifully in this poem from the blacksmith's shop.

"The Anvil of God's Word"

Last eve I paused beside the blacksmith's door,
And heard the anvil ring the vesper chime;
Then looking in, I saw upon the floor,
Old hammers, worn with beating years of time.

"How many anvils have you had," said I,
"To wear and batter all these hammers so?"
"Just one," said he, and then with twinkling eye,
"The anvil wears the hammers out, you know."

And so, I thought, the Anvil of God's Word
For ages skeptic blows have beat upon;
Yet, though the noise of falling blows was heard,
The Anvil is unharmed, the hammers gone.

SEPTEMBER

"*Lift up your eyes and see that the fields are white for harvest.*"

PSALMS 97 & 98
September 1

"*Seeds of Light*"

*"Light is sown for the righteous, and joy for the
upright in heart."* (Psalm 97:11)

The Lord has several guiding principles that are taught throughout Scripture. Of these, there is probably none that is shared more often or upheld more fundamentally than the principle of "sowing and reaping." This principle is not only etched, time and again, into the revelation of Scripture, but the Lord has also made it operational to the existence of life itself on earth. The essence of most of the vegetation around the globe exists in its *seeds*. That life reproduces itself as the seeds are scattered and, in some way, "planted" each year. The harvest is in the nature of the seeds that are sown in the planting taking place months before.

The harvest is not accomplished overnight, or even in a short period of time, but it is an axiom of God's laws of nature that the harvest will come in proportion to the *type* of seeds and the *number* of seeds sown in the planting season. This law of God not only guides *biological* life, but it also exists in the guiding principle of *spiritual* life as well, "For whatever one sows, that will he also reap" (Gal. 6:7b).

Our entire lives are, in reality, a season of sowing and reaping. In the ultimate sense, eternity will be the harvest that is produced from our lifetime of planting. "For the one who sows to his own flesh will from the flesh reap corruption, *but the one who sows to the Spirit will from the Spirit reap eternal life*" (Gal. 6:8). Eternity will be the harvest of the seeds sown in this lifetime. It will be heaven or hell, but in that place, the proportion of award of righteous living in Christ, or sinful living in the flesh, will be experienced in the *eternal* harvest.

However, this lifetime is also a season of sowing and reaping, planting and harvest. If we plant negativity and unbelief, we will reap a harvest of darkness and depression. If, on the other hand, we plant seeds of kindness, love, and compassion, then we will experience the harvest described in Psalm 97. We will know the light of joy and the blessing that comes for the righteous. "Light is sown for the righteous, and joy for the upright in heart. Rejoice in the Lord, O you righteous, and give thanks to his holy name" (Ps. 97:11-12). What seeds are you planting?

PHILIPPIANS 1
September 2

" *Worthy of the Gospel* "

"Only let your manner of life be worthy of the gospel of
Christ..." (Philippians 1:27a)

There is an ancient story that is told about the famed Greek conqueror, Alexander the Great. After an extremely fierce battle against the Persians, a young soldier who was accused of cowardice and desertion in the fall of the enemy was brought before Alexander. The soldier who was still in his teens admitted to his failure of duty and pleaded with tears and sobbing for mercy and another opportunity to prove his worthiness in battle.

Alexander was moved by the young soldier's earnest pleading and granted him clemency. As the incredibly relieved soldier walked out of the judgment hall, Alexander called to him, "By the way, young man, what is your name?" The pardoned soldier smiled at his commander and said, "My name is Alexander, sir, just like yours." With the youth's reply, Alexander the Great leaped to his feet and exclaimed, "Soldier, either change your name or change your behavior!"

As believers, regardless of what our given name might be, the name we bear is the name of Christ. In this chapter, Paul challenged the Philippians, and through the inspiration of his words by the Holy Spirit, challenges us today to never forget that. Sadly, the term "Christian" has become practically meaningless in the world today, however, it can never be anything but precious to those of us who recognize whose name it is, the name of our blessed Savior and Master. When the reality of the worth of the name we bear is in our hearts, it is all the motivation we need for a "worthy walk."

It is an amazing thing to think that we serve a God who desires to identify Himself with His people. "I am the God of Abraham, Isaac and of Jacob" (Exod. 3:6). Paul's term "manner of life" in verse 27 of today's Scripture literally means "behave as citizens." When we remember our citizenship, we live in a way that makes worthy descendants of those of our forebearers marked out in Hebrews Chapter 11, "But as it is, they desire a better country, that is, a heavenly one. Therefore God is not ashamed to be called their God, for he has prepared for them a city" (v. 16). Let's walk worthy, brothers and sisters.

PHILIPPIANS 2
September 3

"Our Daily Work Out"

*"Therefore, my beloved, as you have always obeyed, so now, not only
as in my presence but much more in my absence, work out your own
salvation with fear and trembling."* (Philippians 2:12)

Some of you who raised children in the 1990s and early 2000s, or many of you who grew up in that time period will certainly remember the animated characters in the *Veggie Tales* series in television programs, movies, books, music, and every form of marketable items. It seemed like the *Veggie Tales* characters were everywhere. Of course, raising three children in those years, my wife and I became very familiar with all the items associated with the *Veggies Tales* phenomenon (and all the costs)!

We also became quite knowledgeable of the *Veggie Tales* songs. *Very* knowledgeable. It seemed the music played in our house and our cars on an almost continual basis! I have to admit, as hard as I tried not to let it happen, some of the songs sung by those "armless vegetables" got into my mind and played there over and over. I can even remember one of them as I write these words today. It was sung by a group of vegetable sailors known as, "The Pirates Who Don't Do Anything." I used to laugh and sing along with our kids the pirates' theme song: "We are the pirates who don't do anything; we just stay at home and lie around; and if you ask us to do anything, we'll just tell you we don't do anything." I know, pretty sad that after all these years I can write those silly lyrics from memory!

What is truly sad is that many people profess to know Jesus Christ as Master and Savior whose theme song could be, "We are the Christians who don't do anything!" Paul challenged the believers in Philippi and those of all the ages with the deep theology of a very small word, "Work." Paul strongly condemned the false gospel of "faith plus works," but he endorsed, in the strongest way, the importance of possessing and practicing a "faith that works." As believers, we are to be "working out" our salvation because God is "working in" our lives performing *His* salvation. The idea of "Christians who don't do anything" is, in reality, a contradiction in terms and denial of New Testament Christianity. At the very least, it is the theme song of a wasted life. Take some time to reflect your faith today. How is that working for you?

PHILIPPIANS 3
September 4

"The Mathematics of Joy"

"But whatever gain I had, I counted as loss
for the sake of Christ."
(Philippians 3:7)

Both of my parents were incredibly wise people even though they had not been privileged to receive much formal education. My father attended school until he was about 11 years of age, and my mother had to leave school to work on the small family farm and help care for her brothers and sisters when she was about 14. I remember when I was in my late elementary school years asking them individually to help me with my math homework. I was surprised that each of them gave me the same answer, "Oh, that is that new math, and I don't know how to do it the way your teacher wants." So, off I went to find my brother, and he was able to help me figure things out. Now, I never did discover exactly what my parents meant by that "new math." It was clear they were able to arrive at the correct answer, but they did not get there using the formula that was described in my textbook.

In many ways, Paul shares his personal testimony in our reading today in terms of learning a revolutionary new system of mathematics, the "new math" of the gospel of grace. In verses 4-6, he shares how he used to "keep score" using the "old math" of adding up his self-righteousness in a system of *works religion*. However, all of his addition never produced the sum of a clear conscience. Paul's "old math" of law-keeping was replaced by the "new math" of grace when, by the mercy of Christ, he received the free gift of salvation through faith alone. Not only did he stop using the "old math," he threw that textbook into the garbage heap. "Indeed, I count everything as loss for the surpassing worth of knowing Christ Jesus my Lord" (v. 8a). The "new math" of the gospel completely transformed Paul's entire value system.

Following Jesus, as our teacher, means we live by the "new math" of the Kingdom. Yes, sometimes the "homework assignments" can be challenging, and none of us are the "honor students" we would like to be. But the lessons we are learning from our beloved teacher are joy-filled and graduation will truly be out of this world! How are you doing lately with the "new math?"

PHILIPPIANS 4
September 5

"The Grace of Receiving"

*"And my God will supply every need of yours according to
his riches in glory in Christ Jesus."*
(Philippians 4:19)

I am sure most of us are familiar with the statement of Jesus, "It is more blessed to give than to receive" (Acts 20:35b). More importantly, I hope each person, reading these words today, has also experienced the reality of that blessing in his or her own life. It truly is amazing to sense the joy that comes from giving to meet someone's need. I have often thought the experience gives us just a tiny portion of the joy our Lord is constantly experiencing as He meets the spiritual, emotional, financial, and physical needs of multitudes of people around the world every single second.

Generosity truly allows us, as one of my dear friends now in heaven used to say, "To get in on what God is up to." Yes, it is a blessing to give, but it takes more grace to receive.

Have you ever considered that unless we experience the grace of receiving, others cannot express and experience the blessing of giving? This means that at times on our journey with Jesus, He is going to let us experience a season of need in order for us to grow in grace by receiving gifts from others. Our receiving provision for needs will be God's grace to us, and results in a growth in the *grace of humility*. Our receiving from others, will be a gift of joy to those whom the Lord motivates to give. Isn't it wonderful how the Lord uses giving and receiving to share His grace and His joy with all His children?

Paul is expressing this very chain reaction of grace and joy in the final chapter of Philippians. He has *learned* to be content in every situation (v. 11) through a process of being in need, and at other times, in a season of plenty. Each season has allowed him to experience God's grace in special ways. His times of need have brought the joy of giving and the unity of partnership with fellow believers like the Philippians, who have shared with him personally and in his ministry (vv. 16-18). Out of his personal experience, he can assure them that God will meet *their* needs (v. 19).

There are so many lessons for us in this chapter, but perhaps our takeaway today should be what Paul learned. He learned that contentment is not something that is *achieved* in life by what we *earn*, but something that is *received* through what we *learn* in the season of giving and receiving.

COLOSSIANS 1
September 6

"Giving Thanks"

Many years ago as a child, I remember giggling out loud during the pastor's sermon. If my memory serves me well, I also remember that moment of laughter resulting in a firm thump on the back of my head from my mother! However, I couldn't help it because what the preacher said about giving thanks at mealtime struck me as so funny. The pastor, in a crescendo of fervor declared, "Some people are not as thankful as hogs when it comes to gratitude. At least a hog will grunt his thanks to the Lord as he eats his food!" That still makes me chuckle, even if mom didn't understand!

Giving thanks is one of the most important expressions of worship and means of grace that our Lord shares with us in His Word. If you take a few minutes to do a study on "giving thanks" in the Bible, you will be amazed. Offering thanks to God is not just something we should do at mealtime, although that is so significant. Expressing gratitude to God is a crucial expression of worship and also part of our spiritual formation for growing in godliness.

We are not, by nature, a grateful people, even as Christians. That is the reason the Apostle Paul prayed for the Colossians and for all who would read this letter to practice thanksgiving. Note that last phrase, "practice thanksgiving." Giving thanks is a spiritual discipline that needs to be just as much a part of our growth in the Lord as reading the Bible, attending church, or praying. In fact, Paul prayed that *we would pray with thanksgiving*. He even gave us an outline of thanksgiving that we could incorporate in our prayer time. Let's follow his outline in our prayers right now.

1. Give thanks for your *inheritance*: "Giving thanks to the Father, who has qualified you to share in the inheritance of the saints in light" (v. 12).
2. Give thanks for your *deliverance*: "He has delivered us from the domain of darkness and transferred us to the kingdom of his beloved Son" (v. 13).
3. Give thanks for your *forgiveness*: "In whom we have redemption, the forgiveness of sins" (v. 14).

Great job! Now let's keep practicing!

PROVERBS 22
September 7

" *Ancient Landmarks* "

*"Do not move the ancient landmark that your
fathers have set."* (Proverbs 22:28)

One of the first things you will notice when you visit the country of Israel is that it is a land of rocks. There are rocks everywhere; not just the large rock formations of the hills and mountains, but it seems as if the whole land is pushing up rocks to the surface of the ground! In spite of this, it is once again, as in ancient times, a land that is rich and abundant with fields of vegetables, vineyards, and fruit-bearing trees.

In Bible times, to mark the boundaries of these fields, the rocks were collected to make stone walls. At the corners of a family's property, large piles of stones would be erected to mark the portion of the land that the Lord had given as their inheritance in the "promised land." Moving one of these markers was considered a serious offense not only because it was a form of robbery, but it was also a rejection of a decision and boundary that had been revealed by God.

Solomon is probably referring to the application of both these principles in verse 26. He is sharing the wisdom of a warning against treating a neighbor with selfish disrespect for his possessions. Solomon was also instructing that respecting these boundary markers was expressing honor to God in recognizing that the land was not theirs but His. Going beyond the boundaries God had set was going against His will.

These landmarks are not "ancient" and therefore irrelevant, but they are from the "Ancient of Days," God Himself, and therefore always relevant and totally "up to date." The "ancient landmarks" are always trustworthy because they are true, and they are true because they are established by the God of truth. Truth is not established by mankind's opinions and decisions, which are in a constant state of flux. Truth is determined by the only just and unchanging source in the universe, God Himself. The "ancient landmarks" are not interesting relics of a bygone era, they are the eternal boundaries between right and wrong, good and evil, truth and lies. Solomon's wise challenge of 3,000 years ago should be on our minds every day of our lives, "Do not move the ancient landmarks that your fathers have set" (v. 28).

PSALMS 99 & 100
September 8

"*Serve the Lord with Gladness*"

*"Serve the Lord with gladness! Come into His presence
with singing!"* (Psalm 100:2)

Abraham Lincoln is known as one of the greatest, if not *the* greatest, of all the presidents in the history of the United States. He holds that level of esteem, of course, because he almost, single-handedly, held together the union of the states during the darkest, bloodiest days our nation has ever known. Lincoln possessed an amazing gift of verbal eloquence to express the loftiest ideals of the American republic using the simplest of terms. Phrases from his speeches are woven into the very fabric of the symbolism expressed in our nation's flag.

What many people do not know about Lincoln is that in spite of his tendency toward emotional melancholy, he was an avid collector and dispenser of funny stories and witty sayings. One humorous proverb that Lincoln shared often had to do with a person's countenance, "Every man over forty is responsible for his face," he insisted. Now, that might seem unfair, but what Lincoln referred to was the reality that a person's spirit has a way, over time, of etching itself on his face. The modern discovery of "cell memory" lends some scientific support to Lincoln's belief. The issue is not the physiology of facial beauty, but the emotionality and spirituality of it.

There truly is, I believe, a physical impact on the face of a person who is filled with the Spirit of the Lord. We are told in the *Book of Acts* that even in his trial and suffering, the people noted of Steven "that his face was like the face of an angel" (Acts 6:15). The reality of Christ and His presence was displayed on the countenance of that first Christian martyr. Sometimes our faces are going to be etched with lines of pain and sorrow. However, what spirit is *most commonly* expressed in our countenance?

It has been said of some believers that they probably have Jesus in their hearts, but their faces just don't know about it. Gloominess and pessimism have never been good advertisements for the gospel. The psalmist challenges us to serve the Lord with "gladness" not "sadness" (v. 2). The Lord may or may not have blessed you with physical beauty, but *if you are a believer in Jesus, the beautiful Spirit of God is within you.* May our desire and prayer today be, "And let the beauty of the Lord our God be upon us..." (Ps. 90:17a KJV).

COLOSSIANS 2
September 9

" Public Notice "

"And you, who were dead in your trespasses and uncircumcision
of your flesh, God made alive together with him, having forgiven
us all our trespasses, by canceling the record of debt
that stood against us with its legal demands.
This he set aside, nailing it to the cross."
(Colossians 2:13-14)

The first job I ever had, other than mowing yards, was working in a small grocery store just down the road from my high school. It was a good place to work; a number of my friends were employed there as well. Since I lived in a small town, lots of people from the community did their shopping there. That is the reason the "board of shame" above each of the cash registers was so embarrassing, and, I must admit, quite effective. It was known by the employees as the "board of shame" because that is where the owner of the store would staple the checks that were returned from the bank stamped with the words "insufficient funds." As everyone passed through the checkout line, they could see the names on the checks that had been returned.

While bagging their groceries, I used to observe the reactions of people as they saw the names of acquaintances, neighbors, and sometimes relatives tacked up on the "board of shame." I was determined never to have my notice of debt publicly displayed like that. But it did happen and I am forever grateful that it did! In fact, I truly hope you can say the same.

Paul in our reading today tells believers that our record of debt has been posted on the "board of shame." The *record of debt* is the incredibly long list of all our sin debts, and the "board of shame" is the cross of Jesus. However, Paul tells us that written on that record of our debt are not the words "insufficient funds" but rather "paid in full." The nails that pierced the body of Jesus have publicly displayed forever the canceling of all our debts to God, and the record of payment is inscribed with the precious blood of Christ! In Horatio Spafford's song, "It Is Well With My Soul," he writes, "My sin, oh the bliss of this glorious thought! My sin, not in part but the whole, Is nailed to the cross, and I bear it no more, Praise the Lord! Praise the Lord! Oh, my soul!"

COLOSSIANS 3
September 10

"Open House"

In our entire marriage, my wife and I have attended just a handful of open houses for homes on the market, and we have never hosted an open house in selling a home. I consider both of these things to be a gift from God and a blessing to our marriage! I have never really enjoyed attending open houses, and I can't even consider the stress of hosting one. Just imagining preparing for people to visit all the rooms in my home and then allowing total strangers to do it, quite frankly, sends chills through my body. It is one thing to have guests in your house and tell them "make yourselves at home," and quite another thing to actually have them do it! The reality is that our homes do have areas or objects within them that are reserved just for family members.

Privacy does have appropriate applications, but privacy is never helpful when it comes to the Master of our lives, Jesus Christ. The reality is that nothing can be kept from His all-seeing eyes and His all-knowing mind. But more than that, it is not helpful for any of us to attempt to keep things private from our Lord and Savior. Wherever Jesus goes, He brings His blessing with Him. Any door we keep closed to Him is actually to our own loss.

This is the reason Paul tells us in our reading today, "Let the word of Christ dwell in you richly..." (v. 16a). The word the Apostle uses here for "dwell" means literally "to be at home." He is encouraging us to "open all the doors" of our life to the Word of God. Connecting God's Word to every area of our lives is how we do this. It means we do not have any part of our lives in which the door is closed to Jesus.

Trusting His loving intentions, we can experience the joy of His good and perfect will "richly overflowing" into all areas of our life. It not only enriches us but is also priceless to the relationships we share in the body of Christ. When we shut the door to Jesus in our own lives, we also hinder the good influence of His presence in us impacting the lives of those around us. Take a few minutes today in prayerful meditation and reflection to invite Jesus on an "open house tour" of your life. Trust him with every room, closet, container, etc. His free access will truly "bring value" to your home!

COLOSSIANS 4
September 11

"A Door for the Word"

*"At the same time, pray also for us, that God may open to us a door
for the word, to declare the mystery of Christ, on account of which
I am in prison—that I may make it clear, which is how I
ought to speak."* (Colossians 4:3-4)

As Paul closes his letter to the believers in Colossae, he asks them to remember him in prayer. This, in itself, is not surprising, but what *is* amazing, and also very touching, is what he asks his brothers and sisters to bring before God in prayer for him. He asks them to pray for an open door for the Word of God, and for the ability to make the message clear. Typically, we would expect a man sitting in prison to request prayer that his cell door open, but then Paul was not your typical inmate! He knew he was in prison on account of his ministry of sharing the gospel, but he also knew that this prison experience was affording him new ways and new audiences through which he could share the message of God's love.

Prison bars could never hold captive the Word of God. There were the other prisoners to hear of freedom in Christ, there were soldiers to learn of the Captain of the faith, there were condemned criminals who needed to know, like the thief on the cross, that the day of their execution could be their first day in paradise. Also, in prison, there was plenty of time for Paul to pray and think and to correspond with churches and workers around the world. A good portion of the New Testament was written from prison.

Every situation in our lives is an opportunity for the gospel. There are no closed doors through which the Word of God cannot pass. What we think might be our most limiting situation or confining experience, can often be the *most public platform* we have had in witness. The Word of God is spoken, and it is also written, and sometimes the Word of God is lived. Today, whether we witness in words or actions, may we pray that our Savior help us to "make it clear."

1 THESSALONIANS 1
September 12

" *Gospel Echoes* "

"For not only has the word of the Lord sounded forth from you in
Macedonia and Achaia, but your faith in God has gone forth
everywhere, so that we need not say anything."
(1 Thessalonians 1:8)

When we read the first chapter of 1 Thessalonians in conjunction with the account of Paul's ministry in that city recorded in Acts 17, the thanks the Apostle offers for these believers becomes even more significant. From that passage in Acts, we learn that Paul's ministry in Thessalonica was very brief and very turbulent. In fact, the opposition to Paul's ministry caused a riot to break out, with the mob complaining to the city council, "These men who have turned the world upside down have come here also" (Acts 17:6b). Paul's ministry lasted only three weeks before the believers in Thessalonica sneaked him out of the city by night for his own safety.

As much as the message of Paul and his team turned the city "upside down," it also "turned around" the lives of many people as they "turned to God from idols to serve the living and true God" (v. 9b). The work of ministry also "turned up" the volume and impact of the gospel. Paul, writing back to this beloved church, lets them know that the gospel they received has "sounded forth," that means literally "has echoed" from their lives and has been heard all the way to where Paul is currently serving in Achaia.

I am sure the Thessalonians, as they gathered in worship, were amazed to hear this as Paul's letter was read to them. They never thought that what the Lord was doing in their lives, personally, would impact others so drastically. The British writer, John Donne, famously wrote, "No man is an island." By that, he meant in part that each of our lives is connected to other lives. All of us have an influence and impact on others. That is a sobering thought, but it is also an exciting gospel realization. Our words and actions have "sound waves" associated with them. What kind of echo are we sharing? We have heard the gospel many, many times; how clearly and distinctly are we reflecting those "sound waves of life?" Let them ring, brothers and sisters! Let them ring!

1 THESSALONIANS 2
September 13

"How to Make an Impact"

As we noted yesterday, Paul did not have a lengthy ministry in Thessalonica. His time with those first believers lasted no more than three weeks. However, the influence of Paul on these people dramatically changed their lives. It was so significant that people, hundreds of miles away were talking about the radical transformation that had occurred in their conduct.

What was it that Paul and his associates did that produced such results? It would seem that there must be some significant insights into leadership that are shared by Paul as he rehearses what impacted these people so deeply. First of all, Paul's leadership was sacrificial; he and his friends were willing to suffer physical and emotional hardship for the sake of the people. As leaders, they were *givers,* not *takers* (vv. 1-2). Secondly, Paul and his teammates were *humble* in their leadership. They were *gentle* to those whom they served (v. 7). Thirdly, they were *compassionate*; they were *warm-hearted* and *caring* in their interactions with people (v. 8). Then, these servants of God were people of *integrity*. They did not just "tell" others what to do; they "showed them" by example how to live their lives. Finally, these servant leaders were *willing to exhort* and *encourage* people to walk in "a manner worthy of God" (v. 12). They cared enough to "call them out" and to "call them up" to a better and higher way of life. Above all, Paul and his teammates became personal patterns for others to follow. They called people to live as they lived.

These first two chapters in 1 Thessalonians are the greatest manual on leadership ever written; but before it was written, it was lived. Someone has said if you don't *live the example*, then you are not leading; you are just taking a walk. Leadership is serving others. We make the greatest impact on our knees. "Rather, let the greatest among you become as the youngest, and the leader as one who serves" (Luke 22:26b). That is leadership 101.

PSALMS 101 & 102
September 14

" *Unchangeable* "

"Of old you laid the foundation of the earth, and the heavens are the work of your hands. They will perish, but you will remain; they will all wear out like a garment. You will change them like a robe, and they will pass away, but you are the same, and your years have no end." (Psalm 102:25-27)

I have never experienced an earthquake, and I am perfectly fine with that! People who have endured that trauma have told me it is probably the most terrifying experience they have ever had. During an earthquake, all that you have known as fixed and certain for your entire life suddenly isn't. It is one thing to experience the rising and falling sensation when you are on the water in a boat or in the air in a plane; but when the ground beneath your feet rises and falls reality is completely changed. I can imagine that someone who has experienced an earthquake has, to some extent, had their sense of the stability of the earth forever changed.

In some ways, that might be a good thing. We so easily forget that we are all riding a huge rock covered with shifting plates over a molten core and spinning through space over 25,000 miles per hour! That doesn't sound exactly predictable. It can change at any moment, and in fact, it will change drastically.

The psalmist reminds us the foundations of our existence, the earth beneath us and the atmosphere above us, will one day perish and be worn out like a garment; but the one who formed them will never change. "But you are the same, and your years have no end" (Ps. 102:27). God never changes. He is immutable and eternal. He had no beginning and He will have no end. He is, "I Am." This Eternal One has formed us in His image and placed eternity in us.

There never will be a time when we are not. God alone is from everlasting to everlasting, but every human being once given life by Him becomes eternal. So, what should we live for? The only answer that makes any sense at all is to live for what is eternal, the God of eternity, and those who will live for all eternity. The days of this earth are numbered, and our days on this earth are numbered, but our existences continue forever. Let's live today for the Eternal One and for those who will live forever.

PSALMS 103 & 104
September 15

"God's Benefit Plan"

"Bless the Lord, O my soul, and forget not all His benefits, Who
forgives all your iniquity, who heals all your diseases."
(Psalm 103:2-3)

One of the things that concern people most regarding a potential employment opportunity is the benefits package. The hourly pay or salary is, of course, really important; but also very significant are additional benefits like vacation, retirement plan, health insurance, profit sharing, expense account, etc. Sometimes the benefits package is even more important than the basic salary as people consider their decision. In Psalm 103, David is encouraging himself to bless and worship the Lord and "forget not all his benefits" (v. 2). No song or volumes of songs could ever express even a fraction of all the benefits God shares with His people. However, just meditating on two of His benefits listed in verse three is enough to thrill any fainting heart, "Who forgives all your iniquity, who heals all your diseases." Those two benefits encompass all the needs we can possibly have, either spiritually or physically.

Spiritually, He forgives all our iniquity. The wonderful word here is "all"; God forgives *all* our iniquity. Everything we have ever thought, said, or done that was sinful, and all the things *undone* that we should have done; all of these have been forgiven by God for Jesus' sake. Amazing!

Then, all the physical ailments that plague us have been healed. "By his stripes we have been healed" (Isa. 53:5). It might seem that this health benefit is really not true; after all, we do get sick and we do experience physical ailments. However, this is not true for our "retirement." The physical distresses only extend for this temporary earthly body we inhabit, but the "new and improved version" will never experience sickness or pain. Yes, He has healed all our diseases; we will be free from them forever! What a benefit plan we have been given, and we haven't worked for it or earned it! The free gift of God is eternal life through Jesus Christ our Lord (Rom. 6:23). Bless the Lord, O my soul!

1 THESSALONIANS 3
September 16

"*Vicarious Living*"

"For now we live, if you are standing fast in the Lord."
(1 Thessalonians 3:8)

I remember the first time I ever heard the word, "vicarious." As a new Christian I happened to be in attendance at a worship service where a creed was being recited (also a first for me) affirming Christ's "vicarious atonement" for the sins of mankind by His death on the cross. I asked my brother, Lonnie, about the word and he explained to me that "vicarious" meant "on behalf of others." I fell in love with the word from that moment as I understood that it conveyed the self-sacrificing devotion of Jesus toward me a sinner.

After all these years I still love that word, but I have also come to understand that "vicarious" is always an expression of Christian love. We simply cannot know the love of God and have a disinterested attitude in the welfare of others. As believers, love is never just theoretical. Love is a living, pure and powerful force that has been poured out in our hearts by the Holy Spirit (Rom. 5:5). This love not only flows up to its source in God but also out from Him through us to all who are made in His image. It was for this that Paul prayed, "May the Lord make you increase and abound in love for one another and for all..." (v. 12).

Love fulfills all of God's commands, for love is the fulfillment of the Law (1 John 3:23). Someone once asked his pastor if he had to love everyone, to which the pastor replied, "Of course not! You only have to love three kinds of people: those who are like you, those who are not like you, and those who don't like you." Amen, Pastor! Love is not, in its essence, emotional; it is volitional. More than being something we feel; love is something we choose to do. Love does. "Love" is a verbal noun; it communicates action. Love that does not act is a contradiction in terms. Take some time today to evaluate your love life. Is your life really demonstrating vicarious love? If not, you are really not living, for a life only lived for self is really not life at all. "Vicarious"...its a great word for a great life.

1 THESSALONIANS 4
September 17

"No One Left Behind"

"But we do not want you to be uninformed, brothers,
about those who are asleep, that you may not grieve
as others do who have no hope."
(1 Thessalonians 4:13)

One of the commitments that our military personnel and also our first responders make to their brothers and sisters is "no one left behind." That is a promise that expresses the bond of commitment these brave men and women have for one another. They are a team, a unit, a family, and no one will be left behind.

Paul is writing in 1 Thessalonians 4 to make the same pledge to his brothers and sisters in Christ. There was great concern among these first believers in Macedonia that their loved ones who had already died in the faith had missed out on the promises associated with the Lord's return. Paul writes to assure them that nothing could be further from the truth. Paul explains that a special honor awaits those who have passed away, "The dead in Christ will rise first. Then we who are alive, who are left, will be caught up together with them in the clouds to meet the Lord in the air, and so we will always be with the Lord" (vv. 16b-17).

"No one left behind," that is the Lord's promise. The whole family of God is going home! Untold millions that have lived before us will rise at the shout of Jesus and the sounding of the trumpet. Then from all the nations and people groups around the earth, the living believers will be caught up with them. The words "caught up" in the Latin version is "rapturo"; the word "rapture" comes from this. It means to be "snatched up." All this will happen in a "moment," literally in an "atom" of time like the instantaneous reflecting of light on our eyes (1 Cor. 15:52). We will be "out of here" that quickly. We will meet our Lord and Master with "no one left behind." We can only imagine! But it helps us to imagine it and to talk about it with each other. "Therefore encourage one another with these words" (v. 18).

1 THESSALONIANS 5
September 18

"Children of the Light"

"For you are all children of the light, children of the day. We are not of
the night or of the darkness. So then let us not sleep, as others do,
but let us keep awake and be sober."
(1 Thessalonians 5:5-6)

In our reading today, the Apostle Paul continues addressing the topic of the Lord's return. Evidently, the believers in Thessalonica were struggling to understand the promise of the second coming of Jesus with regard to the intense persecution they were experiencing. Is this the great tribulation which Jesus and the prophets and apostles predicted? How would they know when Jesus was about to return? How should they prepare themselves if the time was near?

These questions and no doubt so many others were being asked, and evidently, the different opinions on the subject were causing great confusion in the church. Paul knows the importance of his response to the issues regarding Christ's return; that is one of the reasons he insists that this letter be publicly read. "I put you under oath before the Lord to have this letter read to all the brothers" (v. 27). His answers are just as important and applicable for us today.

Paul reminds believers that we do not need (nor will we receive) special information to determine the times or seasons connected with Christ's return. What we need to focus upon is *how* our Lord will return and *how* we should live in light of His coming. "In light" is exactly how we should determine to live. Our Master will return like a "thief in the night," that is, He is coming unexpectedly. Those who are spiritually sleeping will be unprepared for His coming because they are "children of the night." They will be living in self-deception that they are peacefully secure with no need to be concerned about judgment (vs. 3, 7).

Knowing *how* our Lord will return should motivate us who have experienced the light of His salvation to live as "children of the light, children of the day" (v. 5). He is coming like a thief in the night, so this is no time for sleeping and no time for partying (vv. 6-7); it is time to stay alert and stay focused on serving our Lord. "So then let us not sleep, as others do, but let us keep awake and be sober" (v. 6). Amen.

2 THESSALONIANS 1
September 19

"Relief Is on the Way!"

"God considers it just to repay with affliction those who afflict you,
and to grant relief to you who are afflicted as well as to us, when the
Lord Jesus is revealed from heaven with His mighty angels."
(2 Thessalonians 1:6-7)

Many years ago, there was a popular bumper sticker displayed on many vehicles that proclaimed three words, "Jesus is coming!" Honestly, I saw it on so many cars, trucks, and vans that, as much as I affirmed the truth being communicated, I thought the stickers were becoming ineffective. I probably should not have laughed out loud, but I did one day when I saw a similar bumper sticker that said, "Jesus is coming and boy is He mad!" I know; my wife, Susan, said my attitude was wrong, too! However, the bumper sticker with its shock value did convey a much-needed message.

It is the same Jesus that is coming back to earth, but He is definitely not returning with the same mission. Paul told the Thessalonian believers, and he tells us, that Jesus is coming "in flaming fire, inflicting vengeance on those who do not know God and on those who do not obey the gospel of our Lord Jesus. They will suffer the punishment of eternal destruction, away from the presence of the Lord and from the glory of his might" (vv. 8-9). These are dreadful words indeed and terrible to contemplate, but they do remind us that our merciful and compassionate Jesus is also the Judge of all the world and the God of vengeance. His deliverance of His people will also mean the destruction of His foes.

We can take comfort from these words, but the truth of Christ's return should never make us complacent. Every time we are encouraged in the New Testament about the second coming of Jesus, we are also challenged about how to live in anticipation of His return. The challenge is always the same, *living in anticipation* means *living in sanctification.* "To this end we always pray for you, that our God may make you worthy of his calling and may fulfill every resolve for good and every work of faith by his power, *so that the name of our Lord Jesus be glorified*" (vv. 11-12). Jesus is returning to be glorified on earth one day; and until that day arrives, may we make all of our days on earth now serve for the glory of His name.

2 THESSALONIANS 2
September 20

"Security about His Second Coming"

"We ask you brothers, not to be quickly shaken in mind or alarmed,
either by a spirit or a spoken word, or a letter seeming to be from us,
to the effect that the day of the Lord has come."
(2 Thessalonians 2:1b-2)

Some things never change. Since the days of the apostles, there have been religious frauds who have caused alarm, unrest, and division in the churches through false predictions regarding the Lord's return. In the years of my own ministry, on several occasions, men and women claiming "revelations about Christ's return" have through their books and broadcasts brought concern and confusion to so many young or immature Christians.

These "prophets for profit" are not true messengers of God...ever. In Thessalonica, a barrage of false prophecies regarding the Day of the Lord was being disseminated in letters and messages of teachers claiming a special spirit of revelation (v. 2). Evidently, these teachers were declaring that the Day of the Lord had arrived, and people were to expect Christ's appearing among them very soon. Paul writes this authoritative letter to refute these false teachers and their claims.

Before Christ returns in glory, Paul informs believers that the "man of lawlessness," the antichrist, must first be revealed. This is the final and false Christ that the prophets and Jesus Himself declared would come in the last days, working signs and wonders with the power of Satan (v. 9). He will oppose the God of heaven, even to the point of demanding to be worshiped as God incarnate (v. 4). His deception will be incredibly powerful, and the Lord will allow the deception to seal the doom of those who refuse to believe the truth of God's Word but delight in a religion without rules of righteousness (v. 12).

How can believers possibly overcome this kind of deception? By the sovereign grace of God and the sanctification by His Spirit, God's people are enabled to "stand firm and hold to the traditions that you were taught by us..." (vv. 13-15). No deception or deceiver is more powerful than the wisdom provided by God through His Spirit and His Word. Jesus promised, "You shall know the truth and the truth shall set you free" (John 8:32). The truth that *sets* us free, *keeps* us free. It also keeps us *safe* and *secure*. We need not fear deception or the antichrist when we are devoted to the Word and the Almighty Christ. Stand firm!

PSALMS 105 & 106
September 21

" *Relentless Love* "

*"Nevertheless, He looked upon their distress, when He heard their cry.
For their sake He remembered His covenant and relented according
to the abundance of His steadfast love."*
(Psalm 106:44-45)

Our reading today from Psalms 105 and 106 is an overview of the history of the nation of Israel spanning a timeframe of about 1500 years. Psalm 105 begins as a song of God's sovereign love expressed to Abram when he was a pagan idol worshiper living in the Ur of the Chaldees. The song continues through Psalms 105 and 106 until it reaches the time of Judah's defeat and captivity in Babylon that culminated in 586 BC. These two psalms form an epic, musical narrative of God's relationship with the people of Israel over the centuries.

There are two primary themes that characterize not only the song but also the character of God and His people over the ages—His *faithfulness* and their *faithlessness*. Time and again, the people would cry out under the oppression brought on them by their own sin, and time and again they would cry out to God and He would rescue and restore them. How could God do this to a people so faithless, and how does He still respond this way to us today, as faithless as we so often are? The answer to that is not in His people then or in us now; the answer is in Him. "For He is good, for his steadfast loves endures forever" (Ps. 106:1b).

God is good. He is good in every way. He is good every day. When we are not good, He is. When we are faithless, He is faithful. This is why we as believers have any hope at all. "For I the Lord do not change; therefore you, O children of Jacob, are not consumed" (Mal. 3:6). Yes, we truly are the "children of Jacob," a man as unreliable and shifty as sand. We love the Lord but love ourselves. We trust Him, but we depend on our abilities. We accept His provision but doubt His promises. We wrestle with Him, and we fight our dearest Friend. What can we do? *We* can do nothing. *He* can do anything; even the greatest, most gracious miracle of all...saving us from ourselves.

PSALMS 107 & 108
September 22

" *Tell It* !"

*"Let the redeemed of the Lord say so, whom He has
redeemed from trouble."* (Psalm 107:2)

He would say it every time. *Every time.* Pastor Snavely, whom I served with for nearly seven years in Ohio, loved a testimony service. He would regularly make them a part of the Sunday evening services at Calvary Baptist Church. He always started them and kept them going with the same exhortation, "Let the redeemed of the Lord say so!" He was an intense and devoted follower of Jesus; he talked about the Lord to everyone all the time, and he loved to hear others do the same. Whether it was a sermon, a song or a testimony, Pastor Snavely delighted to hear the praises of the Lord.

It is amazing how much of the Book of Psalms is given over to the same purpose. A huge amount of these songs are testimonials recounting the mighty works of God in the life of the nation of Israel and in the lives of His people individually. The works of the Lord were the oral history of God's greatness and grace recounted from generation to generation for ages before Moses ever recorded a single written word of the first five books of the Bible.

God's Word is the only inspired and infallible expression of God's redemption story. However, each one of us as believers is part of that story and, in fact, are a story of God, "a letter from Christ" (2 Cor. 3:3). The power of God is in His Word in a completely unique way, but His power is also in each of *our stories* as His children. This is the reason we are "witnesses" of Christ. As witnesses, we do not share the story of others; we share what we have personally experienced in Christ, and with Christ I have observed that power so many times.

People usually listen intently when I teach from the Bible, but it is when I share a personal witness that I can actually see many people "lean in" to what I am saying. It is not that my stories have anything like the power or authority of God's Word, but they are *my story, my witness.* How often do you speak the witness of your stories? Take a moment to consider that seriously. What are people, who interact with you, learning about the Lord just from listening to your conversations? Of all the things we can ever share, nothing compares to the significance of our witness. Your life stories have incredible power! Take it from the Psalmist and from Pastor Snavely, "Let the redeemed of the Lord say so!"

2 THESSALONIANS 3
September 23

"Actively Waiting"

*"Now we command you, brothers, in the name of our Lord Jesus
Christ, that you keep away from any brother who is walking in
idleness and not in accord with the tradition
that you received from us."*
(2 Thessalonians 3:6)

Paul was certainly not the person who coined the phrase "an idle mind is the devil's workshop," but he certainly would have agreed with that evaluation. Paul challenges the Christians at Thessalonica to work diligently and also gives them the stern warning directed toward those who were idle. Apparently, there were people teaching that since the Day of the Lord was imminent, believers should just wait for Him and not be distracted by "unspiritual" work. Well, Paul didn't exactly agree with that position! In fact, he challenged them to "change their position" by getting up and getting busy.

Contrary to what some believers seem to think, work was not a result of Adam and Eve's sin and it is not a curse. In fact, we are told that Adam and Eve were to actively care for and oversee the garden where they lived. Even in the life to come in the new heaven and the new earth, we are told that with our glorified bodies we will serve the Lord. Idleness, Paul says, is outside of God's will (v. 6), it should not be encouraged (v. 10), and those who are idle should be admonished and avoided in regard to close fellowship (vs. 6, 14-15). The coming of Christ should never be mistaken for a reason to "retire," but as an incentive to "refire." The promise of Christ's return in Scripture is always a motivation to actively serve Him.

None of us know how many days we have until the Lord comes to us or comes for us, but one thing is certain, we have one less day than we did yesterday. Our spirit should be the same as our Master who recognized the limited amount of time He had to fulfill His Father's will. "We must work the works of him who sent me while it is day; night is coming, when no one can work" (John 9:4). Working hard is the best way we can invest in eternity. "'Blessed are the dead who die in the Lord from now on.' 'Blessed indeed,' says the Spirit, 'that they may rest from their labors, for their deeds follow them'" (Rev. 14:13).

1 TIMOTHY 1
September 24

" *The Wonder Of It All* "

"The saying is trustworthy and deserving of full acceptance, that
Christ Jesus came into the world to save sinners,
of whom I am the foremost."
(1 Timothy 1:15)

Nearly 150 years ago, the internationally renowned evangelist D.L. Moody held a lengthy evangelistic campaign in England, accompanied by his long-time worship leader, Ira Sankey. One day the two of them were afforded an opportunity to visit a gathering of Romanian people, often referred to as gypsies. After the service concluded, Moody and Sankey were preparing to leave when a young mother came running with a small baby in her arms. She lifted up the little boy to Sankey and asked him to pray for her son.

The worship leader sensed in his spirit he should pray a special blessing on the little one. Sankey placed his hand on the baby and called on the Lord Jesus to one day not only save the little boy, but also use him to bring thousands to faith in Jesus. The Lord heard Sankey's prayer, and in time that little baby became a devoted Christian and then a powerful preacher of the gospel. In his long ministry, the evangelist "Gypsy" Smith, as he was called, did see the Lord use him to bring thousands of people to Christ. In fact, it is estimated that he crossed the Atlantic Ocean 47 times in his ministry that spanned nearly 70 years.

On one occasion when "Gypsy" was very advanced in years, a young preacher came to ask his hero, "Gypsy" Smith, to what he attributed the length and fruitfulness of his ministry. The old man was thoughtfully quiet and then with tears streaming from his eyes, he said, "Perhaps it is this; I never lost the wonder of it all." The wonder of God's gracious salvation still moved his heart after all the years.

Paul certainly felt the same way. He considered himself to be the "foremost" of sinners and the most unlikely of converts. His gratitude fueled his praise, "To the King of the ages, immortal, invisible, the only God, be honor and glory forever and ever. Amen" (v. 17). Paul had never "lost the wonder of it all" either. How about you today, my friend? God's grace is amazing, but does His grace toward you still amaze you today?

1 TIMOTHY 2
September 25

"*One For All*"

"For there is one God, and there is one mediator between God and men, the man Christ Jesus." (1 Timothy 2:5)

Many years ago, I had the opportunity to speak to a lady about her personal relationship with Jesus Christ. I remember very well her answer to my question about her confidence in going to heaven after this life. She responded, "Well, I like to think that just like there are many roads to my home in New York City, there are many ways for people to get to heaven." I replied to her, "Yes, you are correct. There are many roads that lead to New York City, but there is only one way that leads to heavens. Jesus said, 'I am the way, the truth and the life and no one comes to the Father except by me'" (John 14:6).

I am not sure if that lady ever came to Christ, but I am thankful I could share with her the only way to *come to heaven* and that is by *coming to Christ*. There are thousands and thousands of religions around the world, but there is only one mediator between the one true God and all mankind, and that is the man Christ Jesus.

The word "mediator" has the idea of an "umpire" or a "go-between" for people who are alienated from each other. Jesus Christ is the one and only mediator between God and mankind, because he is the only one who is fully God *and* fully man. Of all the billions of people who have ever lived on earth, and the innumerable angelic beings, Christ alone can completely bridge the infinite chasm that exists between a holy God and rebel sinners. Jesus is that one bridge because of who He is and what He has done. He alone as the perfect God-Man could be the one to pay the awful price for reconciling an offended God with sinful humanity. Jesus paid the debt of sinners and the payment was Himself. He is the one and only Mediator because He is the Redeemer *and* the Ransom. Is He all those to you today? How blessed to be able to lift this song, by Philip P. Bliss, in praise!

> *"I will sing of my Redeemer, and His wondrous love to me;*
> *On the cruel cross he suffered, From the curse to set me free.*
> *Sing, oh, sing of my Redeemer, With His blood He purchased me;*
> *On the cross he sealed my pardon, Paid the debt, and made me free."*

And all God's people said, "Amen!"

1 TIMOTHY 3
Septembre 26

" The Gospel on Display "

*"I hope to come to you soon, but I am writing these things to you so
that, if I delay, you may know how one ought to behave in the
household of God, which is the church of the living God,
a pillar and buttress of the truth."*
(1 Timothy 3:14-15)

Right belief is always inseparable from right behavior. The theologians say it this way, orthodoxy (right belief) should always be displayed in orthopraxy (right behavior). There is no greater proponent of this union than Apostle Paul. In fact, that is why Paul wrote what we would call "The Pastoral Epistles," 1 and 2 Timothy and Titus, so that his protégés in ministry, and those they were discipling, would understand how essential it is for right beliefs and right behaviors to be maintained in the church.

The reason this is so important is that the local church is a "pillar and buttress of the truth"(v. 15). The "truth" here refers to the revelation of God; it means all the teachings of the Lord and, in particular, the message of the gospel. The local church is "the pillar" and "the buttress" for this truth. As "the buttress," the local church keeps safe and secure the truth against all the lies of the enemy. As "the pillar," the local church upholds the truth to display the gospel in the midst of the dark world.

Humanly speaking then, the local church is the hope of the world. So, do we understand what happens when the "behavior" of the members of the church does not compliment the "beliefs" of the truth? That's right, the truth is undermined in regard to its integrity, and the gospel is overwhelmed in regard to its illumination. The truth is shaken, and the gospel is shuttered. Ultimately, this is a personal responsibility for each believer; for what is a church but a gathering of individual believers? That is why Paul made his challenge personal to Timothy as he instructed him so that "you may know how one ought to behave in the household of God, which is the Church..." (v. 15).

Let's take it personally today. Is the local church, of which you are a member, standing stronger for the truth and shining brighter for the gospel because of you? How strong, how bright would your church be if all the members behaved like you? Yeah, it's a big deal.

" *Get in the Gym!* "

Have you ever wondered how so many large and expensively equipped fitness establishments can possibly afford to stay open? Well, the cost of memberships and the expense of providing services for the active members has much to do with making the business model work. The average monthly fee for a gym membership in the United States is currently around $70, and currently there are about 60 million people in America who hold gym memberships. If you do the math—60 million people at an average of $70 per month—it is quite clear that it is a lucrative market.

However, you must also factor into the business model that 67% of the memberships go unused. That's right, owners of gyms and fitness centers know that, on average, only 33 out of 100 members will actually use their facility. Yes, they bank on the knowledge that their buildings will never be filled with *good intentions*. Good intentions don't make people physically fit, and the same can be said for getting and staying *spiritually fit*.

Paul told Timothy, the young pastor of the church in Ephesus, that bodily exercise would be helpful for him but that *spiritual* exercise was essential. Godliness is a gift of grace, but no believer experiences the fullest personal progress of growing in godliness without determined self-discipline. "Train yourself for godliness" (v. 7b) is a call to committed action to practice the spiritual disciplines that will result in growth in godliness. My experience is that for most believers, this struggle is not one of "mind over matter," but honestly, "mind over mattress!" You have got to get up earlier to spend time with God before the day begins. Also, sleeping in on Sunday is not a sin, but attending "Bedspread Baptist" is never going to provide the consistent fellowship and worship with other believers that every Christian needs for growth in godliness.

Spiritual health, just like physical health, requires a determined "workout" program. "Work out your own salvation with fear and trembling." You are not alone "for it is God who works in you, both to will and to work for his good pleasure" (Phil. 2:12-13). Yes, exercise requires discipline, but the benefits of spiritual exercise are priceless. It is "of value in every way, as it holds promise for the present life and also for the life to come" (1 Tim. 4:8). Let's get moving!

" *Chasing Money* "

"Do not toil to acquire wealth; be discerning enough to desist.
When your eyes light on it, it is gone, for suddenly it sprouts wings,
flying like an eagle toward heaven."
(Proverbs 23:4-5)

I once heard a comedian say, "Yes, it is true that 'money talks,' but all it
has ever said to me is, 'Bye, Bye!'" Many of us may smile at that line, but
sadly it is probably a "knowing smile" of personal experience. Yes, our
money talks, but there is often so little of it that it only whispers!
Solomon knew a lot about money; he was probably the wealthiest man
the world has ever known. However, Solomon was also the wisest of
men, and although he did not say that money talks, he did warn us that
it has the ability to fly away. In verses 4 and 5, he uses the humorous
word picture of someone who becomes fascinated with wealth and
begins chasing it, only to see the "bird of wealth" suddenly sprout wings
and fly away like an eagle.

Solomon is not saying that wealth is, in and of itself, evil or contrary
to God's law. It is clear from reading the Bible that many faithful
servants of the Lord were quite wealthy. It is the *life pursuit* of wealth
that is so dangerous.

Jesus said living for money *disqualifies* a person from being a
disciple. "No one can serve two masters, for either he will hate the one
and love the other, or he will be devoted to the one and despise the
other. You cannot serve God and money" (Matt. 6:24). Jesus did not say
it was *difficult* to serve God and money; He said it was *impossible*. We
have to choose. Also, the Apostle Paul warned that pursuing wealth was
a path of *deception and danger*. "But those who desire to be rich fall
into temptation, into a snare, into many senseless and harmful desires
that plunge people into ruin and destruction. For the love of money is a
root of all kinds of evil..." (1 Tim. 6:9-10a).

Yes, Paul agrees with Solomon that chasing money is foolish, for
while it may sprout wings and fly away, we find ourselves, by chasing it,
plunging over a cliff into ruin and destruction. If money "comes to us"
as we serve the Lord, then we can receive it with gratitude; but if we
"chase after it," then we are not following Him, but pursuing folly and
that never has a happy ending.

PSALMS 110 & 111
September 29

" *Liberty and Security* "

*"He sent redemption to His people; He has commanded His covenant
forever. Holy and awesome is His name!"*
(Psalm 111:9)

To me, one of the most beautiful of the memorials on the Mall in
Washington, D.C., is the Jefferson memorial. It is not as easily
accessible as some of the other monuments, but the walk around the
beautiful tidal basin, to reach the memorial, is part of the enjoyable
experience. The monument is a columned rotunda that resembles
Jefferson's home, Monticello, and also the architecture of the first
building for the University of Virginia, which Jefferson also designed.
Encircling the bronze statue of Jefferson are etched some quotations
from his writings. I remember being particularly struck by one of them:
*"God who gave us life gave us liberty. Can the liberties of a nation be
secured when we have removed a conviction that these liberties are the
gift of God?"*
     God is truly the giver of life and the giver of liberty—physically,
nationally, and spiritually. The ultimate of all these liberties is the
liberty of *spiritual life*. The Psalmist is thinking primarily of the
national liberty that God provided Israel and secured with the covenant
at Mount Sinai. Believers in Jesus have been graced with the incredible
freedom of redemption confirmed through the New Covenant that our
Lord Jesus ratified on Mount Calvary. The people of Israel were
redeemed from the destruction of Egypt by the sacrifice of a lamb. We
have been rescued from the judgment of God on sin and freed from the
slavery of sin by the sacrifice of The Lamb. God "sent redemption" (v. 9)
to us and made us "his people" forever. This relationship is completely
of His gracious work. He initiated it and He will preserve it; in fact, He
"has commanded his covenant forever."
     Our spiritual freedom is secured forever by the commanding word
of all powerful God. Our freedom and liberty will be maintained as long
as God sits on the throne of heaven. Through the circling ages of
eternity, our liberty will be secure, for encircling the throne of eternal
God shines a beautiful rainbow—the symbol of His covenant keeping
love forever and ever (Rev. 4:3). God is the "Author of Liberty" and He
"remembers his covenant forever" (Ps. 111:5). Amen!

1 TIMOTHY 5
September 30

"*Practical Holiness*"

"In the presence of God and of Christ Jesus and of the elect angels
I charge you to keep these rules without prejudging,
doing nothing from partiality."
(1 Timothy 5:21)

One day, a man was showing his friend an amazing machine in his garage. It was a hobby he had been working on for years and had only recently completed. It had dozens of moving parts, whirling gears, and flashing lights. It was truly amazing to his friend as he watched and listened to it for several minutes. Finally, the friend said to the inventor, "This is simply awesome! What does it do?" To which his creative friend replied, "Oh, it doesn't do anything, but isn't it something!" The Church of the Lord should never be like that.

Our God is infinitely creative in His works, but He is also extremely *purposeful*. All of His works are intended to work. The Church is God's supreme creation. We are told it displays His glory on the earth and to the eyes of men, women, and angels. The church is the visible expression of the invisible Kingdom of God. As the song says, "How beautiful is the Body of Christ." Not only is the Church beautiful, it is also to be very practical. There are things God wants the church to do. These things are so important that Paul commanded Timothy (in the presence of God, Christ, and the angels), to see that they were done without prejudice or partiality.

The list includes all commands in this entire letter regarding church gatherings, teaching, leaders, false teachers, widows, relatives, ordination, etc. Now if the church is to do these things, that means that Christians are to do them. A spiritual and practical church is produced by spiritual people who practice their faith. I remember on one occasion walking around our auditorium while I delivered a message on "what our church ought to be doing." I held a large mirror in my hands, as I walked and spoke, so the reflections of the people in the congregation could be seen. I reminded all of us that when we say "our Church should" or "our Church ought to," we first need to look in the mirror, for in looking in the mirror, we are looking at the Church. Selah.

OCTOBER

" *The grass withers, the flower fades,
but the word of our God
will stand forever.* "

1 TIMOTHY 6
October 1

" *Enjoy and Employ* "

"They are to do good, to be rich in good works,
to be generous and ready to share."
(1 Timothy 6:18)

When you think of God's hands, how do you envision them? Perhaps you have never considered that. I know, God as a spiritual being does not have hands; but in order to communicate with us about Himself, God often uses human characteristics to do so. The Bible speaks often of God's hands; so, how do you envision them? Let me be more specific. Do you see God's hands as open or do you see them as clenched fists? Of course, we know that our God is a giving God, but how often do we really trust His generosity and how do we respond to His generosity? Are His hands really open in our thinking, and are our hands truly open in practice?

Recently in our nation, the term the "top 1%" has often been used in reference to policies about enacting tax reform legislation. It is easy for the vast majority of us to imagine what we would do if we were in the top 1%. However, have you ever considered that you might be much closer to that level than you think? You may very well already be in the top 1%. In 2018, any person making more than $32,400 per year was in the top 1%. That's right, 99% of the 7 billion people on this planet make less than $32,400 per year. We need to let that set in for a moment. We are so blessed by the Lord!

Most of us enjoy a lifestyle that the vast majority of the world cannot begin to imagine. In comparison to the multitudes on this planet now and those who have lived before us, we are "the rich in this present age" to whom Paul refers in verse 17. God "richly provides us with everything to enjoy." The way to *enjoy* God's gifts, even more, is to *employ* them for the good of others. "They are to do good, to be rich in good works, to be generous and ready to share" (v. 18). There is no shame in being rich through the blessing of the Lord, but the *greater riches* are in experiencing the joy of the Lord in helping others by sharing God's gifts. God honestly wants us to be "rich and living it" by *enjoying* His gifts and *employing* them for others.

2 TIMOTHY 1
October 2

" *Fan the Flame* "

"I am reminded of your sincere faith, a faith that dwelt first in your grandmother Lois and your mother Eunice and now, I am sure, dwells in you as well. For this reason I remind you to fan into flame the gift of God, which is in you through the laying on of my hands..." (2 Timothy 1:5-6)

I can't possibly remember all the times my dad quoted "that phrase" from the Bible to me. Once my dad became a believer, he also became a devoted reader of the Bible. One day when I was about eleven years old, he came across 2 Timothy 1:5 and noted the phrase "your *mother Eunice* and now, I am sure, dwells in you as well." You see, my mother's name was Eunice and my dad, in his unique way, thought this verse would encourage me to be a "Timothy" in serving the Lord.

I was 42 years old when my dad passed away, and he quoted this phrase to me just a few weeks before he died. It is certainly an incredible blessing from the Lord to have the heritage of faith passed down from parents and grandparents. Whether that is true for you or not, I'm certain you have had people in your life that were used by God, either literally or figuratively, in the blessing of spiritual mentoring and influence. Likewise, for all of us, it is important to be reminded, just as Paul did Timothy, of our spiritual legacy and gifting, to "fan into flame the gift of God" (v. 6).

Timothy had become a "Timid Timothy" because of the great responsibilities and significant opposition that was upon him. The "fire of his faith" seemed to be burning low, and his mood was beginning to shift from optimism to negativity. Paul knew this was not of God, and Timothy needed to know it as well. "For God gave us a spirit not of fear but of power and love and self-control" (v. 7). Persecution, Timothy needed to recognize, was not just a trial to be endured; it was also an honor to be embraced. The only shame would be the shame of fear-filled silence. "Therefore, do not be ashamed of the testimony about our Lord, nor of me his prisoner, but share in suffering for the gospel by the power of God" (v. 8). The key words for Timothy and for us are "the power of God." We have a bright resource greater than any dark opposition that can arise from the world, the flesh, or the devil. The fire in us is from the altar of God Himself. Now fan the flame!

2 TIMOTHY 2
October 3

" *The* 222 *Principle* "

*"And what you have heard from me in the presence of
many witnesses entrust to faithful men, who will
be able to teach others also."*
(2 Timothy 2:2)

I did not believe the math, so I tested it several times. It didn't seem possible, but sure enough, there it was right in front of me on the calculator. You see, I was testing the math of a statement made by a speaker on evangelism. The man shared this scenario: If you were the only Christian in the world, and you won one person to Christ in the next year, then if you and your convert did that each year, and each successive convert did the same, the entire world could be won to Christ in 33 years. Mathematically, that is a demonstration of the power of multiplication. Evangelistically, that is the reality of the power of making disciples.

Of course, I recognize that many will say that the Bible does not teach that believers will ever reach all the people in the world. While that may be true, that does not set aside our responsibility to do *all we can* to share the gospel. It has been well said that the great commission has not failed; it has just never been attempted.

The great commission is not about *making converts*; it is about *making disciples*. Making converts is a process of addition, whereas disciple-making is a process of multiplication. Imagine the impact if every true follower of Jesus would just pray and then work to reproduce himself or herself in one other person in the next two to three years! This is what Paul is challenging Timothy to do, and the Holy Spirit is challenging each of us through the words of Paul to reproduce. It is the challenge of 2 Timothy 2:2, or as I like to call it, the "222 Principle."

The challenge is for each of us to invest the things we have been taught and learned about Christ and the Christian life, into the lives of a few others who will then repeat the process. It is God's way of spiritual reproduction and gospel multiplication. It is the plan of our Lord's Great Commission. It begins in our own families, but it also reaches into our friendships. It works and it has to be done. Disciples are made one person at a time. Who is your disciple?

2 TIMOTHY 3
October 4

"God-Breathed"

*"All Scripture is breathed out by God and profitable for teaching, for
reproof, for correction, and for training in righteousness, that the
man of God may be complete, equipped for every good work."*
(2 Timothy 3:16-17)

The Apostle Paul was seldom at a loss for words; sometimes, however,
the words were at a loss for Paul. The incredible truths that the Lord
gave to Paul sometimes conveyed concepts for which no human
language had yet created the words. When that would happen, Paul
would create a new word to accomplish the task. That is the case in the
verses above. As Paul tried to communicate the divine and living quality
of Scripture, there existed no word to express that concept. So, Paul
created the word "theoneustos," which means "God-breathed" or
"breathed out by God." It means the words of Scripture are God's
words; they do not originate with man. It means that God's words are
eternal; they are forever settled and unchangeable. It means God's
words are *living* words. In them is the life-giving power from God's
Spirit. It means that the words of Scripture are perfect and without
error; they are infallible.

The fact that the words of Scripture are "God-breathed" also means
they are all-sufficient. Everything that is needed to equip a man or
woman, boy or girl, to know the will of God and do the will of God is
contained in the Bible. That is the reason there is no book like *The
Book*. It is the revelation of the mind of God. It is the compass for every
life. It is the food that proceeds out of the mouth of God that alone can
provide for the nourishment of our souls. That is the reason we preach
it, teach it, sing it, pray it, and memorize it. That is the reason we
defend it against all additions or subtractions; for it is perfect and
anything added to it or subtracted from it corrupts it.

We do not judge the Bible; the Bible judges us. We do not conform
it to our lifestyle; we conform our lives to its truth. How precious is the
Word of God! How precious is it to you? Untold millions of people
around the world would give anything to possess even a few chapters in
their own language. May the Lord awaken your soul to the treasure of
His *inspired* Word, and may He awaken your appetite so that, like Job,
you treasure "the words of his mouth more than [your] daily
bread" (Job 23:12).

PROVERBS 24
October 5

"You're Not Home Yet"

Over one hundred years ago, an elderly missionary was returning to the United States after decades of serving the Lord in the continent of Africa. His health had failed through a battle with a dreadful virus that had also taken the life of his beloved wife. She was buried in Africa, where they had labored faithfully through the years, alongside the graves of two of their children who died decades earlier.

As the ship cruised into New York harbor and approached the wharf to dock, the old man heard music playing. Looking below, he saw a large band and an enormous crowd of people holding banners, waving flags, and cheering enthusiastically. The faithful missionary was dumbfounded; he had no idea that his friends were aware of his arrival and that they would assemble such a welcome. The old man took off his hat and waved back to the cheering crowds. That is when he recognized that they were not looking at him. No, this large and joyful celebration of welcome was not for him at all.

It just so happened that on this same vessel, Theodore Roosevelt, former President of The United States, was returning from a hunting expedition in Africa. He was the one receiving the hero's welcome. Slowly the old missionary made his way down the ramp and, as he expected, there was no one on the dock to greet him. Just then, it seemed the Spirit of the Lord brought a much-needed message to His faithful servant's mind. "Cheer up my child; you are not *home* yet."

So often in the Book of Proverbs, we are admonished not to envy the prosperity of people who do not seem to know God. We are reminded again that it is the blessing of God that makes a person rich. We know this in our hearts; however, it is so difficult at times to not find ourselves "envious of the wicked" (v. 19). It is as we take the long view, the eternal view, that things really come into perspective. "For the evil man has no future; the lamp of the wicked will be put out" (v. 20). The future for us is as bright as the promises of God; and if we listen well, we can hear our Father's voice softly saying, "Cheer up my child; you are not *home* yet."

301

" *The Dawn of the Righteous* "

*"Light dawns in the darkness for the upright; He is gracious,
merciful, and righteous." (Psalm 112:4)*

I once heard a preacher say that five of the most blessed words in all the Bible are these, "And it came to pass." We can all smile at those words because we have all been through seasons so difficult that it was an incredible blessing just to have them come to a conclusion. Some people reading this page right now might be taking those five words by faith because this present dark season has lasted so long, and as yet there has been no glimmer of a new day. The *ability to hope* is such a gift from the Lord.

To have hope is not *to wish*; it is so much more than that. *To wish* is to desire something for which there is no objective basis in reality. Unlike a wish, hope is reality. It is simply a reality that has not yet been experienced. Unlike a wish, hope is based on objective truth, the ultimate truth, the promises of God. Hope is the present experience of faith that takes hold of God's promises and delivers them to His people. "Now faith is the substance of things hoped for, the evidence of things not seen" (Heb. 11:1). It is this objective reality, hope, that is experienced by faith.

Hope is the "light" which "dawns in the darkness" for a believer. Ultimately, the light which we have in the deepest trials has its source, not in the "SUN" but the "SON" God's light in His Son has shined and continues to shine in the darkness, and the darkness has not been able to overcome it (John 1:5). By God's gracious salvation, He has shined into our hearts "the light of the knowledge of the glory of God in the face of Jesus Christ" (2 Cor. 4:6). We, who were once darkness ourselves, have become light in Christ (1 Thess. 5:5). This light is so inextinguishable that, even in the darkest seasons, we can overcome it with being "gracious, merciful, and righteous" (Ps. 112:4). Yes, at times we walk in the night seasons, but by God's grace, we don't have to let the darkness reign in us. "Light dawns in the darkness for the upright" (Ps. 112:4).

2 TIMOTHY 4
October 7

"Victor in the Darkness"

From the time I was a small boy, I was fascinated by the stories of the Roman Empire. I am not sure where that interest began, but it was the impetus for reading many books about Rome, taking two years of Latin in high school, and some courses on the history of Rome in college.

When I was young, I used to envision what it would be like to stand in the Colosseum and stroll through the ruins of the famous Roman Forum. After many years of anticipation, I was finally able to do these things and also enjoy them with my wife and several members of our church. It was an amazing experience, but nothing moved me so deeply as visiting a sight not even included in most of the sightseeing tours of Rome. That moment took place as I stooped in the lowest dungeon of the Mamertine Prison located under the small church named San Giuseppe der Falgenamis. It was in this dark, dreary vault that the Apostle Paul, and also perhaps the Apostle Peter, spent their last days. I could imagine the elderly Paul struggling to stay warm while writing his final words recorded in our Scripture section today.

He knows his time is short, so he encourages his son in the faith, Timothy, to come as quickly as he can. Paul has already stood before Emperor Nero and boldly shared with him, and all assembled, the story of his testimony and the message of the gospel. Nero needs scapegoats to cover his thwarted, maniacal plan to burn and then rebuild Rome, and the Christians are easy candidates with their strange teachings and their predictions of a coming judgment on the earth.

Paul has not yet been formally sentenced, but it is a foregone conclusion that he will be executed. Paul writes to Timothy surrounded by darkness, but the light of the Lord shines through the dungeon gloom and into his heart. The glory of God is in him and it flows from his quill as he writes this final epistle. Paul is the victor. Rome has crumbled and is gone; today people name their sons Paul and their dogs Nero. May the Apostle's testimony that day be our own epitaph one day: A Fight well Fought, A Race well Run, A Faith well Kept, A Crown well Won.

TITUS 1
October 8

"It's Not About Me"

"Paul, a servant of God and an apostle of Jesus Christ, for the sake of God's elect and their knowledge of the truth, which accords with godliness." (Titus 1:1)

We are told by the demographic experts that there are currently five generations making their impact felt on American society: "The Silent Generation," those born between 1925-1945; the "Baby Boomers," born between 1946-1964; "Generation X," born between 1965-1984; the "Millennials," born between 1985-2000; and "Generation Z," born in the early 2000s. Where do you fit in these generational descriptions? Perhaps a bigger question might be, "Just who in the world created these definitions?" Is there a significant difference between people born in 1966 and those born in 1964?

The culture and world in which we live is in a constant state of change, but pressing these arbitrary generational markers into making distinctions in people cannot be helpful for us to maintain a Biblical worldview. If we were to give a more scriptural description of all generations, it might be to designate all of them as the "Me Generation." The result of the sin nature, which has been passed from Adam and Eve to all their descendants, is a natural tendency to selfishness. We are guided by an internal GPS that is calibrated and centered on "me." It is through the regeneration of our natures, accomplished by God's grace in salvation, that we are able to re-orient our lives in two correct directions —upward and outward. Through Christ, we become God-oriented and others-oriented.

In Paul's introduction of this letter to Titus, he gives us the vocabulary of a life that is no longer part of the "Me Generation." Paul, which means "little," used to be Saul, which was the name of the "big King of Israel." Notice how this great Jewish leader describes himself—"a servant of God" and an "apostle of Jesus Christ." He considers himself "God's slave" and "Jesus' sent one." He serves God and His Son as a slave, and he serves for the "sake of the faith of God's elect." Paul's life is oriented around God and others. That is the GPS of "love," for love leads us to live for God and live for the sake of others. In effect, love says I'm no longer a part of the "Me Generation," but I'm a born-again member of the "Him and them" generation. Now that is truly a wonderful birthright!

TITUS 2
October 9

"Grace's Classroom"

It is an interesting thing to me when I recall the teachers I had in elementary school that I do not recall a single one of their lesson plans. Of course, it comes as no great surprise that I do not remember their lessons, because I was notorious for not paying attention in class. My report card also tended to reflect that tendency of mine! What I do remember about each of my teachers is this—I remember *them*. I remember their names, their personalities, their faces; I even remember the way they used to dress or wear their hair. I often share this reality when I am encouraging teachers, group leaders, or aspiring pastors. People do not remember much of what we say, but they do remember *us*. Making disciples is more something that is *caught* than *taught*.

In our reading today, Paul uses the analogy of the classroom and the teacher that is part of God's training plan for all of His children. Not only does *every* believer attend this class and learn from this teacher, but *no* believer ever graduates from the course that is being taught. The teacher of the class is "Grace," and the subject matter of the course is "Christian Living." "For the grace of God has appeared, bringing salvation for all people, training us to renounce ungodliness and worldly passions, and to live self-controlled, upright, and godly lives in the present age, waiting for our blessed hope, the appearing of the glory of our great God and Savior Jesus Christ" (Titus 2:11-13).

The image here is that of the grace of God as our teacher. Contrary to the false teaching that was rampant on the Island of Crete where Titus was ministering, and all over the empire, the grace of God was not a license for a life of sin. It was the liberty for a life of *sanctification*. God's grace is a life-long teacher for us, and we are to be life-long students in the school of *Christlikeness*. For that is the goal of our Christian education, to make us more Christlike.

Our teacher, Grace, directs our focused growth in these directions: *outwardly* as we learn to "renounce ungodliness and worldly passions;" *inwardly*, as we learn to live "self-controlled, upright, and godly lives;" and *upwardly*, as we expectantly are "waiting for the blessed hope" of our Lord's return, although we never graduate from Grace's class. It is good to check our progress from time to time. So, let's take a pop quiz today. Ask the "Headmaster" how you are doing in His school. He will let you know.

TITUS 3
October 10

" *Works-aholics* "

"And let our people learn to devote themselves to good works,
so as to help cases of urgent need,
and not be unfruitful."
(Titus 3:14)

I attended a pastor's conference once in which was offered a break-out session led by a very well-known pastor, author, and Christian leader. During the Q&A session that followed his remarks, someone asked him whether he ever repeated any of his sermons. His response was priceless: "Well, I have always believed that a sermon not worth hearing twice, was probably not worth preaching once." Loved it! Of course, continual repetition is not helpful, for it is usually either a sign of amnesia or much more likely, a lazy preacher.

The Apostle Paul certainly did not struggle with either of those issues, however, he did see a repetition of certain themes as vitally important to his listeners or readers. Usually, what he repeated was connected to the specific needs of his audience. In the epistle to Titus, Paul is speaking indirectly to the needs of the Cretans. He is committed in love to addressing their most prevalent spiritual challenge—they are lazy! Even one of their own prophets said so, "Cretans are always liars, evil beasts, lazy gluttons." Paul is quoting from the poet and philosopher, Epimenides, which in and of itself is interesting to note that Paul, a Jewish Rabbi turned Christ-follower, was very aware of the writings of the cultural influencers of his day. But that is a topic for another day.

The main thing Paul sought to address was that the believers in Crete were not to reflect the values of their society, which was one of *self-focused leisure*. These island-culture-believers were to radically re-orient themselves to a life of work—good works. In fact, they were to "devote themselves to good works" (vs. 1, 8, 14). Paul repeats this theme three times in the closing chapter alone and refers to "works" eight times in this brief letter. Paul's instruction is clear to them and to us; we are not saved by grace *plus* works, but we are saved by a *grace that works*. Our good works are the way we "adorn the doctrine of God our Savior" (2:10). Our work for the practical needs of others attracts people to the spiritual message we share. What a great reason to go to work today! A desperately needy world is waiting and watching.

PHILEMON
October 11

"*Charge That to My Account*"

*"If he has wronged you at all, or owes you anything,
charge that to my account."* (Philemon v. 18)

It has been said that the most valuable gifts come in small packages. That proverb is true when it comes to our Scripture reading for today. The Epistle to Philemon is a "small package," only 25 verses, but Philemon is filled with a beautiful and touching appeal from a beloved mentor to his disciple. Also, intertwined with this letter of compassion and appeal, is an amazing, living allegory of the gospel of forgiveness and redemption.

Paul is writing from Rome during the time of his first imprisonment, which is recorded in Acts Chapter 28. His letter will not be mailed but rather hand-delivered by Onesimus to Paul's friend and protégé in Colossae, Philemon. Now, this is where the story is a little awkward, and truly amazing. You see, Onesimus is a runaway slave whose master is Philemon. Evidently, Onesimus had stolen property or money from Philemon and fled, as thousands of runaways often did, to hide among the teeming crowds of Rome.

While in Rome, Onesimus had somehow crossed paths with the Apostle Paul and through Paul's witness had been gloriously converted. As the apostle pieced together the life story of his new disciple, he realized that Onesimus's master, Philemon, was one of his beloved converts as well. As an apostle and a spiritual father to Philemon, Paul could demand that he release Onesimus. However, he uses this event to appeal to a higher motivation and to produce a glorious illustration. Paul even uses Onesimus's name as part of the story. Onesimus means "useful," and Paul says this one who once would have become "useless" to many (v. 11) has now become *very* "useful" through God's gracious salvation. He is, in reality, no longer a "slave" but a "brother" to Philemon (v. 16). He is also Paul's child in the faith so he challenges Philemon to "receive him as you would receive me" (v. 17). In this tiny letter, we see the huge impact of the gospel on all relationships.

The love of Christ flowing into our lives should open our eyes and our hearts toward *all* people. We are *all* former slaves to sin who have been set free by the Lord Jesus. We are now people with only one obligation—to love others (Rom. 13:8). Love is the repayable debt that makes us completely free to treat others as Christ has treated us. He paid our debt, forgave us, and set us free!

PSALMS 114 & 115
October 12

" The Worship Makeover "

*"Those who make them become like them; so do all
who trust in them"* (Psalm 115:8)

It would be hard to determine where and when the first project was recorded, but today there exists an entire field of communication that could be called "renovation media." The examples are endless, but the process is basically the same: buy a run-down property, fix it up, and then flip it, sell it, rent it, love it, leave it, keep it. Well, you get the picture. Now, the reason all these programs exist is because there is great interest in property renovation. It is interesting and truly amazing to watch the transformation of a house take place through insight, investment and yes, hard work.

In Psalm 115, we are told about a transformation that is even more powerful than that which can ever take place to a property—that is the personal transformation accomplished by trust. The psalmist reminds us that people become in character what they trust in spirit. In his song, the writer compares the impact on devotion to idols to the results of trusting in the Lord. Of course, the idols cannot speak, see, hear, feel, or walk (vv. 5-8). But the worship of these senseless and stationary idols is very influential, "those who make them become like them; so do all who trust in them" (v. 8).

This is a startling but enlightening revelation; we become like what we worship. That means the primary focus of our lives will form our lives. That is the reason the psalmists so enthusiastically challenge those who hear this song to trust, fear, and praise the Lord. He is completely worthy of adoration and also doing so produces the most wonderful transformation (vv. 8-18).

Yes, our worship not only honors God, but it also changes us. "And we all, with unveiled face, beholding the glory of the Lord, are being transformed into the same image from one degree of glory to another. For this comes from the Lord who is the Spirit" (2 Cor. 3:18). Worship is ultimately, by faith, "beholding the glory of the Lord"; it is focusing our minds on Him. When we worship, we "are being transformed into the same image"; we are becoming more like Christ. That is the most "extreme makeover" of all, and its value is priceless and eternal.

PSALMS 116, 117 & 118
October 13

" *The Outcast Returns* "

"The stone that the builders rejected
has become the cornerstone."
(Psalm 118:22)

Many of the Psalms are filled with praise, but Psalms 116, 117, and 118 stand out as a unique trilogy of joyful thanks expressed to the Lord. The cause of this worshipful celebration is apparently centered in David's return to Jerusalem after he was forced to flee because of the treachery of his son, Absalom. Truly, David had feared for his own life and those of his loved ones and loyal followers (Ps. 116:3). By God's miraculous intervention and deliverance, David returned to open the "gates of righteousness" (Ps. 118:19) and be like "the stone that the builders rejected has become the cornerstone" (Ps. 118:22). David wrote these lyrics out of his own experience of deliverance, but he also wrote them as a prophet.

For over 1000 years after he composed them, his greater Son, Jesus of Nazareth, would proclaim these words as fulfilled in His rejection, crucifixion, resurrection, and glorification. "Have you not read this Scripture: 'The stone that the builders rejected has become the cornerstone; this was the Lord's doing, and it is marvelous in our eyes'?" (Mark 12:10-11) Also, Peter and Paul, along with the early disciples, would cite this Psalm of David as proof of Messiah's rejection and exaltation.

The gospel is the message of "him who for a little while was made lower than the angels, namely Jesus, crowned with glory and honor because of the suffering of death, so that by the grace of God he might taste death for everyone" (Heb. 2:9). For our Savior, it was first the cross, then the crown and coronation. Jesus' path is ours as well; but as the old gospel song reminds us, "The way of the cross leads home." How wonderful to think of arriving at the New Jerusalem and declaring, "Open to me the gates of righteousness, that I may enter through them and give thanks to the Lord!" (Ps. 118:19) Then, how wonderful to hear the reply to us from within that glorious city, "Blessed is he who comes in the name of the Lord! We bless you from the house of the Lord" (Ps. 118:26).

HEBREWS 1
October 14

" The God Who Speaks "

"Long ago, at many times and in many ways, God spoke to our
fathers by the prophets, but in these last days He has spoken to us
by His Son..." (Hebrews 1:1-2a)

The theologian and philosopher, Francis Schaeffer, made a significant impact on evangelical thinking in the last part of the 20th Century. Especially influential were his books, *The God Who is There* in 1968 and *He is There and He is not Silent* in 1972. The titles of these two books capture the fundamental truths of the Bible, and in particular, the message of the Book of Hebrews—there is a God and this God speaks. By that, the writer of Hebrews wants us to know that God is "knowable." God is there and He is not silent; God speaks. God speaks in creation. "The heavens declare the glory of God, and the sky above proclaims his handiwork" (Ps. 19:1). God speaks in our conscience. "For what can be known about God is plain to them, because God has shown it to them. For his invisible attributes, namely, his eternal power and divine nature, have been clearly perceived..." (Rom. 1:19-20a).

God speaks in the communication of His prophets. "For no prophecy was ever produced by the will of man, but men spoke from God as they were carried along by the Holy Spirit" (2 Pet. 1:21). However, the greatest and clearest message of God about Himself is in the revelation of His Son, Jesus Christ. "He is the radiance of the glory of God and the exact imprint of his nature..." (Heb. 1:3a). All that God has to say to us is summed up in Jesus. He is not just "a word" from God, He is "The Word" of God (John 1:1).

It is so important that we take this truth literally and personally. The only way we can know God and His plan for our lives is through focusing on Jesus: listening to Him and observing Him in the Word of God, and then devotedly following Him as we obey His Words and the promptings of His Spirit. He is here and He is not silent. Jesus' invitation to follow Him and know God through Him is just as sincere today as it was the night He shared it with His disciples, "If anyone loves me, he will keep my word, and my Father will love him, and we will come to him and make our home with him" (John 14:23). God is speaking. If we follow Jesus closely, we can hear what He has to say.

HEBREWS 2
October 15

"Our Sympathetic Savior"

*"For because He himself has suffered when tempted, He is able
to help those who are being tempted."*
(Hebrews 2:18)

We use the word "synonym" to describe two words that have very similar meanings. One example of a synonym could be the words "empathy" and "sympathy." Both of these words have at their root the word "patheo," which means "to feel." Often, these two words are used interchangeably; however, there is a significant difference. The difference is in the distance. When we "empathize" with someone, we can imagine what they are experiencing, and yet we are not actually personally involved. However, when we "sympathize" with someone, it means either we have experienced their situation, or we are personally impacted and sharing.

It's a big difference because it removes the sense of distance. Just think of what it means to our connection with our creator. To have an "empathetic" God means that He is caring and concerned, which is truly wonderful. But to say that we have a "sympathetic" God is amazing and infinitely comforting! It means our God not only *knows us*, but He knows what it means *to be* one of us. The Lord of heaven in His plan to save us determined to become completely like us. "Since therefore the children share in flesh and blood, he himself likewise partook of the same things, that through death he might destroy the one who has the power of death, that is, the devil" (v. 14). This is more than sympathy; this is entering into our very identity.

Our God is not remote and distant; He has so aligned Himself with us in Christ that He calls us "brothers" and "children" (vv. 12-13). When we come to our God in prayer, we need to remember this! He is eternal and infinite, yet He is so personal and intimate. No matter what you may be experiencing in this season of life, not only does God *know* all about it, He *understands*, too. He sympathizes with you. So, go ahead, my friend, cast all your cares upon Him because He cares for you (1 Pet. 5:7).

HEBREWS 3
October 16

" *Today* "

"But exhort one another every day, as long as it is called 'today,' that
none of you may be hardened by the deceitfulness of sin."
(Hebrews 3:13)

Someone has knowingly said, "Today is the tomorrow we worried about yesterday." All of us can understand the humor and insightful wisdom of that statement. Worry truly does rob of us of our present and future at the same time. Jesus challenged his disciples on many occasions not to "be anxious about tomorrow, for tomorrow will be anxious for itself. Sufficient for today is its own trouble" (Matt. 6:34). Jesus said to focus on today, and the writer of Hebrews challenges us to do the same in this chapter. Three times we are challenged about "today" (vs. 7, 13, 15). In each of these challenges, the emphasis is on listening to the Lord with a readiness to respond.

This is what the Israelites, who had been delivered from Egypt, refused to do. They "heard" the voice of the Lord, but they refused to "listen." Each time, this failure to listen is connected to the condition of their "hearts" (vs. 8, 10, 12, 15). They heard with their ears, but they did not obey from their hearts. The result was that their exodus from Egypt became a forty-year funeral procession, and an entire generation did not enter into the promised land—the "rest" that God said He would give them if they were faithful to His covenant.

The writer of Hebrews reaches 1400 years into the past to share, by the Holy Spirit, a challenge for all the ages to the people of God. "Take care, brothers, lest there be in any of you an evil, unbelieving heart, leading you to fall away from the living God. But exhort one another every day, as long as it is called 'today,'..." (vv. 12-13a). *Wilderness wandering* is any journey that takes us "away from the living God." Our experience of "rest" is only experienced in God's presence and following His path through this desert of the world. We can all become disoriented in this wilderness, and that is why we need companions on our journey so we can "exhort one another every day, as long as it is called, 'today,'..." (v. 13). We all need the voices of true friends encouraging us to listen to the wisest and most loving voice of all. Yes, we really need to listen *up*...today.

HEBREWS 4
October 17

" *The Throne of Grace* "

*"Let us then with confidence draw near to the throne of grace,
that we may receive mercy and find grace to help
in time of need." (Hebrews 4:16)*

The throne of God is an awe-inspiring scene. Though none of us has yet seen the throne room of heaven, everything about it is infinitely majestic. We are told that around the throne, the highest of the angels, the Cherubim and Seraphim, constantly exalt and glorify God for His all-surpassing holiness (Isa. 6). Before the throne of God, an innumerable throng of angels and the redeemed souls of the ages worship and praise the Lord (Rev. 5:11-12). In the throne room of God, there is offered up one continual shout of "Glory!" (Ps. 29:9).

It is not a place to be entered casually; in fact, it is not a place that any mere mortal could enter at all and live. Yet, the writer of Hebrews encourages us to draw near to God's throne with bold confidence. How is this possible? It is possible because of the One who is seated on the throne. This throne of God is the throne of the Son (Heb. 1:8), and the Son has a name—Jesus (Heb. 3:1).

The one seated on the throne is our dearest Friend, our Redeemer, Jesus Christ. He is the King of Grace, and His throne is a throne of grace for us as His people. On the throne sits the *glorified* Jesus, but he is still the *same* Jesus. The love that bound Him to the cross for us still binds Him to us as He wears the crown. The scars of His eternal love for us still remain in His hands, His feet, His side. He is grace personified, so His throne is a place of glory and that is what we obtain there, "grace to help in time of need" (v. 16).

I do not know what time of day or night you are reading this page, but I do know what time it is—it is a time of need. What do you need right now? What do you need physically, spiritually, mentally, emotionally, financially, or relationally? Whatever the need, there is grace, His grace that is infinitely greater than any need you might have. John Newton wrote, *"Thou art coming to a King, large petitions with thee bring, for His grace and power are such none can ever ask too much."*

HEBREWS 5
October 18

" The Ultimate Security Clearance "

Until I moved to Knoxville, Tennessee, many years ago, I don't think I had ever heard the term "Q clearance." However, I had not been here very long until I not only was familiar with the term but also was interviewed as a character reference for a person needing a higher level of Q clearance.

Many people who work in fields related to the Department of Energy projects at the nearby Oak Ridge complex require an incredibly rigorous background check before they can have access to classified information connected with national security. They cannot carry out their responsibilities until it has been determined they are qualified to handle such sensitive information.

Our reading in Hebrews Chapter 6 today details the highest security clearance that has ever been required of any human being. In fact, the security of our salvation itself is determined by the passing of this qualification test. Thank God we are not the ones needing to pass the test! Can I get an "Amen" to that? We would definitely fail the test and so also would every other person, because it is the security clearance for the Great High Priest of all mankind. This High Priest must meet the qualifications of both God and mankind. To represent God, He must be *like God*, and to represent mankind, He must be like mankind. In effect, He must *understand* God and understand humanity. Jesus Christ alone meets the "security clearance" for the position of Great High Priest. He knows what it means to *be* God because *He is God*, and He knows what it means to be a human being because *He is a human being*.

To be qualified to represent us to God, our Lord had to endure "on the job training." This means He had to learn human obedience and human suffering. "Although he was a son, he learned obedience through what he suffered" (v. 8). Jesus had to "learn obedience," not because He was ever disobedient, but as a man and our representative, He had to express obedient submission to God the Father and fully identify with us through the suffering due to our sins. Jesus passed the clearance test! He is fully qualified to serve as the perfect High Priest. Take some time today to praise and thank Jesus for what verse 9 shares about the qualification test He passed: "And being made perfect, he became the source of eternal salvation to all who obey him."

PSALM 119
October 19

" *Light for the Darkness* "

"Your word is a lamp to my feet and a light to my path."
(Psalm 119:105)

I do not like being in the dark. Now, let me be specific; it is not being *afraid* of the dark, but more a real dislike of being *in* the dark. There is something deeply unsettling about not knowing where you are and where you are going.

Many years ago as a youth minister in Ohio, following one of our evening outreach events, I had to take several teenagers home. The last young man lived many miles out of town on a farm. I got the student safely home, then started making my way back to the city by way of narrow country roads. It was early fall before the corn had been harvested, so I was literally driving through tunnels of corn, standing thick and higher than my head for acres and acres. That is when it happened. The lights on my car began to dim, the dashboard sensors began to flutter, and the engine began to lurch then stopped altogether. The alternator had gone out. This could not have happened at a worse time because it was a cloudy night without a moon, and it was dark. And this was before cell phones so there was nothing I could do but start walking...or really shuffling, because that was the only way I could stay on a road that I literally could not see.

I shuffled and stumbled along in the dark for what seemed to be a *very* long time until I finally arrived at a crossroad of two country lanes. That is when I saw it. Far off in the distance, a farmhouse had a light shining on the front porch that gave me a sense of direction. I shuffled toward that light, and the closer I came, the more light shined on the gravel road in front of me. I finally made it to the front porch and discovered the home was occupied by a very nice couple with a very mean dog...but that's another story. Since that night, I have never read or heard quoted Psalm 119:105 without a deeper appreciation of the value of a "light to my path" in a time of darkness. That is what God's Word is for us—light in the darkness.

The Bible does not fully illuminate every moment of our lives with a floodlight of complete understanding, but God's Word does keep us headed in the right direction and gives light to take the next step in dark seasons. The key is not just having God's Word *with* you but having it *in* you. The darkest place the Bible illuminates is our own minds. We don't usually stumble because of the darkness of the world but because of the darkness of our mental pathways. God's Word brightens our lives from the inside out. There is no denying that the darkness in us and around us is real, but God's Word is also real and brighter than any darkness!

PSALMS 120 & 121
October 20

" *Look Up* !"

"I lift up my eyes to the hills. From where does my
help come? My help comes from the Lord,
who made heaven and earth."
(Psalm 121:1-2)

Your Bible may include a notation over these two psalms in today's reading that identifies them as "Songs of Ascents." These songs were specifically written to be sung by pilgrims as they made their way toward the temple in Jerusalem to worship Jehovah. In particular, Psalm 121 was written for singing during the final part of the journey to the House of the Lord. If you are familiar with the topography of Jerusalem, you will recall that the City of David was established on Mount Zion, a steep rocky crag surrounded on three sides by deep valleys. So, when people approached the Temple Mount, they were literally making an "ascent" as they came to worship.

The pilgrims would first see the spectacular panorama of the Holy City from one of the surrounding hills, but as they descended into the valleys they would "lift up" their eyes to the hills. Those valleys were incredibly deep-like ravines, and dark shadows would abound there even in the light of day. But as the pilgrims kept walking through those shadows, rising up and shining above them were the gleaming walls and gates of God's Temple. That beautiful sight, as they gazed upward, would remind them of the faithfulness of God and His steadfast love. The one who formed these hills was their Helper. They might be footsore, but He would keep them from falling. It was dark in the valleys, but their God was always wide awake. These mountains and their shadows would remind them that He is their shade of rest and refreshment from the burning sun of long days.

Yes, the valleys could be dark and scary, but as they see the Temple gleaming above them, they would find comfort in knowing that the One who dwells there is their Guardian from all evil. They are worshipers of the God who is always with them so that whether coming from or going to His House, they are never out of His loving presence. Now, that song of ascents is one for the ages! It is a call to us as worshipers this day to, "Look Up!"

HEBREWS 6
October 21

"Standing on the Promises"

"For when God made a promise to Abraham, since He had no one greater by whom to swear, he swore by Himself."
(Hebrews 6:13)

Someone has well said, "A promise is a check written on the bank of a person's character." Just as money deposited in a bank is only as secure as the solvency of that institution, likewise a promise is only as trustworthy as the character of the person who makes the promise. Sadly, a significant portion of our nation's total economy and part of every small business plan has to be allocated to the reality that many people cannot be trusted. But, God can. In fact, when God makes a promise or pledge, His very existence, in a sense, depends upon it.

Our reading tells us today that when God made His promise to Abraham since He could not take an oath on any person or power greater than Himself, He secured His promise by swearing to His own Name (vv. 13-17). The promise made to Abraham was also made to all His descendants. Those promises are inherited by all who are the spiritual descendants of Abraham through faith in Messiah Jesus. So, just as the writer of Hebrews says, for each of us as believers, the promise of God gives us "strong encouragement" and is "a sure and steadfast anchor of the soul that enters into the inner place behind the curtain" (vv. 18-19). This means that all the promises God makes are anchored to the "Rock of Ages," Jesus Christ. You cannot get more secure than that! The absolute security of every promise God makes is the reason that we are able to *stand* in faith and to *move* in confidence.

I once heard a preacher say, "You are not standing on the promises if you are only sitting on the premises." Ouch and amen! The promises of God are the anchor for our soul, but they are also the propeller for our service. God's promises are the engine of our faith that empowers our service for God. Jesus made the promise to His disciples of all the ages that all authority had been given to Him and that He would always be with us, and then He told us to go in His Name and share what He taught us with others. How are you responding to Jesus' promise in your life? Are you "going with the promises" or just "standing on the premises?"

HEBREWS 7
October 22

" *Meeting Melchizedek* "

*"This becomes even more evident when another priest arises in the
likeness of Melchizedek, who has become a priest, not on the basis
of a legal requirement concerning bodily descent,
but by the power of an indestructible life."*
(Hebrews 7:15-16)

There are so many people I look forward to meeting when I get to heaven. Of course, first and foremost, I long to see Jesus. I also look forward to meeting the person who is the focus in our reading today, Melchizedek. We know so little about this unique and shadowy figure. He is only briefly mentioned in the book of Genesis, but he is incredibly huge since the writer of Hebrews cites him as the prototype of the new and eternal priesthood that Jesus Christ has inaugurated.

Melchizedek is unique in that he is both a king and a priest, just like Jesus. Also, there is no record of the beginning of his life or the ending of his life, also like Jesus. He is shown to be even greater than Abraham in status since Abraham paid tithes to him, again, just like Jesus. The main point of the writer of Hebrews in citing Melchizedek is to show that Jesus has established a high priesthood that surpasses and sets aside the priesthood established under the law. Jesus is the King and the High Priest without beginning of days or ending of life. He reigns forever over the Kingdom of God, and He mediates forever for the people of God. Everything established by the Law was imperfect because of the human limitations of those who performed its service. However, because the new priesthood is based on the credentials of Jesus, His priesthood is endlessly perfect.

So, what does that mean for you today? A lot. In fact, it is the confidence of your salvation and that of every person who believes in Jesus. "But he holds his priesthood permanently, because he continues forever. Consequently, he is able to save to the uttermost those who draw near to God through him, since he always lives to make intercession for them" (vv. 24-25). There are many things you may lack in this life, but you *will never* lack a loving King who is your interceding High Priest before the presence of Almighty God. How blessed you are! Me, too!

HEBREWS 8
October 23

"New is Better"

*"But as it is, Christ has obtained a ministry that is as much more
excellent than the old as the covenant he mediates is better,
since it is enacted on better promises."*
(Hebrews 8:6)

Over the last couple of years, my wife and I have been "downsizing" from a much larger home in which we raised our children to a significantly smaller home on the same street. Now, it is just simple mathematics to calculate that all the items collected over the years and brought into a larger home are not going to fit into a smaller one. Simple math maybe, but not simple to do! It is hard to let go of some items because they have so many memories and experiences associated with them. Now, just imagine letting go of something that had been precious to your family and handed down for over 1500 years!

Susan and I did not have to face that kind of decision, but the Jewish believers in Jesus did. Slowly but surely, they began to understand that Jesus, their Messiah, had changed everything. He was not merely an addition to all that they and their ancestors had practiced and cherished for centuries. He had established something completely new. He had inaugurated a New Covenant. What the writer of Hebrews is declaring to them is that it is not only a "new" covenant; it is an infinitely "better" covenant as well.

It was truly "new," but it should not have been "unexpected" because the prophets of the Old Covenant had told them a New Covenant was coming in verses 8-13 of our reading today. The writer quotes extensively from Jeremiah and Isaiah who, hundreds of years earlier, had shared God's promise of a New Covenant. It would be new, and it would be better because it would be *internal*, *personal*, and *eternal*. This is the covenant every believer shares with God.

It is *internal* in that God's words are not written on stone but on our hearts and in our minds. It is *personal* because this covenant relationship is brought to us by a new birth experience by the Holy Spirit that brings us life and binds us to God and to our brothers and sisters in faith. It is *eternal* because there will never be another. It will last as long as the One who made it lives, and Jesus will live forever. Jesus does not just make the old things better; He makes all things new (Rev. 21:5). New is definitely better.

" Take a Good Look "

My father-in-law was an amazing craftsman, especially when it came to woodworking. After his retirement, he turned his garage into a workshop and from that favorite spot, over the next 30 years, came a steady stream of every imaginable type of wood construction project. Cabinets, bookcases, walking sticks, dollhouses, mantelpieces, pulpits (lots of pulpits!), toys, etc., all took shape out of the ingenious mind and strong, steady hands of Dad Bittner.

One time, he presented me with something to keep on my desk in my study. As I unwrapped it, I thought that Dad Bittner was definitely losing his touch, or maybe losing some brain cells. I was looking at a black block of wood that seemed to have several jumbled, lighter pieces of wood glued onto it. I can still recall his sly smile and twinkling eyes in watching my confused expression as I turned it over in my hands. With a chuckle, he said, "Just look at it for a few moments." So, I did just that for several seconds, and to my amazement, the jumbled lighter pieces of wood seemed to magically produce a name right before my eyes —"Jesus."

He laughed in delight at the stunned and amazed expression that came over my face. I still have that curious looking block of wood and treasure it and his memory. I have focused my eyes on it countless times and watched "Jesus" appear.

In our reading today from Hebrews 9, the writer sums up the essence of our faith by reminding us to focus on three "appearings" of Jesus. They are past, present, and future appearings. Jesus "has appeared once for all at the end of the ages to put away sin by the sacrifice of himself" (v. 26). Christ is now appearing "in the presence of God on our behalf" (v. 24). And one day our Lord "will appear a second time, not to deal with sin but to save those who are eagerly waiting for him" (v. 28).

Our faith becomes clear and certain when we *look back* at what Jesus has done, when we *look up* at what Jesus is doing, and when we *look forward* to what Jesus is going to do one day. Yes, Dad Bittner was right; things become much clearer when you focus on Jesus.

HEBREWS 10
October 25

"The Lettuce Challenge"

Maybe you have had this experience—a speaker or teacher shares something in such a strange or eccentric manner that you simply can't forget it. I hope none of the members of our congregation are thinking about any of my messages right now! For nearly forty years, I have rarely read through Hebrews Chapter 10 without recalling what a professor shared during a graduate course in Greek that included translating the book of Hebrews. In his *very* dry, professional humor, he said something like this, "Gentlemen, whenever you teach through this passage, don't forget to pick the lettuce."

My classmates and I exchanged some glances that, "translated," we thought the old-timer was losing it. Then, with the joy of having mystified another class of seminarians, he called our attention to verses 22-24. "Don't forget to share the lettuce," he said. "*Let us* draw near," "*Let us* hold fast," and "*Let us* consider." Yes, I can almost hear you groaning just like we did. Now, see if you can forget it! The professor's humor may have been a little silly, but his exhortation was saturated with wisdom; we don't ever want to forget the "*let us.*"

These three phrases from the writer of Hebrews are the first words of a personal challenge since he began this very lengthy doctrinal section starting in Chapter 6, verse 1. How should we respond to the amazing revelation about God's New Covenant and its privileges, promises, and exalted mediator, Jesus Christ? We should not fall back in fear as the people of Israel did at Mount Sinai, but we should "draw near with full assurance of faith" (v. 22). We should "hold fast the confession of our hope without wavering" (v. 23). We should "consider how to stir up one another to love and good works" (v. 24). The realities of our New Covenant privileges should draw us to worship, strengthen us to stand firm, and compel us to encourage others. The New Covenant is the constitution of our new identity in Christ. It is the charter of our freedoms and responsibilities. The New Covenant is a life to be lived. And as we live it, don't forget "the lettuce."

PSALM 122 & PROVERBS 25
October 26

"*Getting Back or Getting Blessed*?"

"If your enemy is hungry, give him bread to eat, and if he is thirsty, give him water to drink, for you will heap burning coals on his head, and the Lord will reward you." (Proverbs 25:21-22)

The poet Edwin Markham was only a thirteen-year-old boy in Oregon when Abraham Lincoln died in 1865, but the great president's example and character had a huge impact on the young boy that lasted all his life. When Markham was 70 years old, he was honored to personally read his lengthy poem "Lincoln, Man of the People" at the dedication of the Lincoln Memorial in 1922.

One of the qualities that so impacted Markham was the way Lincoln treated his enemies. Lincoln once asked a harsh anti-confederacy critic, "Do I not destroy my enemy when I make him my friend?" Historians have noted that it was Lincoln's gracious and magnanimous treatment of people who opposed him and his policies that made him one of the greatest, if not *the greatest*, of all American Presidents.

Lincoln's wisdom in doing that was like King Solomon's wisdom recorded in verses 21-22, but the practicing of it is grace in action. It is the most natural thing in the world to seek to punish an enemy, but it is the most divine-like thing to respond to an enemy with kindness and love.

We were all once enemies of God and rebels to His gracious rule. Yet, in His great love with which He loved us, He did not just withhold His wrath, but He gave us His grace and mercy. He made us His friends. We are not responsible for the *actions* of our enemies, but we are responsible for *our* reactions. The key part of that last sentence is "actions." Love does not express itself in what we *feel*, but in what we determine *to do* for our enemies. Whether or not our enemies "feel the heat" of a guilty conscience and reconcile with us, we cannot know. But what we can know is the certainty of our Lord's favor and our own freedom. The poet Edwin Markham wrote,

> *"He drew a circle that shut me out –*
> *Heretic, rebel, a thing to flout.*
> *But love and I had the wit to win:*
> *We drew a circle that took him in!"*

" *The Power of His Name* "

*"Our help is in the name of the Lord, who made
heaven and earth."* (Psalm 124:8)

Names in the Bible are very significant. They carry with them important information concerning the events surrounding the birth of the child, or perhaps an expression of the hope or faith of the parents regarding the child. Names were considered to be very important. That is certainly the case when it comes to the names of God. In one sense, no one could ever name God because God is the *uncaused cause* of all creation. No one ever preceded Him because He had no predecessors. God has always been the eternal first. So, the names of God are the qualities He wants to communicate about Himself.

God does this because He wants us to *know* Him. This does not mean to just know a title for Him, but to *know Him in experience.* Our experiences of God become the means by which we truly "know His name." These experiences of God are sometimes known at the physical level, in the events of our life on earth. Some of these experiences of God are those we encounter in the realm of faith. By trust and reliance in Him, we experience the life of His Spirit strengthening our spirit. Either in the spiritual or physical realm, we experience what today's Psalm proclaims, "Our help is in the name of the Lord, who made heaven and earth" (v. 8). Notice, it is the "name" of the Lord that is our "help." Sometimes it is very "helpful" just to meditate on some of the names of the Lord shared with us in Scripture. Take some time now and throughout the day to ponder, pray, and praise these names of our God.

El Shaddai	Lord God Almighty
El Elyon	The Most High God
El Olam	The Everlasting God
Jehovah-Nissi	The Lord My Banner
Jehovah-Raah	The Lord My Shepherd
Jehovah-Rapha	The Lord My Healer
Jehovah-Shammah	The Lord Who is There
Jehovah-Tsidkenu	The Lord My Righteousness
Jehovah-Shalom	The Lord My Peace
Jehovah-Melech	The Lord My King

"The Hall of Faith"

Do you know what happens to a major league baseball player who manages to stay active for fifteen years or so, in spite of the fact that he fails 70% of the time he goes to the batter's box? That's right, they induct him into the Hall of Fame in Cooperstown, New York! How is it possible that someone who fails on his assignment 70% of the time is given such an honor? Because hitting a small, round ball traveling at over 90 miles per hour with a wooden stick is an incredibly difficult thing to do!

The Hall of Fame is not for perfect players, but it does recognize those who were consistent at a very difficult sport for many years. Today, what we have read is often referred to as "The Hall of Faith" of the Bible. Some of the men and women whose names have been inducted here by the Holy Spirit are very famous; some of them not so well known, or not even named at all. However, there is a common bond that unites these very diverse and different people: each one of them, in the face of significant trials and opposition, expressed faithfulness to the God they had never truly seen.

Yes, several of them experienced incredible revelations of His presence and power, but so much of their life responses were based on confidence and conviction that the One who had made promises to them and the things He had promised were real.

"Now faith is the assurance of things hoped for, the conviction of things not seen" (v. 1). Faith is being guided and motivated by an unseen reality. The true reality is not the passing, transient existence of this physical world, but the invisible and eternal substance and value of the Kingdom of God. The people in this chapter are written down as examples for us. Some of them are deeply flawed, just like us. They are honored by God not for the *perfection* of their lives, but for the *direction* of their lives. Their view and their values were consistently upward and forward. They were *worshiping* God, *walking* with God, and *working* for God.

You see, for people of faith, the ultimate reward is God Himself. He is the ultimate reality. May the Lord in His grace help us to live a real-life today, by faith focused on the unseen realities of God and His Kingdom.

" The Lack of Faith "

On Sunday morning, January 6, 1850, one of the worst snowstorms in decades swept over the southern section of England. Because of the terrible weather, most of the houses of worship in Colchester were closed and shuttered. However, one 15-year-old young man, trudging through the drifts and leaning into the wind, was determined to find a place where God's Word was being preached. He did this because a heavy sense of guilt for his sinfulness and despair for his soul filled his thoughts.

While plodding along Artillery Street, the young man heard a few voices singing hymns. He discovered the singing came from a handful of hearty Methodists who had gathered in their small chapel. The weather was so severe that the preacher for the day could not reach the chapel. Finally, an elderly deacon decided to attempt sharing some Scripture and a few devotional thoughts. He took as his text, Isaiah 45:22, "Look to me and be saved, all the ends of the earth! For I am God, and there is no other." After some minutes of exhortation, the eyes of the deacon fixed on the young man with the gloomy face sitting in the back of the chapel. To the young man's amazement, the old deacon spoke directly to him, "Young man, you indeed look miserable. Look, young man! Look now!"

Years later, the great preacher Charles Spurgeon, recalling that moment, said, "Then I had a vision—not a vision to my eyes, but my heart. I saw what a Savior Christ was." That day Charles Spurgeon looked to Christ and lived. His life and history itself were never the same. The old deacon challenged that teenager with the same exhortation as the writer of Hebrews challenges us... "Look!" "Looking to Jesus, the founder and perfecter of our faith, who for the joy that was set before Him endured the cross, despising the shame, and is seated at the right hand of God" (v. 2).

Here we have the clearest expression of the essence of faith. *Faith is looking to Jesus.* Faith is the gaze of the soul on Jesus. Faith is begun by Jesus and built up by Jesus in the lives of those people who are *looking* to Him. The only place we find faith is in looking away from ourselves, our circumstances, and surroundings, and focusing on Jesus. Faith is not confidence we work up; it is a confidence Christ works in us as we focus on Him. Whatever your age, the exhortation of that old, Methodist deacon is still one we need to hear this day, "Look, young man! Look now!"

HEBREWS 13
October 30

"Sacred Sacrifices"

"Do not neglect to do good and to share what you have, for such
sacrifices are pleasing to God." (Hebrews 13:16)

The primary purpose of guiding the writer of Hebrews was to demonstrate, in a systematic fashion, why the New Covenant is better than the Old Covenant. Ultimately, the reason why the New Covenant is so much better is that all the aspects of the symbolic forms and practices of worship in the Old Covenant have found their fulfillment and completion in Christ. Just as Jesus said in His Sermon on the Mount, He did not come to destroy the Law, but to fulfill it—to fulfill all rituals and requirements of the Law in Himself. As Paul declares, "Christ is the end of the law for righteousness to everyone who believes" (Rom. 10:4). The Law, with all of its forms of worship, has been set aside in the finished work of Christ on the cross.

That is why, with His shout of "It is finished!", the tapestry in the Temple, before the Holy of Holies, was torn from top to bottom and flung apart. All that the tapestry represented, the sacrificial system itself, was ended forever. "For by a single offering he has perfected for all time those who are being sanctified" (Heb. 10:14). We no longer have or need a sacrificial system as followers of the Lord.

However, this *does not* mean that there are no longer any sacrifices that are required in our faith. There are no longer sacrifices *for* our salvation, but there are definitely sacrifices to be offered *because of* our salvation. The Apostle Paul pleads in his Epistle to the Romans for our very lives to be offered daily as "living sacrifices" to God (Rom. 12:1).

As the writer of Hebrews closes this letter, he challenges us to be living sacrifices by making offerings to God in two expressions: through giving *praise* to God and through *providing* for others. These "sacrifices are pleasing to God" (v. 16). We are to offer these sacrifices "continually" (v. 15). Praising God and providing for others should be as natural for us as breathing. They should not be limited to a day in the week, but they should be a way of life. Let's take a "selah moment" as we close today. Stop and think about this. When is the last time you talked to the Lord just to praise Him? How often during the day do you praise Him? When did you last meet a need for someone else, financially, emotionally, or physically? It's a new day for New Covenant sacrifices!

JAMES 1
October 31

" *Faith at Work* "

"But be doers of the word, and not hearers only,
deceiving yourselves." (James 1:22)

As a little boy in Sunday School, I can still recall singing a song often in our opening assembly. Although I don't remember all of the words, I do recall one line that captured my attention: "Do you know, O Christian, you're a sermon in shoes." "A sermon in shoes..." The Apostle James would have liked that for he truly believed in and preached the "shoe leather" kind of religion, a faith that is not just talking but also walking.

Years ago, I heard a preacher say, "Your walk talks louder than your talk talks." That is a real tongue twister, but James would have liked that too. James had an amazing testimony. He was the half-brother of Jesus; his biological parents were both Mary and Joseph. Yet, James did not believe that his oldest brother was the Messiah. However, those doubts were shattered when his crucified brother appeared to him after His resurrection. Think of it—James trusted in his earthly brother as his heavenly Lord and Savior!

According to ancient church tradition, James was known by the nickname, *Camel Knees*, because he spent so much time in prayer that the skin over his knees had thickened. Yes, James was serious about his faith, and he called other believers in his day, and us today, to a serious faith. That is the reason from the opening words of his letter he deals with serious subjects: trials, temptations, temper, and the tongue. James calls us as believers to work on and work through these issues. James talks so much about works that the former monk turned reformer, Martin Luther, referred to James as "an epistle of straw." By that, Luther meant that he found James's emphasis on works rather tasteless and hard to digest.

Well, some things that are not tasty are still very nourishing and healthy. James is definitely in the category of the "solid food" of the Word. It is not milk for the unskilled but solid food for the mature (Heb. 5:12-14). James is a short letter, but it should be read with long periods of reflection. As we read his inspired words, James will hold up the mirror of God's Truth before our face. Our reflection may not be perfect, but the mirror is "the perfect law, the law of liberty" (v. 25). It is a mirror of liberty because, after showing us our dirty face, it also shows us the greatest cleanser of all—the precious blood of the Lamb of God, Jesus Christ!

NOVEMBER

"*Give thanks to the Lord,*
for he is good."

JAMES 2
November 1

" The Real Deal "

*"You see that a person is justified by works
and not by faith alone."*
(James 2:24)

It may be that over the centuries of the church, there has been no passage of Scripture more misused or misapplied than James Chapter 2. It has been used as a proof text by many legalists who have seen in it a validation of their teaching that faith alone is not sufficient for personal salvation. These teachers say that James clearly teaches that just faith is not enough. Some authors have gone so far as to say that James and Paul do not share the same message at all. What is the solution to this apparent contradiction about faith and works and the message of Paul and that of James?

Well, the answer is that there is no contradiction because Paul and James are not talking about the same faith. Paul asserts that salvation is by faith alone, but he never teaches that faith remains alone; it always produces good works. "For we are his workmanship, created in Christ Jesus for good works, which God prepared beforehand, that we should walk in them" (Eph. 2:10). James, on the other hand, is denouncing a faith that does not produce works. That kind of faith, he flatly says, is dead; that is, there is no living reality to it. It is just words and nothing more. Paul and James are completely agreed that we are not saved by faith *plus* works, but by a faith *that* works. These works are not legalistic because they are the expression of the "royal law." "If you really fulfill the royal law..., 'You shall love your neighbor as yourself,' you are doing well" (v. 8). James called this the "royal law" because it reigns over all the others and fulfills all the others. The royal law is the law of love.

Every responsibility that we have to God toward our fellow man is contained in those four letters, L-O-V-E. Jesus said love is doing to others what you would want them to do to you (Matt. 7:12). The "golden rule" is the "royal law." It is simple, but it is not easy, because it is all-encompassing. It takes in everyone without partiality (v. 9). Love crosses the man-made boundaries of race, social status, political persuasion, appearance, or gender. Expressing love to others is a big deal; in fact, it demonstrates whether our faith is "the real deal."

PROVERBS 26
November 2

" *The Boasting of Fools* "

"Do you see a man who is wise in his own eyes?
There is more hope for a fool than for him."
(Proverbs 26:12)

Several years ago, a successful businessman sold his company for a huge amount of money and decided to fulfill his dream of owning a large ranch out west. After a lengthy search for just the right property, he finally selected his dream homestead. It was located along a lovely river with an incredible view of the majestic mountains. During the construction of his dream home, the man came across several large stones on his ranch. They were a beautiful light gray color with black lines coursing through them. Immediately, the wealthy man decided the stones would be *perfect* for the construction of the immense fireplace that would be the centerpiece of the sprawling mansion. At the completion of construction, the businessman invited a large number of his friends and business associates to attend a celebration party for his massive home. The highlight of the evening was the lighting of the first logs in the fireplace. The flames roared upward in the beautiful fireplace made of the unique stones, and the gathered guests laughed and applauded to the delight of the wealthy and proud host.

Very soon, however, the laughter turned to gasps and screams as flames erupted all around the fireplace and soon engulfed the house. Days later, the inspectors determined that the cause of the fire was the fireplace itself. Those beautiful black lines in the stones were actually oil deposits, so the material of the construction project *fueled* the destruction of the rich man's dream house. That is a true story; but in reality, it was not the oil deposits in the rocks that destroyed the house. It was the pride deposits in the man's heart.

To the rich or the poor, pride always brings the same results—destruction. Pride is the origin of sin because it was the original sin in the heart of Lucifer who was guided by "I will" rather than "God's will." Whatever we build in life with a spirit of self-will has, within the brick and mortar, the proud fuel of its own destruction. It will burn up one day. Humility does not cause a person to work less or produce little; humility causes us to rely on God and realize that all we accomplish is for His glory and the good of others. That spirit produces things that last forever.

PSALMS 125 & 126
November 3

" *Shouts of Joy* "

*"He who goes out weeping, bearing the seed for sowing, shall come
home with shouts of joy, bringing his sheaves with him."*
(Psalm 126:6)

In the little church, I attended as a boy, two books guided the service—
the King James Bible and the blue-backed Baptist Hymnal. I can still
remember the sound of dozens of those hymn books being pulled out of
their wooden holders on the back of the pews at the same time. Those
dear folks at Immanuel Baptist Church sure loved to sing those hymns
and gospel songs. One of the favorites that we sang often and loudly was
"Bringing in the Sheaves." As a little boy, I enjoyed singing that song
very much.

One day I realized that I didn't know what "the sheaves" were and
why exactly we were singing about "bringing them in." City boy. That
day on the way home in the car, I asked my mom about it. She
explained it was a song about the harvest, gathering the wheat and
winning souls into the kingdom. I don't know if I made the spiritual
connection, but I remember learning a little more about agriculture and
what those tall and bound stacks in the fields were that I had seen in
books. Eventually, I came to recognize that Psalm 126 was the source
for the image in that great gospel song.

These verses have often been used with an application toward
winning people to Jesus Christ. It is a beautiful thought and an
appropriate application. However, the Psalm is a song of praise for
those who have waited long for deliverance for the people of God and
their city of Zion. When God finally brought deliverance, it was like the
rain on the mountains of Judah causing streams to flow in the
wilderness. It is a song of steadfast hope. No matter how long it is
delayed, the Lord will bring deliverance to His people. Like farmers who
have planted their final seeds with tear-stained faces, when the Lord
brings the life-giving rain, those who have toiled with tears shall reap in
joy. They come home in the harvest time with loads of wheat shouting
for their family and friends to rejoice with them. It is a beautiful image.

As you read it today, perhaps you can hear the words of the Apostle
Paul as he challenges us about the great harvest of the resurrection.

*"Therefore, my beloved brothers, be steadfast, immovable, always
abounding in the work of the Lord, knowing that in the Lord your
labor is not in vain." (1 Corinthians 15:58)*

JAMES 3
November 4

"Taming the Tongue"

*"For we all stumble in many ways. And if anyone does not
stumble in what he says, he is a perfect man,
able also to bridle his whole body."*
(James 3:2)

Of all the epistles in the New Testament, James is the one that focuses most on the practice of true religion. For James, faith is not just a *belief system* it is also a *behavior system*. James has no patience for the finer points of orthodoxy if it is not expressed in a relentless orthopraxy. "Practice what you preach" is not a saying coined by James, but he would most definitely respond to it with a hardy "Amen!"

In the chapter we have read today, it is very clear that when James calls us to a faith that is more than just words, he does not want us for a moment to think our words don't matter. This is definitely his goal in this lengthy passage that focuses on "the tongue." He is not challenging us about the small muscle in our mouths but about the thoughts it communicates. James would strongly affirm the insightful epigram, "What is in the well of the heart comes up in the bucket of the mouth." It is our words that reveal the condition of our souls. James was well aware of what his oldest brother said, "...for out of the abundance of the heart his mouth speaks" (Luke 6:45b). For that reason, we need to reflect on our regular conversations in order to conduct a thorough heart inspection.

Our first concern should not be what our words say, but what our words say about us. How often are our tongues used to speak to God in prayer and praise? How often are they employed in speaking for God in sharing His witness or communicating His Word? How often does God's name or the name of Jesus cross our lips? We speak easily about those we love; how naturally do we speak of our Lord?

The Bible says that life and death are in the power of the tongue (Prov. 18:21). So, we need to make a personal commitment to choose life. No one has the power to determine the words that come from our mouth. We alone are responsible for what we say, and we will be judged by the Lord accordingly (v. 1). Perhaps the best use we could make of our tongues is to right now talk to God about them. Our tongues are a small part of our bodies, but they are a big part of our lives.

JAMES 4
November 5

" *Planning or Presumption* "

*"Instead you ought to say, 'If the Lord wills, we will live
and do this or that.'"* (James 4:15)

Although James did not believe that his brother Jesus was the promised Messiah until after the resurrection, it is very clear in reading this epistle that James was quite familiar with his older brother's teachings. There is much in what James writes in his letter that echoes things the Lord taught His disciples.

One of Jesus' most famous stories was the parable of "The Rich Man." The rich man boasted about how well he was doing in his business endeavors and how he would build even bigger warehouses, sit back, and watch the money flow in. But God spoke to this man's pride saying, "Fool! This night your soul is required of you, and the things you have prepared, whose will they be?" (Luke 12:20) It is exactly that kind of greedy presumption that James condemns in verses 13-15 of our chapter today.

A life lived with a God-consciousness recognizes, "you do not know what tomorrow will bring. What is your life? For you are a mist that appears for a little time and then vanishes" (v. 14). The greatest way to fail in planning for your future is to not recognize the uncertainty of life and the certainty of how much we need to submit our plans to God. This true submission goes far beyond tacking on the phrase "Lord willing" to our plans. When James says, "If the Lord wills, we will live and do this or that" (v. 15), he means that our plans are aligned with God's will, that is, making sure our plans are in agreement with the Words of Scripture, the spirit of the Scripture, and affirmed in our hearts by the Holy Spirit Himself. Goal setting is wise and powerful but only when those goals are worthy.

Success is more than the accomplishment of goals; it is the pursuit of *worthy goals*. King Solomon accomplished every goal that he set for himself; but after achieving them, he found they were only "vanity" and "a chasing of the wind." What use is it to fill your life with goals that will never fill your heart? I think a couple of questions would be appropriate for us to consider in light of our reading today. First, what are the significant goals you have in your life right now? Second, have you checked and cleared those goals with God? That would be smart, really smart!

JAMES 5
November 6

"*He is Near*"

"You also, be patient. Establish your hearts, for the
coming of the Lord is at hand." (James 5:8)

The initial recipients of this letter from James were experiencing a season of great trials. Since he addresses the letter "To the twelve tribes in the Dispersion" (Jas. 1:1), it would seem that James is writing to his fellow Jewish believers in Messiah Jesus. They have scattered from the area of Judea because of the persecution that arose against the followers of Jesus after the stoning of the deacon Stephen (Acts 8:1). These believers had fled from persecution into persecution because the Jewish authorities in Jerusalem had made it clear that these "heretics" were to be afforded no acceptance among the community of "the faithful."

No doubt about it; life was hard for these "strangers and pilgrims." Times such as they were experiencing can cause even devoted believers to lose hope in life and especially lose patience with each other. So, how do you encourage and exhort tired and touchy Christians? One primary way—tell them that the Lord is near, very near. The Lord is "at hand" and He is just "at the door." James tells these struggling disciples not to forget *Jesus is coming* and *Jesus is listening*. Christ is the unseen guest at every table and the invisible listener to every conversation. "The Judge is standing at the door" (v. 9b).

Christ said that people would give an account for every idle word (Matt. 12:36), and He is the Judge who is also the court recorder of all that is being said in His presence right now. That is a sobering thought, and James certainly intended it to be taken that way. If our witness to the world is in how we love one another, then grumbling against each other invalidates the power of Christ we profess. Just as strongly as James exhorts and rebukes, he also encourages and reminds... "the Lord is at hand" (v. 8b).

One of the greatest encouragements in hard times is knowing that they won't last forever. These trials of life will pass, and they will pass forever as we pass through the skies to meet our Lord. Yes, we can press on knowing it won't be very long until "He will wipe away every tear from their eyes, and death shall be no more, neither shall there be mourning, nor crying, nor pain anymore, for the former things have passed away" (Rev. 21:4). Maranatha!

"Kept and Guarded"

"An inheritance that is imperishable, undefiled, and unfading, kept in heaven for you, who by God's power are being guarded through faith for a salvation ready to be revealed in the last time."
(1 Peter 1:4-5)

Not long ago I heard an expression that I had not heard in a long time, "safe as the gold in Fort Knox." Of course, that is a reference to the large reserves of gold bullion owned by the United States government and secured in the U.S. Army base at Fort Knox, Kentucky. That expression caused me to begin wondering just how much gold is stored in Fort Knox. Having done a little research, it appears that the latest estimate as I write these words is approximately 148 million ounces. With the price of gold currently at about $1,400 per ounce that means the value of the gold in Fort Knox is... Well, you can do the math. It's a lot of zeroes! I cannot begin to imagine how securely that treasure is guarded!

However, Peter tells us in our reading today that the security of the gold in Fort Knox is nothing compared to the security of our inheritance in Jesus Christ. Not only is our inheritance protected for us, but we are also being guarded for our inheritance. Peter uses two different words to communicate this "double-security." In verse 4, he says our inheritance "has been kept and is still being kept in heaven for you," for that is the sense of the perfect tense verb he uses. Not only is it being kept for us, but it is also being perfectly maintained, "...imperishable, undefiled, and unfading..." (v. 4) As if that were not enough security, Peter then says we are actively being guarded to ensure we will receive our inheritance, and guess who is actively standing guard around us? *God Himself!* (v. 5)

It is impossible to imagine greater security than that which Peter is describing. The idea of one of God's children missing their heavenly inheritance or one of His beloved ones being taken from Him is beyond even the term "impossible." This security has nothing to do with our merit; it is totally based on the mercy and sovereign grace that was given to us through "the foreknowledge of God" (v. 2) before the world began. Yes, we are exiles right now, but we are "elect exiles" who are being guarded and guided home by our Heavenly Father!

1 PETER 2
November 8

" *The Freedom of Servants* "

*"Live as people who are free, not using your freedom as a coverup
for evil, but living as servants of God." (1 Peter 2:16)*

Let's face it; some things are written in the Bible that make no sense at all. Okay, I admit it; that statement did have a little bit of intentional shock value to it! However, there is definitely Biblical support to what I just said. The Lord makes it very clear that the truths of His Kingdom are foolishness to those who are not converted (1 Cor. 2:14). Read the verse cited at the top of this page again. *Live as people who are free by living as servants?* That is the ultimate oxymoron. To the value system of the world, it would go beyond the pale of foolishness and be personally degrading. After all, our freedoms were purchased at the sacrifice of countless brave men and women, and to surrender our personal freedom is to dishonor them.

That makes perfect sense if we are talking about our *civil* liberties. Yes, we treasure them and gratefully acknowledge our debt to those who secured them for us. However, Peter is describing our *spiritual* and *ultimate* liberty as citizens of God's holy nation (v. 9). Our citizenship in His Kingdom was provided for us by His Son, who has purchased us with His blood (1 Pet. 1:19). In doing so, our Lord has made us truly free indeed (Gal. 5:1). There is no greater freedom than being a servant of Jesus. You see, we don't serve Him because we *have to*, but because *we get to*. We are not bound to the Lord by shackles of oppression but with *cords of love*. Love is the greatest freedom of all because "the love of Christ controls us" (2 Cor. 5:14a).

When we do what Jesus says because of love, then we are truly free. This liberty frees us to "Honor everyone. Love the brotherhood. Fear God. Honor the emperor" (v. 17). Honor everyone, even the emperor, Nero. How could they possibly honor that sadistic megalomaniac Nero? Honoring his position, was not the same as honoring his character. The believers in the first century needed to be reminded that civil authorities were sovereignly instituted by God (Rom. 13:1). Recognizing that authority was an expression of respect for God. Nero had no power over the most humble believer. Why? Because they were children of the Lord God Almighty! They were free. Nero was the slave to his own debauchery. As believers in the 21st century, we too are completely free —free to do the will of God and by doing good "put to silence the ignorance of foolish people" (v. 15b).

PSALMS 127 & 128
November 9

"*Sacred Sleep*"

"It is in vain that you rise up early and go late to rest,
eating the bread of anxious toil; for He gives to
His beloved sleep." (Psalm 127:2)

One Sunday morning, just before the worship service began, I was strolling up the aisles of the auditorium welcoming people. To my surprise, and their embarrassment, a couple in the congregation were finding their seats as I approached them, and they were carrying pillows! Well, this provided lots of ammunition for some wonderful banter with them. For the life of me, I can't remember exactly why they had pillows with them. I am certain it had nothing to do with the sermon! Sleeping in service may sometimes be unavoidable (I'm not certain about bringing pillows!), but sometimes sleep is sacred.

Our reading today in Psalm 127 tells us that restful, peaceful sleep is a gift from God (v. 2). There can be many legitimate reasons for us not to get a good night's sleep, but stress, fretting, and worry is not one of them. God has certainly ordained the virtue of work and working to the best of our abilities. But burning ourselves out with no margins for family, friends, and the enjoyment of life is simply not God's will. The Lord wants us to live at a "pace for grace" (Ps. 46:10). The *law* of the Sabbath is not binding on believers in the New Covenant, however, the *principle* of sabbath is not a law, but a gift. Jesus said man was not made for the Sabbath, but the Sabbath was made for man (Mark 2:27). He meant that it was a gift so that rest, reflection, and time with family could be a sacred part of His people's lives.

Sleep is a form of sabbath. It is rest from the toil of the day, but it is also an opportunity to express trust in God's care and watchfulness over His people. "He who keeps Israel neither slumbers nor sleeps" (Ps. 121:4). God is able to accomplish more while we sleep than we could in a lifetime. When we have done our work and done our best, we can leave the results with Him.

I have yet to have anyone tell me at the end of their life they wish they had spent more time at work. However, I have had many people tell me they wish they had spent more time with family and friends and trusted God more with their work. So, don't just stand on God's promises; lie down on them! "In peace I will both lie down and sleep; for you alone, O Lord, make me dwell in safety" (Ps. 4:8).

339

PSALMS 129 & 130
November 10

"Grace that is Greater"

"O Israel, hope in the Lord!
For with the Lord there is steadfast love,
and with Him is plentiful redemption."
(Psalm 130:7)

As one of the Songs of Ascent, Psalm 130 was a hymn sung by people as they approached the temple in Jerusalem. If you could be transported back in time to stand on the steps of Solomon's Temple or Herod's Temple in Jesus' day, you would have heard groups of pilgrims, and individuals as well, singing this psalm as they came to worship. It is a beautiful anthem of contrition and faith. Everything about the magnificent temple reminded the pilgrims of the awesome holiness of the God of Israel and their own awful sinfulness.

Yes, they came to worship, bringing the required sacrifice to offer. But, how could the blood of their bleating goat or sheep possibly be the basis of their pleas for the forgiveness of their sins? It couldn't. They did not deserve God's forgiveness, and they certainly could not earn it. Yet, it was to this Sovereign God, Maker of heaven and earth, that they must be reconciled, or they would most certainly perish. If they were to be forgiven, it was only on the basis of His "steadfast love" and "plentiful redemption" (v. 7).

"Steadfast love" in Hebrew is the equivalent of the Greek word for "grace" in the New Testament. There has always been only one basis for the forgiveness of sin, and that is God's unmerited, undeserved love. Paul spoke the gospel truth for all the ages when he said, "for it is by grace that you have been saved" (Eph. 2:8). Yes, God's marvelous, infinite, matchless grace has always been the basis of the plea and the praise of the people of God.

> Marvelous grace of our loving Lord,
> Grace that exceeds our sin and our guilt,
> Yonder on Calvary's mount outpoured
> There where the blood of the Lamb was split.

Continued...

340

Dark is the stain that we cannot hide,
What can avail to wash it away?
Look! There is flowing a crimson tide;
Whiter than snow you may be today.

Marvelous, infinite, matchless grace
Freely bestowed on all who believe;
You that are longing to see His face,
Will you this moment His grace receive?

Grace, grace, God's grace,
Grace that will pardon and cleanse within;
Grace, grace, God's grace
Grace that is greater than all our sin.

*("Grace Greater Than Our Sin," written by
Julia H. Johnston)*

1 PETER 3
November 11

" *Good Answer, Good Attitude* "

"Always being prepared to make a defense to anyone who asks you for a reason for the hope that is in you; yet do it with gentleness and respect, having a good conscience..."
(1 Peter 3:15b, 16a)

Sometimes it is almost humorous to listen to people detail why they base their lives on "reason and science" and not on "blind faith." After hearing those people explain how the universe was created and on what basis this infinitely complex world is sustained, I often come away thinking they have more faith than I do! Human reason can never comprehend fully the issues of faith; however, our Christian faith is reasonable. The advances of science and the discoveries of antiquity only continue to verify the reliability of God's Word. There is no contradiction between being a complete realist and a real Christian.

Peter encourages us in our reading today to "be prepared to make a defense to anyone who asks for a reason" for the basis of our hope in Christ. You may be aware that the word for "defense" is "apologian," from which we derive the term "apologetics," meaning the defense of the Scriptures and the faith. It has the idea of being able to share *what* you believe and *why* you believe. However, we must be certain we don't attempt to defend the faith by being offensive. We are to share the reasons for our faith with "gentleness and respect."

Expressing a *right doctrinal position* with a *wrong personal disposition* is never a good witness. It has been well said that only the devil wins an argument over religion. Witnessing is not debating. We must make it our aim to both *live* the gospel as well as *give* the gospel. Paul challenges us, in a crooked and perverse world, to shine as lights for Christ (Phil. 2:15). As believers, we must practice "show and tell"; we "show" the gospel to people in the way we live and how we relate to them and then we "tell" them the good news of salvation in Jesus. It is the gospel, not our presentation or persuasiveness that is "the power of God to salvation" (Rom. 1:16).

The message of Jesus has within it the "inherent power" to save lost souls. We can till the soil in someone's heart with our thoughtful explanation and our gentle disposition, but it is only the life-giving seed of the Word of God that can bring salvation (1 Pet. 1:23). *Know* the Word. *Show* the Word. *Sow* the Word. Amen.

1 PETER 4
November 12

" *Lose Your Gift* "

"As each has received a gift, use it to serve one another, as good stewards of God's varied grace." (1 Peter 4:10)

I loved it. At a recent mission board meeting, I was privileged to hear the testimony of a couple giving their final report as they retired from serving for 42 years, sharing the gospel with isolated tribal people in New Guinea. Their report of what the Lord had accomplished was amazing, but what nearly caused me to laugh out loud was when the wife shared the results of a "spiritual gifts test" she had taken before they were commissioned as missionaries. The test revealed that she had no spiritual gifts! What irony! Over four decades of incredible, fruitful service for the Lord, yet without any discernible spiritual gifts. Thank the Lord the dear lady trusted the Holy Spirit and not a spiritual gift test!

I hope no one has trusted in the spiritual gifts test that I used to administer years ago. Perhaps they have had value to some people; but I have come to recognize, from my experience, they were not helpful for most people. What I have come to understand is that a *spiritual gift* is the expression of the *spiritual gift—the gift of the Holy Spirit*. A spiritual gift is "the manifestation of the Spirit" (1 Cor. 12:7). It is a "gift of grace," a "charismata" (1 Cor. 12:1). It is absolutely clear of Christians that "each has received a gift" (v. 10), but the expression of this gift and the understanding of this gift is in serving one another (v. 10).

The best way to discern our spiritual gift is not in getting to know *ourselves*, but in getting busy *serving others*. Our gifts are *from Him* and *for them*. That missionary couple 42 years ago had very little training and no obvious "gifting," but what they did have were surrendered hearts and servant-like spirits. Today, there are countless souls in New Guinea, and from New Guinea now in heaven, who would say that their lives were a priceless gift to them. *You see, our spiritual gifts aren't gifts at all until we lose them by giving them away.* "Freely you have received, freely give" (Matt. 10:8).

1 PETER 5
November 13

"A Humble Wardrobe"

*"Clothe yourselves, all of you, with humility toward one another, for
'God opposes the proud but gives grace to the humble.'"*
(1 Peter 5:5b)

Peter talks a great deal about humility in his epistles. No doubt, that is because the "Big Fisherman" had learned that *self-confidence* was not compatible with *God-reliance*. Too many times, he had spoken those contradictory words to his Master, "Not so, Lord." He found out very powerfully that he could not lead and follow Jesus at the same time. That is the reason Peter did not want other believers to make his mistakes. He knew just how essential humility is to faithfully and effectively serve Christ. He also knew how evasive humility can be. Humility is the quality that just when you are certain you have acquired it, you have lost it.

Our hearts are so deceitful, we can become proud of how humble we are! So, if that is the case, how do we pursue humility as the Lord has instructed us? The answer is, we become humble by *doing* humble things. Notice, Peter challenges us to "clothe yourselves, all of you, with humility..." (v. 5). Humility is not something that is "worked up" with prayer and meditation; it is "put on" with decision and determination.

Very probably, as Peter instructed us to clothe ourselves with humility, he was remembering the scene in the upper room where Jesus rose, took off his robe and wrapped a towel around His waist in order to wash the disciples' feet. Could he ever erase from his memory the One he had confessed as "the Christ, the Son of the living God," kneeling at his feet as a servant with a basin and a towel? Jesus was not *acting* like a servant; He *was* a servant. Jesus became a servant so that we might become the sons and daughters of God.

Jesus *was* meek and humble. He *did* humble things. Humbling ourselves in surrendered service is where we experience the favor of God. The virgin Mary sang in her Magnificat that the Lord "lifts up the humble" (Luke 1:52). James promised that if we humble ourselves in the presence of God, He will lift us up (Jas. 4:10). Peter says in verse 6 that if we humbly put ourselves under God's hand, that same mighty hand will, at the proper time, exalt us. The virtue of humility is hanging in every believer's closet. May the Lord give us the grace to put it on each day.

2 PETER 1
November 14

" *Absolutely Certain!* "

"And we have the prophetic word more fully confirmed, to which you will do well to pay attention as to a lamp shining in a dark place, until the day dawns and the morning star rises in your hearts."
(2 Peter 1:19)

The most compelling evidence that can be entered into a court case is that of eyewitnesses—people who, under oath and subject to the charge of perjury if they lie, bear witness to what they saw and/or heard. Peter declares that he is exactly that kind of witness. 2 Peter is the personal testimony of the leader of Jesus' disciples against the false testimony that is being spread within the Church by heretical teachers. As it is with almost all false forms of Christianity, the attack is being made against the truth of the Divine nature of Jesus.

Peter denounces this heresy by affirming that he and James and John were "eyewitnesses of his majesty" on the Mount of Transfiguration, one of the greatest divine revelations in human history. They heard the voice of God the Father bearing testimony to his beloved Son (vv. 16-17) That is a very compelling witness from Peter! But if we are not careful, we can fail to recognize the significance of Peter's astounding assertion. He tells us that we have an even more trustworthy witness. What can possibly be more certain than Peter's incredible experience? Let him tell us: "the prophetic word" and "the prophecy of Scripture" (vv. 19-20). Now, that is truly astounding and so comforting. Peter says that his ultimate confidence, and ours as well, is not based on *personal* experience but on the *Word of God*. The reason for this confidence is that the Scriptures were not "produced by the will of man, but men of God spoke from God as they were carried along by the Holy Spirit" (v. 21).

Peter tells us that we have two all-sufficient resources to provide us with everything we need in order to know the Lord, serve the Lord, and know His will. We have *His Divine nature inside of us* and we have *His Divine Word in front of us* (vs. 4, 19). No child of God is deficient for whatever He desires him or her to be or do. Certainly, we are not sufficient for the challenges of a single day, "but our sufficiency is of Christ" (2 Corinthians 3:5). What a gracious God we serve! "His divine power has granted to us all things that pertain to life and godliness, through the knowledge of him who called us to his own glory and excellence" (v. 3).

" Spared Not "

*"Then the Lord knows how to rescue the godly from trials,
and to keep the unrighteousness under punishment
until the day of judgment." (2 Peter 2:9)*

On many occasions, I have heard people who profess to be Christians say that they don't believe in a God of fire, judgment, and damnation. I have often wondered just what Bible they are reading? The Bible and the God of the Bible warn of all these realities, both in the Old Testament and the New. In fact, no one in the Bible warned more of the judgment to come and the reality of a fiery hell than Jesus. It was Jesus who admonished us, "And do not fear those who kill the body but cannot kill the soul. Rather fear him who can destroy both soul and body in hell" (Matt. 10:28).

Our reading today in 2 Peter is a fearful condemnation on those who corrupt the gospel of Jesus Christ and use their persuasiveness to lead others into the same ungodly lifestyles which they glorify. Peter reaches far into the past to bring forward examples of what awaits these deceivers in the future. If God "did not spare" the rebel angels, the ancient world, and Sodom and Gomorrah, then neither will He spare these wicked and lawless deceivers. They may speak loudly of freedom, but they will not escape the certainty of the just and awful vengeance of an offended God.

However, from the darkness of the ancient examples of God's judgment, Peter brings forward two shining examples of God's unfailing grace for His people. He is a God who "spared not" those wicked people, but He also is the God who "preserved Noah" and "rescued righteous Lot." Great words—"preserved" and "rescued." Both Noah and Lot are trophies of God's grace. If Peter did not say that Lot was "righteous," we might question if he really was.

Lot is most definitely an example of grace, the unmerited favor of God. And, are not we as well? Yes, what a dark, desperately wicked and deceitful world we live in, but the Lord "preserves" and "rescues" His own. Thank God that even though at times it seems that the foundations of our society are crumbling, the foundation and the Founder of our faith never will!

> "That soul that on Jesus has leaned for repose,
> I will not, I will not desert to his foes;
> that soul, though all hell should endeavor to shake,
> I'll never, no never, no never forsake."

("How Firm a Foundation," attributed to George Keith)

PSALMS 131 & 132
November 16

" *Reminding God* "

"Remember, O Lord, in David's favor, all the
hardships he endured..."
(Psalm 132:1)

God, by virtue of His very nature, has no limits whatsoever. He is infinite. Nothing limits God, but we are certainly limited in our ability to perceive in our finite minds, even a speck of all the glory of His infinite greatness. It is very clear through the Psalms and the other prayers and praises of Scripture that God takes a Father's delight in His infant children communicating with Him in their very limited understanding and vocabulary. If the Lord were not the completely good, gracious and kind being that He is, He might take offense at some of the things we say to Him in our sincere prayers, like asking Him to "remember."

Think about it, reminding all-knowing God! However, God loves it; so much so that He has chosen to record some of these "less-than-theologically-accurate" prayers in His eternal Word. Psalm 132 is a wonderful example of this delight of our Heavenly Father.

The psalmist writes perhaps generations or centuries after the Lord made a covenant with David and declared promises He would keep for all of David's sons who honored Him. In this psalm, one of David's sons lays hold of that covenant and reminds the Lord of what He had said. "The Lord swore to David a sure oath from which he will not turn back: 'One of the sons of your body I will set on your throne. If your sons keep my covenant and my testimonies that I shall teach them...'" (vv. 11-12).

We don't know which of David's descendants sent this "prayer mail" reminder to God, but he is a wonderful example to us. The old gospel song is so encouraging, "Standing on the Promises of God," but we also need to often practice "kneeling on the promises." After all, we can certainly have confidence in our prayers when we are praying God's own promises back to Him! God's Word is filled with hundreds perhaps thousands of promises. God did not record these only to inform us of what God has done in the past but also to inspire us about what He will do today. He made an eternal record of these promises so we can reflect on them, respond to them and, at times, remind Him of them. When is the last time you reminded the Lord of one of His promises? Go ahead, He won't mind at all!

PSALMS 133 & 134
November 17

"The Smell of Unity"

When you think of heaven, what do you think about? No doubt the Lord Jesus comes to your immediate thoughts and perhaps also the incredible joy of seeing your family and friends who are there. The sights and sounds of heaven are definitely beyond our wildest dreams, but have you ever thought about what it *smells* like? Since in our glorified bodies we will have all the physical senses that are part of our existence on earth, I am sure included in the indescribable and endless joys of heaven will be the absolutely wonderful smells. Imagine, that first moment of inhaling the atmosphere of glory!

Truly, we can only imagine for now. However, we do have recorded in Psalm 133 a description of what smells a little bit like heaven on earth—unity among the family of God. The inspired psalmist tells us that unity among the family members of the Lord is amazingly "good and pleasant." It is like the secret, sacred perfume that was used to anoint Aaron's head as high priest and would drip down upon his beard and saturate his robes. So, as Aaron, and the high priests after him, went about their duties in the presence of God, the amazing aroma would waft behind the curtain to God's dwelling place in the Holy of Holies. It would also be carried outside and smelled by the gathered worshipers. It must have smelled amazing!

As New Testament believers, we now understand that everything about the service and worship in the Tabernacle was representative of Jesus. That means it is not saying too much to understand that the reason this unity of the family of God is so wonderful is that it carries with it the fragrance of Jesus. The unity we share in Christ has been provided by the blood of the Son of God. As we preserve this unity by the power of God's Spirit, our fellowship is a fragrance to the Father of His beloved Son. It brings such joy to His heart that where this unity is expressed, there the Father has commanded His life-giving blessing. How important the unity among God's people truly is! We must also consider what division and strife among His children smell like to God. If unity smells like Jesus, then division must smell like the devil! We cannot imagine how distasteful that is to our Lord. All of us, in our personal relationships, are expressing an aroma to God. What do your relationships smell like?

"God's Got This!"

*"They will say, 'Where is the promise of His coming? For ever since
the fathers fell asleep, all things are continuing as they were
from the beginning of creation.'"* (2 Peter 3:4)

A basic premise that underlies practically all areas of scientific inquiry today is a belief system known as *uniformitarianism*. This concept is also known as the "doctrine of uniformity." That is the assumption that the same natural laws and processes that operate in our present-day scientific observations have always conducted themselves the same way in the past. The key words to this definition are *belief* and *assumption*. This system is not based on science but on faith. It does not even follow the principles of the scientific method because it is not ultimately based on data that can be confirmed by observation and measurement.

Science, as it is popularly called today, does not include in its consideration that there exists an external force that deliberately began these processes, has intervened in these processes in the past, and could do so in the future. There is a "deliberate overlooking" of this possibility Peter tells us in our reading today (v. 5). The reason for this willful rejection is that there is a name for the intelligent, intentional force that could do such a thing—*God*.

Peter is encouraging the saints and refuting the scoffers at the same time in this last chapter of his writings. He declares that the heavens and the earth were formed by the Word of God and that they are being preserved by the constant will of His Divine Mind. The former world was destroyed by His Divine intervention (vv. 5-6), and the present world is being preserved until He intervenes again on the Day of the Lord (v. 10).

Yes, evil exists and abounds; some of the worst expressions of this are the scoffing of the so-called intellectuals of the age. Why does our Lord delay? Why has He waited so long? God waits because His patience means salvation. "The Lord is not slow to fulfill his promise as some count slowness, but is patient toward you, not wishing that any should perish, but that all should reach repentance" (v. 9). Aren't we all forever grateful that the Lord waited and patiently came to us before He came in judgment! Perhaps His waiting is a gift to someone reading this page today. It is His day of grace. Come. And for all of us who have come to Christ, it is another day to "grow in the grace and knowledge of our Lord and Savior Jesus Christ" (v. 18).

1 JOHN 1
November 19

"What a Fellowship!"

*"But if we walk in the light, as He is in the light, we have fellowship
with one another, and the blood of Jesus His Son cleanses us
from all sin." (1 John 1:7)*

John knew Jesus. No one was closer to Christ, with the exception of His mother than the Apostle John. John was introduced to Jesus by John the Baptist. John was personally called with his brother James from their fishing business by Jesus to become "fishers of men." John was with Jesus, day and night, for over three years. From Galilee to Golgotha, John was there. John rested his head on Jesus' chest in the upper room, and Jesus' mother buried her head on his beneath the cross. John saw the empty tomb, he "heard" and "touched" his risen Master and He gazed on Him as He ascended back to heaven.

Yes, John knew quite a bit about fellowship with Jesus, and he wrote this letter so we could experience it as well. How wonderful that this *greatest of earthly treasures* is expressed in the simplest of human vocabulary! The simplest child can read and share it, but the wisest of all can never fully comprehend. John does not really target our minds at all; he aims at our hearts. That is the reason this is called the "Epistle of Love," and John uses that wonderful four-letter word about fifty times. John knows that "love changes everything," because it is a love that brings "life" (v. 1), "joy" (v. 4), "light" (v. 5), and "truth" (v. 6). All of these qualities are "otherworldly," that is, they were brought to this "darkness" by the Eternal Word, the Logos, God Himself incarnate in Jesus of Nazareth.

The Son of God came to this earth to bring the sons and daughters of Adam back to paradise. And what is paradise? *Fellowship. Fellowship* is paradise restored and regained for us through our Redeemer Jesus Christ. The ultimate experience of paradise restored will not take place until all the redeemed family of the Second Adam is glorified and this creation is delivered and reborn with us.

The "first-fruits" of that perfect relationship can be experienced by us in this life as we enjoy "our fellowship, which is with the Father and with His Son Jesus Christ" (v. 3). "Fellowship" means "shared life," and how infinitely more valuable and real that is than just a "religion." May God save us from religion! Don't rush the reading of John's words. They are an invitation and initiation into the joy of divine fellowship with Jesus.

1 JOHN 2
November 20

"Talk to Your Attorney"

"My little children, I am writing these things to you so that you may not sin. But if anyone does sin, we have an advocate with the Father, Jesus Christ the righteous."
(1 John 2:1)

One of the most fundamental rights enjoyed in the American justice system is that of the attorney-client privilege. This entitles every citizen to be represented by an attorney, and it also includes the confidentiality of communication shared between the citizen and his or her legal representative. Without a doubt, one of the truly incredible privileges granted to every believer is the best legal representation that could ever be imagined. In fact, as believers we are graced with dual representation; we have an attorney on earth and we have one in heaven. John tells us about both of them.

Here on earth, we have an attorney who never leaves us and is always providing perfect counsel; He is the comforter, the Spirit of truth, the Holy Spirit. (John 15:26) In heaven, before the ultimate Supreme Court, we have to represent us "an advocate with the Father, Jesus Christ the righteous" (v. 1). Can you possibly imagine a better legal team?! And, they both work with complete, unhindered unity and understanding on our behalf. This is especially true when it comes to the issue of our sin. John is writing this letter to help us not sin, but he also recognizes we will sin, and he includes himself in that sad reality (v. 1). But, this is where our perfect "team of counselors" work on our behalf. The Holy Spirit, in His severe mercy, confronts, convicts, and condemns our wrong attitudes, actions, and inactions. He relentlessly pursues us like a determined prosecutor. Why does He do this, to prove our guilt? No, when we sin, our guilt is already determined because we have broken God's law. Our earthly Attorney becomes our prosecutor so that we will confess our sin to our Advocate in heaven.

However, we cannot "make a plea deal." We have to confess, which means literally to "say the same thing." We have to come clean and agree with God against ourselves. When we do this and throw ourselves on the mercy of the court, that is when our Advocate in heaven takes our case. He does this in His completely gracious way; for He does not plead for us on the basis of our merit but on the basis of His own. He shows in the Supreme Court that He bears, in His own body, the marks of our punishment. Justice has been served! Praise God! Let's have a confidential talk with our Attorney today.

1 JOHN 3
November 21

" *Already, Not Yet* "

*"Beloved, we are God's children now, and what we will be has not yet
appeared; but we know that when He appears we shall be like him,
because we shall see him as he is."* (1 John 3:2)

Any of my family members can tell you that I really enjoy Christmas. I
mean, I *really* enjoy Christmas. I'm certain I am not alone in this
because we all have a special opportunity each year to celebrate our
Lord's birth. However, when it comes to the gift-giving aspect of
Christmas, I have to be careful (my wife helps with this!) because I can
really get carried away.

One of the things I enjoy doing is a special way of giving "the big
gift" to each of my children and to Susan. I write a poem of clues for
each of them to read in order to find their gift hidden in the house. Each
one of them has to read the poem out loud as they try to discover where
I have hidden the gift.

Now, I am a terrible poet, but I am awesome at hiding gifts in
unique places! This has become a fun tradition in our family, but
honestly, it just magnifies the joy of Christmas for me. I enjoy finding
the gift to purchase, hiding the gift, writing the silly poem, and then I
really enjoy watching each one hunt for the present. Most of all, I love
seeing the joy on their faces as they discover and unwrap their gift. The
whole process is like Christmas before Christmas. I am already
celebrating as I am *anticipating*.

In the same way, the Apostle John tells us that we live in the
experience of *celebrating* while *anticipating*; we are already the
children of God, but we are not yet all we are going to be (v. 2). The
reformers centuries ago referred to this as the "already, not yet" quality
of the Christian's salvation. By the grace of God, we are completely
justified, declared not guilty, and made righteous through the imputed
merit of Christ to our account (2 Cor. 5:21). However, we are not yet
glorified. We still anxiously await receiving a body like that of our risen
Savior and seeing Him in all His radiant majesty.

Our salvation is already *fully accomplished*, but it is not yet *fully
experienced*. We live in hope. Hope is the yet unexperienced reality of
all that is ours as the children of God. This hope is powerful as we focus
on it. "And everyone who thus hopes in him purifies himself as he is
pure" (v. 3). It has been said some people are so heavenly minded they
are no earthly good. Quite frankly, I have never met one of those people.
Perhaps, like me today, you need to pray to be more *heavenly minded*
in order to be *earthly good*. Focusing on His Advent, we are *celebrating*
while *anticipating*.

" Victorious Love "

*"There is no fear in love, but perfect love casts out fear. For fear has to
do with punishment, and whoever fears has not been perfected in love.
We love because He first loved us."*
(1 John 4:18-19)

"**D**addy, catch me!" That was the excited call I used to hear from each
of my children when they were very small. They loved to climb up on
the stairs, or any other steps they could find and fling themselves out
into the air for me to catch them. I'm not sure how they ever came up
with the idea that this was a safe or fun thing to do. Okay, so maybe I
had a little something to do with it! I just know that once Ruth tried it
for the first time, she was hooked on the thrill and eventually passed it
on to her brother and sister. They loved it, and I must admit, I did too.

It was a sad day when the youngest, Jessica, passed the weight limit
for old dad's tired arms! It is quite an amazing thing to have another
human being express such absolute confidence in you that he or she
would risk his or her safety in trust of your protection. Now, what was
the basis of my children's trust in me? Love. Yes, they definitely *loved
me*, but that was not what caused them to defy gravity in playing our
risky game. No, it was *my love* that gave them such trust. Each of them
knew that my affection for them was greater than any danger. They did
not even sense danger as they jumped toward me; they only
experienced a delightful joy. "Perfect love casts out fear" (v. 18).

My deep love for my children is not perfect, but they each know that
they can trust me and they don't have to be afraid. Imagine, how much
more infinitely perfect our Heavenly Father's love is for each of His
children. Truly, the only perfect love is that in His infinite heart, and all
of that devotion is focused on each of His little children. What
confidence this should give us! That song so many of us learned as
toddlers contains assurance for all of our lives and all of eternity; "Jesus
loves me this I know for the Bible tells me so." Yes, God's loving arms
are opened wide, as wide as those of Jesus on the cross. Those
outstretched arms of the Son of God are broader than all our fears, and
He says to each of us, "Fear not."

PROVERBS 27
November 23

" *A Hungry Soul* "

"One who is full loathes honey, but to one who is hungry
everything bitter is sweet."
(Proverbs 27:7)

A number of years ago, I recall listening to a couple describe a "parental showdown" they had experienced with their youngest son. It seems that the boy, about 6 or 7 years old, decided that he only wanted to eat food that he enjoyed. It did not matter that his mother had worked diligently to provide a good and nutritious meal; all the son wanted to eat was junk food. Imagine that! Well, this abstinence led to numerous unpleasant and tear-filled battles of will, during the time the family was gathering together for meals.

Finally, the mother and father devised a plan. They would not force their son to eat what was placed on the table for dinner, but that plate of food was all that would be provided at any meal. It would be kept in the refrigerator and reheated for the next meal. Of course, the young man tested this plan. He sat glumly through dinner looking at the food on his plate while the other family members enjoyed theirs. The next morning, he bounded in for breakfast only to be dismayed that the meal from the evening before was placed in front of him again, all the while his siblings enjoyed his favorite brand of cereal.

At lunch, the warmed-up plate of food was placed in front of him yet again as the other family members enjoyed sandwiches. Guess what? An amazing thing happened at dinner that evening when, after several minutes of watching his family eat their food and enjoy conversation, the boy slowly, gingerly picked up his fork and began eating the meal from 24 hours prior. Yes, Scripture was fulfilled at that dining room table, "To one who is hungry everything bitter is sweet!" I'm not sure if the mom and dad high-fived each other, but I know they did so on the inside!

You see, the boy's sense of hunger performed a miracle on his taste buds. Just as this is true *physically*, it is also true *spiritually*. People who are hungry for the Word of God aren't too concerned if the teacher's lesson is illustrated cleverly or if the pastor's message is a little long. They just want the food of the Word. Also, hungry people don't get overly concerned about the name of the church or where the leaders attended seminary. When you are really hungry, the name of the restaurant and the training of the cooks don't seem to be important as long as there is good food and lots of it. Let's stay hungry, my friends!

PSALMS 135 & 136
November 24

" *Repetitious Praise* "

"... for His steadfast love endures forever." (Psalm 136)

He was a fine Christian man, but at that moment he was a little upset. As my friend and brother stood before me in the church auditorium that Sunday morning, he had a sincere complaint he wanted to share with me. One of the songs we had sung in worship that morning had included a phrase that was used many times in the song.

"Pastor, to me that just sounds like vain repetition in worship," he said.

I appreciated his honesty, and as I said, he was a godly man and a good friend. I replied to him, "So what you are saying is that you don't want to hear a phrase repeated over and over again in a song?"

"Exactly," he replied.

To which I responded, "For example, like Psalm 136."

"What do you mean?" he asked.

"Well, you do know that the psalmist repeats the phrase, 'His mercy endures forever,' 26 times in that Psalm?"

My dear friend smiled his sweet smile and said, "Well, you've got a point there, pastor."

What a dear man! He's in heaven now, and I'm sure the repetition of "Holy, Holy, Holy is the Lord of Hosts" is not bothering him at all. Vain repetition in worship does not refer primarily to the repeating of the same words frequently; it refers to the danger of only expressing words when our mind and our heart are not actively engaged.

Jesus told the woman at the well in Samaria that the acceptable worship is offered "in spirit and in truth" (John 4:23, 24). This describes true worship as "all that we are" responding to "all that He is." Both our thinking and our emotions are to be connected as we worship. What makes this type of worship so *wonderful* is that it is so *portable*. Again, Jesus told the Samaritan woman that the true worshipers would neither be limited to a mountain in Samaria or Jerusalem (John 4:21).

Worship is not determined by the location or position of our bodies but by the disposition of our souls to God. When the God of Israel and the Savior of the world has captured our affections, the exalting of His love that endures forever will be our continual refrain. Like the psalmist in our reading today; we will recount the victories the Lord has given and sing over and over again the wonders of His love and the triumphs of His grace. We may not be able "to carry a tune in a bucket," but we will lift up our praises for Him in intentional, worshipful repetition.

1 JOHN 5
November 25

" *Look What I've Got* !"

"And this is the testimony, that God gave us eternal life, and this life is in His Son. Whoever has the Son has life; whoever does not have the Son of God does not have life." (1 John 5:11-12)

A noted Christian author had the opportunity to attend the gathering of a very elite literary society and discuss the information in his latest work. He was extremely humbled by the invitation and as the day for the event approached, his nervousness increased. Finally, the day arrived, and as he shared his material with the extremely well-educated and sophisticated audience, he struggled with stage fright and disjointed thinking as he never had before. When the event concluded in the large city, he walked outside and hailed a cab to take him back to his hotel. Slumping into the vehicle, it seemed to him as if the devil himself got in with him and began to mercilessly accuse him of what a complete failure he had been.

Just at that moment, like a shining light in the darkness of his gloom, the author sensed the Spirit of God reminding him of all that Christ had done for him and of the assurance of his acceptance into God's family. Overcome with joy, the man loudly exclaimed, "Look what I've got!" This so startled the driver, who thought that his passenger had a gun, he almost wrecked the cab. After he regained his composure, the driver said, "Buddy, you almost scared me to death!" To this, the rejoicing author responded, "Oh my friend, I am so sorry. I was talking to the devil!" Well, this did not exactly reassure the cab driver, and for the rest of the ride, he kept his eyes fixed suspiciously on his passenger through the rear-view mirror!

What a treasure we have in Jesus, and why should we be so reticent to rejoice about this Gift of all gifts? "Whoever has the Son has life." This is not a future promise, it is a present reality. Eternal life is the quality of life that is found in only the Prince of Life, God's Son. Eternal life is not found in a church, a sacrament, ritual or even in prayer. Eternal life is in Jesus, and when by faith we embrace Him, His life is transferred to us. Just as God breathed into Adam's nostrils the breath of life, likewise the Spirit of God blows the life-giving breath of God into our spirit when we trust Jesus. This is amazing grace. It is the simple, saving promise, "Whoever has the Son has life." The ultimate question then is "Got Jesus?" If you do, then you can shout at the devil, "Look what I've got!"

2 JOHN
November 26

"Hold Your Blessing"

"If anyone comes to you and does not abide in this teaching, do not
receive him into your house or give him greeting, for whoever greets
him takes part in his wicked works."
(2 John 10-11)

"God bless you" is a very sweet expression; it has also become a very common one. It is used when we sneeze or when we leave. It is used in the church house and used on the game show. People often don't notice it being used at all. However, the words themselves are very important. They invoke the favor and help of the Lord upon people. This is wonderful if they are involved in activities that God can bless.

In our reading of 2 John today, John the apostle is very clear about this. As he writes these words, he is *very old*, and he is also *very bold*. He powerfully expresses his joy in the godly manner of life he has witnessed among many members of the church family (v. 4); however, he is alarmed at the lack of discernment that has been shown by many others as they have opened their doors and their arms to embrace and affirm some incredibly dangerous people. Oh, their words are very spiritual, comforting and assuring, just like the soothing and melodious tones of the serpent in the garden. John says to beware of them for they rob the unsuspecting of the full reward of their labor in Christ (v. 8). They seek acceptance and affirmation; but John says that if people "greet them," meaning if they "bless them," they will actually become an accomplice in their wickedness.

What is so dangerous about these people? They destroy churches and damn souls with a false message of Christ. They are antichrists. So, if these deceivers are so convincing and so subtle, how can we recognize them? We do this with one decisive diagnostic question. "Who is Jesus?"

Ask that question, and then carefully listen to the answer. Every true messenger of the Lord will *fully* confess the identity of Jesus of Nazareth. They will clearly affirm that He is "the Christ, the Son of the living God" (Matt. 16:16). They will declare from personal experience that Jesus is "the true God and eternal life" (1 John 5:20b). The name of Jesus, the message of the gospel, and the eternal souls of men and women and boys and girls are far too precious not to be guarded at all cost. Your blessing is powerful; use it carefully and prayerfully.

357

3 JOHN
November 27

"Gospel Hospitality"

"Beloved, it is a faithful thing you do in all your efforts for these brothers, strangers as they are." (3 John 5)

God has a purpose for everything He does. Perfect as He is in wisdom, it is impossible for Him to do anything without purpose and plan. Perhaps like me, you have often struggled to comprehend what His purposes are. Sometimes, this can extend to wondering just why the Lord included some of the passages that are contained in His Word. Our reading today of 3 John could appear to be one of those curious passages. Why would God include such a brief and personal note from the apostle John introducing his friend Demetrius to another kind and gracious friend, Gaius? Also, why would the specific information about a prideful church leader named Diotrephes be included in this letter, which would eventually be included in our Bibles?

Well, as always, some time in thoughtful consideration and meditation reveals again that God knows what He is doing and what we need! In the previous letter of 2 John, the Lord warned us about receiving into our homes or assisting anyone who does not bring "the teaching of Christ" (2 John 9-11). In including 3 John in His Word, God reminds us that this caution should in no way limit our hospitality. "Hospitality" is a very significant word in relation to our faith; it literally means "loving strangers."

We often think of hospitality in regard to being a thoughtful host in caring well for people who come into our homes, but it is much broader and much more active than that. Hospitality is the gospel in action. It is love that reaches to people outside our circle of community, and often outside of Christ, to care for them physically, emotionally, and spiritually. John saw this in Gaius, loved him for it, encouraged him "walking in the truth" and by his hospitality living "in a manner worthy of God" (vs. 4, 6). People who are not hospitable to strangers are guided by a "me and mine" proud and selfish spirit, just like Diotrephes "who likes to put himself first" (v. 9).

When our children were small, we always cautioned them, when they were away from us, to "beware of strangers"; "stranger... danger" was a motto we used. However, we also introduced them to people who were strangers to them, and we entertained and welcomed many strangers in our home. Part of growing up physically and spiritually is growing in "the love of strangers." That is what God's love is, and that is what God's love does.

JUDE
November 28

" *Take A Stand* "

"I found it necessary to write appealing to you to contend for the faith
that was once for all delivered to the saints." (Jude 3)

This was not the letter Jude wanted to write, but it was the letter he
was compelled to write. It had been Jude's desire, as a long-time
believer in Jesus (who was his oldest brother as well), to encourage
other Christians regarding the mutual salvation they shared. However,
sometimes hard letters have to be written and tough things need to be
said; there is just too much at stake. That is certainly the situation that
prompted Jude's very forceful letter to be sent to the churches.

Word had reached him about "spiritual creeps." "For certain people
have crept in unnoticed who pervert the grace of our God into
sensuality and deny our only Master and Lord, Jesus Christ" (v. 4). The
key phrase is "crept in," because it tells how these false teachers gain
entrance into churches then and still do today. The image is like that of
a slinking, voracious animal that stealthily slips in among the
unsuspecting flock. These are "the wolves in sheep's clothing" (Acts
20:29) that Paul had warned about and that the other leaders, like Peter
and John, had denounced and unmasked.

Now, it was Jude's turn, and what a flowing and forceful judgment
he calls upon them! He shows that these spiritual reprobates are
descended from the wicked enemies of God from ages ago (vv. 4-11),
and Jude then describes what awaits them in the future (vv. 12-16).
Truly, their fate causes us to shudder as we read it. How should we
respond in our day to Jude's ancient, but living words?

First of all, we must make sure that faith is *protected* (v. 3). Once we
allow the integrity of God's Word to be undermined, it will not be long
before the testimony of the gospel falls. Secondly, we must make sure
that false teachers are *rejected*. We are commanded to "test the spirits
to see whether they are from God" (1 John 4:1). Teachers who do not
express fidelity to Christ and His Word are to be exposed as frauds.
Thirdly, we must be careful that our own lives are *inspected*. Personally
and collectively, we must build ourselves up in our holy faith with the
help of the Holy Spirit (vv. 20-21). Finally, we must be merciful to those
who have been *infected* with doubt and led into deceitful living, as if
"snatching them out of the fire" (vv. 22-23). Yes, Jude is serious about
the security of the faith and the safety of souls...and we must as well.

REVELATION 1
November 29

" The Big Reveal "

"The revelation of Jesus Christ, which God gave him to show to his
servants the things that must soon take place..."
(Revelation 1:1)

On a number of the television programs that feature a total home, or sometimes a personal "make-over," the moment finally arrives often referred to as the "big reveal." This is the long-awaited experience of seeing the finished product of all the renovation work. If you have ever watched one of these programs, then you are aware of just how amazing and transformational the changes can be. When it comes to the narrative of Scripture, this final book of God's Word can be considered "the big reveal." As you can see, the word "reveal" is included in the title of this epistle.

The actual source of the word is the Greek term "apokalipsis" which means to uncover or unveil something or someone. In these final chapters of the Bible, both of these applications apply. This book is the apocalypse or the "unveiling" of Jesus Christ and the things that will soon take place (v. 1). The apostle John was shown this unveiling when, as a very old man, he was living and working as a political prisoner exiled to the tiny, rock-like Island Patmos, located about 45 miles off the western coast of modern Turkey. There, John saw Jesus, but as he had never seen him in all the days they shared together.

Jesus was "unveiled" before John in the splendor of His divine glory and with the awe-inspiring symbols of His priesthood (v. 13), eternality and omniscience (v. 14), and His sovereign judgeship (vv. 15-16). The glory of Christ the Son was too much for the old disciple's heart, and he collapsed at His feet as a dead man. But then, John felt the familiar touch that he had not sensed in over 60 years; it was the touch of the Master's hand and he heard His sweet friendly voice saying, "Fear not, I am the first and the last, and the living one. I died, and behold I am alive forevermore, and I have the keys of Death and Hades..." (vv. 17b-18).

Notice that it was the right hand of Jesus that lovingly touched John; the same hand that, moments before, he saw holding the *seven stars*. The hand of total Lordship was also the hand of tender friendship. The Sovereign Jesus was the same Jesus! How John would need to remember that as the things of the future were revealed to him, and my friend how we need to remember that as well. Come what may, He is the same Jesus "yesterday, today, and forever" (Heb. 13:8).

PSALM 137 & PROVERBS 28
November 30

" *A Believing Boldness* "

*"The wicked flee when no one pursues, but the righteous
are as bold as a lion."* (Proverbs 28:1)

During the early days of World War II's "Battle of the Bulge" in mid-December of 1944, all available units of the United States Army were rushed forward to stem the tide of the surprise Nazi onslaught. The epicenter of the attack converged on the town of Bastogne, Belgium. Leading one of the battalions of 101st Airborne Division was Major Richard Winters of Pennsylvania.

As his men prepared to move forward to the front, they were met by a group of shell-shocked soldiers moving back from the lines. One of the men, a lieutenant, informed Major Winters that the road behind them was about to be cut off by a German Ranger division and that it looked like the Major and his men would be surrounded. To this information, Major Winters responded, "We're paratroopers, Lieutenant; we're supposed to be surrounded." Great statement.

This was not just bravado on the part of Major Winters; it just reflected a calm acceptance of what their identity and their mission naturally required. At times as believers, we can certainly sense that the evil and hatred of the world system has us surrounded. It is in those moments that we need to remember our identity and our mission. *We are Christians; we are supposed to be surrounded.* Our identity is *not* of this world; it is *not* our home, and we are foreigners in it. However, our mission is *in* this world. Jesus said He was making us lights for this world, and lights have their mission illuminating the darkness. It is why we are here.

Indeed, knowing our identity and mission does not mean we are automatically prepared for it. Fear is the most dangerous enemy any military unit faces in times of conflict. Fear can turn even the best-trained soldiers into cowards. What is the quality that produces boldness in battle? It is faith. "The righteous are as bold as a lion" (v. 1). Righteousness is based on faith; but then, what is the basis of faith? Faith rests on reality. It may be an unseen reality, but it is reality—"the assurance of things hoped for, the conviction of things not seen" (Heb. 11:1). Yes, it is true we are surrounded, but it is also true that those who surround us are also surrounded!

Here is the reality, my friend, and the basis of our faith—*we are not alone.* Like Elisha's servant, we need our eyes opened "for those who are with us are more than those who are with them" (2 Kgs. 6:16). Yes, we are surrounded, and praise God for that!

DECEMBER

"Glory to God in the highest."

PSALMS 138 & 139
December 1

"The Sanctity of Life"

"Your eyes saw my unformed substance;
in Your book were written, every one of them,
the days that were formed for me,
when as yet there was none of them."
(Psalm 139:16)

The "right to life" and the "right to choose" is a battle constantly being fought in the political arena and the courts of America. However, in the heart of a Christ-follower, there should be no turmoil on this issue. The Supreme Court has already ruled. *THE* Supreme Court. The judge of all the earth has already issued His decree, "All souls are mine" (Ezek. 18:4).

When do the lives of people belong to the Lord? At birth? No. According to His Word through King David, the lives of people belong to the Lord from the moment of conception. "For you formed my inward parts; you knitted me together in my mother's womb" (v. 13). "Your eyes saw my unformed substance..." (v. 16). The word for "unformed substance" is only used here; in Hebrew, it means "embryo." God says from conception, every life is His and He Himself forms each human being. Not only does God form us, but He also forms the days of our lives. "In your book were written, every one of them, the days that were formed for me, when as yet there was none of them" (v. 16).

Life is sacred from conception to completion, and each life has purpose to the One who gave it. This means *your* life is sacred. Say this today (out loud if at all possible), "I am *personally* created by God. I am *precisely* created by God. I am *purposefully* created by God." Think on those words "personally," "precisely," "purposefully." Your life really matters. This day really matters. *Really matters.*

REVELATION 2
December 2

" I Know" (Part One)

In the first chapter of The Revelation, John describes for us, to the best of his limited ability, the transcendent glory of the Son of God. Three things John noted about the glorified Jesus is that He had eyes like flames of fire (Rev. 1:14), that He holds seven stars in His right hand (Rev. 1:16) and that He stands in the midst of seven golden lampstands (Rev. 1:12-13). We are told that the seven stars are the angels of the seven churches and that the seven lampstands are the seven churches (Rev. 1:20).

In Chapters 2 and 3, we learn that these angels (probably best understood as the "messengers," that is, "pastor-teachers") and the churches each receive a specific message that is initiated by the Savior's words, "I know." These churches are literal, local churches, but the number "7" also indicates they are representative of the Lord's church on earth. The sobering words "I know" tells us that the Lord is intimately aware of what is taking place in the entire church collectively and each church individually. It follows then that what the Lord says to the churches He also says to the members. We learn from what the Lord says, He *sees,* and *knows* about the churches, and what He *wants* from us as His children.

- From Ephesus we learn: Christ wants a *passion* for Him above all.
- From Smyrna we learn: Christ wants *perseverance* in the face of trials and opposition.
- From Pergamum we learn: Christ wants *preservation* of the faith from false teachers.
- From Thyatira we learn: Christ wants *purity* of mind and body by His people.

"He who has an ear, let him hear what the Spirit says to the churches." (Revelation 2:7, 11, 17, 29)

REVELATION 3
December 3

"*I Know*" (*Part Two*)

When John reflected on the life and ministry he shared with Jesus, he summed up the experience with these words, "And the Word became flesh and dwelt among us, and we have seen his glory, glory as of the only Son from the Father, full of grace and truth" (John 1:14). The qualities that most reflected to John of Christ's divine nature is that He was "full of grace and truth." John, in this Revelation of Jesus Christ given to him on the Island of Patmos, sees Jesus manifested with visible expressions of His sovereign Lordship that he had never seen as they walked in Galilee and Judea together.

However, in all His radiant splendor, He is still the same Jesus, "full of grace and truth." "Grace and truth" are exactly what Jesus expresses to the three churches mentioned in today's reading, and that is what He expresses to us as "He knows" all about us. The truth He speaks to us from His Word is always perfectly balanced with grace because His Word is an expression of His nature. So, what is it that the Lord wants from His churches and Christians then and now?

- From Sardis we learn: Christ wants us to *restore* the neglected areas of spiritual growth in our lives (v. 2).
- From Philadelphia we learn: Christ wants us to *resolve* that we will trust Him as the one who opens and closes doors of service (vs. 7, 8).
- From Laodicea we learn: Christ wants us to *repent* of a lukewarm devotion to Him and His cause (vs. 15, 16, 19).

"He who has an ear, let him hear what the Spirit says to the churches." (Revelation 6, 13, 22)

REVELATION 4
December 4

"What A View!"

"After this I looked, and behold,
a door standing open in heaven!"
(Revelation 4:1)

A few years ago, Susan and I were privileged to spend a week in fellowship and the study of God's Word with a group of about 150 church leaders in Romania. What a wonderful time we shared! Our return flight was booked through Munich, Germany, and since we had never traveled in that area, we decided to stay a few days and enjoy some vacation.

We rented a German car with plenty of head and legroom for me and started driving through Bavaria, the southern section of Germany. The car came equipped with all the "bells and whistles." Sadly, all of these, and the voice of the directional system were in German! Not to be deterred, my lovely wife pushed every button and flipped every switch until finally, after many miles of buzzers, flashing lights, activated wipers, adjusted mirrors, and opened and closed windows and sun-roof, we were cruising down the Autobahn with a pleasant voice guiding us in English!

The rest of the trip was magical. Over the next four days, we traveled through the indescribably beautiful terrain of Bavaria, Austria, and Switzerland. Countless times, as we would round a curve or crest a hill, we gasped at the glory of the scene before us. It was hard to imagine that there could exist such fairy-tale splendor on a planet that includes so many scenes of hateful ugliness.

Our amazing experience, however, cannot begin to compare with the overwhelming transformation John experienced as he was caught up from the squalor of his existence on Patmos to the overwhelming glory of the atmosphere surrounding God's throne in heaven. There, in an environment of complete peace, inexpressible beauty, and ceaseless praise, John would watch unfold on earth the cataclysmic events of the Great Tribulation. While on earth the most dreadful and terrible days in all of human history are transpiring, from heaven God still reigns undisturbed and is accomplishing His sovereign purposes.

My friend, what will be true in those days to come is true on this day as well. God reigns infinitely and intimately. He is the God who causes empires to rise, and He is the God who knows when the sparrows fall. He numbers the stars, and He numbers the hairs on your head. He knows all things, and He controls all things. He is too good to be unkind, and He is too wise to be mistaken. That is a fact that has to be embraced by faith. Perhaps the tempest of trial is swirling around you today. Fear not, the "Son" is always shining, just above the clouds, and that's no fairy tale!

REVELATION 5
December 5

" The Lion is a Lamb "

John has been translated from the pit of human suffering to the pinnacle of divine glory. In the throne room of heaven, he is overwhelmed by the power and praise displayed before him. Quickly, however, John is overcome with sorrow; for there in the presence of wonderful majesty, his focus is intentionally directed to the most awful problem. A seven-sealed scroll in the right hand of God cannot be opened by anyone who is in heaven or on earth or under the earth (vv. 1-3). This scroll that is sealed seems strange to us, but it was very familiar to people in ancient times. The scroll is a title deed of ownership. The writing on the inside and outside defines the terms that must be met before the property can be reclaimed.

The fact that the scroll is seven-sealed and resting in the hand of God means that the creator Himself must be satisfied that the demands of the redemption have been met. This is the title deed of all creation, and not one of Adam's sinful race is qualified to meet the requirements of God. But, the Second Adam is qualified! This is the cause of the triumphant proclamation by one of the elders, "Weep no more; behold, the Lion of the tribe of Judah, the Root of David, has conquered, so that he can open the scroll and its seven seals" (v. 5).

John looks up from his sorrow to see this Lion, but what he sees is a Lamb having a terrible slaughter-wound; yet, He stands in complete perfection as is testified by the seven horns, seven eyes, and seven spirits. This is the Lamb of God that John the Baptist heralded by the banks of the Jordan River, who the disciple John saw sacrificed on Calvary, who resurrected from the tomb, ascended from the Mount of Olives, and now worshiped in heaven. He has redeemed God's property and God's people, and now has stepped forward to reclaim the inheritance for His family so that they may rule and reign with Him. What a moment! No wonder all the inhabitants of heaven break forth in praise, "Worthy is the Lamb who was slain, to receive power and wealth and wisdom and might and honor and glory and blessing. To him who sits on the throne and to the Lamb be blessing and honor and glory and might forever and ever!" (Rev. 5:12) And let all the people of God on the earth say, "Amen!"

REVELATION 6
December 6

" The Wrath of the Lamb "

*"Fall on us and hide us from the face of Him who is seated on the
throne, and from the wrath of the Lamb, for the great day of their
wrath has come, and who can stand?"*
(Revelation 6:16-17)

As we have already seen in our reading of The Revelation, it is filled
with symbols. However, the fact that there are symbols does not mean
they do not describe literal events. When God gives us symbols in His
Word, these symbols are either explained in the context or understood
by other uses of those messages to the seven churches. Then, in
Chapters 4-22, John communicates the events that Jesus said, "are
those to take place after this."

Our reading in Chapter 6 today brings the focus of what the Lamb is
doing in heaven down to earth. In heaven, Jesus opens the seals, and
the final judgments on earth begin. Satan is not in control, the Savior is.
As the Lord begins to reclaim His rightful possession, the long foretold
day of His wrath begins. It is the wrath of the Lamb who is the Lion.
Under His sovereign oversight and control, one with a bow and who
had been given a crown rides forth conquering everywhere (v. 2). This is
no doubt the antichrist, who comes forth suddenly in the last days
promising peace but bringing war. Under his brief but terrible
authority, the dreadful consequences that follow warfare come upon the
earth—famine, pestilence, and death.

But, in this awful season, the Lord has many faithful witnesses,
faithful unto death (vv. 10-11). When these first six seals have been
opened, then the culminating day of the "wrath of the Lamb" has come
to the earth, and from His holy vengeance, none can hide (vv. 15-17).
However, as in all the times of God's judgment recorded in the Bible,
the Lord knows how to deliver the righteous. We are not looking for the
coming of the antichrist, but the return of Jesus Christ who has
promised, "I will keep you from the hour of trial that is coming on the
whole world, to try those who dwell on earth" (Rev. 3:10). Praise Him
for that promise today!

PROVERBS 29
December 7

"The Song of Freedom"

"An evil man is ensnared in his transgressions,
but a righteous man sings and rejoices."
(Proverbs 29:6)

Toward the end of his long career, a well-known entertainer in North America would sing at his concerts and performances, "I Did It My Way." The music of the song is beautiful, and the singer, with his voice and captivating stage presence, could certainly make it a "show-stopping moment." I can still recall as a young boy being riveted to the screen of the television. However, as I grew up and became aware of the performer's turbulent and even scandalous lifestyle, I remember thinking, "Well, how did that work out for you?" Not very well, really, for him or the family, friends, and people associated with him. His life's theme song, "I Did It My Way" was belted out with the bravado of boastful freedom, but the man wasn't free; he was the prisoner of his own self-absorption.

Truly, he confirmed Solomon's wise statement, "An evil man is ensnared in his transgressions" (v. 6a). The righteous man or woman, on the other hand, may have no vocal or musical abilities whatsoever; but they can always sing because "a righteous man sings and rejoices" (v. 6b). Joy is the song in the soul of a truly free person. Freedom is not "doing your own thing" but "doing the right thing," and joy is the product of "doing what is right" because "you are right" with God. Both freedom and joy are gifts from God for "if the Son sets you free, you will be free indeed" (John 8:36), and the fruit of the Spirit is joy (Gal. 5:22).

When we are freed from our sins through faith in Christ, we are then able to experience and share with God His freedom. The Lord is the one, completely free being, in all the universe and He is a God of joy. That is why the angels could sing, "Joy to the world" (Luke 2:10) because Jesus would bring the joy of salvation to the people of God. It is not wrong to live for joy. The Lord actually commands us to rejoice in Him (Phil. 4:4) and serve Him with gladness (Ps. 100:2). Can you imagine the unspeakable joy awaiting those who are welcomed by Jesus into heaven and hear Him say, "Well done, good and faithful servant" (Matt. 25:23)! In effect, what will He be saying? He will be exclaiming, "You Did It My Way!"

PSALMS 140 & 141
December 8

" *Painful Kindness* "

*"Let a righteous man strike me—it is a kindness; let him rebuke me
—it is oil for my head; let my head not refuse it."* (Psalm 141:5)

Pain is not enjoyable. Pain can be awful, and some who are reading this page today are in the grip of it. Physically, or perhaps emotionally, it is there and very real. In a season of giving and receiving gifts, certainly none of us would look forward to unwrapping a gift of pain this year. Pain is not pleasant, but it can be good for us. That is the reason King David in the verse above speaks of the "kindness" of being struck by the rebuke from a friend. David's son Solomon, who would be the wisest of men would say, "A friend loves at all times and a brother is born for adversity" (Prov. 17:17).

A true friend loves and is kind, and sometimes that means loving enough and being kind enough to rebuke us, to tell us not necessarily what we *want* to hear, but what we *need* to hear. The experience may not be pleasant, but the expression may be true. Valuing the insight and valuing the individual who loved us enough to give it, is wisdom. God uses pain as a kind gift of His severe mercy. The British scholar and author C.S. Lewis wisely said, "God whispers to us in our pleasures, speaks in our consciences, but shouts in our pains. It is his megaphone to rouse a deaf world."

Part of our fleshly nature is that we usually require the shouts of pain before we can hear the whispers of love. We usually do not count our blessings until we have felt our bruises. Some of these bruises are caused by the words of a friend who has found it necessary to rebuke us. If you have such a friend in your life who will give you that kind of *gift*, at times, then count yourself truly blessed! Friends like that are treasures themselves.

A question to consider in light of today's Scripture is to ask who can count us as such a friend? If we truly love someone, we will not withhold what is in their best interest, even if it may cause some temporary pain. Paul challenged us, "If anyone is caught in any transgression, you who are spiritual should restore him in a spirit of gentleness..." (Gal. 6:1). The word Paul uses for "restore" means "to put back in place" like a dislocated bone. Sure, it's going to hurt, but if it helps a brother walk straight, how kind is that?!

REVELATION 7
December 9

"Salvation in the Tribulation"

It has been revealed, time after time through the centuries, that during the most terrible times people often lift up their heads and cry to God for His mercy. Truly, broken hearts and lives are often the plowed soil for receiving the seeds of the gospel. This will definitely be the case during the horrendous days of the great tribulation. God will save and appoint His sowers of the gospel seed, and the result will be perhaps the most abundant harvest of evangelism in the history of mankind.

The apostle Paul declared that because of the rejection of the gospel of Messiah Jesus by most of the Jewish people, the message of salvation has come to the Gentiles. He goes on to say that when the Lord, in His sovereign grace, brings Israel to trust in Messiah, it will only serve to expand the grace of God flowing to the nations (Rom. 11:11-15). This prophecy of Paul seems to fit precisely with what was revealed to John and what he recorded in our reading today in Chapter 7.

In verses 1-11, John sees multitudes from all the tribes of Israel marked by the seal of God. Immediately afterward, he is shown a "great multitude that no one could number, from every nation" (v. 9) gathered before God's throne. He is told, "These are the ones coming out of the great tribulation. They have washed their robes and made them white in the blood of the Lamb" (v. 14). Truly God, in this day of His wrath, remembers mercy (Hab. 3:2).

The gospel is the power of God to bring salvation (Rom. 1:16). It is so alive with life and light of the Son of God that no darkness can overcome that radiance (John 1:5). We need to claim what the Lord promises about Himself and His gospel when we witness to people who may seem engulfed in darkness. At times, we can begin to doubt whether they will ever come to faith, but let this chapter encourage our hearts today! The God of all grace who is able to bring millions to Himself during the great tribulation is doing the same right now, for when sin has abounded "grace abounded all the more" (Rom. 5:20).

God has set His seal on all of us who believe. We are His lights for the present darkness, and He will use our witness to "give the light of the knowledge of the glory of God in the face of Jesus Christ" (2 Cor. 4:6).

REVELATION 8
December 10

" *The Seventh Seal* "

"When the Lamb opened the seventh seal, there was silence in heaven for about half an hour." (Revelation 8:1)

We use an expression in English that on the surface is a contradiction in terms but is used intentionally to communicate the uniqueness of the atmosphere in a room or space. We will say, "The silence was deafening." "Deafening silence" is an oxymoron in speech but it communicates clearly. A deafening silence is a situation in which the absence of sound only serves to heighten the awareness that something is very different.

What is described in verse 1 of our reading today is completely unique throughout all the ages of time, and even before the beginning of time—*there is silence in heaven.* The atmosphere of heaven is never silent and never has been; it resounds incessantly with the sounds of the saints and angels worshiping Almighty God in praise and adoration. However, when the glorified Jesus opens the final seal on the title deed of creation, an immediate and complete hush of all sound pervades the throne room of God. This unprecedented silence, cloaking completely every noise for a space of thirty-minutes, is a gripping, focusing prologue to what is preparing to happen. Jesus, in opening the seventh seal, is starting in motion all the awful and awe-inspiring events that must take place for the complete reclaiming and redeeming of the earth and the fulfillment of God's purposes.

Out of the opening of the seventh seal and the "deafening silence" that follows will resound the seven trumpet judgments and the outpouring of the seven bowl judgments in accomplishing God's vengeance of the Day of the Lord. The trumpets begin to sound, one by one, after the angel offers incense on the altar with the prayers of the saints (v. 3). God is answering the prayers of His suffering people through the ages. "O, Sovereign Lord, holy and true, how long before you will judge and avenge our blood on those who dwell on earth?" (Rev. 6:10) The fire from the altar that is thrown on the earth (v. 5) is God's answer to those prayers.

Dear friend, the Lord our God is long-suffering and patiently waits, withholding judgment, while the opportunity is given for people to repent. But have no doubt, "the day of the Lord will come like a thief, and then the heavens will pass away with a roar..." (2 Pet. 3:10). Pray and be ready. *Pray and be ready.*

374

REVELATION 9
December 11

"Out of the Abyss"

Again, the imagery and symbolism used in the sharing of The Revelation with John are pervasive throughout all he records and communicates with God's people. John uses incredibly vivid and graphic details in writing the message in Chapter 9, but we need to keep in mind that a total understanding of everything he shares is not possible. John is using images and terms available to him as an inhabitant of the 1st century to describe events that clearly involve spirit beings and that are taking place in the distant future. Nevertheless, the symbols used and the information conveyed enables us to understand the events described, and they are indeed frightening.

The scene begins with a star falling from heaven and that star has been given the key to the bottomless pit. We know in Scripture that *Lucifer* means "shining one" and *angels* are referred to by the image of "stars." We also know that Lucifer was expelled from heaven, so this reveals to us the identity of this star as Satan. Under the sovereign control of God, he is permitted to release the demonic beings imprisoned there who bring horrific plagues of physical pain on many of the earth's inhabitants. These plagues are reserved for those who do not belong to the Lord (v. 4). Their king's name "Abaddon" or "Apollyon" means "destruction" or "destroyer" and is probably another reference to Satan.

The blowing of the sixth trumpet brings the release of four more angelic beings from captivity who are associated with a terrible plague that many Bible teachers believe to be a description of terrible weapons of war. Others view the scene as a symbolic description of an awful assault by demonic forces. Regardless, the results are unimaginably horrible as one-third of mankind perishes in the horrific attacks. In spite of all these awful judgments, the people who survive continue to practice their ungodly and immoral lifestyles.

It is reminiscent of "the days of Noah" when, in defiance of God, mankind continued to devote itself to wickedness up to the day the flood began. Knowing that days such as these are coming, how much should we be like faithful Noah in continuing to work for the Lord and be a witness of His grace! There is a flood of fiery judgment coming, but there is an Ark of salvation in Jesus Christ. Let's keep pointing people to Him, the open door.

REVELATION 10
December 12

" *Mighty Angel and Little Book* "

The action described in the Book of the Revelation is an alternation of scenes taking place in heaven with those taking place on the earth. Also within the book are sections that are pauses in describing activity and in them we are given more information about what is being shared, similar to the use of parentheses in a sentence. Chapter 10 is one of these parentheses amid the narrative.

John sees a mighty angel in amazing splendor descend from heaven. The imagery describing him is a combination of God's glory and faithfulness and also those of divine judgment. With a roar, this enormous angel descends, and in the vision places one foot on the sea and the other on dry land, representing the entire world. He raises his right hand and declares that by the authority of the One who created both land and sea there will be no more delay, but that in the days of the seventh trumpet about to sound, the final revelation of God's purposes will be completed.

John heard seven thunderous messages from heaven accompanying the angel's appearing, but he was forbidden to reveal what was shared. The appearance of the angel and the prohibition for disclosing messages is very similar to what Daniel experienced and recorded in Chapters 8 and 10 of his prophecy. Attention is drawn to the "little scroll" open in the angel's hand; it is described as "having been opened" in a literal translation. This connects this scroll as the same as the seven-sealed scrolls in Revelation Chapter 5. This is the title deed for the final redemption of God's creation.

The days of the concluding events in the final judgment and renewal of all things are about to begin. This is the reason John is told to eat the little scroll, which tastes so sweet in his mouth but becomes terribly bitter to his stomach. What he is about to share is the ultimate salvation of God's people and the triumph of the Lamb; this is truly sweet to John indeed. However, his revelation will also include the final destruction and eternal doom for untold multitudes of unsaved sinners, and this is very bitter to the loving John's soul. It is not an easy thing to be God's messengers because we must be faithful to share His entire message. It is one of free grace and salvation for all who believe, and judgment and eternal doom for all who reject the Lord. May the Lord find us to be faithful and true messengers.

REVELATION 11
December 13

" The Two Witnesses "

Our reading today contains the description of two very important events that take place during the middle of the terrible days on earth recorded in the Book of the Revelation—the ministry of God's two special prophets in the city of Jerusalem and the blowing of the seventh trumpet in heaven. God never leaves Himself without faithful witnesses, even during the darkest of times of persecution of His people. For 3 1/2 years, some of the most powerful witnesses for Christ the world has ever known will be shared during the season of the great tribulation around the world. These two witnesses are given miraculous powers by the Lord to perform signs and wonders that very much resemble those of Moses and Elijah during their ministries.

Many Bible scholars believe that these two witnesses truly are Moses and Elijah returned as last-days prophets for God, because of the nature of their miracles, because Moses and Elijah represent the Law and the Prophets in God's Word, and because Moses and Elijah appeared with Jesus on the Mount of Transfiguration. Regardless, these two servants of Christ will be the cause of many conversions to the Lord; but they will also be the two most despised people, especially by Satan and his evil servant, the beast, that is, the Antichrist (v. 7).

When His prophets have fulfilled their mission, God will allow the antichrist to kill them; however, the worldwide celebration of their deaths will be interrupted as, by the power of God, they are resurrected and then ascend back to heaven. The accompanying deadly earthquake will rock Jerusalem, but also the events will lead to a huge number professing the Lord (v. 13). These amazing events will be followed by the dramatic blowing of the seventh trumpet in heaven. As this takes place, the sounds of judgment and worship mingle in the presence of God within the temple of heaven. The shout of triumph rings through the glory, "The kingdom of the world has become the kingdom of our Lord and of his Christ, and he shall reign forever." These words, used by the composer Handel in his "Hallelujah Chorus," proclaim that the final consummation of God's redemption plan is about to begin.

Many events are involved in this final climactic process, but the outcome is already an established fact. The Lord reigns supreme and unchallenged, and we will share in His victory. Go ahead, sing the "Hallelujah Chorus" today!

PSALM 142 & PROVERBS 30
December 14

" The Prayer of a Caveman "

*"Bring me out of prison, that I may give thanks to Your name!
The righteous will surround me, for You
will deal bountifully with me."*
(Psalm 142:7)

When visiting Israel, I have been blessed on many occasions to stand in a spot of one of the famous scenes of the Bible and imagine the events that transpired there. Viewing the geography makes the description of it in God's Word so much more real and personal. Psalm 142 takes on that added dimension today as I recall walking along the river in the oasis-like surroundings of En Gedi. Looking across the stream and above the tree line, you see the orange-tinted, craggy cliffs of the Judean wilderness. It appears the only inhabitants are the eagles and the groups of ibex, sometimes referred to as gazelles, that somehow survive on the tiny tufts of grass growing there and also somehow survive the death-defying leaps they make from rocky crag to crag.

It was in this wilderness oasis that David and a few of his loyal men hid from the soldiers and the deadly hatred of King Saul. David was considered public enemy number one, and he knew that there was only a step between him and terrible death. However, hiding in the darkness of his prison-like cave, David grasped the light that shined in his heart, if not in his cave. It was the glowing rays of assurance of the power and faithfulness of his God, Jehovah. His sad lament was true, "no refuge remains to me; no one cares for my soul" (v. 4).

This was the truth of how he felt, but it was not the truth of the ultimate reality; he was not alone. The invisible, but ever-present One was there with him. David's refuge was not in a cave but in the Rock of Ages. David knew this and He made a choice to declare it, "I cry to you, O Lord; I say, 'You are my refuge, my portion in the land of the living'" (v. 5). We know the rest of David's story, but we don't know the rest of ours. Perhaps today you are sitting in your house or your car, but it seems like you are sitting in a dark cave; it feels like solitary confinement. You truly feel alone...but you aren't. He is there. The Lord never leaves nor forsakes His people. This "caveman's psalm" was recorded for times just like this. Sing it today and embrace His light in the darkness.

PSALMS 143 & 144
December 15

"*Streams in the Desert*"

"Blessed are the people to whom such blessings fall! Blessed are the people whose God is the Lord!" (Psalm 144:15)

The opening words to Charles Dickens' classic novel, *A Tale of Two Cities,* are considered some of the finest in English literature, "It was the best of times, it was the worst of times...." Those are great words for the beginning of a great book, but I have often come to think over the years that those words are usually an apt description of where most people find themselves on just about any day. Things are great in some areas, and they are terrible in others. I have often jokingly responded to many people when they ask me how I am doing, "Oh, I'm just living the Tale of Two Cities!"

The truth is that most of us on most days are experiencing situations and even emotions that fluctuate between both ends of "the best of times, the worst of times" spectrum. It's called "life." The critical issue for us as followers of the Lord is to be guided by the absolutely reliable compass during the changing emotional terrain of our days. How wonderful it is that each of us possesses that compass with the "true north" for both our mountaintop and wilderness seasons.

David's words in the two psalms for today's Scripture reading are a wonderful example of how to use that perfect compass of God's character and faithfulness in the conflicting experiences of "the best of times and the worst of times." That is where David is living in this season. He is experiencing the protection and provision of God as never before in his life, and yet he is also being wrongly accused and pursued by King Saul. David is not in denial, and he specifically shares with God all that is happening and all that he is feeling in his fear.

However, also notice all the times he declares, "I remember," "I stretch out my hands," "I meditate," "I am your servant," "I take refuge," and "I will sing." David knew how to look to his "God compass." True north for him was not what he was feeling at any given moment but rather the fixed point in his universe was the north star of God Himself. Today is probably "the best of times and the worst of times" for many of us; but in all the times of our life, there is the timeless God who declares, "I am the Lord and I do not change" (Mal. 3:6). Let's keep our eyes on Him in "the best of times and the worst of times."

REVELATION 12
December 16

"*A Play Within a Play*"

*"And a great sign appeared in heaven: a woman clothed with the
sun, with the moon under her feet, and on her head
a crown of twelve stars."* (Revelation 12:1)

Many people consider William Shakespeare to be the greatest writer in the history of the English language. His impact has truly been phenomenal. So many phrases that have made their way into the fabric of modern English had their origin from the quill of "The Bard of the Globe Theatre" in Elizabethan England. One of Shakespeare's most famous literary devices has come to be known as the "play within a play." Shakespeare used this in both his renowned works *Hamlet* and *A Midsummer Night's Dream*. He uses the characters of the play to create and watch a play as part of the overall production being viewed by the theatre audience. So, the people attending the play are watching the actors produce and act in their own play. Through this device, Shakespeare brings out greater information and insight into the characters as they, themselves, view and interpret characters in a play. Brilliant.

In a real sense, this is what the Lord is doing in Revelation Chapter 12. Amid the "unveiling drama of the end of the age," that is, the Book of the Revelation, He introduces a play-like allegory of the main characters involved in God's whole story of redemption. These characters are presented in symbolic form: Israel is the woman clothed with the sun (v. 1), the red dragon is Satan (vs. 3, 7, 9, 12-17), the stars are angels deceived by Satan who rebel against God (vs. 4, 7-9), the male child is Christ (vs. 5, 11), Michael is the archangel who leads God's loyal angels in battle against Satan and his angels (vv. 7-9), and finally, "the brothers" are the people who have faith in Israel's Son, the Messiah Jesus. The brothers are faithful and victorious over the devil through the blood of the Lamb and their testimony for Him (vs. 10, 11, 17). What a play!

This divine "play within a play" serves to remind the Christians of the ages, and especially the believers who come to faith during the Great Tribulation, that the events of the final days are part of a much bigger and eternal story of redemption. The battle is spiritual in the heavenlies, the struggles on earth are at times horrific and bloody, the warfare is relentless, but the outcome is never in doubt. Salvation comes. Christ the King-Lamb has defeated Satan, the dragon. And we are more than conquerors who overcome that lying fiend by the blood of the Lamb! Let the play continue for we know the final scene!

REVELATION 13
December 17

" *The Beast Rises* "

*"And I saw a beast rising out of the sea, with ten horns and seven
heads, with ten diadems on its horns and blasphemous names
on its heads."* (Revelation 13:1)

Our reading in God's Word today is one of the most noted chapters in
the Book of the Revelation, and it also contains some of the most
significant forms and uses of symbolism in the entire epistle and, for that
matter, all of Scripture. As we have learned so far in interpreting the
message of the Book of the Revelation, the symbols used in the message
are explained either within the context of the passage or within the text
of the rest of Scripture. Therefore, it is vitally important that we adhere
to the historical, literal, grammatical method of interpreting passages
like Chapter 13.

Our attention is particularly called to two terrible personalities and
one enigmatic number. The first is the dreadful beast with ten horns and
seven heads rising out of the sea. In this case, key chapters in Daniel such
as 2, 4, 7, and 8 are so insightful because they clearly refer to a similar
prophecy and symbol. The beast in verse one is clearly the Antichrist,
who, seen rising out of the seas, will rise out of the peoples of the earth in
the last days. He will rise to prominence because he is empowered by the
furious cast-down dragon who is clearly identified as Satan (vs. 2, 4). His
seven heads represent that as Daniel also saw the beast and his kingdom
is the final expression of the seven great world empires of the Middle
East and west. The Antichrist appears to be aligned with a final leader or
nation confederacy. These leaders transfer their submission to
Antichrist, who has miraculously survived a deadly wound or disaster
(vs. 3, 4; Rev. 17:9-13). This unites power under Antichrist, as the eighth
and final world kingdom of the earth (Rev. 17:11).

The rule of Antichrist is closely associated with a false religious
expression led by an individual who is symbolized as rising out of the
earth, which probably means in contrast to the sea, that is a symbol of
the Gentile nations. The land here represents either Israel or the lands of
the Bible narrative in the Middle-East. This false prophet has the power
to work miracles, causing people to actually believe the Antichrist is the
long-promised Christ or Messiah. Loyalty is required to be pledged to the
Antichrist by the rise of an identification system for all commercial
transactions (vv. 16-17). The symbolism of the mark is 666. This is *man's
number* in contrast to *God's number,* 777. It is the number of defiant,
rebel, humanism in opposition to God. Antichrist is 666 but he is about
to discover he is no match for 777!

REVELATION 14
December 18

" *The Shouts of Angels* "

*"Fear God and give him glory because the hour of his judgment has
come, and worship him who made heaven and earth, the sea and
the springs of water."* (Revelation 14:7)

As the narrative of the Book of the Revelation continues to unfold, the
speed in which the events take place increases, and a crescendo in the
volume as well. All this activity and sound is initiating from the center
of the throne room on the heavenly Mount Zion. Before the Lamb are
standing with Him 144,000 people who know Him in salvation, who are
also representative of all those of the ages who have been redeemed by
Christ (v. 3). The number 144,000 is symbolic for the sum of 12 x 12,
the same number of the tribes of Israel and the apostles of Christ. We
are told later in the epistle that the New Jerusalem has 12 gates and 12
foundations and that the city symbolizes The Lord's espoused wife, His
Church.

These 144,000 are also connected to the declaration by the angel of
the eternal gospel (v. 6). Again, the angel is not a literal gospel preacher,
but as an angel, he is a messenger of God sharing "the eternal good
news" of God's ultimate salvation that is now at hand. Just as angels
heralded the first coming of Jesus, they also celebrate the spiritual
harvest of the gospel around the world. Another angel announces the
wonderful, awful news that the harvest of the earth has come. God's
people are about to be gathered into the eternal Kingdom, and the
wicked are about to be judged in everlasting judgment.

The strange announcement about the fall of Babylon the Great is the
announcement of the ending of mankind's system of rebellion against
God, which first began at the Tower of Babel and has existed through
the ages in opposition to the rule of God as "Babylon." The glorified
Lamb is coming as the Crowned Conqueror. The final bloody winepress
of Armageddon is soon to become full of the grapes of the wrath of God.
Judgment and deliverance are coming!

Although, as believers, we are told of these things that are certain to
come to pass, there is a call to action inherent in the message being
communicated. We are part of these representative 144,000 sealed for
God. We are also saved and sealed to serve. We serve as messengers of
the eternal gospel, the message of salvation from the coming judgment.
Paul said knowing the "terror of the Lord," we should, by all means,
persuade people to repent and believe the gospel (2 Cor. 5:11). Let us
work in the harvest while it is yet day, for the night is coming when no
man can work (John 9:4).

REVELATION 15
December 19

"*Songs of Victory*"

"And they sing the song of Moses, the servant of God,
and the song of the Lamb..." (Revelation 15:3)

The narrative of the Book of the Revelation is paused momentarily in our reading taken from Chapter 15. It is another passage that is described as a "sign." These visions are given to us as a way of understanding more clearly the "big picture" of what is being accomplished by God through these culminating events of the last days. The sign consists of the preparation for the coming of the final "plagues" of God's judgment on the kingdom of Satan. The fact that these are the "last" plagues means that "with them the wrath of God is finished" (v. 1). Also, the description of them as "plagues" reminds of the judgment of the plagues that wreaked havoc on Pharaoh and the empire of Egypt. By these plagues, the enemies of God were punished, and the Israelites were liberated from centuries of slavery and redeemed as Jehovah's covenant people. By the waters of the Red Sea, the nation that had crossed through baptism and escaped from certain death to new life stood and sang with Moses a song of deliverance and worship.

Now in Revelation Chapter 15, another redeemed people, the freed former slaves of spiritual bondage, stand by the sea of glass in heaven and sing the Song of the Lamb. It is also a song of praise for God's glorious works on behalf of His people. This vast throng sings both the Song of Moses and the Song of the Lamb, demonstrating that they represent the redeemed of the old covenant and the new. It is a wonderful thing to note that a saved people are also a singing people.

The grace of God that opens the heart in faith also opens the mouth in praise. "I waited patiently for the Lord; he inclined to me and heard my cry. He drew me up from the pit of destruction, out of the miry bog, and set my feet upon a rock, making my steps secure. He put a new song in my mouth, a song of praise to our God. Many will see and fear, and put their trust in the Lord" (Ps. 40:1-3). It is songs like this, and that of Moses and the Lamb, that only those redeemed from the pit of destruction, despair, and slavery can sing. In heaven, we will all have glorified vocal cords to sing the songs as we would desire. But until then we should still sing, as rescued slaves, the songs of redemption. No matter the quality of your voice, the Lord will enjoy the sound.

REVELATION 16
December 20

"*It is Finished*!"

The greatest words of triumph that have ever been proclaimed on the earth are, "It is finished!" Of course, they were shouted with all the ebbing strength of the Lord Jesus as He finished His hours of suffering on the cross. Those words of Jesus were a declaration that all that was required to bring both the rebel sons and daughters of Adam to the Father had been accomplished. With that shout, the earth, and especially the city of Jerusalem, rocked and quaked. Salvation had come.

In our reading today, the same shout is proclaimed but this time by an angel in heaven. In response, the heavenly Jerusalem erupts in lightning, thunder, and earthquakes. Salvation has come. The Lord has fulfilled His ancient promise to judge the world's idolatrous, rebellious system of Babylon. The seven final plagues of the bowl judgments have poured forth all the fullness of the cup of God's wrath. Also, God's judgments are preparing for the final confrontation between the forces of Antichrist and the authority of Jesus Christ.

The evil of the dragon, the beast, and the false prophet are even sovereignly controlled by God to assemble the nations of the earth to the final conflict. The lying deception of the arch-enemy of God will actually turn to his own kingdom's destruction as all the armies of the earth converge on a place called Armageddon.

Armageddon literally means "the hill of Megiddo." Megiddo is one of the most significant cities in Israel and, in fact, in all of the Middle-East. For millennia the city has guarded the crossroads of the Valley of Jezreel in northern Israel. If the country of Israel is the land bridge connecting the continents of Europe, Asia, and Africa, then Megiddo is the gate of that land bridge. All the roads for armies on three continents must converge in this long, broad Valley of Jezreel. The emperor Napoleon, gazing out upon the valley in front of Megiddo, exclaimed, "This is the greatest battlefield on the face of the earth!"

And so it will be one day when the Lord assembles the representatives of the nations of the earth to meet with Him there. It will become the epicenter of the conflict of the ages that will culminate with the return of the King, who reminds us, "Behold I am coming like a thief!" Completely unexpected, the Lord Jesus will return in power and glory. He will be unexpected by the world, but the Lord wants us to expect Him and stay alert and stay pure so we will not be ashamed at His appearing. Let's stay ready my friends! The King is coming!

PSALMS 145 & 146
December 21

" *Infinite, Intimate God* "

The nature of God is such that God is not only everywhere, but He is all there everywhere. Theologians refer to this truth as the immanence of God. Because God is omnipresent, He is also completely present everywhere. God is infinitely simple, which means He cannot be subdivided into pieces. God is in every place, and all of God is in every place. It was this infinite and intimate nature of God that David adored and celebrated so often in his songs. David praised the God of Israel as the One who the heavens could not contain but also worshiped Jehovah as the loving and concerned companion who was aware of his every emotion. This is the God of the ages, who is also the Heavenly Father revealed fully to us by His Son, Jesus Christ.

In these two Psalms of David, we are given the opportunity to express worship to our infinite, intimate God in word and deed. In our praise and prayer today, there is nothing too big nor anything too small that we cannot bring it to him. We are speaking to the One for whom nothing is so big that it causes Him the slightest challenge, and there is also nothing so seemingly trivial or insignificant that it is beneath His concern or full attention.

In Psalm 145, we join David as we praise the Lord saying, "Your kingdom is an everlasting kingdom, and your dominion endures throughout all generations" (v. 13). We also worship God today as we imitate His concern for the most vulnerable members of society, "The Lord watches over the sojourners; he upholds the widow and the fatherless..." (Ps. 146:9). The Lord of the universe is concerned with those who are most overlooked in the world.

People who truly love God must express the care for those about whom the Lord cares. Looking out for the immigrant who may not be a fellow citizen but is our fellow man is the way of God's will for us. Upholding the cause and care for the widows and the fatherless is how we uphold the faith. The Lord is glorified when our minds are filled with His infinite glory and our hearts are full of His intimate loving concern for the most at-risk. May we be people today who worship God well by serving others well in His Name.

PSALM 147 & 148
December 22

"*Heaven and Nature Sing*"

In this season, all around the world the songs are constantly being played and sung that celebrate the messages of Christmas. Sadly, so much of that music in this age leaves the "Christ" out of the "Christmas." The madness of the materialism surrounding the holidays often replaces the wonders of the worship in what should certainly be "holy days." Perhaps the days of this week are a good time for us to refocus our concentrated worship of the One for whom "Heaven and Nature Sing."

David certainly was not familiar with the carol, "Joy to the World," but that could be a title for Psalm 148. This Psalm is remarkable in the manner that David sees every aspect of heaven and nature proclaiming a joyful anthem of praise to God. Notice the progression from the highest to the lowest in David's praise. Heavens, heights, angels, and heavenly host lead the worship (vv. 1-2). Then, the solar system and the atmosphere, stars, sun, moon, and skies praise the Lord (vv. 3-4). From the earth, the ocean life and depths, the fire, hail, snow, mist, and wind all obey God (vv. 7-8). The wildlife and geography of mountains, hills, fruit trees, cedars, beasts, livestock, along with the flying birds, and creeping insects all worship and praise Jehovah (vv. 9-10). Then the inhabitants of the earth from the most powerful kings, princes and all peoples, the old men and young men, the maidens and children all join in praising the Lord (vv. 11-12).

It is an amazing Psalm that tells us much about David's worldview. He clearly saw life through the lens of a worshiper. Life for David was, in all its expressions, resounding with the praise of God. What is most revealing is that David could hear the song because he saw the Lord in all things. He saw God because he was listening. *Heaven and Nature Sing*—they truly do, but are we looking in such a way that we can hear the praise of our God?

> *"Joy to the world, the Savior reigns;*
> *Let men their songs employ;*
> *While fields and floods, rocks, hills and plains*
> *Repeat the sounding joy,*
> *Repeat the sounding joy,*
> *Repeat, repeat, the sounding joy."*

("Joy to the World" words by Isaac Watts)

386

REVELATION 17
December 23

" *Babylon on the Beast* "

God has promised a special blessing on those who read and those who listen to the message of the Book of the Revelation (Rev. 1:3). However, it is also very clear that God caused John to use a great deal of symbolism in communicating the message. There are certainly reasons the Lord did this. One is that, like the parables used by Jesus, the symbolism involved would only be understood by those who seriously desired to discern God's will with a sincere desire to serve Him. Secondly, since much of the information conveyed in this epistle could be misinterpreted by the Roman authorities during the early days of the church, some of the symbolism used offered safety to the Lord's disciples because the message would not be understood by pagan-minded people.

Revelation Chapter 17 is the most symbolic passage in the book and perhaps in all the Bible. The scarlet beast is the same as that in Chapter 13, representing the final confederation of nations led by the Antichrist. However, we are introduced to a woman who is described as a harlot named "Babylon." She is responsible for intoxicating and seducing kings, and her influence covers the whole world. She is fabulously wealthy and is said to be "drunk with the blood of the saints, the blood of the martyrs of Jesus" (vv. 1-6). This woman is closely associated with the rise and support of the Antichrist and his deception. She will be key to the prominence of the Antichrist and his associates. However, when he gains complete strength, the Antichrist and his league of nations will destroy the harlot and claim her wealth.

The chapter ends with the revelation that this harlot, Babylon, is directly connected to the city of Rome and the empire that is ruling the world in the first century. As stunning as it seems, the interpretation of this chapter is clear to those who carefully read the history of western paganism and its origin and continuation through the centuries. The origin of false worship began in Babylon and continued through the centuries through all empires of the Middle-East and West until the time of Rome in John's day. With the adaptation of Christianity as the religion of the empire after Constantine, paganism infiltrated the western world through the religious continuation of the Roman Empire, in the Roman Church, and grew out of the ancient, original paganism of Babylon continuing through the Roman Empire's rise and fall. It is the false Christianity of Rome that is the murderer of millions of God's true saints. This false system will empower the Antichrist, but he will turn on it when he declares himself the incarnate God (2 Thess. 2:3-5). Religion, my friends, is of the devil but redemption is of Christ!

REVELATION 18
December 24

"*Babylon Has Fallen!*"

Our reading today may seem a strange one for Christmas Eve; but on further reflection, it can be seen to be the perfect passage for the day. On the night of Jesus' birth, the angels of the Lord proclaimed that the Lord of Glory had been born in Bethlehem. The startling announcement of their song was that God Himself had come to bring salvation to the world. His salvation would deliver the souls of countless millions of people who were enslaved in the bondage of false religion that could bring no freedom. This man-centered and Satan-initiated form of religion was first established in ancient Babylon. Since that time, the idolatrous and adulterous paganism of false religion has been the curse of mankind and the source of enrichment and enslavement by despots over mankind.

With the rise of the gospel of Christ bringing light and liberty to the oppressed peoples of the earth living in darkness, the deceiver, the devil, substituted a false gospel and false Christianity that only brings spiritual bondage and death. This false Christianity is the masterpiece of Satan that the apostles and prophets of God forewarned and cursed (Gal. 1: 6-9, etc.). This awful and idolatrous religion of greed and power has no connection whatsoever with King Jesus; although its leaders claim to be ministers of God, they are actually demonized deceivers (2 Cor. 11:15).

The song of the angel in Revelation 18 is the proclamation of the "good news" of the destruction of this ancient Christ-less Christianity. How fitting that the Antichrist himself should be the one to destroy it in an effort to be worshiped as the god-man. The Lord uses the wrath of His worst enemies to accomplish His sovereign purposes. This attack by the Antichrist against false Christianity will be the epitome of our Lord's control in the worst of times on earth. The worship of ancient Babylon and the system of the false faith will be destroyed. Many on earth made rich by it will weep and wail, but the people of God and the angels and martyrs in heaven will join with jubilation in the vengeance brought by God and the judgment of this great oppressive system.

So, this song of desolation in Revelation Chapter 18 is a fitting carol to celebrate the birth of the divine Redeemer and King, Jesus Christ. Babylon will be destroyed, and the Baby of Bethlehem will reign forever!

ISAIAH 9
December 25

" The Lord Has Come!"

For unto us a child is born, to us a son is given; and the government shall be upon His shoulder, and His name shall be called Wonderful Counselor, Mighty God, Everlasting Father, Prince of Peace. Of the increase of His government and of peace there will be no end, on the throne of David and over His kingdom, to establish it and to uphold it with justice and with righteousness from this time forth and forever more. The zeal of the Lord of hosts will do this." (Isaiah 9:6-7)

Never has there been such a birth announcement as this one! It is made even more amazing because it was made 750 years before the baby was born. In fact, the entire passage of this incredible declaration of the arrival of the Son of the Highest is written in *past tense*. How appropriate this is because the promise comes from the Eternal One with whom there is no past, present, or future. For the Lord, the past is prologue and the future is pre-written history.

The glad news came in the darkest days of the nation. The invasion of the Assyrians covered the entire region of northern Israel in the shadow of gloom and death. However, out of this land of shadows, covering people in despair and darkness, the light would dawn. Yes, from Galilee, the region of Gentiles, would come to Israel the Redeemer and King who would be a light to the nations and the glory of His people, Israel (Luke 2:32). The tromp of the invaders and the oppressors would only mimic the march of the time until the deliverer would come quietly who would rule over the earth, breaking the yoke of oppression, and destroying forever the garments of war (v. 5). The one promised would be a child born but also the son given (v. 6). As a baby, He would be born to mankind; but as the eternal Son, He is given to the children of Adam. His coming would be from the everlasting ages of eternity past (Mic. 5:2), and His days will extend through the ever-cycling ages of eternity.

The Child is born, and the Son is given; He is the gift of a Wonderful Counselor who guides the meek in the ways of mercy and justice. He is the gift of the Mighty God who provides protection with the strength of omnipotence. He is the incarnate Everlasting Father who, age to age, cares for the people of His inheritance. The child born to us is the Prince of Peace for us. By His stripes, the chastisement that brings peace that will never fail will come to our souls. His government shall rest securely on the shoulders that bore our cross. The Son of David born in the city of David will bring David's Kingdom to this world, and we will rejoice and reign with our King forever and ever. What a gift! Merry Christmas!

REVELATION 19
December 26

"Two Dinner Invitations"

A dinner invitation can be a source of excitement and expectation, or it can also cause a great degree of anxiety and apprehension. Usually, this is determined by the source of the invitation and also the sort of food that is going to be prepared! This chapter in the Book of the Revelation contains two dinner invitations, and there is no question for which meal we want to be included.

The first invitation is for human beings to enjoy the marriage supper of the Lamb. It is truly the feast of all the ages as the heavenly Bridegroom, Jesus Christ, has invited people from around the world and through the ages. To accept the invitation to this meal is to actually become the most honored of the celebration, the Bride of the Lord. The people of faith in Jesus are united with Him in love; they are His beloved bride. Using the beautiful image of the eastern, ancient marriage practices, the groom has paid the purchase price for His espoused bride. For Christ, the price was His own sacrificial death. He has resurrected and returned to His Father's house to prepare a dwelling place for His beloved bride. Christ promised to return and take His people, His Bride, to live with Him forever. When He calls His church away in the rapture (1 Thess. 4:13-18), then together we will celebrate the marriage supper of the Lamb. The greatest of blessings is to take part in this feast, which is, in fact, heaven itself.

The second invitation in this chapter is not for human beings but for the birds of the air to feast on the flesh of human beings who are the defeated enemies of Christ (v. 17). This is the awful result of the Lord's return as King of Kings and Lord of Lords. It is the victory of His conquest of the Antichrist, the false prophet, and the armies of the world gathered to make war with Him. This is the moment of the final destruction of the rebel power of the Antichrist and his followers. It is truly one of the most horrible images in all of Scripture, but it is the true depiction of the Day of God's wrath and the vengeance of the King of Kings.

Thank God that those of us who accept the Lord's invitation to His marriage supper rejoice with Him in heaven and return in triumph with Him in victory. Make certain of your reservation for both of these events through faith in Christ alone!

REVELATION 20
December 27

"The First Resurrection and The Second Death"

In this passage we see the culmination of all the events that transpire during the great tribulation on the earth reaching their climactic moment when the Lord Jesus, having returned in glory, now establishes His Kingdom on earth. This literal and physical reign of Jesus is often referred to by Bible scholars as the *millennium* or one thousand years. Many theologians see the references to a thousand years as symbolic of an age of peace when the gospel of Christ will hold sway over the nations. However, there is no reason to interpret this period other than how it is plainly presented—a thousand-year reign of Christ on the earth.

This was the promise of the Jewish prophets and the hope of the faithful followers of the Lord in both the Old Testament and the early centuries of the Church. Not until the spiritualization of the "City of God" by Augustine in the 4th century was the promise of the millennial reign of Christ understood in any way other than a literal thousand years. Those who enter His Kingdom appear to be the surviving saints of the tribulation along with the resurrected martyrs of those years; they are said to be the *blessed ones* who take part in the first resurrection (v. 6). During the 1000 years, Satan is bound and imprisoned. After the 1000 years, he is released for a season and once again he gathers rebels from among the millions who are born during the thousand years. Yes, even in the wonderful atmosphere of the Kingdom on earth, apart from regenerated hearts by faith, the nature of mankind is to rebel against the loving rule of the Lord.

Like all rebellions against almighty God, it utterly fails; and at last, the lying serpent, the devil, is cast into the everlasting destruction of the Lake of Fire. Now, the time of the inauguration of the age of the New Heavens and the New Earth has finally arrived, but first, the final judgment of the Great White throne must reveal the identity of the true sons and daughters of God. The Lord Jesus Himself judges humanity based on the record of their deeds and ultimately whether their names are recorded in the Lamb's Book of Life, the roster of names of all who have been redeemed by the blood of the Lamb.

What a dreadful scene as untold multitudes of people are judged for their rebellion, sin, and unbelief and are dragged from the presence of God and cast into the Lake of Fire! My friend, are you certain today that your name is written in the Book of Life? If not, waste not another moment but repent of your sins to God and call upon the Lamb for Salvation. Rest assured, all those who call in faith on His Name have their names recorded in the Book of Life.

PROVERBS 31
December 28

" A Mother's Wisdom "

*"The words of King Lemuel. An oracle that
his mother taught him."* (Proverbs 31:1)

Abraham Lincoln once said, "All that I am or ever hope to be I owe to my dear mother." Nancy Hanks Lincoln died when her son, Abraham, was only 10 years old; but she made an incredible impact on him and the world, *through* him. Any man or woman who has been blessed with a godly mother has been given, from God, a treasure of incalculable worth. I know personally and will always praise the Lord for the good and godly mother He gave to me.

We are not told the specific identity of Lemuel or his mother, but most Bible scholars agree that Lemuel is a spiritual title for King Solomon and that his mother is the famous Bathsheba. She was a very wise woman because she mentored her young son by teaching him oracles, that is, specific instructions of wisdom based on God's Word. Sadly, some of the things she taught Solomon slipped from his grasp later in his life as he failed in some of the very areas she instructed him —focusing his energies on relationships with many women who turned his heart from the Lord. Also, Solomon pursued a life of parties and pleasure for a season that undermined his faith and integrity. When anyone, especially a leader, is distracted by self-focused living, he or she cannot be the advocate for the poor and destitute who desperately need the focused concern and efforts of God's servants.

Solomon's mother spoke to him with wisdom as a youth; and in later years, he spoke of her with the highest affection and admiration. In fact, the remainder of this last chapter of Proverbs is an oracle on the character and conduct of a godly woman, wife, and mother. Solomon describes, from his own mother's life, the qualities of a virtuous woman. The Lord inspired his words and inscribed them in the Bible for all ages. What a testimony of grace and redemption is given in these words from Bathsheba and Solomon's words about her. As a young woman, she knew abuse by King David in his lust and the loss of her dear husband by David's deception. But in the grace and strength of the Lord, she overcame the abuse and became a blessing to her family and an example for the ages of a woman who fears the Lord. The same God and the same grace are available for every abused and used person today.

PSALMS 149 & 150
December 29

"Sound His Praises"

"Let everything that has breath praise the Lord!
Praise the Lord!" (Psalm 150:6)

I dearly love these two final psalms of praise to God. When you read them out loud, you can also hear and feel the exuberance of the throngs of worshipers in the temple as they sing to the Lord with all their might. It is noisy praise, with every type of instrument making melody to God. The worshipers are not still and expressionless, but they are engaged in every part of their being in rejoicing before the Lord. Some of them are so filled with joy that they begin to worship the Lord with dance (Ps. 149:3).

I know some people may secretly wish that verse was not in the Bible, but there it is! These two psalms have so helped me to recognize the importance of expressing praise to God with freedom and exuberance. Did you notice how many different and varied instruments are used in these songs of worship? Tambourine, lyre, trumpet, flute, harp, strings, pipes, cymbals, and clashing cymbals. This is worship loud and big! What is the inspiration for such worship? A heart overwhelmed and awe-struck at the glory, majesty, and love of God. Most of all, it is the overflow of gratitude and thanks for the personal deliverance and salvation from sin and bondage through God's grace.

Fannie Crosby was an amazing woman. Although blinded by an illness at the age of six, she determined that her disability would never be permitted to limit her zeal for education, musical training, and service to God. She wore the Victorian era dresses and also the darkened glasses of the blind, but her poems and lyrics were filled with light and joy. Fannie knew Jesus, and her joy was exuberant and contagious. I often think of Fannie Crosby when I read these final stanzas of the Psalms. Clearly, Fanny loved these psalms as well, and they inspired one of her beloved gospel songs, sung loudly by millions of God's people joyful in their worship.

Continued...

"Praise Him! Praise Him! Jesus, our blessed Redeemer!
Sing, O earth, His wonderful love proclaim!
Hail Him! Hail Him! Highest archangels in glory;
Strength and honor give to His holy Name.
Like a shepherd Jesus will guard his children—
In his arms he carries them all day long:

Praise Him! Praise Him! Tell of His excellent greatness!
Praise Him! Praise Him! Ever in joyful song!"

Praise Him! Praise Him, Jesus, our blessed Redeemer!
For our sins He suffered, and bled, and died.
He our Rock, our hope of eternal salvation,
Hail Him! Hail Him! Jesus the Crucified.
Sound His praises! Jesus who bore our sorrows,
Love unbounded, wonderful, deep and strong.

Praise Him! Praise Him! Tell of His excellent greatness!
Praise Him! Praise Him! Ever in joyful song!"

("Praise Him! Praise Him! Jesus, Our Blessed Redeemer,"
words by Fanny Crosby)

And the people of God said, "Amen!"

REVELATION 21
December 30

"We Can Only Imagine"

There are times when a scene is so beautiful, or an experience so wonderful, that words fail any attempt to describe it. John must have felt that way on the Island of Patmos as he tried to frame into words, written with quill and ink on parchment, the sights and sounds of what he experienced in his visions of the new heaven and the new earth. How can words express what the mind cannot comprehend?

However, in what John does share, he transports us to a world that is beautiful beyond the telling, and yet it is *our home*. It is where we belong and where we long to be. It is the holy city, the new Jerusalem. In this Jerusalem, there is no temple "for its temple is the Lord God the Almighty and the Lamb" (v. 22). God dwells unhidden in the midst of His people. It is a brand new world made for us, His people. It is so new that the way John attempts to describe it is by sharing what is *not* there.

There are no tears, no death, no mourning, no crying, and no pain. There is no more curse, no evil or evildoers, and there is no temptation or tempter. There is no more night; but there is no sun, for the Son, the Lamb, fills the city with light. And what a city it is with gates of pearl that never shut and open to the streets of gold like transparent glass. The walls and the foundations are made of the most beautiful and costly stones so that the city flashes like a multi-colored jewel. This is the shining city of the King, the capital of His eternal Kingdom, and our hometown forever and ever.

The New Jerusalem is surpassing in glory far beyond anything this world has ever known, but what will truly make it heaven for us is the fact that Jesus is there. We will see Him, face-to-face, and know Him in a way the angels never can because He still bears in his body the scars of His loving sacrifice and suffering for each of us. Truly it will be Jesus who is the glory of heaven to our souls.

The bride eyes not her garment, But her dear Bridegroom's face;
I will not gaze at glory, But on my King of Grace—
Not on the crown He giveth, But on His pierced hand:
The Lamb is all the glory Of Immanuel's land.

("The Sands of Time Are Sinking," written by Anne R. Cousin)

REVELATION 22
December 31

"Come, Lord Jesus!"

*"The Spirit and the Bride say, 'Come.' And let the one who hears say,
'Come.' And let the one who is thirsty come; let the one who desires
take of the water of life without price."*
(Revelation 22:17)

The story of the Bible is the story of redemption. It is the story of paradise lost and paradise regained. The Bible opens in a garden with the Creator and His children living together in the perfect joy of unhindered and unbroken, loving fellowship. God's image-bearers were fully alive and free. They reflected His glory, and His life flowed within them, and through them in limitless joy. The Tree of Life nourished them and also was the living symbol of life with God. Tragically, all of paradise was lost by the terrible traitorous rebellion of sin.

However, the Creator Himself, in His amazing grace, redeemed the earth and guilty sinners through His own substitution and sacrifice. The Lord became the Lamb. In the closing scenes of the Bible, we see the glorious vision of paradise restored. Once again, perfect harmony permeates all creation. God's sons and daughters rejoice in His presence and are surrounded by a garden world in which, once again, the Tree of Life flourishes. Now, nations of redeemed souls fill the new creation, all strife is healed, the wars are ceased forever, and there is no more curse. No songs of mourning or wails of grief are ever heard again. There is no night, only eternal day that radiates from the *SonLight* of the Lamb, Jesus Christ.

The nations of the new earth will bring their tributes of love and devotion to Christ the King. Of His government and peace, there will be no end. The eternal, infinite joy of the servants of God will be to look on His face. Paradise is indeed restored. All who desire may share in this eternal joy that has been purchased and provided by Jesus. Freely, He offers to share His Kingdom of love with all who desire.

Our Lord closes His Revelation with an invitation and a promise. The invitation is, "Come!" "Come and take of the water of life without price." His promise is, "I am coming!" And our prayer as we leave this year and enter another is, "Amen. Come, Lord Jesus!"

Author's Biography

PASTOR SAM POLSON is the Lead Pastor of West Park Baptist Church in Knoxville, Tennessee, and featured teacher with the SonLight Radio media ministry. He also serves as Chairman of the Board of the Association of Baptists for World Evangelism and previously served for many years on the board of Shepherds Ministries, an educational ministry for adults with developmental disabilities. Sam was born and raised in New Castle, Indiana, where he met and married his wife, Susan. He earned his Master's degree in theology from Bob Jones University and then served seven years as an assistant pastor at Calvary Baptist Church in Findlay, Ohio. The Polsons then moved to Knoxville, where Sam has served as Lead Pastor for more than 33 years. He advises the pastoral team and staff, teaches in large and small group settings, and is the most energized by witnessing people come alive to the reality of the gospel. His first book, *In His Image*, explores the purpose for which we were all created and is available online in English, Romanian, and Mandarin. *By Faith*, Timeless Insights for Staying on Course from Hebrews 11, is available in English and Romanian.

"For what we proclaim is not ourselves, but Jesus Christ as Lord, with ourselves as your servants for Jesus' sake."
(2 Corinthians 4:5)

About Climbing Angel
Publishing

Climbing Angel Publishing exists for the purpose of sharing stories of hope and encouragement, aiding in the gathering together of community, and supporting the process of betterment. The following CAP books are available worldwide through internet bookstores.

Adult Books: *(Romans 8:28-30)*

In His Image (*Also available in Romanian & Mandarin*)
By Faith (*Also available in Romanian*)
My Birthday Gift to Jesus
Without Ceasing
SonLight Daily Devotional

Children's Books: *(Philippians 4:8)*

The Christmas Tree Angel
The Unmade Moose
Thump
Somebunny To Love (*Also available in Mandarin*)

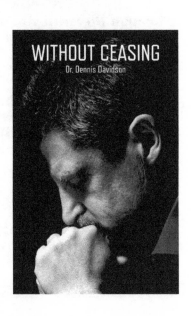

CPSIA information can be obtained
at www.ICGtesting.com
Printed in the USA
LVHW091832060120
642659LV00006B/99/P